T0339456

ANALYZING MODERN BUSINESS CYCLES

ANALYZING MODERN BUSINESS CYCLES

Essays Honoring
Geoffrey H. Moore

Edited by Philip A. Klein

Routledge
Taylor & Francis Group

LONDON AND NEW YORK

First published 1990 by M.E. Sharpe

Reissued 2018 by Routledge
2 Park Square, Milton Park, Abingdon, Oxon OX14 4RN
711 Third Avenue, New York, NY 10017, USA

Routledge is an imprint of the Taylor & Francis Group, an informa business

A Library of Congress record exists under LC control number: 89038689

ISBN 13: 978-1-138-04596-5 (hbk)
ISBN 13: 978-1-138-29927-6 (pbk)
ISBN 13: 978-1-315-17167-8 (ebk)

Photograph of Philip A. Klein supplied through the courtesy of Alan Klein.

Contents

Charts

Tables

Foreword

Solomon Fabricant

As I contemplate writing about Geoffrey Moore and the NBER, I'm reminded of last spring's 50th anniversary meeting of the NBER's Conference on Research in Income and Wealth when Martin Feldstein asked me to say some appropriate words about the history of the conference. As I approached the dais with what must have seemed to be a thick pad of notes, Marty hastily added: "You have one minute, Sol!"

Well, Geoffrey Moore joined the National Bureau in 1939. This means that we are celebrating not only his 75th birthday but also his 50-year association with the Bureau. It is an association that has progressed through many levels—research assistant, staff member, associate director of research, director of research, vice president of research, director of business cycle research, and most recently membership on the Bureau's Board of Directors and its Executive and other Committees. It's a long record to cover in just one minute, and I find it frustrating not to have time to quote a bit of Shakespeare (which might fit in) and ask at which stage Geof acquired his "fair round belly with good capon lined"—which a quick glance seems to deny, however—or to try to match the stages of his career with growth cycles, business cycles, or at least the phases of a Kondratieff wave.

There is much that I could recount about Geof in each of his stages, but I must be brief. Rather than hurry through what Geof has meant to the Bureau at each stage, simply note that in his own research, in the research he directed or helped with, and in the directions he tried to influence policy, Geof kept firmly in mind and held fast to the principles and standards on which the Bureau's reputation rests—a reputation for impartial scientific research on important economic problems and research that truly could serve to strengthen the basis on which sound economic policy might be built. I'm not suggesting that his role was that of a Wesley Mitchell or an Arthur Burns—Geof would not want me to say it was or

Solomon Fabricant was with the National Bureau of Economic Research and was Professor Emeritus at New York University. Solomon Fabricant died September 13, 1989 before he was able to proofread this foreword.

that others did not contribute. To be as cautious as Geof tries to be, I won't go beyond saying that nothing he did could have served in any way to diminish the high reputation of the Bureau—which is no small praise.

A record of 40 or 50 years of close affiliation with just one institution (except for the 3 or 4 years at the BLS and some incidental relationships elsewhere) raises an interesting question. "During a typical 40-year career," we are told in a very recent NBER research paper, "the average American man holds 10 jobs"—which means nine shifts between employers—"and doubles his pay." We'd better not inquire too closely into Geof's pay, but we can't help noting the striking difference between his mobility and the mobility of the average American. It surely can't reflect lack of enterprise on Geof's part; or lack of opportunities elsewhere; nor, from what I remember of payrolls at the National Bureau, could it have been a princely salary rising twice as fast as the Consumer Price Index. There must have been other values, values that count, that made the experience at the National Bureau so rewarding. What were they?

I can be pretty sure what thoughts must be echoing through Geof's mind as he thinks back over the years. They run through my mind, too, as I look back. Geof and I put some thoughts down on paper some 35 years ago, when we had both had enough experience at the Bureau (about 15 years in his case, a little more in mine) to know what the experience was already worth to us, and what we expected it would be worth in the years ahead.

In 1953, Geoffrey and I put our heads together and decided on a special publication of the NBER. The occasion was Arthur Burns's departure for Washington, leaving the Bureau in our charge. He was responding to President Eisenhower's call to serve as Chairman of the President's Council of Economic Advisers—a call that came also to Martin some 30 years later. The publication we had in mind would consist of Arthur's reports on the work of the National Bureau during his tenure as the Bureau's Director of Research, along with a number of his papers on closely related subjects. Publication of the volume would be a fitting tribute to Burns's own contributions to economic knowledge and also to his role in shepherding the Bureau's research staff through the research on which he reported each year. Also important, the volume would have value beyond the immediate occasion. It would help inform the general public of the objectives of the Bureau as well as the principles and policies on which it sought to realize its objectives. In particular, the volume would help convey the kind of environment within which the staff worked, and the moral and scientific tone that had been set at the Bureau by Wesley Mitchell. In one of his papers in the volume, Arthur stated the working habits it fostered, including a sense of social responsibility, precision of thought and expression, a repugnance of shoddy work, the ability to profit by criticism, and a passion for objective evidence.

We entitled the volume *The Frontiers of Economic Knowledge* and in our Foreword, pursuing the analogy expressed by the title of the volume, likened the work of the Bureau to an adventure into the unknown by a company of explorers bound together, so to say, in a pact of mutual assistance in which collegiality really meant something. It was this prospect of exciting adventure at the frontiers of economic knowledge in the company of a congenial group of like-minded men and women that kept Geof, and myself and others also, attached so loyally to the Bureau for so many years.

I would also like to mention business cycle analysis and related studies that Geof has pursued and continues to pursue so patiently and so assiduously despite the vagaries of fashion. In 1970, when the Bureau celebrated its 50th anniversary, a session was devoted to business cycles in which Geof participated, although then at the BLS. It is easy to forget that many economists—perhaps most—believed that the business cycle had become obsolete, or at any rate of trivial significance and no longer worth serious attention. The business expansion that had begun in 1961 was still continuing—the longest on record; to strengthen the view that it would continue indefinitely, generally received theory had led economists to believe they knew the causes of business cycles and how to deal with them. This opinion was voiced in the discussion when Geof, Ilse Mintz, and others among us read papers on the subject at the anniversary meeting. The expansion of 1961–69 was continuing, but it seemed to us that a slowdown was evident, and the possibility that the growth recession under way might mark the beginning of a classical recession—as turned out to be the case—should not be neglected. One prominent economist expressed the opinion that business cycles, though once as terrible as dinosaurs, were now more like small lizards, and the Bureau had worked itself out of a job. Another discussant belittled the idea of a growth recession as a contradiction in terms. Much has happened since 1970 in the economy and in economic theory to alter opinions, academic and other. We have been experiencing an expansion so far, about as long as the expansion of 1961–69, but now there is little talk of the obsolescence of business cycles and much more concern over the possibility of a recession in late 1989 or in 1990. Geof and others studying business cycles haven't yet worked themselves out of a job.

As he looks back, Geof must certainly consider himself lucky to have been associated so closely and so long with the National Bureau—lucky beyond his merits, Geof might modestly say. But few would agree with him. We feel *we* were lucky to have had Geof as one of our company at the National Bureau—not the smartest, or the handsomest, or the slimmest, or the most modest, or the best tennis player—but if you take an average of these attributes, weighted or unweighted, Geof would rank up with the best of them: Geoffrey, a colleague to cherish, and more, a friend to treasure.

Foreword

Gottfried Haberler

I greatly appreciate the opportunity of joining this distinguished group to salute Geoffrey Moore on the occasion of his 75th birthday. The grand masters of the National Bureau of Economic Research (NBER), Arthur F. Burns and Wesley C. Mitchell, put modern business cycle measurement on the map with their landmark publication *Measuring Business Cycles* in 1946. The creation, development, and continuing improvement of a system of leading, lagging, and coincident indicators was an achievement of greatest importance. Geoffrey Moore has been prominently involved in that work right from the beginning.

The whole approach has been criticized for lacking a theoretical foundation. One competent reviewer of *Measuring Business Cycles*[1] calls it "unbendingly empirical."

To my mind, this criticism is unjustified. The study of any subject, say astronomy, starts with prescientific or pretheoretical observations and descriptions. That the pretheoretical descriptions in *Measuring Business Cycles* provide an indispensable basis for theoretical work on business cycles is proven by the fact that they are widely used in such master works as Milton Friedman's and Anna Schwartz's *Monetary History of the United States*, which has a strong theoretical foundation and makes full use of the facts and figures presented in *Measuring Business Cycles*.

Of Geoffrey Moore's numerous publications, I mention a few to indicate the wide range of his work: *A Significance Test for Time Series* (with W. A. Wallis), 1941; *Production of Industrial Materials in World Wars I and II*, 1944; *The Quality of Consumer Installment Credit* (with P. Klein), 1967; *How Full is Full Employment*, 1973; *An Inflation Chronology*, 1977; *Business Cycles, Inflation and Forecasting*, 1983; and *Monitoring Business Cycles in Market-Oriented Countries* (with P. Klein), 1985.

Gottfried Haberler is Galen L. Stone Professor of International Trade Emeritus, Harvard University, and Resident Scholar, American Enterprise Institute, Washington, D.C.

A most impressive life work. We look forward to more contributions.

Note

1. See Tjalling C. Koopmans, "Measurement Without Theory" in *The Review of Economic Statistics*, Vol. 29, No. 3, August 1947.

Acknowledgments

I have been unusually fortunate in being able to enlist the participation of the group of economists represented in this volume. It goes without saying that their purpose has been to honor Geoffrey H. Moore, but I have nonetheless been the fortunate recipient of a very great deal of dedicated work as well as cooperation in meeting the various deadlines involved. I owe an enormous debt of gratitude to all the authors involved.

Two of the participants are due particular thanks, Ernst Boehm and John Cullity. They originally approached me with the suggestion that we take the project on, and they have provided help and encouragement for which I am very grateful. Additionally, much of the Introduction reads better, thanks to Cullity's blue pencil.

I should also like to thank Solomon Fabricant, not only for writing the Foreword, but also for his wise counsel at all stages of this project. I have relied heavily on his judgment and editorial skills.

I want to express my special thanks to Gottfried Haberler for agreeing to have his words included in this volume, which will be published an incredible fifty-two years after the publication of his pathbreaking *Prosperity and Depression.*

My secretary, Mrs. Donna Mae Weber, and her colleagues who have typed or worked with a good many parts of the manuscript have my thanks. So, too, does Claire Kreider, the indispensable computer expert in the Department of Economics at Penn State. I should also like to express my appreciation to a veritable army of secretaries to contributors to the book. They all have been unfailingly cooperative and a joy to work with. Finally, Richard D. Bartel, Economics Editor at M. E. Sharpe, and his associates have been very helpful.

Philip A. Klein
University Park, Pennsylvania

I
INTRODUCTION

1

Geoffrey H. Moore and His Impact on Modern Business Cycle Research

Philip A. Klein

"Which way is the economy headed? What do the indicators show?" While much of the modern science of economics continues to be regarded as esoteric by the public, these basic questions always predominate. The monitoring of the business cycle is an activity that the public is aware of and in which it shows much interest and concern.

The two most prominent current forecasting techniques are probably the leading indicator method and the construction and interpretation of econometric models. After an early period of presumed competition between the two methods, it is now clear that the two techniques are complementary, both assisting in the complex task of monitoring business cycle developments. Moore has long spearheaded careful and detailed monitoring of business cycle developments and the application of the resultant insights to forecasting future activity. It is unlikely that there is anyone today whose research has had a greater inpact on making the public and the economics profession aware of the potential usefulness of analyzing business cycles with economic indicators than Geoffrey H. Moore—to whom this volume is dedicated. The usefulness of the business cycle indicators is widely acknowledged.

In his position as Associate Director (later Director) of Research at the National Bureau of Economic Research, Moore did, of course, influence the scope and direction of much of the research of the National Bureau at the time. But it is in his influence on the construction, interpretation, and use of business cycle indicators in which Geoffrey Moore has made his largest impact. This work exemplifies the careful, dispassionate, detailed analysis of economic time series which Wesley Clair Mitchell, the remarkable Columbia University economist whose seminal influence did much to point economics toward empirical investigation, had in mind when he founded the National Bureau of Economic Research in 1920.

This approach led to the collection and interpretation of a wide variety of economic series in a manner which proved invaluable to economists of all persuasions. The National Bureau's business cycle chronologies and indicators have proven to be helpful in analyzing diverse economic questions. The National

3

Bureau, moreover, played no small part in the creation of a reliable statistical data base for the United States, one which surpasses that of any other country in the world. Many contributed to this effort, but few more significantly or over a longer period than Geoffrey Moore.

Moore was born in Pequanock, New Jersey on February 28, 1914. He grew up in New Jersey and attended Rutgers University, graduating with a B.S. in agricultural economics in 1933. He obtained a Masters Degree from Rutgers in 1937, continuing his interest in agriculture in his thesis, "The Use of Credit by Dairy Farmers." Subsequently, he went to Harvard University and received a Ph.D. in 1947. His doctoral dissertation was entitled "Harvest Cycles."

He joined the Senior Research Staff at the National Bureau of Economic Research in 1939 and worked in that capacity until 1948 when he was made Associate Director of Research. In 1965, he became Director of Research and remained in this position until 1968. His research activities at the Bureau continued until 1979, except for a brief period at the Bureau of Labor Statistics. He is currently on the Board of Directors of the National Bureau and is a member of its Executive Committee.

While Moore has spent the greater part of his professional career at the National Bureau, he has often accompanied his research with teaching. He was an instructor in agricultural economics at Rutgers from 1936 to 1942. He taught at New York University in 1947 and 1948, at Columbia University in 1953 and 1954, and at the Colorado School of Mines in 1984. These periods of formal teaching do little justice to his interest in education, because along the way he has organized or participated in a host of seminars, workshops, and short courses devoted to teaching others the techniques for analyzing time series to which so much of his own work has been devoted.

The most notable change from the focus of his career at the National Bureau was his tenure as Commissioner of Labor Statistics from 1969 to 1973 at the Bureau of Labor Statistics (BLS). His experience as well as his outstanding reputation made him a prime candidate for this position. His tenure at the BLS provided him with the opportunity to disseminate the fruits of his research to a larger audience. Moore was able to apply many of the ideas about the proper analysis of economic statistics, developed during his many years of research at the Bureau, in a new setting. He was in a position to apply the techniques to new data and to use the results to broaden the development of sound public attitudes toward critical problems. In brief, Moore's service in Washington confirmed his view that objective analysis of data was also the best basis for the formulation of public policy.

Moore's approach to economic statistics and the analysis of economic data was shaped under the influence of Arthur F. Burns, who brought Moore to the National Bureau. Moore was instrumental in fleshing out a viable research agenda of the sort that Mitchell envisaged when he established the National Bureau. In all of its publications, readers were told that the Bureau was set up to "ascertain and present to the public important economic facts and their interpretation in a scientific and impartial manner." Its reports state that "The National Bureau seeks not merely to determine and interpret important economic facts but to do so under such auspices and with such safeguards as shall make its findings carry conviction to all sections of the nation."

This is precisely the sort of approach with which Moore has always been most comfortable. His work carries credibility because his reputation has been built on attention to detail, accuracy, objectivity, and straightforward calculations designed to reveal what is intrinsically shown by time series data rather than attempting to bend them to demonstrate any particular type of results. His primary interest has always been economic analysis rather than economic policy. The major challenge for Moore has been how to treat time series so as to bring out the significant relationships embedded in the statistics.

Moore's interest in improving statistical measures was revealed in his very first publication for the National Bureau, *A Significance Test for Time Series and Other Ordered Observations*, written jointly with W. Allen Wallis and published by the Bureau in 1941. His concern that statistics reflect accurately what they were designed to reflect was shown in his 1944 study, *Production of Industrial Materials in World Wars I and II*. The latter study focused on measuring output in an economy radically altered by war and was devoted to testing how accurately the Federal Reserve's Index of Industrial Production measured during wartime the commodities on which it was based. From the 1940s through the 1960s, there was scarcely a National Bureau study which did not acknowledge the advice and support of Moore. He was thus an active participant in the particular development and presentation of statistical analysis with which the Bureau was most closely associated at that time.

His later work increasingly revolved around the development of business cycle indicators. Out of Wesley Clair Mitchell's view of business cycles as "congeries of interrelated phenomena" came the notion that in addition to dating business cycles, we could find measures of economic activity which preceded these business cycle turning points with reasonable reliability as well as other indicators which succeeded (lagged) and confirmed them. This perspective reflected Mitchell's view of how a dynamic market-oriented industrial economy could be understood. The notion that instability in market-oriented economies consisted of a patterned sequence of changes reflecting leading, roughly coincident, and lagging indicators was, therefore, a major insight growing out of Mitchell's work. One major milestone in the evolution of this approach was the publication by the Bureau in 1947 of Arthur F. Burns and Mitchell's *Measuring Business Cycles*.

Building on the Burns and Mitchell seminal work, Moore devoted his efforts to improving the techniques for selecting business cycle turning points and to developing up-to-date lists of leading, coincident, and lagging indicators for these turning points. The first such list was constructed by Burns and Mitchell in

1938. Furthering this work, Moore wrote important monographs in 1950, *Statistical Indicators of Cyclical Revivals and Recessions*, and in 1960, *Leading and Confirming Indicators of General Business Changes*. A third Moore study of the indicators, conducted jointly with Julius Shiskin in 1967, presented a technique for scoring them quantitatively. This study, entitled *Indicators of Business Expansions and Contractions*, also included a revision of Burns and Mitchell's list of most reliable indicators. In all of these revisions, Moore was a critical player.

Much of the essential work of developing indicators through the early postwar years was included in the two-volume *Business Cycle Indicators*, edited by Moore; in addition to his own work it included papers by a number of other economists working on business cycle measurement. It was at this time that the Bureau's critical role in monitoring U.S. business cycles under the leadership of Burns and Moore was recognized by the Department of Commerce's agreement to accept the National Bureau as the official arbiter of business cycle turning points in the United States. The Commerce Department also decided to publish a monthly report on the current status of the leading, coincident, and lagging indicators. This report, originally titled *Business Cycle Developments*, was subsequently retitled *Business Conditions Digest* in the mistaken belief/hope that business cycles might have been rendered obsolete during the long expansion of the 1960s. Julius Shiskin, Moore's successor as Commissioner of Labor Statistics, played a prominent role in the development and launching of this publication. To this day, it remains the major governmental publication monitoring business cycles in this country. The Department of Commerce is now responsible for revision of the indicators but others, including a number of contributors to this volume, have played major roles in this ongoing work. Furthermore, Geoffrey Moore has always counselled on these changes.

In his last decade at the National Bureau, Moore devoted his energies largely to developing a set of business cycle indicators for other industrialized market-oriented economies along the lines of the system by then firmly established and widely followed in the United States. This time the work was expanded to embrace the concept of "growth cycles," cycles in rates of growth as well as in absolute levels of economic activity. Growth cycle chronologies and indicators came into being and then into prominence in Europe and Japan as well as in the United States, as many analysts found them useful for studying instability in countries experiencing the rapid growth common to many market economies in the first quarter century after the Second World War. This work was accelerated after Moore established the Center for International Business Cycle Research in 1979 following his retirement from the National Bureau. This work also resulted in the 1985 publication of *Monitoring Growth Cycles in Market Oriented Economies*, in which I joined him as co-author, and in *International Economic Indicators*, a careful description of the data underlying in the indicator systems for other countries. In the latter publication, he was joined as co-author by his wife, Melita H. Moore.

The recession of the early 1980s showed that the absolute expansions and contractions in the level of economic activity, now called "classical cycles" were hardly a thing of the past. We recognize that the modern world is unhappily plagued by both classical and growth cycles, and that the presumed demise of classical cycles in the 1960s was a case of wishful thinking. It became clear that in the modern world it would be advisable and arguably necessary to monitor both classical cycles and growth cycles. As we have seen, *Business Conditions Digest* continues to monitor classical cycles in this country. Growth cycles are similarly monitored monthly at Moore's Center for International Business Cycle Research now at Columbia University. At the same time, Moore continues to work on furthering our understanding of both kinds of cycle through his ongoing research.

Working with Victor Zarnowitz, he has devised a set of "triggers" based on reasonably consistent historical interrelationships among leading, coincident, and lagging indicators. Monitoring the occurrence of these triggers should prove useful in improving the forecasting of cyclical turning points in the economy. In addition, he has developed techniques for tracking historical patterns during recessions and recoveries, and special indicator systems for forecasting employment, inflation rates, and stock market changes. He has also developed weekly indicator systems designed to improve short-run forecasts.

In all of these activities he has continued to do what he always did at the National Bureau. He has brought younger economists to his Center and interested them in his work, involved them in improving the measures, and helped them to become independent contributors to the ongoing task of enriching and improving our ability to understand instability in the modern world. The measures developed and the analyses performed at the Center for International Business Cycle Research are reported on television and radio, and in national magazines and the press. The publications of the Center are increasingly influential and regarded as highly helpful to a broad mix of readers.

Today he has a significant impact on the public's perception of business cycle developments, and his influence can be readily observed. He is one of the country's most widely consulted economists, most especially on interpreting the ongoing signs of cyclical movement in the economy. His views are sought by government officials, businesses and trade unions, journalists, and academic economists. Through all these relationships, Moore continues to support many types of research on business cycles and forecasting. As he has devoted much of his own attention to business cycle indicators, he fully appreciates that there is continuing need for more and better statistics, for progress in a variety of methodological approaches, and for increased historical and international analyses, if we are to gain greater control over economic instability. The present volume has been organized so as to reflect this wide influence and appeal.

Throughout his career, Geoffrey Moore has epitomized the careful and dispassionate contributor to basic research. His approach and his contribution were well summarized by Senator William Proxmire at the time of Moore's last testimo iy as Commissioner of Labor Statistics to the Joint Economic Committee. Throughout his tenure in that post he had been adamant in his refusal to do anything which might be construed as politicizing the official statistics, particularly those reporting on the monthly state of employment and unemployment. Said Proxmire,

> I want to take this occasion to express the gratitude of this committee for your fine cooperation. . . . You have made a fine record, it has been very helpful to this Senator, greatly improved my understanding of the unemployment figures and, I think, the committee and the country as a whole. . . . In the years I have been on this committee, and I have been on this committee for 12 or 13 years, I cannot recall any replacement of an economic official which has been more widely deplored by the economic community than in your case. I think it is a great tribute to you.

This volume is an effort to present some of the current thinking on the approach to business cycle research to which Moore has devoted his professional life. We feel that this evidence of continued progress in understanding instability is the greatest tribute we can pay to Geoffrey Moore.

2

Plan of the Book

Philip A. Klein

The present volume was written to honor Geoffrey H. Moore's contributions to business cycle analysis, and it thus reflects his research interests. It also reflects the diverse approaches to economic inquiry influenced by his work. On any given day, he is as likely to be consulted by economics and financial reporters as by government economists. Economists in industry, no less than academic economists, regard his work as crucial to their own monitoring of unfolding economic events. In their diversity, all these economists speak to the usefulness of the work Moore has been so pivotal in developing. Moore's continued application of Mitchell's eclectic approach to business cycle theory has shown the fruitfulness of selecting from a variety of insightful theories and analytical techniques.

The contributors to this volume are, therefore, representative of the wide variety of economists who have incorporated Moore's approach to the analysis of business cycles in their everyday thinking, and who find it a valuable adjunct to whatever other ways of monitoring instability they may also utilize. By including a diverse group of economists in this *Festschrift*, it is our hope that we have provided a volume which will offer up-to-date thinking about instability as well as new insights into the usefulness of indicators in various contexts. In the process, the volume should prove informative to the public as well as to all economists concerned about growth and stability, unemployment and inflation.

Accordingly, this volume contains essays which assess the current state of indicator systems and essays which consider how the indicator systems can be helpful both in forecasting and in analyzing instability. There are contributions which are devoted to specific types of forecasting problems. Several pieces consider ways in which indicators and indicator systems can be improved. Finally, a group of essays illustrate how indicators can be applied to a representative group of both theoretical and policy problems.

In Part II, Ernst Boehm's "Understanding Business Cycles Today: A Critical Review of Theory and Fact" is broadly cast to provide a background for the essays which follow. Boehm considers the objectives of business cycle theory historically, contemplates changes in our views about instability, pays particular attention to some of the more recent developments in business cycle theory, and considers finally the policy implications of this work. Throughout his discussion of business cycle theory, he underscores the necessity of evaluating theoretical developments against the empirical record. Thus, his approach is thoroughly in the tradition of Wesley Clair Mitchell who argued always that first we must examine "the main facts."

From his review, Boehm reaches four major conclusions. First, he underscores anew the individuality of each cyclical episode. Against this individuality, however, he delineates the common features which justify the search for business cycle theory and offer at least modest promise to the pursuit of policy improvements. Second, Boehm reviews the evidence with which to confront the old question of whether business cycles are endogenous, exogenous, or a confluence of both. He concludes (as indeed earlier have Moore and others who have worked with him) that not only is there evidence of both endogeneity and exogeneity in the etiology of instability, but there is evidence of variability in the mix from one cycle to another. He suggests that this empirical record casts doubt on the recent views that cycles can be explained entirely as the result of random events, or of unanticipated monetary shocks, or as the result of random real shocks. Thus, Boehm suggests that the empirical record is not sympathetic either to rational expectations theorists or exponents of real business cycles. Third, Boehm urges as an outgrowth of the second conclusion that more explicit attention needs to be paid to the empirical record in future efforts at developing more useful cycle theory. Finally, Boehm reaffirms, in light of the recent record, the Mitchellian case for developing an eclectic theory of business cycles.

Part III is devoted to four essays which attempt to assess the current state of the indicator system in a number of ways. This is eminently appropriate and such reassessment has always been a regular part of maintaining the indicators. Indeed, as was mentioned in the Introduction, the short list of "most reliable indicators" has been revised at least a half dozen times since Burns and Mitchell produced the first such list in 1938. It is appropriate, therefore, that experts in business cycle analysis should continue to monitor the indicators on an ongoing basis.

In the first essay, Joel Popkin considers why some of the leading indicators lead. He begins by—in a sense—validating the indicator approach, noting that the leading indicators are virtually the only forecasting methodology reported monthly by the Federal government. Thus, this method implicitly has the governmental stamp of approval. He returns to the old charge that the indicators are derived from a methodology reflecting "measurement without theory" and shows that indeed there is considerable theory embedded in the indicator system.

Popkin is particularly interested in the manufacturing sector, and he focuses attention on the speed of adjustment of production in that sector of the economy as it responds to altered demand-supply relations. He examines behavior in this sector as it can be tracked from changes in orders to changes in inventories. He argues that we might be able to improve our leading indicator system by concentrating on developing leaders for manufacturing per se. He constructs an experimental leading indicator of manufacturing capacity utilization based on the relationship between prior unfilled orders and new orders (to represent demand) and current finished goods inventories (to represent supply). He analyzes the ratio of the two demand indicators to the supply series in both current and constant dollars and finds that the ratios in both, on average, form leads at business cycle turning points, although the leads are longer at peaks than at troughs. He concludes with the observation that the cyclical behavior of inventories is a major factor in the timing of leading indexes, and that the development of leaders for the service sector may be more difficult than has been the case for the manufacturing sector. Popkin's work points, therefore, toward a possible direction in which enhanced precision in the indicator system might be achieved.

In the second essay, Werner Strigel considers the potential contribution to monitoring business cycles which can be made by what are known as "qualitative indicators." In contrast to the "quantitative indicators" pioneered by the Burns-Mitchell approach, qualitative indicators are based on surveys of various groups of participants in the economic process. Surveys of entrepreneurs and consumers have been conducted for many years in the United States (e.g., the Michigan Consumer Survey started shortly after the Second World War and the Dun and Bradstreet survey of entrepreneurs also goes back to the late 1940s). As a general rule, these surveys have not been included in U.S. indicator systems. For example, the value of new orders in dollars has been available, and it perhaps did not seem necessary, therefore, to include information from entrepreneurs regarding increases or decreases in new orders. Especially where quantitative data are not available, however, as has often been the case in countries outside the United States, survey data have provided a useful clue to cyclical developments. Europeans, under the leadership of Strigel and the Institute for Economic Research in Munich, which he headed for many years, have popularized such surveys in most European market-oriented countries. The European Economic Commission has collected these national surveys from member countries for some time and publishes a monthly report on consumer surveys and another on surveys of business managers. In each survey, the respondent is asked to assess what has been happening in the immediate past and what is likely to happen in the immediate future. The time frame, both retrospective and prospective, is customarily about four months.

These two surveys have now been combined to produce what Strigel calls an "Economic Climate" Indicator, and he assesses these three indicators in his study. Specifically, he examines the "business climate," the "consumption climate," and the "economic climate" for the European Community, Japan, and the United States, basing his climate indicator for each on available survey data.

The surveys pose their questions on orders, sales, etc., in such form that the respondent can reply "up" or "increase," "down" or "decrease," or "no change." These replies are then netted—that is, we calculate the percentage who say "up" less the percentage who say "down"—and the climate indicators are based on the analysis of the resulting "net balances." Strigel compares movements in his climate indicators to subsequent movements in a comparable quantitative measure of economic activity. Thus, for each of his three geographic groups he relates movements in the business climate to changes in industrial production, changes in the consumption climate to changes in private consumption, and changes in the economic climate to changes in GNP. He finds that the qualitative indicators do a reasonably good job of tracking changes in the quantitative activity to which they pertain, and that the leads of the qualitative indicators are usually longer than the leads in the U.S. leading index. It is important to bear in mind that the net balances are in effect already in the form of first differences of the survey results, which accounts for some of their lead over changes in levels of quantitative activity. However, Strigel has done an interesting job of suggesting the potential for improving our arsenal of forecasting tools were we to combine qualitative and quantitative indicators.

In the third essay, Phillip Cagan presents a careful examination of the impact of the inclusion of various alternative measures of the money supply on the behavior of the composite leading index. He focuses attention on the usefulness of different measures of monetary changes. No measure of monetary change was included in the short list of leaders prior to the 1975 revision. Zarnowitz and Boschan recommended the inclusion of deflated M1 in the 1975 revision. This was replaced by deflated M2 in 1979. Interestingly, as Cagan shows, the leads in M2 became far less clear in the 1980s than had been the case earlier. The change in the money supply is the only leading indicator which reflects actions by monitors of aggregate economic activity (in this case the monetary authorities) rather than the changes in interrelationships developing explicitly (mostly endogenously) in the private sector. As such, it was included originally because it was thought to be a reliable leader itself and to improve the leading qualities of the index. As Cagan notes, the recent deterioration in the lead in this series combined with its increased volatility suggests that reconsideration of the treatment of money in the composite index may be in order.

Cagan examined a variety of monetary aggregates which might be substituted for M2, including M1, nonterm M3, the monetary base, liquid assets, and total debt. When substituted for M2 in the composite index, none of these produces a longer lead at peaks except nonterm M3, which, however, shows greater variability as well.

Cagan argues that recent institutional and other changes account for the altered cyclical behavior of the monetary aggregates and concludes that one can in theory make a case for including either M2 or the monetary base which affects the money supply indirectly. In terms of their cyclical behavior, one cannot support the choice of one more than the other, but Cagan argues we should not include both. In terms of volatility, a case can be made for substituting the base for M2. A question raised by Cagan's analysis but which he does not directly address is whether a current review of all the evidence still ratifies the 1975 decision for inclusion of any monetary aggregate.

In a final essay in this part, Lawrence R. Klein considers the possibilities of including business cycle indicators in econometric models and the potential gain involved. It could perhaps be argued that this constitutes an "application" of indicators and might be properly placed in Part V, but Klein is principally concerned with assessing the temporal characteristics of indicators as they reflect important interrelationships over the cycle. From this perspective, he is asking what the currently regarded "most reliable" business cycle indicators might add to the forecasting properties of econometric models.

Klein begins by noting that one could include indicators in models either by making the composite leading index a variable in the model or by including the individual components of the index separately in different equations of the model. He chooses the latter approach. Individually reviewing the eleven series currently included in the leading index, he suggests that M2 exemplifies an exogenous variable which might be included profitably in econometric models (cf. Cagan's discussion of this above). Next, Klein considers the index of stock market prices and asserts that in his view it represents the one leader which he would classify as a random error variable. Because he regards it as containing a large erratic component, he would not include it in econometric models. The other nine leaders currently on the "short list" are all classified by Klein as endogenous variables, and he considers the possible contribution of each as a potential source of additional information in econometric models. He notes that some of the leaders are already included implicitly if not explicitly in some models.

He also considers the coincident indicators and the lagging indicators, noting that many models contain a number of the major coincident indicators in one form or another. He recalls the earlier work of Irma and Frank Adelman, which in effect concluded that one could simulate cycles, employing the Klein-Goldberger Model, which had cyclical properties similar to those deemed important in the empirical work so closely associated with the National Bureau in the years Moore was active there.

In a final section, Klein considers the potential gains from adding variables which represent anticipations (such as business or consumer surveys) to the evidence of more explicit advance commitment represented in the leading series by, for example, new orders and building permits. Klein's comments are interesting, particularly when compared with the views of Strigel who, as noted, focuses explicitly and in detail on the forecasting properties of this type of information.

A major implicit contribution of Klein's essay is its clear recognition of the complementary nature of work on business cycle indicators and the development of econometric models. Far from suggesting that we choose between these two approaches, Klein instead focuses on the potential gains of combining these two approaches. As such, he has opened a potentially significant avenue for much future research.

Part IV is devoted to a group of essays assessing the usefulness of cyclical indicators in forecasting business cycle developments. The first essay considers the usefulness of indicators in forecasting stock price movements, while the second and third are devoted to an examination of the role of indicators in more general forecasting.

In the first paper, Michael P. Niemira evaluates the leading indicators as an aid in forecasting stock price activity. He begins by suggesting that if one profiles stock price behavior over the cycle by means of the nine-stage pattern introduced by Burns and Mitchell in *Measuring Business Cycles*, one finds that stock market gains are greatest in the early stages of a bull market (stages II and III), while the losses become larger as bear markets move from stages VI through VIII. Recognizing the well-known leading properties of stock market activity at business cycle turning points, he turns to the question of forecasting the turns in this leading indicator. Niemira focuses on a technique developed by Salih Neftci. By examining the period-to-period change in an indicator over past expansions or contractions, the Neftci method predicts turning points by employing sequential analysis to determine when the probability of a cumulative sequence of period-to-period changes exceeds some predetermined statistical confidence level, say 90 percent. As is true of most forecasting techniques, the higher the confidence level used, the smaller the lead in the forecast.

Niemira tests three possible leaders of stock market behavior: a leading inflation index, the inverse of the composite index of the lagging indicators, and the real money supply (M2). Of these three, he finds that the best predictor of stock price behavior is the leading inflation index which he has developed. It is similar to the one developed by Moore and his colleagues at the CIBCR but includes slightly different indicators. Basing a buy or sell signal on historical expansions and contractions and setting the signal at a preset 90 percent confidence level so that the turning point was reached, he concludes that over the past thirty-five years one could have predicted stock market leads by more than thirteen months, on average, and troughs almost seven months in advance. He finds that M2 performs least satisfactorily as an early signal of stock price behavior, a finding that also is relevant to Phillip Cagan's examination of the cyclical behavior of M2 in Part III.

Like many forecasting devices, a principal weakness in forecasting peaks or troughs by this method arises because of the historical variability hidden by focusing on average behavior patterns. But Niemira concludes that applying the Neftci approach to forecasting with leading indicators is useful in the case of stock price forecasting and by extension could enrich other forecasting efforts in this and other areas of the economy as well.

In a second essay, Edgar Fiedler contemplates the state of the science and art of forecasting more broadly, and also from the perspective of those who use forecasts as well as those who make forecasts. He notes the current attitude toward what is possible and contrasts it with the relative and probably misplaced optimism regarding the possibilities of precision in forecasting which was prevalent in the 1960s. Recognizing these recent doubts, he traces the progress he thinks has been made. He argues that we can now generalize about instability sufficiently well to enable us to understand and to quantify, at least broadly, the parameters which apply to the depth, duration, and diffusion of typical postwar cyclical disturbances.

Fiedler offers some views on the probable causes of recent cyclical excesses, and assesses the chances of another episode approaching the dimensions of the 1929 depression. He then focuses on the role of the cyclical indicators in monitoring economic instability. Like several other contributors to this volume, notably L. R. Klein, he stresses the view that the indicators do indeed mirror structural imbalances and distortions which, when examined systematically, can form the basis for useful theorizing. He argues that the theory underlying the indicators is, not surprisingly, an eclectic theory in the tradition of Mitchell, a point also made in the first essay by Boehm.

Finally, Fiedler offers his views on the forecasting record and suggests that while there is clearly room for improvement, forecasters in general do better than would be the case with a naive forecast. There is also some evidence of improved forecasting accuracy. The reader will want to compare Fiedler's views with those of McNees in the next essay.

The last essay in this group is by Stephen K. McNees and deals from several perspectives with the overall accuracy of macroeconomic forecasts of U.S. economic activity. McNees considers both annual forecasts for a thirty-five year period and quarterly forecasts for the past dozen years. He is concerned not only with the overall accuracy of these forecasts, but with the important question of whether forecast accuracy is improving over time. Also addressed are the related questions of whether there is a discernible difference in the accuracy of forecasts of different variables and for different time horizons, and whether accuracy in the vicinity of turning points is significantly different from accuracy during cyclical phases. He considers a variety of forecasting techniques and devotes some attention to which forecasters and which techniques are most accurate.

While his paper is thus rich in empirical detail, several of his general findings seem particularly instructive. First, McNees finds that over time annual forecasts of both real GNP and inflation have improved. The same conclusion is more difficult to substantiate for forecasts of nominal GNP. In general, the private forecasts (e.g., those forecasters surveyed by the American Statistical Association and the National Bureau of Economic Research) do not appear to be significantly more accurate than the government forecasts made by the Council of

Economic Advisers. Conclusions about changes in the accuracy of quarterly forecasts are more difficult to reach, but overall, forecasts based on models of one sort or another generally do better than naive forecasts (e.g., "random walk" or ARIMA models). Finally, there is some evidence that forecasters have done reasonably well in recent cycles in recognizing peaks and have tended to forecast relatively few "false peaks."

Part V is devoted to an aspect of the business cycle indicator approach which has always been of concern to Moore. He believes strongly that any such system is in need of constant reappraisal and improvement if it is to remain useful—let alone become increasingly so—in monitoring instability and in forecasting future directions. Unlike a yardstick, which is immutable, business cycle indicator systems definitionally are never completed, much less perfected. A book reflecting the diverse applications of Moore's approach would scarcely be complete, therefore, without some essays which reflect his methodological, technical, and statistical concerns with improving indicators. Charlotte Boschan and Victor Zarnowitz are two of the economists who have worked prominently both with Moore and independently to improve business cycle indicators over the past thirty years.

In the first essay, Victor Zarnowitz and Phillip Braun make a contribution to our methodological arsenal for monitoring business cycles, but ultimately they do much more. Noting that business cycles in the postwar period have frequently been milder than prewar cycles, they reconsider the usefulness of some of the techniques for studying instability, notably composite leading indexes. They note that these indexes have been refined during the past forty years, and they apply them to the earlier period. Their major methodological effort is to include leading indicators in reduced-form macro models and to apply vector autoregressive analysis to very long time periods. Their work is, therefore, especially interesting in light of the suggestions made earlier in the L. Klein paper.

More specifically, Zarnowitz and Braun examine the interactions within sets of up to six variables representing output, alternative measures of money and fiscal operations, inflation, interest rates, and indexes of leading indicators. Quarterly series are used, each taken with four lags, for three periods: 1949–82, 1919–40, and 1886–1914. The series are in stationary form as indicated by unit root tests. For the early years, the quality of the available data presents some serious problems. They find evidence of strong effects on output of the leading indexes and the short-term interest rate. The monetary effects are reduced greatly when these variables are included. Most variables depend more on their own lagged values than on any other factors, but this is not true of the rates of change in output and the composite leading indexes. Some interesting interperiod differences are noted and discussed.

It is clear that the Zarnowitz-Braun paper has significant and new substantive findings. But it also stakes out some new methodological ground, certainly in terms of the long period covered. The paper is, moreover, closely related to the other work in Part V. Along with suggestions for research made at the end of their paper, one may add the questions concerning the construction of the composite indexes raised in the Boschan-Banerji paper which follows. Also on the agenda for future research, the use of the new leading index going back to 1919 presented by Maltz and Dubrin (see below) raises fascinating possibilities for subjecting that index to the kind of analysis that the Zarnowitz-Braun methodology would permit.

In the second essay, Charlotte Boschan and Anirvan Banerji reassess the way in which composite indexes are constructed. They trace the development of these indexes from their origin in diffusion indexes, through the initial efforts of Julius Shiskin and Moore to combine groups of indicators into an index which would not only reflect the diffusion and duration of the component series but could meaningfully represent their amplitude as well. Because large amplitudes in any one series would dominate simple averages, the problem of reflecting the disparate amplitudes of a number of components in a composite index was confronted by "standardizing" them, that is, by making the average value of the absolute monthly change in each component series over some historical time period equal to one. The components can then be weighted if desired and can also be standardized to make their long-run average change conform to the trend in a target series (e.g., the change in GNP or the coincident index).

The burgeoning use of the computer and the necessity of monitoring both classical and growth cycles have made the construction of composite indexes more complicated, even as new doors were opened for resolving the problems which their development poses. Boschan and Banerji consider the diverse approaches being taken currently to the construction of composite indexes in the United States, Canada, Europe, and Japan, and assess the strengths and weaknesses of each. They suggest an eclectic approach to standardization procedures which, they argue, would improve the comparability of composite indexes across countries, across sectors in a single economy, and over time for both. They conclude with some observations on improving the techniques used for weighting the components of composite indexes. After thirty years of working with composite index construction, we have enough useful experience to cause them to remain hopeful that composite indexes can be made even more helpful in monitoring instability in the future than they have been in the past.

Finally, in this section a new composite index is displayed which has been constructed at the Center for International Business Cycle Research. The long-leading index is presented by Chantal Dubrin and Jean Maltz, two long standing associates of Geoffrey Moore. They have built on the work of John Cullity and Moore who earlier had constructed a long-leading index covering business cycles since 1948. Dubrin and Maltz have pushed an index containing roughly equivalent indicators back to 1919. By linking the two, their index is undoubtedly the leading index covering the longest time span thus far available for the United States. Not only is it a good illustration of the kind of ongoing work with composite indexes pointed to by Boschan and Banerji, but it may well be of interest to researchers focusing on such historical questions as, could we have forecast the Great Depression more accurately had current tools been available then? Several other countries have long monitored instability with both a short- and a long-leading index. The contribution of Dubrin and Maltz, therefore, facilitates some international comparisons. It also illustrates well the ongoing work of the CIBCR designed to improve our techniques for measuring and monitoring instability.

In Part VI, the final part, we have included a group of short essays which display the variety of potential applications of indicators to questions in both economic theory and in policy. In the first, Alfred Malabre considers the conventional business cycle chronology based on the methodology developed originally at the National Bureau of Economic Research. That chronology reflects the efforts noted in Part V which have been made in the past quarter century by Moore and others to keep the methodology timely. Malabre uses this chronology as a background against which to characterize what has transpired in recent business cycles. He focuses on both the severity of recent cycles and their enduring tendency to recur. Echoing the earlier psychological theories of instability, he sees little likelihood of instability disappearing and concludes with the observation that our present stabilization policies may well prove less effective in the future than they have in the past.

A second essay, by John P. Cullity, is similar to the Malabre essay in that it, too, builds upon the approach to explaining instability developed at the National Bureau from its earliest days under Wesley Mitchell and continuing there through Moore's retirement in the late 1970s. So widely are the business cycle indicators followed, it is often forgotten today that in his review of Burns and Mitchell's *Measuring Business Cycles*, Koopmans charged that the indicator approach to analyzing cycles represented what he called "measurement without theory." In fact, the Burns-Mitchell measurement methodology reflected very well Mitchell's theory of instability, sometimes referred to as the "business-economy" explanation. To be sure, Mitchell never got around to writing his long promised book-length theory of cycles, but he spelled out in a number of places his views on what explained cyclical behavior. His theory of instability, which here is newly corroborated by Cullity, was a leading explanation well into the 1930s and was only partially eclipsed by the Keynesian onslaught of the mid-1930s. Mitchell paid a great deal of attention in his theory to the fluctuations in price-cost margins over the cycle, and it is to this phenomenon that Cullity turns our attention. He utilizes a technique widely used by Geoffrey Moore and his colleagues at the

Center for International Business Cycle Research. Called "Recession-Recovery Analysis," Cullity exploits it here to show the relative changes in hourly wages, output per hour, and unit labor costs during three long recoveries, including the recovery still extant in the late 1980s. In an analysis of the 1980s expansion, he argues that the underlying relationship between changes in productivity and changes in wage rates provided an environment which promoted the successful containment of inflation. Cullity contends that when wages increase more rapidly than output per hour, unit labor costs will ineluctably increase and make containing inflation more difficult regardless of the explicit macro-policies surrounding economic performance. (Cullity does not discuss the relationship between explicit macro-polices and changes in unit labor cost.) He argues that there are new forces at work in the economy now affecting price and cost changes. As such, macroeconomic policy will have to adjust to them, or at least take them into account, if it is to prove successful in the future in promoting noninflationary growth.

Cagan and P. Klein take a somewhat different approach and in a pair of essays attempt to demonstrate the usefulness of recent work in business cycles and business cycle indicators in reassessing two old notions in economic theory, the "wealth effect" and "money illusion."

Cagan analyzes the stock market for evidence bearing on the wealth effect. Stock price indexes have long been among the most consistently reliable leading indicators in virtually all market-oriented industrial economies. Indexes of stock prices are found in virtually every country's set of leading indicators. A key concept in the theory of consumer behavior is the wealth effect—the notion that changes in prices will influence consumer attitudes toward their wealth and thus affect subsequent consumption behavior. The concept has most notably found a place in the "life-cycle" theories of consumption developed in the past thirty or so years. These theories have a place for changes in wealth because such changes affect anticipated lifetime income and, therefore, consumption. Cagan focuses on the evidence from the stock market crash of October 1987 as it bears on the notion of a wealth effect. He demonstrates that, in this case, the presumed loss of wealth on the part of stockholders did not result in significant changes in their subsequent consumption.

Cagan notes that a part of the explanation may lie in the concentration of stockholding among that group in the income distribution which can afford to wait until stock prices rise once again. He does indeed get high correlation coefficients for regressions including deflated income, wealth, and stock price changes. But he argues that the results can be and perhaps have been misinterpreted. He utilizes the composite leading index, excluding the stock index (a better leader than stock prices alone), and gets even higher correlation coefficients. He concludes that the high correlation of stock changes with subsequent consumption behavior generally may not be capturing any wealth effect but simply reflecting the tendency for stock fluctuations to act as a proxy for general cyclical fluctuations. That being the case, any correlation between consumption behavior and stock fluctuations is not proof of the existence of any wealth effect but only of the impact of general instability on consumption behavior. (In the process Cagan offers a sobering demonstration that high correlation coefficients do not necessarily support whatever hypothesis is under investigation.) In his analysis, Cagan demonstrates very nicely how one can apply business cycle indicators in the framework which has grown from Mitchell's work to test a variety of concepts in economic theory, here the wealth effect. In this way, work in business cycles can be applied constructively to notions not necessarily derived from cyclical analyses *per se*.

P. Klein attempts to demonstrate the same point with a different example, this time by a new look at another theoretical construct with a long history in economic theory—the notion of money illusion. (Cullity touches on this concept by considering briefly the impact on unit labor costs of rising wages and rising prices.) In the labor sector, money illusion has traditionally suggested that in setting their wage demands, workers may focus too single-mindedly on nominal prices and thereby mistake nominal gains for real gains, a view which data in recent experience does not support very strongly. Klein applies the reasoning behind the notion of money illusion not to labor but instead to entrepreneurs and utilizes qualitative indicators of business confidence in an attempt to discover whether entrepreneurs' confidence is more closely related to real or to nominal changes in aggregate economic activity. Using evidence from four European economies as well as the United States, he finds consistently that entrepreneurs' confidence is more closely attuned to real than to nominal fluctuations, suggesting that modern entrepreneurs are not subject to money illusion. The essay also points out, however, that in earlier work Moore and Klein had found that entrepreneurs' ability to forecast changes in inflation appears, unfortunately, to be very limited at best. They often tend to assume that the inflationary experience of the recent past will continue in the future. Accordingly, even if entrepreneurs do not fall victim to money illusion, their subsequent behavior may cloud this fact especially if they have failed to anticipate inflation correctly.

In yet another study, this one concerned with the international transmission of cyclical disturbances, Anna J. Schwartz and Michael Bordo offer implicitly an example of a point made by Lawrence R. Klein. There is no reason, in principle, not to combine studies of instability based on indicators with those based on econometric models or other types of analysis. In assessing the state of our understanding of the international transmission of instability, Schwartz and Bordo note that there are three types of evidence available on cyclical behavior in response to the transmission of external influences. One type is the set of business cycle studies associated with Moore's work that accepts the NBER reference chronology or the postwar growth cycle chronology. Another type is more recent econometric work. The third type of evidence is historical accounts of individual cycles. The Schwartz-Bordo paper summarizes especially the third type of evidence. As they point out, this approach is not fully satisfactory because it does not distinguish foreign from domestic disturbances, money from real shocks, or the prevailing exchange rate arrangements. Moreover, the evidence, such as it is, intertwines the disturbances and the propagation mechanism within the economy. Covering international instability under varying exchange rates systems (the pre-1914 system, the Bretton Woods world, as well as the current managed floating rate system), they conclude that there is really no consensus among economists on the relative roles of domestic and foreign disturbances in producing the business cyles we experience, nor do we know much about the possible diversity in propagation mechanisms when the disturbances vary. Their implicit conclusion is that with the state of our present knowledge of the complex forces producing international instability, there is room for many methodological approaches to increase understanding.

In the final essay, P. Klein focuses on showing that indicators of both real instability and the inflation rate can be used in the process of analyzing public policy issues. This time, the focus is on the question whether recession as a technique for reducing inflationary tendencies is as effective as many suppose. In particular, he raises the question of whether the popular notion of a "natural rate of unemployment" is useful as an analytical construct as is often claimed, or whether it reflects a rationalization for policy failure. He suggests that logically, one could contemplate with equal cogency a natural rate of inflation below which the unemployment rate is regarded as unacceptably high. One need not agree with the policy implications drawn from this essay to agree that it demonstrates that work on indicators can be useful in policy debates as well as in issues involving business cycle theory and measurement. It is as a demonstration of this point that the essay has been included in this book.

In conclusion, we think that the essays in this volume, taken as whole, demonstrate that the perspective on business cycles taken originally by Wesley Clair Mitchell and the tradition of business cycle research which he spawned and to which Geoffrey H. Moore has contributed so richly, is alive and well. If the debate about stabilization policy has been in some ways rekindled in recent years, it can also be said that we continue to add to our understanding about the causes of instability, albeit more slowly perhaps than we wish. Our techniques of measuring instability have been significantly enhanced in the period since the Second World War, and our development of international indicators of both classical and growth cycles continues to improve both in coverage and to some extent in accuracy. We have noted earlier that the old charge of "measurement without theory" may have largely disappeared as has the equally old debate of whether we could make more significant progress in understanding instability (or more precisely, growth at irregular rates) by proceeding with aggregate rather than disaggregate analysis. Not surprisingly, the answer to the latter question would appear to be that we need both.

Finally, it seems increasingly clear that the tradition of business cycle analysis via indicators and the econometric approach can be combined with potentially fruitful results. Both continue to be developed independently as well. It is also widely appreciated now that progress in understanding instability and in forecasting business cycles is often painfully slow. As such, no methodological school can claim natural superiority or overwhelming advantage. However, it is our hope (and indeed our belief) that these essays attest to the continued value and the future potential of the approach to business cycle monitoring to which Geoffrey H. Moore has devoted his professional life.

II
ANALYZING BUSINESS CYCLES TODAY

3

Understanding Business Cycles Today: A Critical Review of Theory and Fact

Ernst A. Boehm

This paper critically reviews aspects of earlier leading business cycle theories and recent new developments, notably in the United States. The review is made especially in the light of the empirical evidence on business cycles. Some important recent improvements in our knowledge of the facts about business cycles, to which Dr. Geoffrey H. Moore has made a major contribution,[1] appear to have been unjustifiably neglected in certain recent theories. The silence on these empirical findings raises questions about the relevance and usefulness to policy makers of these theoretical developments for the purpose of understanding business cycles today. The recent theoretical developments have centered largely around the subject of rational expectations, which itself has created a great deal of interest in economic theory in general since the early 1970s. Special attention is paid to the recent writings on business cycles stimulated by Robert E. Lucas, one of the leaders of the rational expectations school.

There are four main general conclusions of this review. First, for theoretical and policy purposes, it is necessary to treat each business cycle as an individual. It is important to do so since each cycle varies from one to the next in respect to amplitude and duration; and each varies in the timing and nature of the changes of the co-movements of key variables, which contribute to the variations in ampli-

Acknowledgment is made of financial assistance for this project to the Reserve Bank of Australia from its Economic and Financial Research Fund and to the University of Melbourne through its Committee on Research and Graduate Studies. This paper is a revision of my earlier paper titled "Understanding Business Cycles: A Critical Review of Theory and Fact" which was issued as Research Paper No. 84, Department of Economics, University of Melbourne, June 1982. Its preparation was greatly aided by discussions at seminars given at the University of Pittsburgh in May 1981, the University of Melbourne in April 1982, and Auburn University in June 1984; and its presentation as a paper at the Eleventh Conference of Economists, Flinders University, Adelaide, August 1982. I wish to thank, but in no way implicate, a number of people who have helped in the preparation of this paper, and especially Drs. Jocelyn Horne, Ian McDonald and Paul McGavin for their comments on earlier versions, and Miss Carolyn Ball for valuable assistance in its final preparation.

tude and duration. Nevertheless, one is justified in studying business cycles as a group since "each cycle in some important ways in its decomposition into sectors and in the aggregate bears a close 'family likeness' to earlier cycles" (Boehm and Moore 1984, 35; see also Hicks 1950, 2).

Secondly, interrelated with the first point, there are considerable but varying degrees of endogeneity from one business cycle to another as well as exogenous elements. Hence, business cycles cannot be explained entirely as the result of random events or unanticipated monetary shocks, as suggested by rational expectation theorists (Lucas and Sargent 1979, 14), or of random real shocks to technology as invoked by real business cycle exponents (Kydland and Prescott 1982; Long and Plosser 1983). The concept of the price-cost cycle is briefly reviewed. This recognizes an additional, largely endogenous force which helps to fill an important gap in business cycle theory concerning *why* the main business cycle in industrialized democracies is of relatively short duration.

Thirdly, in formulating an adequate and acceptable theory, more explicit attention needs to be paid to the empirical evidence on business cycles. On the other hand, some empirical evidence itself, or at least the way it has been interpreted, may have contributed to a misunderstanding of the true characteristics of business cycles. This applies to both earlier theorists and the recent rational expectations and real business cycle theorists. Generally speaking, the variety of business cycle theories have, in important respects, fallen significantly short of providing a continuing explanation that is both adequate in the light of what is actually experienced in market-oriented economies and, in particular, in providing a basis which can confidently and continually be relied upon in the formulation of economic policies.

In the light of the history of economic theories of business cycles and of the varying nature of business cycles, a fourth conclusion is that there appears to be a strong case for developing an eclectic theory of business cycles which incorporates essential elements of earlier theories and of the theory of rational expectations, and which also takes into account the price-cost cycle.

The Objectives of Business Cycle Theory

The general objective of any economic theory is to single out for detailed analysis the key economic variables. Though the theory may be an abstraction from reality and oversimplifies the real world, nevertheless, it needs to be sufficiently relevant and credible to be convincing, attractive, and helpful to policy makers. It is an advantage, of course, if the theory can also be intelligible to policy makers so that full or sufficient communication can take place between economists and policy makers in explaining economic phenomena (such as business cycles) and in the choice, if desired, of appropriate policies. The understanding is vital so that policy makers can seek and obtain a consensus in support of any economic and social objective, and so aid the success of government policies. Therefore, one of the main concerns in this paper is to see whether the business cycles that earlier economists talked about in their theories, and the cycles that those recently contributing to the theory of business cycles are talking about, are, in fact, like the cycles actually experienced and identified.

The Changing Interest in Business Cycles

During the 1950s, economists gave considerable attention to questions of economic fluctuations. It was only natural that many economists, in turning their attention from war economics back to peacetime problems should have once again returned to the problems that had occupied them in the 1930s. Evidence that business cycles were prominent in their thoughts seems clearly illustrated by the fact that more than a dozen economists took the opportunity to contribute to the subject through their article-length reviews of Hicks's (1950) contribution. The subject of economic fluctuations also attracted increasing attention during the 1950s and 1960s in the revival of interest among economists in the subject of economic growth. The stimulus for this came largely from Harrod (1948). However, interest in business cycles waned as the experience of the 1960s led an increasing number of economists to raise the question of whether the business cycle was obsolete: witness the conference (Bronfenbrenner 1969) held in 1967 "on the possible obsolescence of the 10-year business cycle and the various patterns of long- and short-term fluctuations that have characterized capitalistic economic life" (p.v).

The question, "Is the business cycle obsolete?" especially reflected the relatively favorable economic situation in the United States but also that in other industrialized countries. For the United States, it was the time of expanding expenditures on President Johnson's "Great Society" including policies to eliminate poverty.[2] It was, in addition, the time of rising expenditures on the Vietnam War which was helping not only to maintain the expansion phase but also to build the rising inflation expectations that continued into and marked the 1970s. These experiences were transmitted in varying degrees to other industrial countries (Boehm and Moore 1984, 47–48). In the 1960s, there was substantial economic growth throughout most of the world and especially in the industrialized countries. Moreover, this growth meant real advances in per capita income which continued in most advanced countries throughout much or all of the 1960s without a setback involving an absolute decline in real output.

Another important reason why interest in business cycles declined after the very considerable debate on the subject in the first half of the 1950s and in light of the strong, general uptrend during the 1950s and 1960s was because models of the business cycle since the publication of Keynes (1936) had generally applied to special cases or economic conditions. For instance, the theories of Kaldor (1940) and Hicks (1950) seem to apply most appropriately to a severe economic depression, as experienced in the early 1930s. More recently, Lucas (1980, 706) has been worried that the 1930s depression does not fit the rational expectations theory of business cycles that he was developing. But he has no need to be worried on this account. The depression of the 1930s was atypical. It was a special case and stands (along with earlier major depressions)[3] apart from the main business cycle.

It is important to see the rational expectations revolution of the 1970s and the development of a new classical theory of business cycles as a consequence and against the background of the spectacular failure of Keynesian macroeconomic models in the first half of the 1970s. This failure occurred in the face of accelerating or high rates of inflation and rising or high unemployment rates. In the 1960s, the application of Keynesian principles to economic policy appeared to be working successfully; hence, as noted above, many economists, business people, policy makers, and others increasingly believed that the business cycle had been made obsolete.

However, illusions about the ability to influence the course and level of economic activity were shattered for many economists by the major world recession in 1974. Indeed, Lucas and Sargent (1979, 1) described the years 1973 to 1975 for "the U.S. economy . . . its first major depression since the 1930s." Before reviewing more fully the new classical theory of rational expectations and recent models of real business cycles, it will be instructive to discuss the empirical evidence of business cycles.

Distinction between Growth Cycles and Classical Cycles

As shown in Tables 3.1 and 3.2, the term "business cycles" is used in this paper to refer to either growth or classical cycles, or both.

Classical cycles are defined as recurring expansions and contractions in the absolute level of aggregate economic activity. Classical cycles historically have been the main concern of business cycle studies at the National Bureau of Economic Research (NBER) in New York. The NBER studies began with the work of Mitchell (1927; see Moore and Zarnowitz 1986). The classical cycle fits the business cycle theories of Kalecki (1939) and Schumpeter (1939). It also fits the hints Keynes (1936) offered about the nature of business cycles; and it is the cycle that is clearly at the heart of the post-Keynesian models of, for instance, Kaldor (1940) and Hicks (1950). Table 3.1 shows that there was no classical contraction in the United States between February 1961 and December 1969, a period of 106 months; Table 3.2 shows a classical upswing continuing in Australia from September 1961 to July 1974, a period of 154 months.

The experience of the 1960s, especially in the United States with no classical downturn between 1961 to 1969, contributed to a revival of interest in growth cycles.[4] Growth cycles are defined as fluctuations in the rate of growth of aggregate economic activity, with periods when the growth rate is above the long-

Table 3.1

Phases of Business Cycles, U.S., 1948–87

	Growth cycles							Classical cycles					
	Date of peaks and troughs by month and year[a]		Average duration in months					Date of peaks and troughs by month and year[b]		Average duration in months			
			Contrac-tion (peak to trough) (3)	Expan-sion (trough to peak) (4)	Cycle					Contrac-tion (peak to trough) (9)	Expan-sion (trough to peak) (10)	Cycle	
	peak (1)	trough (2)			(peak to peak) (5)	(trough to trough) (6)		peak (7)	trough (8)			(peak to peak) (11)	(trough to trough) (12)
	7/48	10/49	15					11/48	10/49	11			
	3/51	7/52	16	17	32	33							
	3/53	8/54	17	8	24	25		7/53	5/54	10	45	56	55
	2/57	4/58	14	30	47	44		8/57	4/58	8	39	49	47
	2/60	2/61	12	22	36	34		4/60	2/61	10	24	32	34
	5/62	10/64	29	15	27	44							
	6/66	10/67	16	20	49	36							
	3/69	11/70	20	17	33	37		12/69	11/70	11	106	116	117
	3/73	3/75	24	28	48	52		11/73	3/75	16	36	47	52
	12/78	12/82	48	45	69	93		1/80	7/80	6	58	74	64
								7/81	11/82	16	12	18	28
Averages:			21	22	41	44				11	46	56	57
Standard deviations:			11	11	14	20				4	30	32	29

Sources: [a]CIBCR 1988a.
  [b]U.S. Department of Commerce 1988, p.102.

Note: The average durations and standard deviations are rounded to full months.

Table 3.2

Phases of Business Cycles, Australia, 1950–87

Date of peaks and troughs by month and year[a]		Growth cycles					Date of peaks and troughs by month and year[b]		Classical cycles			
		Average duration in months							Average duration in months			
		Contrac-tion (peak to trough) (3)	Expan-sion (trough to peak) (4)	Cycle					Contrac-tion (peak to trough) (9)	Expan-sion (trough to peak) (10)	Cycle	
peak (1)	trough (2)			(peak to peak) (5)	(trough to trough) (6)	peak (7)	trough (8)				(peak to peak) (11)	(trough to trough) (12)
4/51	11/52	19				4/51	9/52	17			
8/55	1/58	29	33	52	62	12/55	12/57	24	39	56	63
8/60	9/61	13	31	60	44	9/60	9/61	12	33	57	45
4/65	1/68	33	43	56	76						
5/70	3/72	22	28	61	50						
2/74	10/75	20	23	45	43	7/74	10/75	15	154	166	169
8/76	10/77	14	10	30	24	8/76	10/77	14	10	25	24
6/81	5/83	23	44	58	67	6/81	5/83	23	44	58	67
11/85	3/87	16	30	53	46						
Averages:		21	30	52	52			18	56	72	74
Standard deviations:		7	11	10	16			5	56	54	56

Sources: [a]As for Table 3.1, source (a), and Institute of Applied Economic and Social Research, University of Melbourne.
[b]Boehm and Moore 1984, p. 42, and Institute of Applied Economic and Social Research, University of Melbourne.

Note: As for "note" to Table 3.1.

term trend rate alternating with periods when it is below this long-term value, but not necessarily negative. This enables account to be taken of the important fact that a slowdown may occur when the growth rate, though continuing positive, is slower than the long-term trend rate of growth. Hence excess capacity, notably unemployment, rises. On the other hand, during the expansion phase of the growth cycle, when excess capacity is being absorbed, the actual rate of growth is above the long-term trend rate of growth.

An interesting and important point to note from Table 3.1 is that the peaks of the growth cycle in the United States during the period 1948-87, when there was a corresponding classical cycle, occurred in all cases before the classical cycle peak. Table 3.2 shows that this was true also for three of the six growth cycle peaks for Australia when there was a corresponding classical downturn over the 1950-87 period. In general, the classical peak tends to lag the growth cycle peak, except when there is a sharp downturn as occurred in Australia in April 1951 and June 1981, since the tendency is for the growth rate to remain positive for several months before an absolute fall in aggregate economic activity is experienced and the growth rate becomes negative. By contrast, the troughs in both the United States and Australia occurred at the same time more often than not for both growth and classical cycles. It is also important to note that on three occasions for the United States (namely, 1951-52, 1962-64, and 1966-67) and three for Australia (1965-68, 1970-72, and 1985-87), there was no classical contraction corresponding to the growth contraction; and for the only time since World War II in either country, there was a classical expansion in the United States in 1980-81 but not a growth expansion, that is, the growth rate became positive but remained below trend.

Mistaken and Changing Views about the Nature of Business Cycles

In the recent active pursuit of new ideas and methods in business cycle research (Sims 1977; Lucas 1975, 1977, 1980; Lucas and Sargent 1979; Kydland and Prescott 1982; Long and Plosser 1983; McCallum 1987, 1988), no attention has been given to the distinction between classical cycles and growth cycles. This appears an important omission and potentially serious weakness. It also immediately raises questions and doubts about the extent of the relevance of the theory being promoted and its usefulness to policy makers. For example, it was important and helpful in the United States experience during 1979 to recognize that a growth slowdown was occurring even though the recession of the classical cycle did not begin until January 1980, a lag of 13 months on the growth cycle peak (see Table 3.1).

However, in defense of business cycle theorists, it seems highly likely that at least part of the lack of relevance of business cycle theory to the facts could stem from the shortcomings of earlier empirical work in the identification and explanation of the economic fluctuations that have actually been experienced.[5] This weakness probably applies to the empirical work on business cycles for most countries. For instance, many economists and economic historians have long felt that the United States has the best documented evidence and most reliable chronology of the classical cycle—or the business cycle as it is generally known—dating back to the 1830s, as provided by the NBER. However, Zarnowitz (1981) has cast doubt on whether the NBER chronology of peaks and troughs for the United States, in fact, relates to the classical cycle, as has been generally believed (see also Moore and Zarnowitz 1986). Zarnowitz (1981, 493) states:

> It is important to recall that the expansions and contractions of the early business cycles in the NBER chronology tend to be of nearly equal length—much like the phases of the growth cycles and very unlike those of the later business [classical] cycles in which the expansions are much longer than the contractions.

Table 3.1 shows that since 1948 the contraction (column 3) and expansion (column 4) phases of growth cycles in the United States have been, on average, more alike, whereas the contraction phase of the classical cycles (column 9) with an average of 11 months has been less than one-quarter the duration of the expansion phase (column 10) of 46 months.

Australia's experience, in some important respects, has been comparable (see Table 3.2) to that of the United States for both growth cycles and classical cycles. The contraction phase of the growth cycle of an average of 21 months has been the same in both countries. But the average expansion phase has been longer for Australia, 30 months compared with 22 months in the United States. Hence the average duration of growth cycles in Australia at 52 months both for the peak to peak and the trough to trough cycles has been 11 months and 8 months longer, respectively, than the average durations in the United States.

One consequence of the shorter average duration of the growth cycle in the United States is that between 1951 and 1983, the United States experienced eight growth cycles compared with seven in Australia. But thus far in the 1980s, Australia has encountered an additional growth cycle peak and trough compared with the United States.

With respect to the classical cycle experience, the average contraction phase has been just over half as long again for Australia at 18 months compared with 11 months for the United States. By contrast, the average expansion phase of Australia's classical cycle has been 56 months compared with 46 months for the United States. The relatively long average durations of the classical upswings in both the United States and Australia were influenced greatly by the long classical upswing in the 1960s, which for Australia continued until July 1974. These experiences in Australia and the United States highlight one important aspect (identified by economic indicator analysis) of the changing cyclical variability of business cycles from country to country and one time to another in the same country (see DeLong and Summers 1986b; Moore and Zarnowitz 1986; Zarnowitz and Moore 1986).

The findings in Tables 3.1 and 3.2 do not support the earlier writers on business cycles who generally believed that business activity was subject to 7- to 10-year cycles. For this, writers were much influenced by the timing of commercial crises in nineteenth-century Britain. The accumulating empirical evidence (notably the pioneering work of Mitchell at the NBER) of a short cycle in the United States with a duration of 3 to 4 years led, for instance, Schumpeter (1939) and Hansen (1941, 1951) to write in terms of a "minor cycle" of 3 to 4 years being superimposed on a "major cycle" of 7 to 10 years' duration.

However, the major empirical study of Burns and Mitchell (1946) and later NBER studies (in U.S. Department of Commerce 1988, 102) and Center for International Business Cycle Research (CIBCR 1988a) studies have strengthened the conclusion that the main business cycle in the United States is a short cycle. Burns and Mitchell provided a reference cycle for the United States from 1834 to 1939, with monthly turning points from 1854 forward. The NBER, and also the CIBCR since 1979, have progressively updated this reference cycle. A consequence of the strong evidence supporting only the relatively short cycle was that Schumpeter's and Hansen's idea of minor and major cycles lost appeal. Thus Matthews (1959, 214), after making a detailed examination of "the periodicity of fluctuations in the United States," rejected "the notion of a regular or inherent tendency to fluctuations of 7–10 years' duration." But he concluded that "the tendency to a three- to four-year cycle is well established." By contrast, Matthews (1959, 223) concluded that for Great Britain, "the observed timing of fluctuations conformed surprisingly well to a roughly seven- to ten-year pattern from early in the nineteenth century until World War II." But, for the United Kingdom, as more recently for the United States and Australia, and also for Canada, Japan, West Germany, Taiwan and South Korea, the main business cycle has been a relatively short cycle as can be seen from the summary presented in Table 3.3.

It is of interest to note here that the author's own research work for Australia (Boehm 1971, ch. 3; Boehm 1979, 16–32; Boehm and Defris 1977, 1982; Boehm and Moore 1982, 1984; Boehm 1987a) has led to the conclusion that the main business cycle in Australia over the last 130 years has been a relatively short cycle, generally varying from 2 to 5 years' duration. It seems likely that these cycles also should be appropriately classified as growth cycles. But there is a serious lack of statistical data for periods before World War II to enable one to determine accurately the turning points of classical cycles and growth cycles as are presented in Table 3.2 for the period 1950–87.

A weakness of the above analysis of duration in terms of averages, and the general conclusion in support of the main business cycle being a relatively short cycle, is that it could misleadingly support the view that business cycles are much more alike from one cycle to another than, in fact, they are. For instance, the

Table 3.3

Average Duration of Business Cycles in Eight Countries

| | | | Growth cycles | | | | | Classical cycles | | | |
| | | | Average duration in months | | | | | | Average duration in months | | |
Country (1)	Period (2)	Number (3)	Contraction (peak to trough) (4)	Expansion (trough to peak) (5)	Cycle (peak to peak) (6)	Cycle (trough to trough) (7)	Number (8)	Contraction (peak to trough) (9)	Expansion (trough to peak) (10)	Cycle (peak to peak) (11)	Cycle (trough to trough) (12)
Australia[a]	1950–87	8	21	30	52	52	5	18	56	72	74
S.D.			7	11	10	16		5	56	54	56
Canada[b]	1950–82	10	17	18	36	35					
S.D.			5	10	12	13					
Japan[b]	1953–83	6	21	35	52	56					
S.D.			9	17	18	24					
South Korea[b]	1966–85	4	22	35	57	57					
S.D.			5	11	8	12					
Taiwan[b]	1963–82	5	26	20	40	46					
S.D.			15	9	16	13					
United Kingdom[b]	1951–83	6	28	31	57	62					
S.D.			11	11	11	19					
United States[c]	1948–82	9	21	22	41	44	7	11	46	56	57
S.D.			11	11	14	20		4	30	32	29
West Germany[b]	1951–83	6	30	29	58	59					
S.D.			10	14	13	20					

Sources: [a]As for Table 3.2; [b]CIBCR 1988a; [c]As for Table 3.1.

Notes: The average durations and standard deviations (S.D.) are rounded to full months. Gaps indicate that data are not available.

popular idea in textbooks of a 40-month short cycle (popularized as the Kitchin cycle by Schumpeter 1939) might seem to be approximately verified for the United States according to the growth cycle averages of 41 months from peak to peak and 44 months from trough to trough shown at the foot of columns 5 and 6, respectively, in Table 3.1. But a glance down both columns reveals that the distributions around both averages are considerable, from 24 to 69 months from peak to peak and 25 to 93 from trough to trough. The considerable variability of the individual phase and cycle durations is shown by the relatively high standard deviations in Table 3.1. For Australia, Table 3.2 (columns 5 and 6) shows an average growth cycle duration of 52 months, but also with a big distribution around the average. The biggest variation, as indicated by the standard deviations, was for the trough to trough growth cycles from 24 to 76 months. Furthermore, it needs to be remembered that in both the Australian and U.S. experiences, not all growth cycles developed into a classical cycle.

But it is not only in respect to duration that important and complex differences occur from one cycle to another. Major differences also occur in the amplitude, as is partly allowed for by the distinction between classical cycles and certain growth cycles and noted by the fact that some growth slowdowns do not lead to a classicial downturn (as noted above from Tables 3.1 and 3.2). Empirical analyses have also shown that it is helpful to distinguish between growth contractions which are, for instance, mild or sharp and deep, and expansions which are weak and brief, weak but prolonged, or strong and prolonged, and so on (see Boehm and Defris 1977, 53–60; Boehm and Defris 1982, 63–67; Moore 1980b, 6–7; Boehm and Moore 1982, 19, 53–54; Zarnowitz and Moore 1986, 542). These variations may be partly explained by differences in the strength of the key determinants of aggregate demand, notably real investment and exports. There may, in addition, be changes on the supply side. The differences in these forces influence the timing, nature, and duration of the fluctuations and expectations regarding further fluctuations.

There may also be important differences between cycles and the influences on those cycles from variations in the time in a particular phase when turns occur in the relative changes in costs, productivity, prices, and profit margins. While it seems reasonable to view these characteristics as generally changing in a typical, predictable way during the main phases of a business cycle, and to view them following similar sequences in successive cycles, it is, nevertheless, important to interpret flexibly the actual timing and degree of the relative changes. It is unrealistic to assume as Lucas did (1970, 26–27) that productivity is "fixed over the cycle" (see also Boehm 1986, 34). Detailed evidence justifying a flexible approach regarding the timing and nature of the relative changes in the key variables of earnings, productivity, costs, prices, and profits during business cycles is provided for Australia in Boehm (1982b) and for the United States in Moore (1980a, part II, especially ch. 11 and 14) and Moore (1983, part II, especially ch. 12 and 16). As Hicks (1950, 2) also noted:

> The cycles are not uniform; they differ among themselves quite considerably; but there can surely be no doubt of their family likeness. The definition of their common characteristics is certainly no easy matter.

Meyer and Weinberg (1975, 192) similarly concluded that "the truth seems to be that business cycle experiences rarely repeat themselves in any neat, symmetrical, standard fashion." And in reference to Mitchell (1927), Meyer and Weinberg reminded us that he ". . . always emphasized that business cycles vary widely in character." More recently, Blanchard and Watson (1986, 125) concluded from their examinations of a structural model and the ". . . correlation coefficients between variables and an aggregate activity index" that ". . . *business cycles are not at all alike*" (italics added) (see also DeLong and Summers 1986a, 1986b; Zarnowitz and Moore 1986).

Meanwhile, those of the rational expectations school appear to have exaggerated the extent to which it seems reasonable to view a "family likeness" between business cycles. For instance, Lucas (1977, 9–10), while recognizing that cyclical "movements do not exhibit uniformity of either period or amplitude, which is to say, they do not resemble the deterministic wave motions which sometimes arise in the natural sciences," stated,

> Though there is absolutely no theoretical reason to anticipate it, one is led by the facts to conclude that, with respect to the qualitative behavior of co-movements among series, business cycles are all alike. To theoretically inclined economists, this conclusion should be attractive and challenging, for it suggests the possibility of a unified explanation of business cycles, grounded in the general laws governing market economies, rather than in political or institutional characteristics specific to particular countries or periods.

It seems important to observe that "the facts" which appear to have influenced Lucas were those that had been mostly reported and widely accepted up to the 1950s, notably in the work of Mitchell at the NBER.[6] However, it seems very important to note further that Lucas's (1977, 1980) references to empirical evidence on business cycles do not include studies published in the late 1960s and thereafter, including the substantial contributions by Geoffrey H. Moore over a number of years and collected partly in Moore (1980a, 1983). These studies furnished a better understanding of business cycles including, in particular, the helpful and important distinction between classical cycles and growth cycles.[7] This distinction is neglected by Lucas (Boehm 1986, 35).

But for Lucas, the cyclical experiences since World War II have posed no problem for theoretical purposes as does explaining the severe depression of the 1930s, as noted above. Lucas believed (1980, 706) that a less spectacular but perhaps ultimately more influential feature of post-World War II time series has been the return to a pattern of recurrent, roughly similar "cycles" in Mitchell's sense. If the magnitude of the Great Depression dealt a serious blow to the idea of the business cycle as a repeated occurrence of the "same" event, the postwar experience has to some degree restored respectability to this idea. If the Depression continues, in some respects, to defy explanation by existing economic analysis (as I believe it does), perhaps it is gradually succumbing to the Law of Large Numbers.

Lucas's view that "business cycles are all alike" led him (1980, 699) to assert:

> The idea that one could, with a firm empirical basis, speak of something like a "typical business cycle," divided into stages invariant in character (if not in duration) suggested that a substantial part of observed fluctuations might be explainable at a fairly abstract, or "simple" level, with a single theoretical explanation of *the* (i.e., of all) business cycle(s).

Lucas found support for "this idea" in Haberler (1937) who, it is pertinent to remember, provided a synthesis of business cycle theories before the impact of Keynes (1936). It is interesting to compare Lucas's idea of a "typical business cycle" with the following observation by Mitchell (1927, 383–84):

> The differences among business cycles which have attracted most attention are differences in duration. Quite naturally, the discoverers of the recurrence overstressed its uniformity in this respect as in others. Influenced by the dominant type of economic theory, these discoverers thought of a "normal" cycle and so simplified their problem—a practice still common.

Lucas has ensured that the "practice [is] still common."

We must face the question of how helpful this practice is for government and business economists in their respective roles of advising decision makers. While it seems reasonable to proceed (as a first approximation) on the theoretical basis that there are close family likenesses from one cycle to another, it would seem to be stretching it too far and could be very misleading for both theoretical and policy purposes to view business cycles as "all alike" to the extent that Lucas seems to suggest. Furthermore, variations in duration (which are generally recognized) are themselves likely to contribute to, and to be an effect of, variations in the character and qualitative behavior of co-movements of series during upswings (for instance, whether or not a full boom is experienced) and downswings (for instance, whether a growth slowdown leads to a classical recession). Certainly, knowledge of previous cycles, as provided by the indicator approach, can be very instructive in monitoring the current state of the economy and forecasting the likely course of events (Moore, ed., 1961; Moore and Klein 1977; Moore 1978, 1980a ch. 5 and part III, 1983 ch. 6 and part III; Boehm and Moore 1982, 1984; Klein and Moore 1985; Boehm 1987a, 1987b; CIBCR 1988b, 1988c; Central Statistical Office 1988; Westpac-Melbourne Institute 1988). This knowledge should also help to improve business cycle theory or to check its relevance as an aid in forecasting.

If business cycles were as typical and alike from one to the next, economic forecasting should be much easier and have a much better track record than, in fact, it has: witness the indecision and diversity among economic forecasters over the likely course of the U.S. economy during 1979.[8] With the advantage of hindsight and subsequent statistical evidence, we now know that a growth slow-down began in the United States in December 1978, but there remained considerable uncertainty (with a number of erroneous forecasts meantime) as to whether a classical downturn might occur. In the event, a classical peak was reached in January 1980 (Table 3.1).

Despite the persistence of the short (growth) cycle as the main business cycle, the considerable variability in amplitude and duration from one cycle to another is clearly demonstrated in comparisons that have been made of individual cycles (Boehm and Defris 1977, 1982; Moore 1980b; Boehm and Moore 1982; DeLong and Summers 1986b; Zarnowitz and Moore 1986). The uncertainties about the course of activity apply especially at turning points and usually more so at the lower turning point, as long recognized, and pointed out by Matthews (1959, ch. 9 and 10), and as experienced by Australia "during the years 1975 to 1979 [when] there was considerable 'on and off' speculation about imminent recoveries in the economy" (Boehm and Defris 1982, 66). Moreover, the uncertainty regarding the course of economic activity has considerable significance for the rational expectation thesis of a limited role for economic policy, as discussed below.

In summary, on the evidence available for a number of industrialized market economies (see Table 3.3), it seems safe to draw the general conclusion that since World War II the main business cycle has been a relatively short one, varying on average in duration from 3 to 5 years in terms of growth cycles; and as far as Australia and the United States are concerned, just over 1 to 2 years longer in duration in terms of their classical cycles. But the characteristics and qualitative behavior of business cycles (with respect to duration and amplitude, and generally to a lesser extent the timing of changes of co-movements of key series) vary markedly at times from one country to another and in the same country over time. Any theory that does not allow for these variations and possibilities could not be regarded as entirely relevant or at least as a general theory. The evidence strongly supports the case for a general eclectic theory of business cycles. The variations also have very important policy implications.

Recent Theoretical Developments

The New Classical Equilibrium Theory

The new classical equilibrium theory of the business cycle has its roots strongly embedded in the ideas of rational expectations. The rational expectations hypothesis dates back to the work of Muth (1961). Muth's objective was to explain expectations in the same way as economists explain other economic variables, that is, by assuming that economic agents (consumers, business people, trade union leaders, government, etc.) maximize their objectives subject to the constraints they meet. Muth defined such expectations as rational. This rationality does not mean perfect foresight. There is allowance for mistakes. But people learn, and hence they will not be systematically wrong.

Muth's 1961 idea lay relatively dormant until the early 1970s when Lucas (1972, 1973, 1975, 1976) began to develop his equilibrium model to explain business cycles using rational expectations. Lucas's objective was to understand the relation between inflation and unemployment within a mechanism generating price and output movements resulting from "unsystematic monetary-fiscal shocks, the effects of which are distributed through time due to information lags and an accelerator effect" (Lucas 1975, 1113).

In order to support the classical equilibrium business cycle theory, the rational expectation theorists have recognized that it is necessary to reconcile economic experiences such as the business cycle in terms of the two basic postulates of classical economic theory that Keynes had refuted, namely (a) that markets clear, and (b) that agents act in their own self-interest (Lucas and Sargent 1979, 7). For Lucas, an economy is in equilibrium at each point in time when postulates (a) and (b) are satisfied. In the words of Lucas and Sargent (1979, 8), the research line being pursued is

> to discover a particular, econometrically testable equilibrium theory of the business cycle, one that can serve as the foundation for quantitative analysis of macroeconomic policy. There is no denying that this approach is counterrevolutionary, for it presupposes that Keynes and his followers were wrong to give up on the possibility that an equilibrium theory could account for the business cycle. As of now, no successful equilibrium macro-econometric model at the level of detail of, say, the Federal Reserve-MIT-Penn model has been constructed.

The *a priori* justification for seeking an equilibrium theory of the business cycle is the firm belief in the apparent regularity of the business cycle, as discussed above (Kantor 1979, 1434). Lucas, Sargent, and their disciples recognize that adherence to both postulates (a) and (b) require an explanation of the recurrence of "business depressions" when, with sticky wages and unemployment, it could not be said that markets are clearing and agents (notably the involuntary unemployed[9]) are acting as they would desire. Thus, a key feature of the equilibrium models is the relaxation of the classical postulate that agents have perfect knowledge. It is still assumed that markets clear and agents optimize, but decisions are made on the basis of the limited, partly imperfect information available. It is in this economic climate that agents respond in their demand and supply decisions to their expectations about future relative prices. These prices are, in turn, being influenced by monetary changes.

The key impulses in the equilibrium theory that trigger the business cycle originate from agents' reactions to unexpected changes in variables influencing their decisions. An attractive feature of Lucas's equilibrium theory is his search for a factor that has widespread influence on the decisions of economic agents. It is argued below that the price-cost cycle plays this type of role in influencing economic agents, doing so largely as an endogenous element. However, for Lucas, one important way in which a random shock appears is through unanticipated price changes initiated by unanticipated monetary changes (Lucas and Sargent 1979, 8). The unanticipated money supply changes cause the price changes, with Sims's (1972) causation tests being quoted in support (Lucas and Sargent 1979, 9). In brief, real output and employment changes follow because unexpected changes in money supply trigger general absolute price changes which are mistaken for relative price changes.

The cyclical process envisaged by Lucas and Sargent can be explained in terms of adaptive expectations, as originally used to describe the expectations augmented Phillips analysis. Adaptive expectations closely approximate the learning process of agents under rational expectations (Santomero and Seater 1978, 515–8; Poole 1980, 268–73). The process of adaptive expectations may be described with the aid of Chart 3.1 where $\dot{p}$ is the actual inflation rate, $\dot{p}^e$ in the expected inflation rate, U the unemployment rate, and U_N the natural rate of unemployment.

It is appropriate to recall here that a key aspect of Keynesian macroeconomic models was the assumption of a trade-off between inflation and unemployment; that is, the familiar Phillips relation indicating that the higher the inflation rate, the lower the unemployment rate (or the higher the real output). It is also helpful to note here that the long classical upswing in the 1960s in the United States, Australia, and other relatively developed industrialized democracies supported the false belief that unemployment could be reduced to a minimum and held low indefinitely by expansionary, in fact, inflationary fiscal and monetary policies. The economic dividend was believed to be real economic growth at the cost of only slightly more inflation.

Friedman (1966, 1968) and Phelps (1967) rightly attacked the notion of a stable long-run negatively sloped trade-off (such as PC_1 in Chart 3.1) on the basis that expectations of price and wage changes would eventually catch up to actual

Chart 3.1. **Relation Between Inflation Rate and Unemployment Rate.**

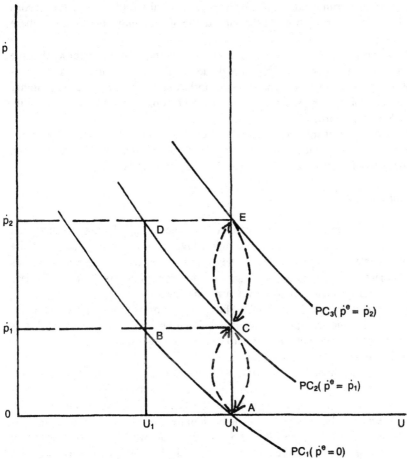

price and wage changes. Their thesis is that, if the government tries to reduce unemployment permanently to U_1, the expectations of inflation will rise making for the continuance of the higher rate of inflation $\dot{p}_1$. And so the cyclical upswing in the short-run, during the period of learning and adjustment to the higher rate of inflation, will be from A toward B. But, in the long-run, the higher rate of inflation would not maintain the lower unemployment rate U_1 because agents' expectations would eventually adjust to eliminate money illusion. The real increases initiated by price increases will be recognized as errors of judgment. Thus there will be a movement back to the long-run equilibrium which, with the now higher price and wage expectations, will be at the long-run equilibrium point, such as C, where the expected and actual price level are equal.[10]

If the government persists on achieving U_1 and continues to expand, the new path in the short-run would be toward D, but eventually settling at E (for reasons explained for C), i.e., settling at the natural rate of unemployment. In short, there is no long-run trade-off.

Further refinements can be made, such as allowing for the possibility that the path ACE will become positively sloped due to costs and inefficiencies of higher inflation, thus making for higher rates of inflation being associated with higher natural rates of unemployment. Friedman (1977) took account of this possibility in his Nobel Lecture.

If a lower rate of inflation is sought, then the government would depress the economy. The unemployment rate would rise above the natural rate and the economy would follow a path such as E to C, or C to A.

Critical Review

There seems to be no doubt that changes in expectations, both short-term and long-term, and changes in prices should play key roles in any theory of the business cycle and as recognized in the new classical theory. Nevertheless, this new theory seems open to serious criticisms on several important grounds. There are seven partly related matters worth noting here.

(*i*) There is the weakness noted above regarding the inadequate empirical basis on which the equilibrium theory has been launched. Associated with this aspect there is the oversimplification of the problem by exaggerating the extent to which business cycles are all alike.

(*ii*) The fundamental role of rational expectations does not seem to be supported by the empirical evidence, nor does the role attributed to the associated long-run concept of the natural rate hypothesis (NRH). In short, the relevance of both concepts seems to be exaggerated. The birth of the NRH (in regard to unemployment) in the latter half of the 1960s is not so surprising when one allows that these were the latter years of the relatively long classical cycle upswing. The concept seems useful for viewing the situation to which the economy would tend in certain circumstances in the long-run. It is comparable to the classical economists' vision of the stationary state. The NRH assumes, or logically implies, the obsolescence of the business cycle. Meanwhile, the business cycle would continue in the short-run which may "turn out to be years or even decades long" (Santomero and Seater 1978, 527).

There is also the important point that adaptive expectations may be a more realistic and consistent manner in which expectations influence the course of real activity, as found by Figlewski and Wachtel (1981). Their examination of the formation of inflationary expectations led to the conclusion that for the United States since World War II, expectations had been formed in a manner inconsistent with rational expectations.

(*iii*) Serious doubts may be held concerning the line of causation postulated whereby prices play the leading role in producing fluctuations in real variables such as output and employment. For Chart 3.1, the traditional assumption is that price changes lead the inflation process and the real fluctuations. Unemployment falls in moving from A to B so long as the expected price level lags behind the actual, thus permitting a lower actual real wage to entice firms to employ more labor on the one hand, and a higher expected real wage to induce workers to join the labor force on the other. But this causation scenario is inconsistent with findings on causation between wages and prices (Boehm 1982a, 1984; Boehm and Martin 1989). For Australia and Britain, wage changes have generally led the inflation process. Though bi-directional causation appears to apply in the United States, nevertheless causation seems to run more strongly from wages to prices (Boehm 1982a). In short, the leading role attributed to prices in adaptive expectations, as originally envisaged by Friedman (1968) and now adopted by the rational expectations theorists, is not supported by statistical tests. Moreover, under rational expectations, it is assumed that equality between the expected and actual price level takes place fairly quickly through the learning process. Statistical tests, however, indicate that price adjustments are more tardy than wage adjustments. This experience further supports adaptive expectations as being more consistent with the formation of inflationary expectations than rational expectations. Meanwhile, the business cycle would be continuing and each turning point—a peak or a trough—means some change in the underlying influences on expectations as between inflation and deflation. Deflationary influences may, of course, manifest themselves in a slowing down in the rate of increase in the inflation rate.

The relatively short span of time taken for the upswing or downswing phases of the growth cycle, suggests *per se* that there is something more than unanticipated price changes initiated by unanticipated monetary changes producing fluctuations in employment and real output. Furthermore, apart from the evidence on causation, it seems *a priori* highly doubtful that significant price illusion would be held by agents in the 1980s following the inflationary experiences since the mid-1960s. This would seem to cast serious doubt on the rational expectation hypothesis that absolute price changes are mistaken for relative price changes.

(*iv*) The serious doubt about the price misperception hypothesis also applies to the associated assumption that unanticipated price changes are initiated by unanticipated monetary changes. But monetary and price statistics tend to be more readily and generally available than Lucas appears to require for his theory. The heavy dependence of the rational expectations hypothesis on a single causal chain with random monetary shocks inducing price misperceptions leading to mistaken production decisions appears generally not supported by the facts (Zarnowitz 1985, 551–62; McCallum 1987, *ii* and 7).

(*v*) The assumption that the impulses which trigger business fluctuations are mainly unanticipated shocks has not been convincingly argued. Intuitively and also after consideration of the qualitative behavior of business cycles, it is difficult to believe that the recurring short (growth and classical) cycles (with family likenesses from one to another) can be largely explained by random shocks. This question is discussed further below in connection with the real business cycle approach. The price-cost cycle (as explained in the section below) and adaptive fluctuations in inventory investment and to some extent fixed investment identify important endogenous forces contributing to the business cycle actually experienced. If growth cycles were largely the result of exogenous forces, it would be hard to explain their persistence as a relatively short cycle with a duration generally of between 2 to 5 years.

(*vi*) An important omission of the new equilibrium theory of business cycles is an explanation of why the main business cycle has tended to be a relatively short (growth) cycle.[11] But this question also has been largely avoided or neglected in earlier theories of business cycles. As argued in the following section, major parts of the explanation on duration appear to be furnished by both the duration of the price-cost cycle and the fluctuations in inventory investment.

(*vii*) Finally, another question that initially was relatively neglected in the new classical theory, as in monetarism in general, was the subject of economic growth. For our purposes here, this meant relative neglect of the interrelationship between trend and cycle as seen by Schumpeter (1939). An important point to consider is that business cycles have taken place against the background of a secular uptrend which has also fluctuated (see Boehm 1979, ch. 2) and, in turn, probably influenced the characteristics of business cycles. The development in the 1980s of real business cycle models as a modification of the new classical economics includes attention to economic growth and hence addresses this previously relatively neglected question.

The Real Business Cycle Approach
and Sticky Price Models

The growing recognition in the early 1980s of the inapplicability of Lucas's equilibrium approach to developed economies (with its unrealistic reliance on random monetary shocks inducing price misperceptions which lead to incorrect production decisions) has led to new developments in two main divergent directions. One involves the real business cycle (RBC) approach (developed by Kydland and Prescott 1982; Long and Plosser 1983; see also Prescott 1986a, 1986b; King and Plosser 1988), and the other is a revival of interest in developing models with sticky prices (or nominal rigidity). As McCallum (1986, 397) observes, the RBC and sticky price ". . . types of models . . . are rather strongly representative of Classical and Keynesian viewpoints, respectively" (see also Gordon 1987).

The RBC theory modifies the new classical equilibrium approach for business cycle analysis by paying greater attention to cycle propogation through the effects of shocks over time. As the name suggests, the shocks are real and not monetary and in particular are shocks to technology (or productivity). Changes in money supply are the consequence of "reverse causation," that is, fluctuations in money supply are an endogenous response to output fluctuations initiated largely by technology shocks. The RBC models concentrate on the behavior of real factors such as consumption, investment, and employment, while nominal variables such as prices, the price-cost cycle discussed below, and monetary and fiscal disturbances are not examined as possible primary causes of cyclical fluctuations.

A favorable feature of RBC models initiated by Kydland and Prescott (1982; see also Manuelli 1986; Prescott 1986a, 1986b; King, Plosser, and Rebelo 1988a, 1988b) is the attempt to develop the RBC model in the context of neoclassical growth theory. This addresses an important question which, as noted above, was previously relatively neglected in the new classical theory and concerns the close interrelationship between trend and cycle.

Dissatisfaction with the new classical equilibrium theory and its outgrowth in RBC models on grounds of empirical invalidity partly explains the revival of interest in sticky price models (see McCallum 1982, 1986, 1987, 1988; Dotsey and King 1987; Gordon 1987). An important characteristic that distinguishes Keynesian macroeconomics from classical theory is that nominal prices may be relatively sticky and may take some time to respond to shocks and changes in the market forces. The fluctuations in nominal aggregate demand generate fluctuations in employment and output that would not occur if flexible prices applied and cleared markets in the classical sense.

Flexible prices, however, appear to be inconsistent with observed market behavior. On the other hand, sticky price models are open to the "Lucas critique" of how does one know that the nominal adjustment process will not occur quickly if one does not understand its nature (McCallum 1987, 8-9). Another problem for sticky price theories (McCallum 1986, 398 and 408-410) is to explain why contracts to a large extent are set in nominal terms.

The RBC approach as an outgrowth of the new classical economics and the renewal of interest in the sticky price approach are very much in their infancy. Some commentators view the debate and conflict between both approaches (see especially Manuelli 1986; Prescott 1986a, 1986b; Summers 1986; McCallum 1987; Gordon 1987) as evidence of the highly unsatisfactory state of macroeconomics. (For a critical review of RBC, see also McCallum 1988). It is clear that both approaches warrant more detailed empirical research, including more attention to the existing wealth of facts on business cycles as briefly reviewed in this paper.

Why the Main Business Cycle
Is a Relatively Short Cycle

It was noted above that theories of the business cycle have generally failed to explain *why* the main business cycle in industrialized democracies has been of relatively short duration (as is shown in Tables 3.1 to 3.3). Whatever duration has been assumed in the variety of theories of the business cycle, the question of duration has tended to be touched upon only briefly and vaguely.

While explanations of the duration of the business cycle have been lacking, there has been general recognition of the fact that fluctuations in inventory investment may play an important part in generating short cycles. For instance, Matthews (1959, 94) noted that "the statistics for the United States show that inventory investment has been particularly important in fluctuations of short duration" (see also Metzler 1947). In fact, "the change in business inventories in constant prices" has been found a reliable leading indicator of business cycles in the United States economy. However for Australia, the National Account series of "increase in stocks, private nonfarm in constant prices" proved unsuitable as a leading indicator (Boehm and Moore 1982, 5, 26, and 28; 1984, 36 and 38).

A major part of the general explanation of why the main business cycle is a relatively short cycle appears to stem fundamentally from its close relation with the price-cost cycle. Empirical evidence of the relationship between the price-cost cycle and the business cycle in Australia, Canada, the United Kingdom, and the United States and the contribution that the relationship provides to business cycle theory have been described in some detail elsewhere (Boehm 1982b). A stylized diagrammatic illustration of the relation between a typical price-cost cycle and business cycle as far as the turning points of both are concerned is provided in Chart 3.2.

The price-cost cycle is derived from the cumulated quarterly net percentage changes in prices and costs. National Account data were used in the empirical work with prices represented by the implicit price deflator and costs by unit labor costs. It is assumed that the percentage change in unit labor cost is a reasonable proxy for the rate of change in total costs. This seems justified, especially on the grounds that wages are a major component of total costs.

The cumulation of the successive quarterly differences between the changes in prices and costs seems a natural technique when allowance is made for the cumulative nature of the endogenous processes which play a large part in cyclical fluctuations. The novelty of cumulating the net changes in prices and costs has two special advantages. First, it captures (implicitly) the varying lags in the relation between changes in costs and prices. Second, it allows (also implicitly) for other factors, notably changes in productivity, influencing the changes in costs and prices.

An upward trend is superimposed in Chart 3.2 to allow for the secular uptrend of real output. The model attempts to represent the empirical evidence with the trough of the price-cost cycle leading the business (growth or classical) cycle trough, on average, usually up to about nine months. This generally precedes the next peak in the price-cost cycle which, in turn, leads the growth cycle peak usually by a little longer period than the lag of the business cycle trough to the price-cost cycle trough. The lag of the classical cycle peak would be a little longer

Chart 3.2. **Diagrammatic Illustration of Relation Between Turning Points of a Typical Price-Cost Cycle and a Business Cycle.**

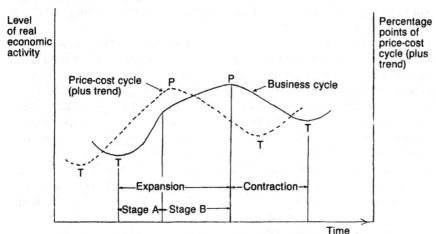

than that of the growth cycle since economic activity generally slows down before it turns down.

The concept of the price-cost cycle seen as a recurring, self-reversing, cumulative process reflecting the total of an industrialized market economy's experiences as expressed in prices and costs (and by implication changes in productivity) appeals as an avenue warranting close attention in the theory of business cycles. An essential aspect is that these economic phenomena generally reflect the normal working of the economic system. This normal process leads to the generation of seemingly inevitable fluctuations in key economic variables in a fairly regular and consistent manner in relation to business cycles. It appears that both cycles would normally be under some influence from each other, though of varying importance at different phases of each cycle.

The forces generating both price-cost cycles and business cycles appear to reveal themselves particularly in the way in which the peak of the price-cost cycle seems to be approximately associated with, or to follow by only a brief period, the slowdown of the expansion in moving from Stage A to Stage B as illustrated in Chart 3.2. Stage A of the expansion phase of the growth cycle takes, on average, about a year. It is a time of fairly rapid advances in real output associated with the initial recovery from the bottom of the recession as unused and underutilized labor and capital are brought into production. In Stage B (which is found, on average, to be about a year in Canada, the United Kingdom, and the United States, but nearly 18 months in Australia), real expansion slows down appreciably, generally because it is reduced to the economy's rate of growth of capacity.

The general timing relation between the turning points of the price-cost cycle and the business cycle stylized in Chart 3.2 is consistent with the use of the ratio of price to unit labor cost in manufacturing as a leading indicator in business cycle analysis of the United States. For Australia, the ratio of implicit price deflator to unit labor cost has been found a reliable leading indicator (Boehm and Moore 1984, 36 and 47).

It should be acknowledged that a close relationship between fluctuations in costs, prices, and profits during business cycles was generally recognized from the beginning of major empirical studies of business cycles. Indeed, the cyclical patterns in these factors were one of the main themes formulated by Mitchell (1913, 1927, 1951) in his business cycle theory. Moore has contributed a great deal to this analysis for the United States and other countries (Moore 1980a, ch. 11 and 14; 1983, ch. 12 and 16). What appears largely to remain is to take into account more fully and formally the continuing interrelation between business cycles and the fluctuations in costs, prices, and profits. The price-cost cycle helps us to achieve such a view of the subject, most notably in providing an important contribution (as mentioned above) toward the explanation of why the main business cycle is a relatively short cycle.

It is important to recognize that price-cost cycles vary from one to the next as do business cycles in key characteristics such as duration, amplitude, and the timing of changes in co-movements. Both price-cost cycles and business cycles probably differ largely for similar and interrelated reasons. However, it seems reasonable to theorize in terms of the typical interrelation of the turning points of the price-cost cycle and the business cycle, as illustrated in Chart 3.2. The similarity of the general picture of the economy provided by the price-cost cycle and the business cycle stems fundamentally from both representing a cumulative, self-reversing process—the business cycle reflecting the general state of economic activity, the price-cost cycle reflecting especially the state of profitability.

Occasionally, there have been false turns in the price-cost cycle for which there have been no matching turns of the growth cycle. This means a shorter average duration of the former cycles. This appears important in another respect, however, since it strengthens the hypothesis that the net weight of the real and monetary forces behind the price-cost cycle would be for the generation of business cycles of relatively short duration. It needs to be allowed that other factors (for instance, changes in fixed investment, inventory investment, exports, capital inflow, credit availability, and economic policy) also may contribute to the generation of business cycles. In the light of the remarkably consistent and strong empirical evidence, nevertheless, it seems reasonable to conclude that the duration of the price-cost cycle plays a key role in the determination of the duration of the business cycle.

It is explained in more detail elsewhere (Boehm 1982b) that the price-cost cycle contributes appreciably to the explanation of the amplitude of business cycles as well as their duration. In particular, the empirical evidence shows that a major downswing in the price-cost cycle is generally associated with a classical recession. By contrast, the occasions when a growth slowdown does not lead to a classical recession are generally marked also by a relatively mild downturn in the price-cost cycle.

Policy Implications

In this section, brief comments are offered only in respect to the above discussions regarding the rational expectations school and the relation between the price-cost cycle and the business cycle.

A major theme of rational expectations within the new classical equilibrium theory is that anticipated policy changes will have no real effects, only monetary effects. This certainly provides a serious challenge to traditional Keynesian stabilization policy. As Poole (1980, 249) explains:

> The proposition that fully anticipated monetary changes produce no effects on output and unemployment is especially important and controversial. If this theory is correct, no monetary policy that is consistent, and therefore predictable, can produce any stabilizing effects on output and employment. Only to the extent that policy is unpredictable and perhaps even capricious will effects on output and employment occur.

However, it is allowed that fiscal and monetary policy changes will have real effects while private agents are learning to overcome misperceptions and misunderstandings (Kantor 1979, 1432). Moreover, an aspect that appears to have been neglected in the writings on rational expectations, or assumed away under the assumption that "business cycles are all alike," is that the business cycle itself has sufficient irregularity and generates sufficient uncertainty to prevent agents from ever possessing perfect information. The business cycle contributes largely to "a *stochastic* equilibrium at the level of the individual firm" that Sutton (1981, 329) found interacts with wage inflexibility to produce, even in the long-run, the Phillips curve trade-off.

An important policy implication of the price-cost cycle is the stabilizing role that it plays. It contributes to the fact that the economic system is normally not violently unstable.[12] Nevertheless, the phenomenon of the price-cost cycle, as of the business cycle, entailing an inevitable ebb and flow of aggregate economic activity does not preclude a continuing role for economic policy (fiscal, monetary, commercial, prices, and incomes) of aiming to mitigate the unfavorable effects of recessions, aiding and speeding recoveries, and preventing the excesses of booms as much as possible. But it must also be recognized that if maladjustments develop and make for a downturn in the price-cost cycle, then any postponement of this downturn or prevention of a significant downturn (entailing a more or less severe classical recession) may only mean a more significant economic downturn later, especially if the forces making for a major downturn continue to cumulate.

In brief, a role for stabilization policy seems to have been firmly restored (Modigliani 1977). On the other hand, the rational expectation theorists are justified in pointing out that policies may themselves prove to be destabilizing and promote bigger real fluctuations and/or greater inflation or deflation than would otherwise have occurred. A careful and continuing monitoring of the business cycle is essential (Boehm and Moore 1982, 1984) to aid the effective programming of policy changes that will mitigate as far as possible the unfavorable and avoidable economic and social effects and excesses of recessions and booms.

Conclusion

The explanation of business cycles has not been found a simple matter; nor have past attempts been highly successful and enduring. Indeed, there is a wide variety of earlier theories summarized in Haberler (1937), Schumpeter's theory (1939), and the variety of post-Keynesian theories, including Kaldor (1940) and Hicks (1950); see also Hansen (1941 and 1951).

Though there are family likenesses from one cycle to another, each needs to be individually recognized for purposes of the successful formulation of economic and social policies. And real factors may play a leading role as well as monetary factors.

The hypothesis of rational expectations imposed in the new classical equilibrium theory of business cycles in conjunction with the NRH appears largely inconsistent with the nature of and interrelationship between the recurring business cycle and the price-cost cycle.

There would appear to be considerable merit in furnishing a general eclectic theory which draws upon the earlier main developments and proven hypotheses in business cycle theory and which also incorporates recent helpful theoretical developments, notably regarding the vital areas of learning and expectations formation (Zarnowitz 1985, 570–71). The objective would be to provide a general theory that could continually be called upon, from its various parts, to help understand and explain the current and prospective state and course of economic activity. This ongoing review of the economy and the development of appropriate economic and social policies could be aided by forecasts furnished by both an econometric model of the economy and an economic indicator analysis.

Notes

1. See, for instance, Moore (1980a, 1983); Klein and Moore (1985); Moore and Moore (1985); CIBCR (1988b, 1988c).
2. See Council of Economic Advisers (1965, p. 8 and ch. 4); Council of Economic Advisers (1966, pp. 4 and 63, and ch. 4).
3. During the nineteenth century these would include depressions in the United States during the latter half of 1810s, early 1840s, mid-1870s, and 1893-95 (see Thorp 1926,

ch. 1); and in Australia, the late 1820s, early 1840s, and 1891–95.

4. This was especially centered on research work at the NBER by Mintz (1969, 1974). Moore has continued and further developed this work. See especially Center for International Business Cycle Research (CIBCR) (1988b, 1988c); and Moore and Moore (1985). See also Moore (1978; 1980a, esp. pp.1–10 and ch.2; 1983, esp. ch. 5 and 6); Moore and Klein (1977); Zarnowitz (1981); Klein and Moore (1985).

5. On the other hand, as discussed in more detail below, a weakness of recent work in the United States on rational expectations and business cycles is the undue reliance of the leaders of this work on the earlier empirical work in which there is no distinction between classical cycles and growth cycles. In short, improvements since the late 1960s in the empirical evidence on business cycles have been neglected. Another important illustration of faulty analysis arising from the failure to recognize the distinction between classical cycles and growth cycles is in Britton (1986). He was misled into believing that the "central tendency" (p. 3), as he put it, toward "a cycle of relatively constant and regular periodicity" (p. 66) is "more marked in the United Kingdom than in the United States" (p. 3). But the United Kingdom trade (or business) cycle that Britton wrote about is the growth cycle which he compares with findings for the U.S. classical cycle. (See Boehm, forthcoming, and Table 3.3.)

6. Apart from Mitchell (1913, 1951), other relevant historical publications referred to by Lucas include Friedman and Schwartz (1963); Gayer, Rostow and Schwartz (1953); Haberler (1937, 1960); von Hayek (1933); Tinbergen (1939).

7. These include, especially, Mintz (1969, 1974); Moore and Klein (1977); Moore (1978; 1980a, esp. ch. 2 and 5; 1983, esp. ch. 4–6); Klein and Moore (1985).

8. *The Economist* (1979a, 33) in its "American Survey," noted:

> The much heralded recession is still not in sight. The country's [real] gross national product . . . is estimated . . . to have expanded . . . at an annual rate of 2.4% in the three months that ended on September 30th. This increase confounded economists' forecasts.

And *The Economist* (1979b, 30) reported:

> Administration economists, usually a dour bunch, looked smug this week. No wonder. According to the early-summer predictions of most independent forecasters, the American economy should now be well down the road to deep recession. In fact, the latest economic indicators show that the rate of unemployment fell in November.

9. However, it should be noted that the assumption in major theoretical papers popularizing the natural rate of unemployment hypothesis is that all changes in employment result from the voluntary decisions of workers. There is no role for involuntary unemployment. See Gordon (1976, 196), Santomero and Seater (1978, 515–25), and Lucas and Sargent (1979, 12). Cf. Modigliani (1977, esp. pp. 6–8).

10. The requirements for the rational expectation thesis to be satisfied may be seen in the equation

$$\dot{p}_t = a + b\dot{p}_t^* + r_t$$

and testing the joint hypothesis that $a = 0$ and $b = 1$, (where r_t is the error term). Similarly, in the wage equation, the requirement is to find a coefficient of unity on prices as the independent variable. It is interesting to note that it was not until the accelerating rates of inflation in the early 1970s entered regressions that values approximating unity were obtained to satisfy the natural rate hypothesis (see Gordon, 1976, 193; 1987, 7–8). As countries experience falling and lower rates of inflation (comparable, for instance, with the 1950s and 1960s), it may be expected that the coefficient on prices will fall and is likely to approximate one-half, as it generally did for the 1950s and 1960s. See, for example, Solow (1969); Gordon (1971); Eckstein and Brinner (1972); Hagger (1977, ch. 3).

11. Okun (1980, 817) concluded: In my judgment, the theory of rational-expectations-with-misperceptions provides an explanation of the business cycle that . . . fails to account for the duration and many key features of the actual cycle.

12. Aspects mentioned here are discussed more fully in Boehm (1982b, 17-20).

References

Blanchard, O. J., and M. Watson. 1986. "Are All Business Cycles Alike?" In *The American Business Cycle: Continuity and Change*, pp. 123-79. Edited by R. J. Gordon. NBER Studies in Business Cycles No. 25. Chicago: University of Chicago Press.

Boehm, E. A. 1971. *Prosperity and Depression in Australia 1887-1897*. Oxford: Clarendon Press.

————. 1979. *Twentieth Century Economic Development in Australia*. 2d ed. Melbourne: Longman Cheshire.

————. 1982a. "Money Wages, Consumer Prices, and Causality in Australia." Paper presented to Section 24: Economics, 52nd ANZAAS Congress, Macquarie University, May 10-14.

————. 1982b. "The Price-Cost Cycle and the Business Cycle." Research Paper No. 85, Department of Economics, University of Melbourne, June.

————. 1984. "Money Wages, Consumer Prices, and Causality in Australia." *Economic Record* 60 (September): 236-51.

————. Review of Lucas (1983) in *The Wall Street Review of Books*, 14 (Winter): 33-37.

————. 1987a. "New Economic Indicators for Australia: A Further Report." Working Paper No. 4, Institute of Applied Economic and Social Research, April.

————. 1987b. "Economic Indicators for Australia's Service Industries." Paper presented to Western Economic Association International's 62nd Annual Conference, Vancouver, B.C., July; in *Leading Economic Indicators: New Approaches and Forecasting Records*. Edited by K. Lahiri and G. H. Moore. New York: Cambridge University Press, forthcoming.

————. "Review of Britton" (1986). *Wall Street Review of Books*, forthcoming.

Boehm, E. A., and L. V. Defris. 1977. "Recurring Periods of Plateau Slumps and Sluggish Recoveries in the Australian Economy: 1950 to 1976." *Australian Economic Review* (1st Quarter): 53-60.

————. 1982. "The Australian Reference Cycle: 1950-80." *Australian Economic Review* (1st Quarter): 63-67.

Boehm, E. A., and V. L. Martin. "An Investigation Into the Major Causes of Australia's Recent Inflation and Some Policy Implications." *Economic Record* 65 (March): 1-15.

Boehm, E. A., and G. H. Moore. 1982. "The Indicator Approach to Understanding Australian Economic Fluctuations 1950-80." Paper presented to Section 24: Economics, 52nd ANZAAS Congress, Macquarie University, May 10-14; and Research Paper No. 94, Department of Economics, University of Melbourne, May 1983.

————. 1984. "New Economic Indicators for Australia, 1949-84." *Australian Economic Review* (4th Quarter): 34-56.

Britton, A. 1986. *The Trade Cycle in Britain, 1958-1982*. The National Institute of Economic and Social Research, Occasional Paper 39. New York: Cambridge University Press.

Bronfenbrenner, M., ed., 1969. *Is the Business Cycle Obsolete?* New York: Wiley.

Burns, A. F., and W. C. Mitchell. 1946. *Measuring Business Cycles*. New York: National Bureau of Economic Research.

Center for International Business Cycle Research (CIBCR). 1988a. *International Economic Indicators*. Columbia University, New York, Appendix A-3, June.

CIBCR. 1988b. *International Economic Indicators*. New York: Columbia University, monthly.

———. 1988c. *Recession-Recovery Watch: A Bimonthly Report Designed to Assist in the Evaluation of Current Business Conditions*. New York: Columbia University.

Central Statistical Office. 1988. "Cyclical Indicators of the United Kingdom Economy Recent Movements of the Indices." London: Government Statistical Service, monthly.

Council of Economic Advisers. 1965. *Economic Report of the President*. Washington, D.C.: U.S. Government Printing Office, January.

———. 1966. *Economic Report of the President*. Washington, D.C.: U.S. Government Printing Office, January.

DeLong J. B., and L. R. Summers. 1986a. "Are Business Cycles Symmetrical?" In *The American Business Cycle: Continuity and Change*, pp. 166–79. Edited by R. J. Gordon. NBER Studies in Business Cycles No. 25. Chicago: University of Chicago Press.

———. 1986b. "The Changing Cyclical Variability of Economic Activity in the United States." In *The American Business Cycle: Continuity and Change*, pp. 679–734. Edited by R. J. Gordon. NBER Studies in Business Cycles No. 25. Chicago: University of Chicago Press.

Dotsey, M., and R. G. King. 1987. "Business Cycles." In *The New Palgrave: A Dictionary of Economics*, vol. 1, 302–10, Macmillan.

Eckstein, O., and R. Brinner. 1972. "The Inflation Process in the United States." A study prepared for the Joint Economic Committee, 92nd Cong., 2 sess., Washington, D.C.

Figlewski, S., and P. Wachtel. 1981. "The Formation of Inflationary Expectations." *Review of Economics and Statistics* 63 (February): 1–10.

Friedman, M. 1966. "What Price Guideposts?" In *Guidelines: Informal Controls and the Market Place*, pp. 17–39. Edited by G. P. Shultz and R. Z. Aliber. Chicago: University of Chicago Press.

———. 1968. "The Role of Monetary Policy." *American Economic Review* 58 (March): 1–17.

———. 1977. "Nobel Lecture: Inflation and Unemployment." *Journal of Political Economy* 85 (June): 451–72.

Friedman, M., and A. J. Schwartz. 1963. *A Monetary History of the United States, 1867–1960*. Princeton: Princeton University Press for NBER.

Gayer, A. D., W. W. Rostow, and A. J. Schwartz. 1953. *The Growth and Fluctuation of the British Economy, 1790–1850*. Oxford: Clarendon Press.

Gordon, R. J. 1971. "Inflation in Recession and Recovery." *Brookings Papers on Economic Activity* 1: 105–58.

———. 1976. "Recent Developments in the Theory of Inflation and Unemployment." *Journal of Monetary Economics* 2: 185–219.

———., ed., 1986. *The American Business Cycle: Continuity and Change*. NBER Studies in Business Cycles No. 25. Chicago: University of Chicago Press.

———. 1987. "Postwar Developments in Business Cycle Theory: An Unabashedly New-Keynesian Perspective." Keynote lecture at 18th CIRET Conference, Zurich, September.

Haberler, G. 1937. *Prosperity and Depression: A Theoretical Analysis of Cyclical Movements*. Geneva: League of Nations.

———. 1960. *Prosperity and Depression*. rev. ed. Cambridge, Mass.: Harvard University Press.

Hagger, A. J. 1977. *Inflation: Theory and Policy*. London: Macmillan.

Hansen, A. H. 1941. *Fiscal Policy and Business Cycles*. New York: Norton.
————. 1951. *Business Cycles and National Income*. New York: Norton.
Harrod, R. F. 1948. *Towards A Dynamic Economics*. London: Macmillan.
von Hayek, F. A. 1933. *Monetary Theory and the Trade Cycle*. London: Jonathon Cape.
Hicks, J. R. 1950. *A Contribution to the Theory of the Trade Cycle*. Oxford: Clarendon Press.
Kaldor, N. 1940. "A Model of the Trade Cycle." *Economic Journal* 50 (March): 78–92.
Kalecki, M. 1939. *Essays in the Theory of Economic Fluctuations*. London: Allen & Unwin.
Kantor, B. 1979. "Rational Expectations and Economic Thought." *Journal of Economic Literature* 17 (December): 1422–441.
Keynes, J. M. 1936. *The General Theory of Employment Interest and Money*. London: Macmillan.
King, R. G., and C. I. Plosser. 1988. "Real Business Cycles." *Journal of Monetary Economics* 21 (March/May): 191–93.
King, R. G., C. I. Plosser, and S. T. Rebelo. 1988a. "Production, Growth and Business Cycles: I. The Basic Neoclassical Model." *Journal of Monetary Economics* 21 (March/May): 195–232.
————. 1988b. "Production, Growth and Business Cycles: II. New Directions" *Journal of Monetary Economics*. 21(March/May): 309–41.
Klein, P. A., and G. H. Moore. 1985. *Monitoring Growth Cycles in Market-Oriented Countries: Developing and Using International Economic Indicators*. NBER Studies in Business Cycles No. 26. Cambridge, Mass.: Ballinger Publishing Co.
Kydland, F. E., and E. C. Prescott. 1982. "Time to Build and Aggregate Fluctuations." *Econometrica* 50 (November): 1345–370.
Lahiri, K., and G. H. Moore, eds. *Leading Economic Indicators: New Approaches and Forecasting Records*. New York: Cambridge University Press, forthcoming.
Long, J. B., and C. I. Plosser. 1983. "Real Business Cycles." *Journal of Political Economy* 91 (February): 39–69.
Lucas, R. E. 1970. "Capacity, Overtime, and Empirical Production Functions." *American Economic Review* 60 (May): 23–27.
————. 1972. "Expectations and the Neutrality of Money." *Journal of Economic Theory* 4 (April): 103–24.
————. 1973. "Some International Evidence on Output-Inflation Trade-Offs." *American Economic Review* 63 (June): 326–34.
————. 1975. "Equilibrium Model of the Business Cycle." *Journal of Politcal Economy* 83 (December): 1113–144.
————. 1976. "Econometric Policy Evaluation: A Critique." *Journal of Monetary Economics* 2 (Supplement), Carnegie-Rochester Conference Series (1): 19–46.
————. 1977. "Understanding Business Cycles." *Journal of Monetary Economics*. (Supplement), Carnegie-Rochester Conference Series (5): 7–29.
————. 1980. "Methods and Problems in Business Cycle Theory." *Journal of Money, Credit and Banking*. Seminar on "Rational Expectations," Part 2 (November): 696–715.
————. 1983. *Studies in Business-Cycle Theory*. Cambridge, Mass.: MIT Press.
Lucas, R. E., and T. J. Sargent. 1979. "After Keynesian Macroeconomics." *Federal Reserve Bank of Minneapolis Quarterly Review* (Spring): 1–16.
Manuelli, R. E. 1986. "Modern Business Cycle Analysis: A Guide to the Prescott-Summers Debate." *Federal Reserve Bank of Minneapolis Quarterly Review* (Fall): 3–8.
Matthews, R. C. O. 1959. *The Trade Cycle*. Cambridge University Press.
McCallum, B. T. 1982. "Macroeconomics After a Decade of Rational Expectations:

Some Critical Issues." *Federal Reserve Bank of Richmond Economic Review* (December): 3–12.

————. 1986. "On 'Real' and 'Sticky-Price' Theories of the Business Cycle." *Journal of Money, Credit, and Banking* 18 (November): 397–414.

————. 1987. "Postwar Developments in Business Cycle Theory: A Moderately Classical Perspective." Keynote lecture at 18th CIRET Conference, Zurich, September.

————. 1988. "Real Business Cycle Models." NBER Working Paper No. 2480, January.

Meyer, J. R., and D. H. Weinberg. 1975. "On the Classification of Economic Fluctuations." *Explorations in Economic Research.* NBER 2 (Spring): 167–202.

Metzler, L. A. 1947. "Factors Governing the Length of Inventory Cycles." *Review of Economic Statistics* 29 (February): 1–15.

Mintz, I. 1969. *Dating Postwar Business Cycles: Methods and Their Application to Western Germany, 1950–67.* New York: National Bureau of Economic Research.

————. 1974. "Dating United States Growth Cycles." *Explorations in Economic Research.* NBER 1 (Summer): 1–113.

Mitchell, W. C. 1913. *Business Cycles.* Berkeley: University of California Press.

————. 1927. *Business Cycles: The Problem and Its Setting.* New York: NBER.

————. 1951. *What Happens During Business Cycles: A Progress Report.* New York: NBER.

Modigliani, F. 1977. "The Monetarist Controversy or, Should We Forsake Stabilization Policies?" *American Economic Review* 67 (March): 1–19.

Moore, G. H., ed., 1961. *Business Cycle Indicators.* Vol. 1, *Contributions to the Analysis of Current Business Conditions.* Vol. 2, *Basic Data on Cyclical Indicators.* NBER Studies in Business Cycles. Princeton: Princeton University Press.

————. 1978. "The Current State of the International Business Cycle: A New Measurement System." Contemporary Economic Problems 1978. Washington: D.C. American Enterprise Institute. Reprinted in Moore (1980a, 1983).

————. 1980a. *Business Cycles, Inflation and Forecasting.* NBER Studies in Business Cycles, No. 24. Cambridge, Mass.: Ballinger Publishing Co.

————. 1980b. "The Case for International Business Cycle Research." *Atlantic Economic Journal* 8 (September): 5–16.

————. 1983. *Business Cycles, Inflation, and Forecasting.* 2d ed. NBER Studies in Business Cycles, No. 24. Cambridge, Mass.: Ballinger Publishing Co.

Moore, G. H., and P. A. Klein. 1977. *Monitoring Business Cycles at Home and Abroad.* U.S. Department of Commerce, National Technical Information Service, PB 283997/A5. Washington, D.C.: Government Printing Office.

Moore, G. H., and M. H. Moore. 1985. *International Economic Indicators: A Sourcebook.* Westport, Conn.: Greenwood Press.

Moore, G. H., and V. Zarnowitz. 1986. "The Development and Role of the National Bureau of Economic Research's Business Cycle Chronologies." In *The American Business Cycle: Continuity and Change*, pp. 735–79. Edited by R. J. Gordon. NBER Studies in Business Cycles No. 25. Chicago: University of Chicago Press.

Muth, J. F. 1961. "Rational Expectations and the Theory of Price Movements." *Econometrica* 29: 315–35.

Okun, A. 1980. "Rational-Expectations-with-Misperceptions as a Theory of the Business Cycle." *Journal of Money, Credit and Banking.* (Seminar on "Rational Expectations") Part 2 (November): 817–25.

Phelps, E. S. 1967. "Phillips Curves, Expectations of Inflation, and Optimal Unemployment Over Time." *Economica* 34 (August): 254–81.

Poole, W. 1980. "Understanding Monetary Policy: The Role of Rational Expectations."

The Business Cycle and Public Policy 1929-80. Joint Economic Committee, U.S. Congress, pp. 245-81.

Prescott, E. C. 1986a. "Theory Ahead of Business Cycle Measurement." *Federal Reserve Bank of Minneapolis Quarterly Review* (Fall): 9-22.

—————. 1986b. "Response to a Skeptic." *Federal Reserve Bank of Minneapolis Quarterly Review* (Fall): 28-33.

Santomero, A. M., and J. J. Seater. 1978. "The Inflation-Unemployment Trade-Off: A Critique of the Literature." *Journal of Economic Literature* 16 (June): 499-544.

Schumpeter, J. A. 1939. *Business Cycles: A Theoretical, Historical, and Statistical Analysis of the Capitalist Process.* 2 Vols. New York: McGraw-Hill.

Sims, C. A. 1972. "Money, Income, and Causality." *American Economic Review* 62 (September): 540-52.

—————, ed. 1977. *New Methods in Business Cycle Research: Proceedings from a Conference.* Minneapolis: Federal Reserve Bank of Minneapolis.

Solow, R. M. 1969. *Price Expectations and the Behavior of the Price Level.* Manchester University Press.

Summers, L. H. 1986. "Some Skeptical Observations on Real Business Cycle Theory." *Federal Reserve Bank of Minneapolis Quarterly Review* (Fall): 23-27.

Sutton, J. 1981. "A Formal Model of the Long-run Phillips Curve Trade-off." *Economica* 48 (November): 329-43.

The Economist. 1979a. October.

—————. 1979b. December.

Thorp, W. L. 1926. *Business Annals.* New York: National Bureau of Economic Research.

Tinbergen, J. 1939. *Business Cycles in the United States of America, 1919-32.* Geneva: League of Nations.

U.S. Department of Commerce. 1988. *Business Conditions Digest.* Washington, D.C.: Government Printing Office, July.

Westpac-Melbourne Institute. 1988. *Indexes of Economic Activity.* Melbourne: University of Melbourne, monthly.

Zarnowitz, V. 1981. *Business Cycles and Growth: Some Reflections and Measures,* Reprint No. 222. New York: National Bureau of Economic Research, pp. 475-508.

—————. 1985. "Recent Work on Business Cycles in Historical Perspective: A Review of Theories and Evidence." *Journal of Economic Literature* 23 (June): 523-80.

Zarnowitz, V., and G. H. Moore. 1986. "Major Changes in Cyclical Behavior." In *The American Business Cycle: Continuity and Change,* pp. 519-82. Edited by R. J. Gordon. NBER Studies in Business Cycles No. 25. Chicago: University of Chicago Press.

III

CURRENT ASSESSMENT OF CYCLICAL INDICATORS

4

Why Some of the Leading Indicators Lead

Joel Popkin

The leading indicators have enjoyed a long and, largely, a celebrated life. Though they have been the butt of criticism sometimes, they are the only forecasting methodology endorsed by the federal government. There is no comparable index of economic time series or results of econometric models that are compiled and released monthly by the government to the public as an indicator of things to come—a leading indicator. Many other countries have followed the U.S. government's leadership in this regard.

Throughout their existence, there have been two main criticisms of the "indicators" approach to forecasting and one that has arisen lately. One criticism is that the indicators have predicted more recessions than have, in fact, occurred. This is due in large part to the inclusion of a stock market price index as one of the (now existing) 11 leading indicators. If that index is excluded, the predictive value of the remaining indicators is not changed much.

Another criticism, the one that has arisen recently, is that the indicators do not reflect the rapidly growing service sector. The extent to which that criticism is valid will be discussed later in this chapter.

Both criticisms are basic to the third and most longstanding of the criticisms of the indicators—that there is no well-articulated theory of what series should be indicators. The major premise of this paper is that there is indeed a basis in business cycle dynamics for the selection of indicators. That basis is set forth and used to specify the content of an experimental leading indicator derived from theory. A measure consistent with that content is then constructed and compared with the leading indicator index. It turns out that the experimental indicator, which shows promise as a leading one, subsumes several components of the present leading indicator index. This suggests the leading indicator index does have theoretical content, which probably has been a key factor in the acceptable forecasting record the indicators have exhibited.

Business Cycle Dynamics

The leading (and the coincident and lagging) indicator indexes measure economic variables that are not part of the national income and product accounts (NIPA) of which the gross national product (GNP) is a part. That the indicators have forecasting content suggests that the NIPAs are not, by themselves, a set of variables that can be totally explained by being cast into a simultaneous set of equations. At least partly, that is because components of the NIPAs contain, in various time periods, unobservable disequilibria.

In any time period for example, total profits may not fully reflect materials cost pass-throughs that are underway. If energy prices have risen because of an OPEC action and domestic crude oil producers match the price rise, their profits should increase, suggesting that total profits in the NIPAs will increase. But while that price increase may be passed through to refiners, it may not be passed through fully to end users during the quarter in which it occurred. Thus, aggregate profits may not rise at first—profits in energy producing sectors will rise but be offset by declines in profits in industrial sectors that purchase energy. Only when the latter sectors raise their prices to pass through the original energy price increase will aggregate profits rise. There is no way to discern the initial imbalance in profits if only the NIPAs are considered. One must look at prices and costs in the industrial sectors behind final demand to observe this.

Inventories provide another example. Inventories will rise when goods are shipped to one sector in anticipation of their subsequent use. At first, inventory investment will rise—if producers keep ordering ahead and using up the goods as planned—intentionally. Inventories might also rise because sales did not meet expectations, but in contrast, that development might lead to production cutbacks undertaken to work off the initial, involuntary inventory rise. The mere fact of a rise in inventories does not indicate whether it reflects disequilibria; more information is needed.

These two examples are intended to point out the need to understand what is happening behind the final demands measured in the NIPAs. Are there behavioral variables in certain intermediate sectors that indicate disequilibria are present, the direction of such disequilibria, and the speed with which they will be corrected?

The first step in finding them is to look at the cycles in large components of GNP. Table 4.1 contains a comparison of the cyclical characteristics of output associated with goods, services, and other major components of constant dollar GNP. Goods output is measured to include distribution margins—wholesale, retail, and transportation. The cyclical differences among the components are clear. The bulk of the business cycle reflects the cycle in goods production and distribution. GNP for goods rises more and falls more than that for structures. And there are no cycles in services, just a slower rate of growth during recessions than expansions.

Table 4.1

Cyclical Behavior of GNP and Selected Components—Percentage Change, Annual Rate

Movement to:		GNP	Goods	Services	Structures	Goods imports	Domestic purchases of domestic goods	Goods exports
Trough	1949 IV	-2.0	-5.9	-0.4	8.4	1.2	-5.7	-8.7
Peak	1953 II	8.0	8.9	7.8	5.6	9.6	9.4	2.8
Trough	1954 II	-3.0	-7.2	-0.5	4.7	-4.5	-8.5	10.6
Peak	1957 III	3.4	3.4	3.7	2.4	6.7	3.0	8.1
Trough	1958 II	-4.0	-9.1	0.7	-1.1	4.4	-8.1	-18.7
Peak	1960 II	4.9	5.6	4.2	5.2	10.9	5.1	10.5
Trough	1961 I	0.4	-4.5	3.8	5.3	-11.4	-5.3	4.1
Peak	1969 IV	4.3	4.4	4.6	2.7	10.2	4.2	5.9
Trough	1970 IV	-0.4	-2.0	1.6	2.4	3.8	-2.7	3.5
Peak	1973 IV	4.6	5.6	3.9	4.1	12.8	4.7	11.6
Trough	1975 I	-3.5	-6.3	2.4	-15.4	-12.9	-7.7	1.8
Peak	1980 I	4.1	4.6	3.5	5.1	7.8	4.1	7.2
Trough	1980 III	-4.5	-7.0	1.6	-19.6	-24.2	-7.8	3.6
Peak	1981 III	3.3	5.8	1.3	2.5	10.5	7.8	-3.1
Trough	1982 IV	-2.6	-5.9	0.9	-5.1	-5.9	-4.7	-4.7
Latest	1988 II	4.3	5.7	3.2	4.0	12.3	4.8	10.4
Average change during:								
Contractions		-2.5	-6.0	1.3	-2.6	-6.2	-6.3	-2.8
Expansions		4.6	5.5	4.0	3.9	10.1	5.4	6.7

Chart 4.1. **Output—Ratio of Cyclical to Control Solution.**

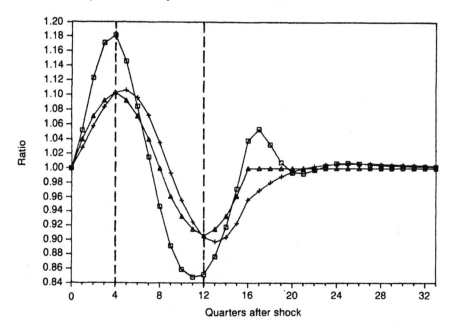

Notes: The ratios are for primary manufacturers (□), finished manufacturers (+), and final commodity (△). The first broken vertical line corresponds to the cyclical peak and the second to the cyclical trough.

Consider how cycles evolve in the goods sector. A retailer has been maintaining a desired level of inventory against expected sales. The sales are disappointing, say 5 percent below the anticipated level. If the retailer adopts this new sales level as his expectation—not an implausible reaction certainly—he will reduce his orders for finished goods manufactures by 10 percent initially. Half of that will reflect the adjustment to the new lower level of expected sales and the other 5 percentage points to work off the unintended inventory build-up. Thus, the presence of inventories magnifies the fluctuations in production.

If the process is repeated between finished goods producers and their suppliers, it also becomes clear that the amplitude of cyclical fluctuations at early production stages is greater than at later ones. This can be seen in Chart 4.1 in the comparison of the output of primary materials producers with that of finished producers and retailers.[1]

Not only does the presence of inventories give rise to this differential pattern of behavior by stage of process, but the timing and amplitude of those fluctuations vary by production stage. In particular, developments in new orders relative to production and sales at early stages of process tend to lead those at later produc-

Chart 4.2. **Ratio of New Orders to Production—Ratio to Control Solution.**

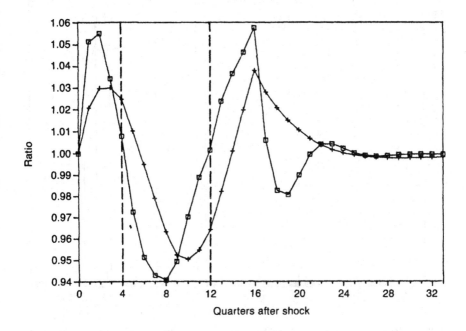

Quarters after shock

Notes: Ratios are for primary manufacturers (□) and finished manufacturers (+). The first broken vertical line corresponds to the cyclical peak and the second to the cyclical trough.

tion and distributive stages. This is shown in Chart 4.2.[2] A necessary condition for this lead during cyclical expansions is that the growth of final demand slows before reaching a peak. Under those circumstances, consider a retailer who anticipated last period's growth rate would persist. He placed orders to meet that increased level of demand and to build inventories to a higher level as well, assuming he had some desired target ratio of stock to sales. If demand rises only two and one-half percent instead of five percent, he will reduce his orders by five percent. Conversely, if a recession ends through declines at increasingly lower rates, production relative to orders at earlier stages of process will rise before final demand does. That is why leading indicators lead at turning points. And their lead is more reliable if the rates of change around turning points are well behaved.

Chart 4.3 depicts the behavior of the FRB's industrial production index for manufacturing as a whole. Official business cycle peaks and troughs are indicated as well. The data are plotted logarithmically to reflect rates of change. It is clear that manufacturing production is better behaved during expansions than contractions. Production usually slows as expansions mature. But in recessions, the

Chart 4.3. **Industrial Production—Manufacturing.**

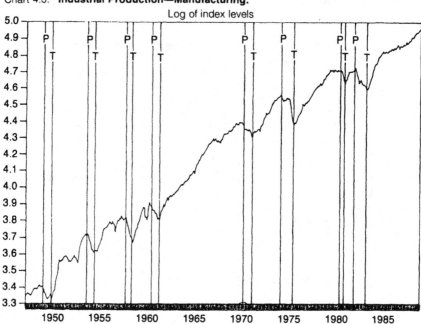

Log of index levels

steepest rates of decline sometimes occur early in the downturn and sometimes late. Adjustment paths during recessions are diverse, suggesting—not unlike the theory of chaos just beginning to be applied to economics—that adjustment processes are complex once the economy turns down. This likelihood is, in fact, suggested by the leading indictor index which exhibits very short leads, if any, at troughs.

A Summary Indicator Based on Business Cycle Dynamics

As a result of the business cycle dynamics described here, there should be considerable informational content in production, inventory, and orders variables relating to the manufacturing sector. Variables for this sector are, in fact, well represented in the list of leading indicators. Six of the eleven leading indicators are so related; they are:

1. New orders received by manufacturing, consumer goods and materials, 1982$;
2. Contracts and orders, plant and equipment, 1982$;
3. Average work week of production workers, manufacturing;
4. Vendor performance; percentage of companies receiving slower delivery;

5. Change in sensitive materials prices, percentage;
6. Change in manufacturing inventories on hand and on order, 1982$.

The six leading indicators reflect various aspects of demand for manufactured goods. All manufacturing orders are reflected in the indicators—those for consumer goods, for materials, and for capital equipment. All unfilled orders are inventories measured in the "on hand or on order" indicator. Unfilled orders are also reflected in the vendor performance indicator. Average weekly hours of manufacturing workers is a proxy for manufacturing production. Changes in production are associated with a change in the work week and/or a change in employment. Typically, hours are adjusted before workers are hired or laid off. Sensitive prices reflect largely those of unprocessed or very partially processed commodities, which are affected by demand before prices at a later stage.[3] The mechanism causing rates of change in sensitive prices to decline is the lead of the new orders—production rates at early production stages, described above.

Therefore, the hypothesis seeking expression in the leading indicators seems to be one that has the demand for manufactures deeply imbedded in it. To test independently the role of the manufacturing sector as a leading indicator, one approach is to construct a comprehensive measure for the sector and compare it with the leading indicator index. Such a measure might take the following form. Demand could be expressed as the sum of unfilled orders on the books at the end of period t–1 plus the orders received in period t. Of course, the supply available to meet that demand needs to be measured. It is the equivalent of finished goods inventories at the end of period t–1 plus the amount of production that could be achieved in time period t. A measure of that would be capacity output. That might overstate potential production because it may be too costly to increase output in the short-run. More needs to be known about the speed of adjustment of production.[4]

The data are available to construct this measure, i.e., the ratio of demand to supply in manufacturing. Most components are taken directly from the monthly Census survey, "Shipments, Orders and Inventories," except manufacturing capacity. The index of capacity utilization in manufacturing is calculated and released by the Federal Reserve Board; manufacturing capacity is the denominator in the index. It is the only measure not available in nominal dollars. Since the experimental measure developed here is a ratio, it can be expressed in either current or constant dollars. Constant dollars estimates are preferable, but it is difficult to construct properly deflated monthly measures of unfilled orders and finished goods inventories because they are stocks which consist of different vintages with different prices. Instead, capacity in current dollars was estimated using shipments and inventories in 1977. It was then calculated for the other periods using the capacity index and a price index of manufactured goods; the producer price index (PPI) for total manufactures was used for this purpose.

Chart 4.4. **Manufacturing Indicator in Current and Constant Dollars.**
Feb. 1967 = 100

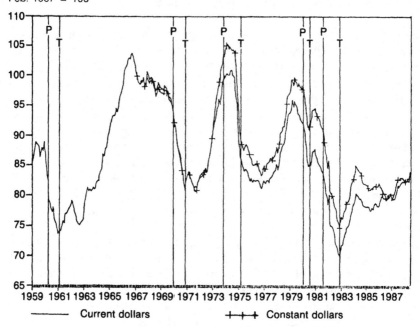

——— Current dollars   +—+—+ Constant dollars

However, a crude constant dollar measure, that did not take account of the vintages in the stock variables, was also constructed. The price index needed to deflate the unfilled orders series was available only from 1967 forward, so the constant dollar series begins in that year. The two series are shown in Chart 4.4 and official business cycle peaks and troughs are indicated. Both experimental comprehensive series show some of the characteristics of a leading cyclical indicator. Certainly, they show the disequilibria that are characteristic of the sector. Demand for manufacturing goods weakens substantially relative to supply. Demand clearly slows and often declines before business cycle peaks. That is because it is sensitive to the slowdowns in final demand that typically occur just before business cycle peaks.

At troughs, the manufacturing sector leads are much shorter; often there is no lead at all or even a lag. But, as discussed above, recessions are not as orderly as expansions.

Table 4.2 shows how each of the two experimental manufacturing sector indicators compares with the leading indicator index. The official index does better at every trough. But even so, the lead of indicators at troughs is quite short. If the indicator must move in one direction for three months to provide a reliable signal, then the leading indicators have not signaled a recovery until it was underway.

Table 4.2

Official Leading Indicator Index vs. Experimental Series Lead in Months

Official dating year and month		Official leading indicator index	Experimental current dollar series	Experimental constant dollar series
1958-4	Trough	−2	0	
1960-4	Peak	−11	−12	
1961-2	Trough	−2	−1	
1969-12	Peak	−8	−8	−8
1970-11	Trough	−1	0	0
1973-11	Peak	−8	+7	+4
1975-3	Trough	−1	+19	+19
1980-1	Peak	−10	−8	−8
1980-7	Trough	−2	−1	−1
1981-7	Peak	−3	−7	−7
1982-11	Trough	−8	0	0

Notes: Peaks and troughs in the offical leading indicator index are selected after screening by a statistical process. Peaks and troughs in the experimental series were determined judgmentally; the selections can be evaluated by studying Chart 4.4.

At peaks, the two experimental indicators and the leading indicator index have almost equal records during the past four expansions that have ended; the official index exhibits an average lead of 7 months and the experimental ones lead 5 or 6 months, on average. The difference arises because neither experimental manufacturing sector measure leads at the 1973–75 recession; but, there are some who think that the date of that particular peak is too early.

Thus, an indicator that is based on business cycle dynamics that involve over- and undershooting, particularly where inventories are concerned, works reasonably well. The leading indicators work better, of course, partly because they have been the subject of considerable useful research and analysis. The fact that over half the indicators relate to goods production and distribution behavior (which accounted for less than half of the economy in 1986–87) indicates that those components, at least, do have a foundation in business cycle dynamics.

Conclusions

There are three conclusions that emerge from this chapter. The first is that the indicators are not without theoretical content, even though their selection is not directly structured to reflect a theory. Thus, it may be that the longstanding criticisms of the index are themselves without firm foundation. The second finding is that broadly defined service sector variables may not have much content for predicting business cycles. The data in Table 4.1 indicate that service sector output rarely declines during recessions; it just rises more slowly. Thus, it may not prove feasible to develop leading indicators from variables in the service sector or to use them to improve the leading indicator index. Finally, because business cycles cannot be represented by well behaved sine curves, but are better behaved during expansions than contractions, the structure of indicators needs to be considered. It may be that separate sets of leading indicators are needed at troughs and at peaks. And because the behavior at troughs is more chaotic, the indicator set which signals that the economy has bottomed out may need expression in higher order changes than the set of variables comprising leading indicators of peaks.

Notes

1. This chart is reprinted from J. Popkin, "The Business Cycle at Various Stages of Process," *Journal of Business and Economic Statistics* 2 (3) July 1984, in which a full, three-stage model of goods demand and supply was specified, estimated, and simulated.

2. Ibid.

3. Ibid.

4. See, for example, G. L. Childs, *Unfilled Orders and Inventories, A Structural Analysis* (Amsterdam: North Holland, 1967); in it, a model is developed that takes into account the fact that a producer may have three ways to initially handle an incoming order—he may do nothing and let it become an unfilled order, he may produce it, or fill it from finished goods inventory.

5

Business Cycle Surveys:
A New Quality in Economic Statistics

Werner H. Strigel

The Challenge

"Most forecasters regard the prediction of turning points as one of the significant challenges in their work," so said Geoffrey H. Moore in a paper presented at the 1968 Annual Meeting of the American Statistical Association in Pittsburgh (Moore 1969). But it seems that neither politicians, economists nor stock-market speculators have always succeeded in satisfactorily meeting this challenge during the last twenty years. We seldom confront explicitly the large degree of uncertainty of business cycle analysis (diagnosis and forecasting), not to mention the underlying decision processes of entrepreneurs and of politicians. We have no *certain* knowledge about the future or even about the present; even knowledge of the recent past is far from complete. Thus, current stock market prices, which are available on a daily basis, fail to transmit a reliable picture because of their largely erratic movements which often do not reflect the basic cyclical trend. The economic data made public by the authorities, and generally rather late at that, in many cases have a provisional character and are sometimes subject to surprising corrections. Moreover, irregularity often results from accidental circumstances like strikes, weather anomalies, shifting holidays, etc. All these can complicate the analyses and give rise to differing interpretations.

Even today, in the age of computers, data banks, and numerous econometric forecasting models, the speed and accuracy of the official economic statistics on which all diagnostic and prognostic efforts are based, leave a lot to be desired. We can illustrate this with a German example: In the Federal Republic of Germany, the *preliminary* quarterly data for GNP usually are not available until three months after the end of the quarter. The *final* figures are determined nine to eighteen months later[1] but may be subject to further revisions as a result of

The author wants to thank Dr. Heidemarie Sherman for her excellent translation, Dr. Georg Goldrian for his valuable help and advice in computing the climate indicators, and the editor Philip A. Klein for his stimulating suggestions.

recalculations. In the period from 1976 to 1985,[2] the final quarterly GNP data displayed, on various occasions, deviations from the preliminary data of as much as 0.5 to 1 percentage point of the real growth rate. Given an average annual real growth rate of roughly two percent in that period, these amount to considerable divergences. The differences are particularly annoying when, compared with the preliminary data, the revised figures show changes in the direction of the cyclical movement or in the slope of the growth path.

Leading indicators as well as forecasting models must try to bridge this information gap between the time of actual cyclical activity and the subsequent publication of preliminary and then final data by the statistical offices. The accuracy of econometric model forecasts of GNP and its major components depends greatly on the accuracy and timeliness of the ex-post data used and the correct assumptions about future developments (e.g., the dollar exchange rate). The introduction into the models of so-called rational expectations as explanatory variables did not noticeably improve the quality of the forecasts (Aiginger 1980; Nerb 1986). It therefore appears more useful to gather ex-ante data at the source, i.e., directly at the enterprises or the households.[3]

Besides econometric forecasting models, leading indicators are still a main-stay of business cycle analysis. It is the author's opinion, however, that in select-ing these indicators and in combining them into composite indicators, insufficient consideration has been accorded to the fact that effective demand is not created until after business managers and consumers have formed judgments and antici-pations. Insofar as these variables do not change simultaneously, i.e., in the same month as demand, they ought to exhibit a lead over demand provided, of course, the corresponding information is available.

Statisticians and economists in the United States may be credited with being the first people to analyze economic time series thoroughly for their sensitivity to the business cycle (leading, coincident, and lagging). Representative for many, names like Burns, Mitchell, Moore, Shiskin, and Zarnowitz may be mentioned. Their work has inspired imitation worldwide, and the leading composite index of the U.S. Department of Commerce, which is based on their research, has achieved great political importance and is frequently used in international com-parisons (e.g., in OECD publications). Despite this and other kinds of progress, the opinion voiced by Moore twenty years ago, that a cyclical turning point can be safely determined only several months after the fact, is still regarded as valid today (Moore 1969).

Postwar Developments

It would be an interesting task to investigate whether the uncertainty of politi-cians, economists, and managers regarding their assessment of future economic activity or their forecasts of either GNP growth rates or their sales chances for the coming five to ten years has diminished markedly as a result of the increased supply of information during the past twenty years. A larger amount of information, which often may point in different directions, can also mean an increase in uncertainty. It is noteworthy, too, that different conclusions are drawn from the available data by different social and political groups. A remarkable example is found in the Federal Republic of Germany, where business anticipated the sharp slowdown in economic growth in the 1970s much earlier than the government (Goldrian and Strigel 1989).

After World War II, the supply of economic statistics was improved in a rapidly increasing number of countries by business and consumer surveys which were predominantly carried out by private organizations. These surveys closed various gaps in both the time and the number of variables covered by the official statistics. In 1950, such business cycle surveys existed in just three countries; by 1988, these surveys were carried out in 43 countries (Strigel and Ziegler 1988). The questions asked in these surveys frequently differ, however, and make international comparisons difficult. For the member countries of the European Community, however, a certain harmonization of the surveys did occur back in the early 1960s (European Community Commission 1967). In addition, for a number of questions international comparisons are possible (e.g., the United States, Japan, EEC), as will be shown later on.

The traditional economic statistics as a rule are quantitative (they tell only how much, e.g., number of employees, value of sales). Business cycle surveys ask similar questions but mainly in qualitative terms (e.g., new orders in the last month have been up, down, or unchanged). In addition, these surveys focus on the coverage of the following kinds of information:

• Judgments (e.g., assessment of an enterprise's business situation or a household's financial situation).

• Anticipations (plans and expectations of businessmen and consumers).

Here are two examples of the formulation of those questions:

We judge our current business situation for product X to be
good _____   satisfactory _____   bad _____

During the coming three months the sales price of product X will be
raised _____   left unchanged _____   lowered _____

Experience has shown that month-to-month or quarter-to-quarter changes in the frequency distribution of answers to qualitative questions determined at the micro level, but aggregated over, e.g., the entire industry or the entire economy, contain useful information on the pace of the upswing or downswing, as well as point to indications of a potential turning point. A prerequisite for this is that the panels chosen for these surveys must be representative of each sector concerned (manufacturing industry, construction, trade, consumers, etc.) and that in aggregating the data, account is taken of the different weights of the individual sectors.

"Climate" Indicators from Qualitative Data

Our work on business cycle surveys has now been underway for more than thirty years. We have developed various kinds of qualitative indicators. Some of the most useful are called "climate indicators" and, by way of illustration of their business cycle characteristics, we shall show several types of climate indicators for the United States, Japan, and the European Community (EEC).[4] We shift our focus on the following indicators (the respective sources are listed in the Appendix A):

• The Business Climate (BC) as an indicator of industrial production activity.

• The Consumption Climate (CC) as an indicator of private consumption.

• The Economic Climate (EC), an aggregate of the business and consumption climates, as an indicator of the overall change in economic activity.[5]

The climate indicators are, as a rule, composed of two pieces of information (see Appendix A for the sources of the variables used):

(*i*) information regarding the assessment of the present situation of the enterprise or the household (ex-post data) and

(*ii*) information regarding the anticipations of businessmen or consumers (*ex-ante* data).

Constructing the climate indicators by combining the ex-post and ex-ante data from these surveys at times has given rise to criticism. Therefore, the rationale for constructing these indicators in this way is summarized briefly from an earlier study (Strigel 1985): ex-post and ex-ante variables are combined into a climate indicator (BC or CC) in order to weight the anticipation variables with a level variable (e.g., assessment of the present business situation). This reveals the cyclical situation in which the anticipations are formed. Thus the ex-ante information "remaining unchanged" has a completely different meaning in a boom phase from the same answer in a recession phase. The percentage shares of the positive and negative answers to the ex-post and ex-ante questions are netted, and the balances are averaged. The time series derived in this way is based on 1980 = 100, seasonally adjusted and smoothed (three-month moving average). The indicators BC and CC are aggregated into the Economic Climate Indicator (ECI), the necessary weights being determined by multiple regressions.[6] This approach has been thoroughly discussed elsewhere (Goldrian 1988).

The use of climate indicators constructed in this manner may be justified on theoretical grounds. Before the actions of businesses and consumers are reflected in the data of the traditional economic statistics there is, as a rule, a phase during which the economic actors form judgments and anticipations. These influence their plans and their ensuing decisions and actions. Changes in businesses' and consumers' judgments and anticipations ought to be reflected in the business cycle surveys. If judgments and anticipations don't change simultaneously in one and the same month (conceivable in rare cases), the climate indicators ought to lead the ex-post data of the official statistics. Numerous well-known economists (e.g., Jöhr, Katona, Keynes, Lindahl, Pigou) have repeatedly referred to the influence of expectations and sentiments on the cyclical process. To be sure, climate indicators (as well as other business cycle indicators) necessarily do not point directly to the causes of changes in the cyclical movement. But they reveal relatively early how changes in financial variables (e.g., the level of interest rates, the exchange rate of the dollar, etc.) or economic policy measures (e.g., changes in taxation) or sudden exogenous "shocks" (e.g., change in oil prices) affect business and consumer "sentiment" (Strigel 1978a and 1978b).

The attempt to fuse the BC and CC indices into a business cycle indicator of the overall economy (ECI) was designed to help answer three questions: (i) Does the movement of the ECI index reflect the trend-adjusted change in overall economic growth? At the very least, does it indicate changes in the direction of the business cycle? (ii) Do the qualitative indicators lead the corresponding quantitative data at the cyclical turning point? (iii) Can we construct a leading index reflecting the predominant cyclical tendency in the entire OECD by combining the ECI indices for the United States, Japan, and EEC (these three regions account for approximately 90 percent of total OECD GNP)?

Answering these questions was not easy because there are diverse approaches taken in the questions, panels, and periodicities of the business cycle surveys in the United States, Japan, and the EEC (see Appendix A). The trend adjustments used for the time series of the official statistics[7] also present some problems at the margin. Despite these and other difficulties, the results of the research to date are surprisingly good. Even the differences mentioned among the individual surveys may be judged positive, as they show that the hypotheses selected prove correct even if the data used are not strictly comparable. This shows that it is possible despite the differences to glean similar, i.e., comparable, indicators representing the business and consumption climates in the three regions from the available information and to construct an ECI index. These endeavors were facilitated by the experiences gained with the Ifo business-climate index (Strigel 1985) and the consumption indicators developed earlier by Katona and his students (Katona 1975; Katona and Strümpel 1978; see also Nicola and Liberatori 1987).

The Results

Before presenting graphically the results of our experiences to date with climate indicators, the selection of the reference time series from the official statistics must be explained briefly. Here, of course, is a wide open field for discussion. May such climate or "subjective" indicators really be compared to "objective" data, and if so, to which ones? Here we tend toward the pragmatic approach. In order to prove that qualitative data are of value as cyclical indicators, one needs the quantitative mirror of the official statistics; there simply is no other mirror.

As the reference variable for the business climate in industry, we selected industrial production (sales or demand figures as well as capital expenditures could also have been used). Private consumption was used as the reference variable for the consumption climate. Here data on monthly retail sales would have been preferable, but they are not available for all regions (e.g., such data are missing for Italy). Private consumption is not really an optimal reference series for the consumption climate as these data are published quarterly rather than monthly. In addition, a large part of consumption as defined in the national accounts statistics is not very sensitive to the business cycle. This is true, for example, of expenditures on food, rent, and education. This fact is reflected in the deviation from trend, which is greater on average for industrial production than for private consumption in all three regions. For the reasons mentioned, perhaps it is not surprising that in several regions the relationship between the consumption climate and private consumption was not as good as the relationship between the business climate and industrial production (cf. Charts 5.1, 5.2, 5.3, and table in Appendix B). In the Japan's case, the reason might be that the CC indicator could be improved further. In combining the two climate indicators (BC and CC) into the Economic Climate Indicator (ECI), these differences are no longer important because the explanatory share of the two indicators is determined by multiple regression while the ECI is adjusted (standardized) to the amplitudes of the deviations from trend to GNP. The reference variable used for ECI is real GNP (adjusted for trend). All official data used are those published by the OECD.

For all three regions (the United States, Japan, EEC) as well as for the total OECD, the Economic Climate Indicator shows a remarkably good relationship with overall economic performance, with the ECI index usually having a considerable lead at cyclical turning points (cf. Chart 5.4 and table in Appendix B). This leading property of the ECI may be demonstrated best by a comparison with the widely followed Index of Eleven Leading Indicators for the United States. This comparison is presented in Chart 5.5, where the U.S. ECI is compared to the trend-adjusted movement of the Index of Eleven Leading Indicators (U.S. Department of Commerce) and the trend-adjusted GNP. The optical agreement of the qualitative with the quantitative leading indicator is amazingly good (see also R squares in Appendix B).

Summary and Outlook

The business cycle surveys developed in many countries after World War II, based on reports from entrepreneurs and consumers, filled several important gaps, but certainly some remain both in our temporal and in our economic information systems. The coverage of economic actors' judgments and anticipations in a qualitative form has opened up a hitherto widely unknown dimension for economists' cyclical analysis. It was our intent to demonstrate here that it is possible to construct an indicator of the overall economic climate from the addition of frequency distributions of judgments and anticipations. Over time, this Economic Climate Indicator (ECI) as a rule correctly reflects not only the

Chart 5.1. **U.S.: Climate Indicators and Official Statistics.**

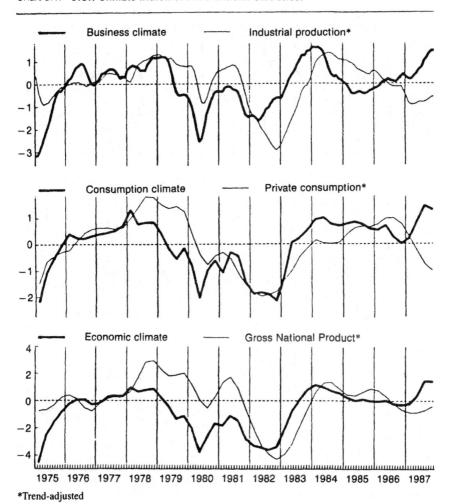

*Trend-adjusted

tendency of the change in trend-adjusted GNP, but it is also available relatively early (monthly data), is subject to fewer random fluctuations, is revised less frequently than GNP, and at the turning points generally has a lead of one or more quarters. Also, it exhibits a remarkably close pattern with the U.S. Index of Eleven Leading Indicators. Compared with the several decades of experience gathered by Moore and others, the thirteen-year period of analysis must certainly be considered modest. On the other hand, the similar positive experiences from several countries—despite certain differences in the surveys used—have shown that the suggested procedure has led to plausible results. After 10 or 20 years, this analysis should be concentrated also on the behavior of climate indicators during

Chart 5.2. **Japan: Climate Indicators and Official Statistics.**

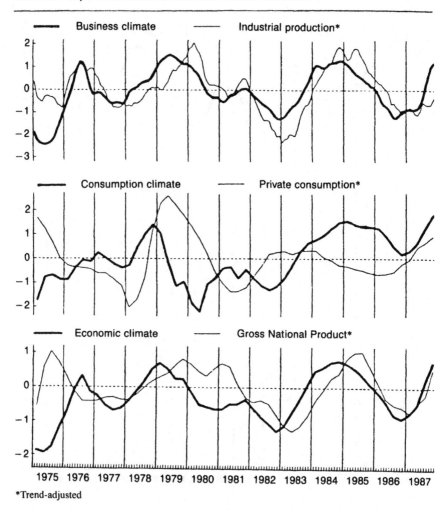

*Trend-adjusted

cyclical revivals and recessions and on cyclical turning points (see Moore 1961).

This positive evaluation of our research results is based on the fact that these climate indicators give us, in general, early hints of changes in the *direction* of cyclical developments. Using a quantitative scale, the correlation between climate indicators and the official statistics is not as good. This is not surprising because we do compare rather different things—qualitative evaluations on the one hand and quantitative facts on the other (see results shown in Appendix B). But considering the average lead time of the economic climate indicator (2 to 4 quarters), the results are rather remarkable. The average time required to eliminate random fluctuations was about the same for the Economic Climate Indicator

Chart 5.3. **European Community: Climate Indicators and Official Statistics.**

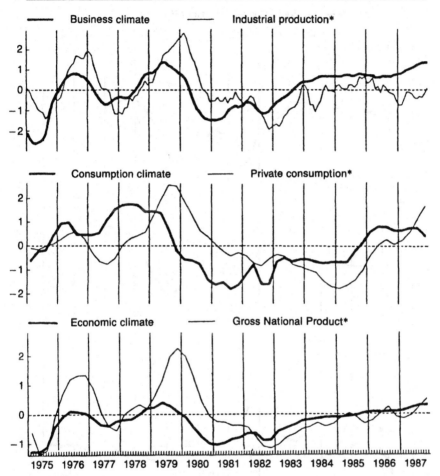

*Trend-adjusted

as for GNP in all four regions under review (three months or one quarter). We should also bear in mind that the ECI consists of monthly data; because of this fact, there is already an informational lead of up to three months over the GNP data. In addition, there are different time lags in publication; in some regions, the official—but preliminary—GNP data are published only several months after the end of the quarter under review. Considering all these factors, the Economic Climate Indicators should be quite interesting to those who like to keep a finger on the pulse of the economy.

Perhaps the reader has received the impression that the true objective of the various business and consumer surveys is the construction of a new leading

Chart 5.4. **OECD: Climate Indicators and Official Statistics.**

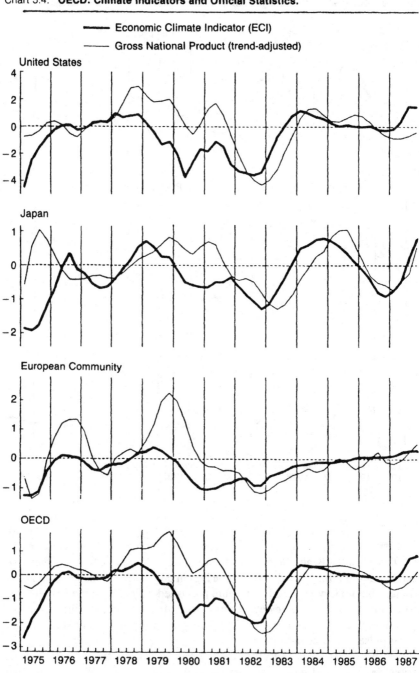

Chart 5.5. **Business Cycle Indicators for U.S.**

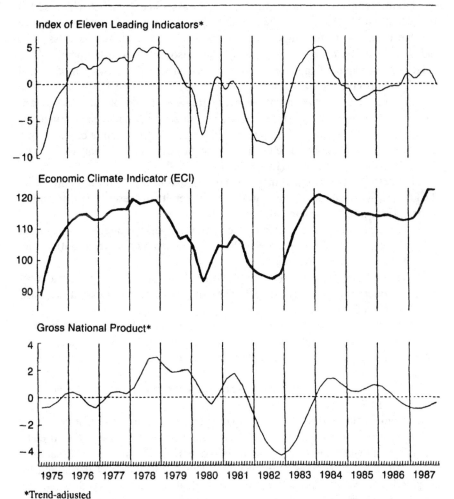

Index of Eleven Leading Indicators*

Economic Climate Indicator (ECI)

Gross National Product*

1975 1976 1977 1978 1979 1980 1981 1982 1983 1984 1985 1986 1987

*Trend-adjusted

indicator (see e.g., the criticism by Schmiedeskamp 1984). In fact, the ECI index is a by-product developed from many years of experience with the gathering of qualitative information. For the Ifo Institute for Economic Research in Munich, with its emphasis on branches of industry, it was initially more important to obtain additional information for the industries it covered. Some examples of the type of information gathered are assessment of the stocks of finished goods, capacity utilization, order stocks in terms of production months, production plans, price expectations, and capital expenditure plans. Each of the items was broken down into up to 500 market segments.

Consumer research institutions, too, were initially more interested in details like buying behavior, the propensity to save, the assessment of a household's level of income, etc. It was only in the course of time that people started to recognize that these surveys have components from which macroeconomic business cycle indicators may be constructed. Initially, they also overlooked the potential for enlarging the input of information to the econometric forecasting models and thereby improving their accuracy (see, e.g., Naggl 1984 and 1989). One of the initiators of these surveys and of the international exchange of ideas and experience in this field (CIRET)[8] did, however, recognize very early the importance of qualitative information. "The social world we are dealing with is basically of a qualitative nature which can be grasped by quantitative methods only to a certain extent but not in principle" (Langelütke 1954).

The users of business cycle analyses and forecasts may possibly be confused by the great variety of information as well as the diversity of presentation for similar information. Some examples might include:

• the verbal analyses of well known economists, perhaps internally consistent but differing nonetheless one from the other in manner of presentation and evaluation of facts and figures.

• the multitude of results reflecting differently constructed econometric forecasting models as, for example, published by the Conference Board (see also Zarnowitz 1986).

• the variations in timeliness (differences between preliminary and final figures) exhibited in the publication of the most recent data on various quantitative leading indicators (not to mention the complication of fluctuations in daily leading indicators such as stock prices).

• and, in addition to the many other pieces of information, the new Ifo Institute's ECI.

As from a voluminous menu, it is up to the individual to select that item from among a large supply which seems to match one's taste. When the author tried to find out many years ago from economists and statisticians in U.S. multinational corporations which sources of information they considered most important, he frequently received the laconic answer "we look at all of them." At the time, the ECI did not yet exist. Perhaps it will enrich the range of information in this area. Depending on the attitudes of those interested, the ECI will either captivate with its simple information (e.g., undiminished expansion) or disappoint because it lacks "precise" information (Morgenstern 1963). It cannot tell us, for example, that economic growth will increase from 2.3 to 2.7 percent (that these figures may later be revised to 2.6 and 2.5 percent, respectively, is usually registered by Ph.D. candidates only).

There is certainly room for improving the method suggested here for constructing an economic climate indicator. This applies especially to those regions where not all the data required for the ECI are available on a monthly basis, like the consumer climate in Japan and the business climate in the United States (see Appendix A). There is also the possibility of expanding the regional coverage to include Australia and New Zealand and the Southeastern Pacific region.

It was the objective of this paper to demonstrate by way of an example how statisticians and economists are trying to meet the challenge stated by G. H. Moore.

Appendix A
Data Sources for the Climate Indicators

Country/ Region	Source	Indicator and area covered[1]	Frequency
United States	National Federation of Independent Business, Washington	Index of Business Optimism (B)	quarterly
	Purchasing Management Association of Chicago, Chicago	Companies reporting slower deliveries (B)	monthly
	The Conference Board, New York	Consumer Confidence (C)	monthly
	Ifo Institute, Munich	Economic Climate (E)[2]	monthly
Japan	The Bank of Japan, Tokyo	Business Conditions, ex-post and ex-ante (B)	quarterly
	The Shoko Chukin Bank, Tokyo	Business Conditions, ex-post and ex-ante (B)	monthly
	Nippon Research Institute, Tokyo	Life satisfaction and buying attitudes for automobiles (C)[3]	6 times a year
	Economic Planning Agency, Tokyo	Consumer Sentiment (C)[4]	quarterly
	Ifo Institute, Munich	Economic Climate (E)[2]	monthly
European Community	EC Commission, Brussels	Industrial Confidence (B)	monthly
		Consumer Confidence (C)	monthly
	Ifo Institute, Munich	Economic Climate (E)[2]	monthly
OECD	Ifo Institute, Munich	Business Climate (B)	monthly
		Consumption Climate (C)	monthly
		Economic Climate (E)[2]	monthly

1. B = Business, C = Consumers, E = Total Economy.
2. Aggregation of B- and C-Indicators.
3. Both indices have been combined to a Consumption Climate Index for the period 1975–1982.
4. This index has been used for the period 1982–1987.

Appendix B
Results of Correlation Analyses

The correlation analyses are based on the same data set which has been used for the construction of Charts 5.1 to 5.5:

—*Industrial Production*: three-month moving average of seasonally and trend-adjusted data,

—*Private Consumption*: three-quarter moving average of seasonally and trend-adjusted data (in real terms),

—*Gross National Product*: three-quarter moving averages of seasonally and trend-adjusted data (in real terms),

—*Business Climate*: three-month moving average of seasonally adjusted data,

—*Consumption Climate*: three-month moving average of seasonally adjusted data,

—*Economic Climate*: three-month moving average.

Before the correlation the data for the climate indicators have been shifted according to their average lead time (see following table):

Indicator and region	Average lead*	Reference variable	Correlation coef.
Business Climate		*Industrial Production*	
USA	4 m		0.57
Japan	3 m		0.74
EEC	4 m		0.65
Consumption Climate		*Private Consumption*	
USA	3 q		0.66
Japan	5 q		0.22
EEC	5 q		0.73
Economic Climate		Gross National Product	
USA	2 q		0.63
Japan	4 q		0.49
EEC	3 q		0.63
OECD	3 q		0.73
United States: Index of eleven leading indicators	2 q		0.72

*m = months; q = quarters

Notes

1. In September of each year the Federal Statistical Office, Statistische Bundesamt, announces the revised GNP figures for the four quarters of the previous year.

2. The Statistische Bundesamt has been regularly announcing quarterly GNP data since 1978 only.

3. In 1989 the Ifo Institute for Economic Research will publish a voluminous handbook on its 40 years of experience in the area of business surveys and on the information content of business anticipations (Oppenländer/Poser 1989); a worldwide compilation of the business cycle surveys existing at present is provided by Strigel and Ziegler (1988).

4. The author reported on an initial attempt at the 16th CIRET Conference, Washington (Strigel 1983). In the ensuing years, this idea was developed further and the method was improved (Strigel 1984; Goldrian and Strigel 1985; Goldrian 1988).

5. Industry and private consumption account for about two thirds of total demand. Cyclical fluctuations are more pronounced in industry than in private consumption. That is why, as a rule, the business climate indicator of industry gets a greater weight when combined with the consumption climate into the ECI.

6. The adjustment between the qualitative indicator and GNP proved to be better when the computation of the weights is not based on the entire period of 13 years but rather on the average of the past five years.

7. The trend adjustment of the time series of the quantitative data from the official statistics is necessary because the time series of the qualitative data cannot contain a trend component; their maxima and minima cannot exceed +/- 100.

8. CIRET is the Centre for International Research on Economic Tendency Surveys. CIRET has about 500 members or correspondents in 48 countries (1988) and organizes an international conference every other year. The 18th CIRET Conference was held in October 1989 in Osaka, Japan. The CIRET Secretariat is attached to the Ifo Institute for Economic Research, Munich, F.R. Germany.

References

Aiginger, Karl. 1980. "Empirical Evidence on the Rational Expectation Hypothesis Using Reported Expectations." Paper presented to the World Congress of the Econometric Society, Aix en Provence.

The Conference Board. *Statistical Bulletin* (monthly). New York.

European Community Commission. 1967. *The Harmonized Business Surveys in the Community: Principles and Methods*. Brussels. (November).

Goldrian, Georg. 1988. "The Aggregation of Climate Indicators into a Composite Indicator." *CIRET Studien* (38): 21–52. Munich.

Goldrian, Georg, and Werner H. Strigel. 1985. "An International Comparison of Cyclical 'Climate'-Indicators." Paper presented at the 17th CIRET Conference, Vienna.

————. "Nationale Gesamtindikatoren." In *Handbuch der IFO-Umfragen*. Edited by K. H. Oppenländer and G. Poser. Berlin-München.

Katona, George. 1975. *Psychological Economics*. New York.

Katona, George, and Burkhard Strümpel. 1978. "Consumer Sentiment and Economic Trends." In *Problems and Instruments of Business Cycle Analysis, 13th CIRET Conference Proceedings*. Edited by W. H. Strigel. *Lecture Notes in Economics and Mathematical Systems*, Vol. 154, pp. 29–46. New York-Berlin-Heidelberg.

Klein, Franz-Josef, and Gernot Nerb. 1985. "The Performance of the EC Composite Leading Indicator and its Components." In *Essays on the Performance of Leading Indicators Based on Qualitative Data, CIRET-Studien* (36): 121–48. Munich.

Langelütke, Hans. 1954. "Integrative Tendenzen in der Wirtschaftsforschung." *Allgemeines Statistisches Archiv* (38): 322. (Translated citation.)

Morgenstern, Oskar. 1963. *On the Accuracy of Economic Observations*. Princeton: Princeton University Press.

Moore, Geoffrey, H. 1961. *Business Cycle Indicators*. Vols. 1 and 2. Princeton: Princeton University Press.

—————. "Forecasting Short-term Economic Change." *Journal of the American Statistical Association* (64) 325: 9.

Naggl, Walter. 1984. "The Anticipations Model: A Short-term Forecasting Model Based on Anticipations Data," pp. 161–91. In *16th CIRET Conference Proceedings*. Edited by K. H. Oppenländer and G. Poser. Aldershot.

—————. 1989. "Verwendung von Konjunkturtestdaten in einem ökonometrischen Modell." In *Handbuch der IFO-Umfragen*. Edited by K. H. Oppenländer and G. Poser. Berlin-München.

Nerb, Gernot. 1986. "Der Konjunkturtest im Lichte neuerer wirtschafts-theoretischer Ansätze." *Ifo Studien* (32) 1–3: 27–40. Berlin-München.

Nicola, E. de and Liberatori L. 1987. "Family's Climate: Its Utilisation for Macroeconomic Analysis." Paper presented at 18th CIRET Conference, Zurich.

Oppenländer, K. H., and G. Poser., eds. 1989. *Handbuch der IFO-Umfragen*. Berlin-München.

Schmiedeskamp, Jay. 1984. "Lessons from our Experience with Consumer Confidence Surveys." Paper presented at the 16th CIRET Conference, Washington, D.C. In *CIRET Studien* (34): 227–91. Munich.

Strigel, Werner H. 1978a. "Fehlendes Vertrauen als Wachstumsbremse." *Ifo-Studien* (24) 1/2: 21–41.

—————. 1978b. "Entrepreneurial Reactions in a Changing World." *Ifo Digest* (1) 4: 21–29.

—————. 1981. *Business Cycle Surveys. Economic Data Based on Business and Consumer Evaluations and Expectations*. Frankfurt-New York.

—————. 1983. "The Potential Use of Qualitative Data by Individual Firms Exemplified with Old and New Surveys." Paper submitted to the 16th CIRET Conference, Washington, D.C.

—————. 1984. "Qualitative Business Cycle Indicators—An International Comparison." *Ifo Digest* (7) 3: 35–43.

—————. 1985. "The Business Climate as Leading Indicator." Memorandum for the 17th CIRET Conference, Vienna. In *Essays on the Performance of Leading Indicators*, *CIRET Studien* (6): 1–56. Munich.

Strigel, Werner H. and Maria Ziegler. 1988. "Trade Cycle and Tendency Surveys—The Current State of the Art. International Synoptic Table." In *World Index of Economic Forecasts*. 3d ed. Edited by R. Fildes. Aldershot.

Zarnowitz, Victor. 1986. "The Record and Improvability of Economic Forecasting." *Economic Forecasts: A Worldwide Survey* (3) 12: 22–30.

6

The Leading Indicators and Monetary Aggregates

Phillip Cagan

The composite leading index includes the monetary aggregate real M2.[1] In recent years the behavior of all of the monetary aggregates has changed, raising questions about their continued usefulness as reliable indicators. This paper evaluates the contribution of M2 and other monetary and financial aggregates to the composite index.

Behavior of the Monetary Aggregates

In the 1980s, the monetary aggregates became less reliable indicators because their growth rates displayed increased volatility, reduced correspondence to business cycles, and less clearly defined cyclical turning points. The cyclical conformity improves when money is deflated by the consumer price index, as presented for M2 growth in Chart 6.1, though the volatility and clarity of turning points still deteriorate in the 1980s.

Actually, the deterioration began earlier. Estimates of a demand function for real M1 display increased residual errors and cumulative departures from predicted values after the mid-1970s.[2] Then, the fairly steady 3¼ percent per year upward trend in M1 velocity (ratio of GNP to M1) abruptly changed in the 1980s into a fluctuating decline that lasted apparently until mid-1987. Since then the trend has turned upward again but at a much reduced rate. Many studies that attempt to reformulate a demand equation for M1 to fit the years since the mid-1970s achieved better success because of their ingenuity and data mining, but none of them satisfactorily fit the entire period since the early 1950s. The change in the behavior of M1 appears to characterize the broader monetary aggregates as well. Though analysis of demand equations for aggregates other than M1 has been less detailed, a clear indication of a change in behavior is the uniform decline in all their velocities in the early 1980s, a decline that exceeds by far any

---

I am indebted to M. Guha for supervising the computer runs at the Center for International Business Cycle Research.

Chart 6.1. **Monthly Percentage Change in Real M2, February 1959–December 1987.**

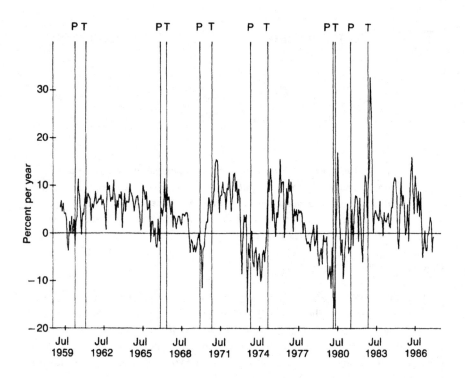

Note: NBER reference cycle peaks and troughs plus mini-recession of November 1966 to May 1967.

previous post–World War II cyclical decline and cannot be adequately explained by the 1981–82 recession.

These changes in behavior are generally attributed to the developments in the financial system that began in the late 1960s and accelerated during the 1970s. The rise in interest rates combined with ceilings on deposit rates led to the introduction of many better-paying financial instruments to compete with the traditional transactions and savings deposits. Among the most successful were negotiated certificates of deposit, repurchase agreements, money market mutual funds, and overnight Eurodollar deposits in the Cayman Islands. Banks met the competition with interest-paying NOW accounts, which originated in Massachusetts savings banks and eventually spread to the entire banking system. The Monetary Control Act of 1980 removed all ceilings on rates in stages by 1986 except for demand deposits. These developments have resulted in massive shifts in the form in which the public holds its transaction balances and savings.

Significantly, the Federal Reserve has reduced the attention it pays to monetary aggregates in its conduct of monetary policy.

Attempts to define a new monetary aggregate with the same behavior as the old M1 and M2 cannot avoid the fact that the distinction between transactions and savings balances, such as it was, has been greatly blurred in the 1980s. The present NOW accounts, which evolved from the super-NOW accounts and have no restrictions, have largely replaced demand deposits for individuals. NOW accounts pay a competitively determined interest rate which makes them attractive for both transactions and savings. Low turnover confirms their appeal as savings. Their turnover rates approximate the previous rates for saving deposits, well below those for checking accounts previously held by individuals. Because they are partially savings, NOW accounts display a greater sensitivity to changes in interest rates available on substitute liquid assets than demand deposits ever did.

One approach to redefining a more useful monetary aggregate is to cover a broader group of assets which internalize the most frequent substitutions and which, therefore, are not affected by such substitutions. Ideally, such a broader aggregate would display the stability formerly shown by the narrower aggregates. A theoretically appealing broader aggregate is nonterm M3,[3] recently defined by the research staff of the Federal Reserve Bank of San Francisco. It comprises the broad range of liquid assets in regular M3 (that is, all the new ones like money market mutual funds, repurchase agreements, Eurodollars, etc.) but includes only the assets available without a set term (that is, excludes repurchase agreements and Eurodollars that are not overnight, and all time deposits). It expresses the notion that a transactions demand for immediately available assets can be distinguished from other liquid assets that have a predetermined maturity of more than a day.

The growth of this nonterm M3 deflated by the CPI is shown in Chart 6.2. It moves similarly to M2 as in Chart 6.1, except that it displays greatly increased volatility in the 1980s and is not clearly superior to M2 as an indicator. A comparison of M2 and nonterm M3 suggests that redefinitions of the coverage of M2 will not improve its performance as an indicator.

Alternative Monetary Aggregates in the Composite Leading Index

We may evaluate alternatives to M2 as leaders by recomputing the composite index with M2 excluded and with substitutions of other monetary and financial aggregates. In addition to the theoretically appealing nonterm M3, the most widely discussed substitutes are M1, the monetary base,[4] liquid assets, and total debt. The present composite index since 1955 is shown in Chart 6.3.[5] Criteria for evaluating alternatives are the lengths of leads, the variation in the lengths of leads, and the prevalence of hard-to-identify rounded peaks such as in 1980.

Chart 6.2. **Monthly Percentage Change in Real Nonterm M3, February 1959–December 1987.**

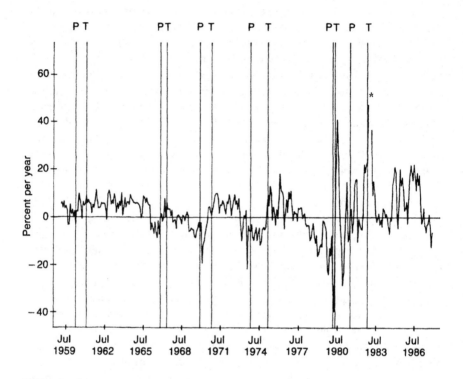

*1983 value for January (199.8) and February (108.4) omitted.

Note: NBER reference cycle peaks and troughs plus mini-recession of November 1966 to May 1967.

Another criterion not examined here is the number of false signals.

The performance of the composite when other series are substituted for M2 displays no major changes, but minor changes of marginal significance do occur. The leads at peaks and troughs for these substitute composites are listed in the Appendix. The turns for the mini-recession of November 1966 to May 1967 (based on the peak and trough in aggregate measures of activity) are included to provide more information. When a cyclical turn is flat, making it hard to select the exact month of the turn without the benefit of hindsight, the ending month of the plateau is also shown in parentheses. The end of such plateaus provides a better measure of the effective lead signaled by the series. Such plateaus occurred in some of the series since 1957 at the peaks of 1969, 1980, and 1981, and at the troughs of 1970 and 1982.

To compare these indexes, an important consideration is the length of leads.

Chart 6.3. **Index of Composite Leading Indicators, January 1955–December 1987.**

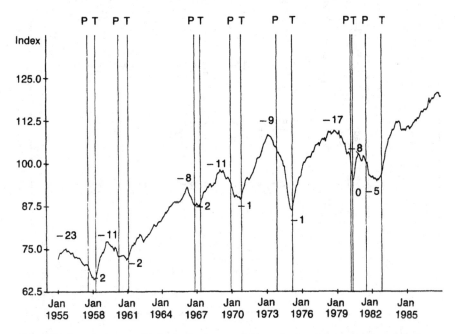

Notes: Numbers denote monthly leads of extreme point in series to subsequent peak or trough. NBER reference cycle peaks and troughs plus mini-recession of November 1966 to May 1967.

Table 6.1 shows the average lead at peaks and troughs since 1957 for various versions of the composite index. The original composite and substitutions for M2 in the top part of the table show some differences in the averages. The only substitution with a longer average lead than the original has at peaks is nonterm M3. The longer lead of nonterm M3 is produced, however, by the 1980 peak which is flat and would probably not have been identified until the plateau ended later, at the same time that most of the other series peaked. At troughs, all the substitutions except liquid assets increase the average lead but only slightly.

The standard deviation of the leads shown in Table 6.1 and the Appendix is slightly smaller for some of the substitute series than for the original. But a small standard deviation is not an unambiguously desirable trait. While a more uniform length of leads makes identification easier, the occasional longer lead gives a more useful signal even though it increases the standard deviation.

Sharp turning points and the absence of plateaus also help identify turns. The present composite index has one turn since 1957 with a plateau—at the 1980 peak. Plateaus are selected at turns where the cyclical high point of the series is followed by nearby values that on a graph appear virtually at the same level.

Table 6.1

Leads at Cyclical Peaks and Troughs in Months 1957–1982

	Peaks				Troughs			
	Average lead		Std. dev.		Average lead		Std. dev.	
	High points	End of plateaus	High points	End of plateaus	High points	End of plateaus	High points	End of plateaus
12 series composite	−12.4	−11.7	5.2	4.8	−1.9	−1.9	1.5	1.5
Substituting for M2:								
M1	−12.4	−11.3	5.2	5.0	−1.6	−1.6	1.6	1.6
Nonterm M3	−13.1	−12.3	6.4	5.3	−1.4	−1.4	1.8	1.8
Monetary base	−12.4	−11.7	5.3	4.9	−1.4	−1.4	1.0	1.0
Liquid assets	−11.4	−11.4	5.7	5.7	−3.7	−2.0	4.3	2.7
Total debt	−11.4	−10.4	5.0	5.8	−1.6	−1.6	1.6	1.6
Excluding:								
M2	−11.3	−11.3	5.1	5.1	−1.4	−1.4	1.0	1.0
Workweek	−12.3	−11.6	5.3	4.9	−1.9	−1.9	2.1	2.1
Unemployment	−11.7	−11.7	4.8	4.8	−2.1	−2.1	2.0	2.0
New orders	−12.3	−11.6	5.3	4.9	−2.3	−1.9	1.8	1.5
New businesses	−12.4	−11.7	5.2	4.8	−1.7	−1.9	1.6	1.5
Stock prices	−13.1	−11.6	6.4	4.9	−2.0	−1.6	2.0	1.6
P&E contracts	−13.4	−11.4	6.2	5.0	−2.0	−2.0	2.0	2.0
Housing starts	−12.1	−10.4	5.4	5.8	−1.4	−1.4	1.8	1.8
Vendor performance	−12.0	−11.3	5.4	5.0	−2.1	−2.1	2.0	2.0
Inventories	−12.4	−11.3	5.2	5.0	−2.4	−2.4	1.8	1.8
Sensitive prices	−12.0	−10.9	6.0	5.8	−2.4	−2.4	1.9	1.9
Credit	−12.4	−11.3	5.3	5.1	−1.9	−1.9	1.5	1.5

Source: Appendix table.

Note: Agreement of paired columns means that all high points and end of plateaus are the same month.

Table 6.2

Variability of Monthly Changes in Monetary Aggregates for Two Subperiods (Annual Percentage Rates)

	1960–1973 (1)	1974–1986 (2)	Ratio (2)/(1) (3)
Real M1	4.0	6.7	1.7
Real M2	3.2	4.8	1.5
Real nonterm M3	3.8	12.2	3.3
Real monetary base	3.5	4.4	1.2*

*Smaller than ratio of figures shown because of rounding.

Sources: M1 and M2 from Washington Federal Reserve, nonterm M3 from San Francisco Federal Reserve, base from St. Louis Federal Reserve via Citibank database, all deflated by urban CPI.

Notes: Method of computation: For the monthly periods indicated, standard deviation of differences between monthly percentage changes in the series and a smoothed version of the monthly changes, both expressed as annual percentage rates. The smoothed version is the change between each month and an average of the preceding 12 months.

Among the substitute series, all but the monetary base and nonterm M3 display plateaus at more than one turn.

Despite the longer average lead of the composite with nonterm M3 substituted for M2, the former series has the disadvantage of appreciable volatility. A measure of volatility of this series and of M1, M2, and the monetary base is presented in Table 6.2 for two subperiods since 1960. The measure is the deviation of monthly changes in the series deflated by the consumer price index from a smoothed version of the changes. The smoothed version is the ratio of each month to the preceding twelve-month average of the deflated series (which gives the change over the preceding 6½ months). Table 6.2 gives the standard deviation of the differences between the monthly and smoothed percentage changes (both expressed as annual rates).

In the earlier 1960–1973 period, the standard deviations of the four series are very similar. In the later 1974–1986 period when the introduction of new financial instruments accelerated, M1 and nonterm M3 display considerably greater volatility. The volatility of M2 and the base also increased in the later period, but by much less than the other series did, and the base by less than M2. This points to a slight preference for the base over M2 as a component of the composite index. Changes in the Fed's base are plotted in Chart 6.4. Perhaps a short moving average of changes in the base would improve its performance as an indicator, but that alteration has not been tried here. Nevertheless, despite its month-to-month variability, the base series clearly tends to lead cyclical turns in business.

Such a preference raises the question, however, whether the relation to aggregate activity is as close for the base as for broader monetary aggregates like M2.

Chart 6.4. **Monthly Percentage Change in Fed Monetary Base, February 1959–December 1987.**

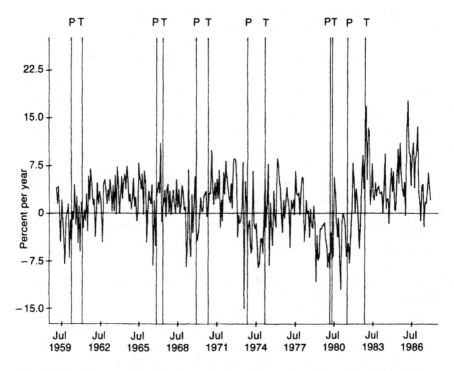

Note: NBER reference cycle peaks and troughs plus mini-recession of November 1966 to December 1967.

While the base represents the outcome of monetary policy actions, it comprises mostly currency, which is supplied on demand and may reflect aggregate activity with a lag and not a lead. Nevertheless, the base appears to be a leading indicator. Moreover, M2 has been affected by financial developments that have changed and obscured its relationship to aggregate activity, whereas the base is not directly affected by the introduction of substitutes or changes in the public's behavior. The base may therefore be considered a serious candidate to substitute for M2 in the composite index. None of the other substitutes considered appears to offer any advantages over M2.

The Composite Index Excluding Individual Components

As shown in the Appendix Table, substitution of the base for M2 hardly changes the length of leads in the composite. This suggests that the choice of either series is immaterial. As a matter of fact, the composite is not sensitive to the exclusion of any one component. The Appendix Table records the leads of the composite excluding each of its components one at a time. The leads differ either not at all or usually by one month at most of the turns. Although the exclusion of M2 makes less difference than the exclusion of most of the others, when the monetary aggregate most affected by recent financial developments M1 is substituted for M2, the behavior of the composite is hardly affected. We can conclude that, in the composite, no one component affects the turning points by much. Therefore, substitutions for one component are not likely to make much difference.

Nevertheless, substitutions can make a marginal difference. The current choice of M2 does better than any other monetary or financial series that might be proposed as an alternative, except for the monetary base which appears equivalent to M2.

Summary and Conclusion

Because recent financial developments have changed the behavior of monetary aggregates, the continued inclusion of M2 in the leading indicators deserves reexamination. The important changes in monetary aggregates have occurred since the late 1960s. The trend-adjusted composite index has been recomputed since 1955 substituting various alternatives for M2 (M1, nonterm M3, the monetary base, liquid assets, and total debt) and excluding each of its present components one at a time. A comparison of leads at cyclical peaks and troughs for the alternatives reveals only marginal differences. Inclusion of nonterm M3 produces the longest average lead. Inclusion of M1, M2 (in the present composite), or the monetary base produces the same average lead at peaks (longer than the lead for total debt or liquid assets) and only a slightly shorter average lead at troughs. Based on a measure of the month-to-month variability for 1974–1986, M1 and nonterm M3 display greater volatility than that for M2 or the base, and M2 greater than the base. This makes the base a candidate to replace M2 in the composite index.

The choice will depend partly on any preference for not changing the present composition of the composite index and partly on the question of which series bears a more reliable relationship to aggregate activity, which the evidence presented here does not address. In monetary theory, the public's money balances reflect and help determine aggregate expenditures, while the monetary base affects expenditures, once removed, by helping determine the money supply. On the other hand, the relationship of the base to aggregate expenditures may be less affected by the introduction of new financial instruments and changes in the monetary system. Since both series reflect the same monetary effects on the economy only one, not both, belongs in the composite index.

Appendix Table

Leads (−) of Composite Index of Indicators at Cyclical Turns (Months)

	Business peaks								
	Aug 57	Apr 60	Nov 66*	Dec 69	Nov 73	May 80	July 81	Average	Std. dev.
12 series composite	−23	−11	−8	−11	−9	−17(−12)	−8	−12.4(−11.7)	5.2(4.8)
Substituting for M2:									
M1	−23	−11	−8	−11(−8)	−9	−17(−12)	−8	−12.4(−11.3)	5.2(5.0)
Nonterm M3	−23	−11	−8	−11	−8	−23(−17)	−8	−13.1(−12.3)	6.4(5.3)
Monetary base	−23	−12	−8	−11	−8	−17(−12)	−8	−12.4(−11.7)	5.3(4.9)
Liquid assets	−23	−11	−8	−11	−4	−15	−8	−11.4	5.7
Total debt	−23	−11	−8	−11(−8)	−8	−12	−7(−3)	−11.4(−10.4)	5.0(5.8)
Excluding:									
M2	−23	−12	−8	−8	−8	−12	−8	−11.3	5.1
Workweek	−23	−11	−8	−11	−8	−17(−12)	−8	−12.3(−11.6)	5.3(4.9)
Unemployment	−23	−11	−8	−11	−9	−12	−8	−11.7	4.8
New orders	−23	−11	−8	−11	−8	−17(−12)	−8	−12.3(−11.6)	5.3(4.9)
New businesses	−23	−11	−8	−11	−9	−17(−12)	−8	−12.4(−11.7)	5.2(4.8)
Stock prices	−23	−11	−8	−11	−8	−23(−12)	−8	−13.1(−11.6)	6.4(4.9)
P&E contracts	−23	−12	−8	−11(−8)	−9	−23(−12)	−8	−13.4(−11.4)	6.2(5.0)
Housing starts	−23	−11	−8	−11(−8)	−8	−17(−12)	−7(−3)	−12.1(−10.4)	5.4(5.8)
Vendor performance	−23	−11	−8	−8	−9	−17(−12)	−8	−12.0(−11.3)	5.4(5.0)
Inventories	−23	−11	−8	−11(−8)	−9	−17(−12)	−8	−12.4(−11.3)	5.2(5.0)
Sensitive prices	−23	−13	−8	−11(−8)	−9	−17(−12)	−3	−12.0(−10.9)	6.0(5.8)
Credit	−23	−12	−8	−11(−8)	−8	−17(−12)	−8	−12.4(−11.3)	5.3(5.1)

Business troughs

	Apr 58	Feb 60	May 67*	Nov 70	Mar 75	May 80	Nov 82	Average	Std. Dev.
12 series composite	-2	-2	-2	-1	-1	0	-5	-1.9	1.5
Substituting for M2:									
M1	-2	-2	-1	-1	0	0	-5	-1.6	1.6
Nonterm M3	-2	-2	-1	-1	0	+1	-5	-1.4	1.8
Monetary base	-2	-2	-2	-1	0	0	-3	-1.4	1.0
Liquid assets	0	-2	-7	-7(-1)	0	+1	-11(-5)	-3.7(-2.0)	4.3(2.7)
Total debt	-2	-2	-2	-1	0	+1	-5	-1.6	1.6
Excluding:									
M2	-2	-2	-2	-1	0	0	-3	-1.4	1.0
Workweek	-2	-1	-5	0	0	0	-5	-1.9	2.1
Unemployment	-2	-2	-5	-1	0	0	-5	-2.1	2.0
New orders	-2	-2	-5(-2)	-1	-1	0	-5(-3)	-2.3(-1.9)	1.8(1.5)
New businesses	-2	-2	-2	-1	0	0	-5	-1.7(-1.9)	1.6(1.5)
Stock prices	-2	-2	-2	-1	0	+1	-5	-1.6	1.8
P&E contracts	-1	-2	-5(-2)	-1	0	0	-5	-2.0(-1.6)	2.0(1.6)
Housing starts	-2	-2	-1	-1	0	+1	-5	-1.4	1.8
Vendor performance	-2	-2	-5	-1	0	0	-5	-2.1	2.0
Inventories	-2	-2	-5	-1	-2	0	-5	-2.4	1.8
Sensitive prices	-2	-2	-5	-3	0	0	-5	-2.4	1.9
Credit	-2	-2	-2	-1	-1	0	-5	-1.9	1.5

*Mini-recession of 1966–67.

Source: Run on computer program of Center for International Business Cycle Research, Columbia University, trend-adjusted option, weights of unity and standardization of components based on 1948–88. See fn. 1 for other new versions of the composite.

Data from Citibank database. Series title and Citibank indentification are as follows: Composite leading index (DLEAD), M1 deflated by CPI (FM1/PUNEW), Nonterm M3 deflated by CPI (FM3 deflated by CPI (FMBASE/PUNEW), Liquid assets deflated by CPI (FML/PUNEW), Debt of domestic nonfinancial sectors (FMND/PUNEW), M2 deflated by CPI (FM2D82), Average weekly hours (LPHRM), Unemployment insurance claims (LUINC), New orders $82 (MOCM82), Business formation (BUS), Stock prices (FSPCOM), Contracts for plant and equipment $82 (MPCON8), Housing starts (HSBP), Vendor performance (percent reporting slower deliveries) (IVPAC), Change in business inventories $82 (4 term weighted moving average) (IVMUT8), Change in sensitive materials prices (4 term weighted moving average) (PSM99S), Change in business and consumer credit (FCBCUC).

Index omits later starting series and links them in when available (M1, liquid assets, and nonterm M3 in 1959, and debt in 1956).

Note: Leads in parentheses pertain to end of plateaus (see text).

Notes

1. See explanatory articles by V. Zarnowitz and L. Boschan in *Business Conditions Digest* for May and November 1975, reprinted in *Handbook of Cyclical Indicators*, 1984, U.S. Department of Commerce, Bureau of Economic Analysis, pp. 67–69. Beginning with April 1988, the published composite index in *Business Conditions Digest* excludes new businesses prior to January 1984 (for a new total of 11 series). All 12 series are included here. The latest version of the U.S. composite leading index of 12 series used by the Center for International Business Cycle Research substitutes corporate profits after taxes and the ratio of price to unit labor cost for new businesses and real M2. These substitutions are not made in this study.

2. See J. P. Judd and J. L. Scadding, "The Search for a Stable Money Demand Function: A Survey of the Post-1973 Literature," *Journal of Economic Literature* 20 (September): 993–1023.

3. See Brian Motley, "Should M2 be Redefined?" *Economic Review, Federal Reserve Bank of San Francisco* 1988 (Winter): 33–51.

4. St. Louis version, adjusted for reserve requirements. High-powered money of the Washington Fed is available more promptly and gives essentially the same results. See "The Monetary Base," appendix to *Monetary Policy Report to Congress*, Board of Governors of the Federal Reserve System, July 13, 1988.

5. Some of the monetary aggregates begin a few years later. They are omitted from the composite and then linked in as they become available.

7

Cyclical Indicators in Econometric Models

Lawrence R. Klein

Motivating Thoughts

In 1959 and 1960, when the Committee on Economic Stability of the Social Science Research Council (SSRC) was planning a project for constructing an econometric model of the United States on a cooperative basis, Geoffrey Moore put forward some ideas that have proved to be unforgettable for me. I have often referred back in my own mind to his contributions to the discussion, either in the form in which they were originally cast, or as stimuli for related ideas that have significance for econometric model construction. While the different committee members were trying to piece together patterns of research personnel and work to be done for relevant sectors (housing, business investment, money market, input-output flows, agriculture, and the like), Geoffrey Moore suggested that it was important to include the leading indicators of cyclical activity explicitly in the composite model.

This suggestion could lead in two different directions. Either the "official" index could be a variable of the model, or the individual components of the index could be separately treated in the different equations of the model. The present (1988) composition of the index includes eleven tested statistical series:

1. average work week in manufacturing (hours)
2. initial claims for unemployment insurance
3. manufacturers' new orders
4. vendor performance
5. contracts and orders for plant and equipment
6. building permits for new houses
7. the change in trade inventories
8. the change in prices of basic materials
9. an index of stock market prices
10. the change in money supply (M2)
11. the change in outstanding business and consumer credit

All these data, to be useful as signals of business cycle developments to come, must be available at least on a monthly frequency; some are available weekly or daily. On the other hand, the SSRC model that was planned in 1959 was to be based on quarterly data, and with very few exceptions, model building for business cycle studies remains at a quarterly frequency.

Of course, monthly indicators can always be averaged by quarters, but they would then be used somewhat differently than if they were to remain purely as signals or early warning indicators. In a model, quarterly or otherwise, the stress is on interdependence among statistical series, while the customary use of indicators is as separate magnitudes describing individual economic time series. There is, however, one kind of interdependence that is investigated by their use, namely, an interdependence of timing. The leading indicators are estimated to move first, especially at cyclical *turning points*, and other indicators, in particular coincident or lagging indicators, are estimated to move afterwards.

The interrelationships of an econometric model are often specified according to abstract economic theory. Principles of optimization (minimization or maximization) are used, together with market clearing, accounting balance, institutional restrictions, and the economic interpretation of the laws of science and technology.

The leading indicators exhibit cyclical turns for good economic reasons, but much of the reasoning is not based on optimization theory, market clearing, or other standard ideas of economic theory. They are related to the dynamics of plans, expectations, and physical constraints. These constraints are, in a sense, very much like the constraints imposed by the laws of science and technology. An order must be placed before a good or service is delivered, and the economic transaction is completed in an accounting sense. Similarly, initial claims for unemployment insurance precede the flow of transfer payments to the unemployed. A building permit is issued before construction activity takes place and before payments are made for work done. Vendor performance shows how long it takes to get orders filled.

Each of the eleven indicators could be justified, through economic analysis, as to why its movements tend to precede those of the economy in general. The tendency to lead is not, however, infallible. Some of the series, particularly the stock market price component, are notorious for giving false signals. Nevertheless, these series have individual and collective content; therefore Geoffrey Moore's suggestion deserves serious consideration.

The variables of typical equations in econometric models fall into these categories:
- endogenous (observed)
- exogenous (observed)
- random errors (unobserved)

The leading indicators are mainly endogenous variables, i.e., they are generated by the process that governs the economic system—the model. In other words, the endogenous variables have influence on the economy and are influenced by the economy. By contrast, exogenous variables influence the economy, but they are not influenced by the economy. The drought of 1988 in the United States, measured by the number of inches of rainfall in critical months in the grain growing area, has influence on agricultural (and other) prices in the economy. This weather-type variable is a typical exogenous variable because the drought was not generated or affected by the state of the economy. It is not in the list of leading economic indicators, but it does have a lead effect. The poor weather conditions of the summer of 1988 caused some higher prices in the autumn and winter, and the conditions of earlier months were visible in prices in the summer. It is not always a consistent indicator; its impact can be highly uncertain, but it does have an impact on the agricultural component of raw material prices. These prices are important components of the leading indicator index, but they are also influenced by other things besides the exogenous weather factor.

A better example of an exogenous variable among the eleven components is M_2, the money supply. It is not directly under control of American monetary authorities (the Federal Reserve Open Market Committee), but it is indirectly controlled through the various exogenous instruments that the Federal Reserve manages, mainly the use of open market operations. To a first approximation, we might say that M_2 could be an exogenous variable in a macroeconometric model of the U.S. economy, but a stricter designation of an exogenous variable would be the monetary base (M_0) or the more conventional money supply (M_1), consisting of circulating notes, coins, and checkable deposits. Whether strictly endogenous or exogenous, M_2 is an excellent candidate among the eleven components to be in a macroeconometric model of the United States. It could be used as an end-of-quarter variable or as a quarterly average. The former is preferable to the latter, since M_2 is a *stock* variable and should best be measured at an instant of time.

The one component among the eleven that could be classified as a random error is the index of stock market prices. A popular economic hypothesis is that stock prices behave according to a random walk process. This could refer to prices of individual issues or to market averages. In my opinion, it is more plausible in the former rather than the latter mode. If we denote stock price, at an instant of time, as S_t, the random walk hypothesis asserts

$$S_t - S_{t-1} = e_t.$$

Thus the change in the stock market price (index) is a random variable. We have random variables in macroeconometric models, but it is far from evident that one of them could be identified as an index of the change in stock market prices. ΔS_t could stand for some random variable in a model, but it would be unusual since the random error variables of the models are not directly observable.

For my own tastes, stock market prices are so unpredictable and we know so little about them that they should not be explicitly included in a model, but some model builders do, in fact, include stock market price indexes directly in model specification. For past history, they can be measured and quantitatively related to other variables in interdependent relationships. I think that since we know so little about stock market prices and since they so often give false signals, they are better left out of models, except for those that deal with the total flow of funds in the economy. By theoretical reasoning, stock market prices should represent the discounted stream of future earnings of the company issuing the stock. Earnings—past, present, and future—do have a role in models; therefore our earnings (profit) variables and discount factors are already in models. Stock market prices often gyrate wildly; therefore, they are not precisely related to discounted future earnings, which should not exhibit such wild and frequent changes. Whatever is systematic about stock market prices is included in models, but the large erratic component is not. I am sympathetic to the arguments for including many leading indicators in macroeconometric models, but not common stock prices, either as index averages or as individual quotations.

Two components have already been discussed, stock market prices and M2. The former ought not to be an explicit model variable, while the latter should. Let us now turn to the other nine components.

The length of the work week is an extremely important leading indicator, one of the most easily understood and followed by many observers; it is generally commented on when the monthly employment report is delivered. A typical input variable in a production function of a model is a measure of worker hours, the product of employment and the average work week. Not every model would separate the two, but a dynamic version of the Wharton Model (Mark III) distinguished between the fast short-run adjustment process of hours worked and the slower process of number of workers. The data provided plausible and fairly accurate separation between these two processes and enabled this particular version of the Wharton Model to include the work week (hours worked/employees) as a separate model variable.

In further development of the labor market sector of the model, the builders of the Wharton Model subtracted the number of persons employed from the labor force to obtain unemployment. They did not get to such a sensitive variable as initial claims for unemployment insurance; that would be an unlikely variable to find in most models, but total unemployment would be conventional. Total unemployment is a good coincident business cycle indicator, but not a *leading* indicator.

In the inventory sector of many models, there is a distinction among inventories, new orders, production, shipments, and unfilled orders, with separate equations for each, some related by definitional identities. From this subsystem of equations, new orders are generated. It is not likely that *vendor performance*, one of the eleven components, can be estimated by an equation, but some surrogate measures of the order-delivery lag can be determined by statistical estimation of variable lag models, where the length of lag is an explicit function of stage of the business cycle. This is not a very satisfactory result, but is possibly as well as one can do for this particular component.

Orders for plant and equipment can probably be handled in a better way. This variable is made a function of the same variables that are used in an ordinary fixed investment equation—output, unit costs, financial market conditions, and existing capacity. The special feature is that plant and equipment orders can be estimated from longer lags (earlier values) of the explanatory variables. The lengths of lags are empirically determined. Actual investment in plant and equipment is then estimated as a moving average of prior orders for plant and equipment. This procedure has been actually used for *investment intentions* and housing starts but not, to my knowledge, for plant and equipment orders. The same procedures used for anticipations, however, can be used for orders.

Building permits for new houses (or, in some models, housing starts) have been used in much the same way that was described above for plant and equipment orders. As far back as the SSRC cooperative model project, Sherman Maisel designed a sequence for estimating housing starts as a function of traditional variables that were used for residential construction analysis, but with appropriately longer lags. A moving average of starts was then phased into residential construction. This approach was subsequently used in many other models; so there is no question about the use of the permits component of leading indicators. It is an accepted model variable (endogenous).

A great interest attaches to analysis by stage of fabrication in the dynamic process. Many models pay close attention to inventory holdings of raw materials, goods in process, manufacturers' stocks of finished goods, and wholesale or retail holding of inventories. Also there is usually a split between stocks of agricultural and nonagricultural inventories. It is apparent, therefore, that inventories in wholesale and retail trade are explicitly modeled. The inventory-sales ratio is a key variable that is generated in many models in order to appraise cyclical conditions.

The case of raw material prices is very interesting. In the cyclical macroeconometric models there is rarely fine slicing of sectors. Distinctions between agriculture, energy, manufacturing, and various service sectors are frequently made, but detailed industrial specification is usually found in large input-output models, many of which are combined with macro sectors to generate factor income and final demand. Such large systems, frequently of a thousand equations or more, are seldom calibrated to a quarterly time frame; they are usually annual. They have some cyclical content but are more frequently used for intermediate and long-run trend analysis. They do estimate many raw material prices.

There are many specialized models, however, of individual agricultural markets (and also total national agriculture) and individual markets for fuels, ferrous metals, nonferrous metals, and other industrial materials. They are frequently estimated and used in tandem with econometric models and as *satellite* models. There is sensitive commodity price information in national macroeconometric models, but such prices are not fully endogenous within a total model context. They are, however, very clearly monitored in lead-lag relationships with models. All during the 1970s and into the 1980s, food and fuel prices were studied together with macro model information for signals of inflationary tendencies. Given the present interest in commodity prices for international policy coordination and the influences of the 1988 American drought, econometric analysis relies heavily on study of movements of sensitive commodity prices.

Worldwide, there are about 35 sensitive commodities that account for most of the activity at the primary stage of economic production. In the world macro-model system of Project LINK, there has been an effective combination, in full feedback mode, between commodity models and macro models, with trade at all possible bilateral levels among 79 national or regional models.[1] Not only the components of leading indicators, but also many of the constituent series of the index of sensitive commodity prices, are individually generated within the system. Models go very far in connection with the raw material price indicator, but they do this at the global level because commodity markets are truly international in scope.

Apart from stock market prices and money supply, which were already discussed, the only remaining component is that for the change in outstanding business and household credit. In many models, consumer and producer borrowing are included, although not usually in the direct short-run form of this indicator series. Installment credit is certainly included in many macro consumption functions, and business borrowing is studied for both inventory and fixed investment behavior. An earlier version of the Wharton Model contained an elaborate flow of funds system, from where the accounting data for such variables would come on a quarterly time frame. There are few models that have a full national income/product accounting base, together with a full flow-of-funds base, but such systems are possible, desirable, and have been developed. They have not generally been maintained on a replicated basis.

Coincident and Lagging Indicators

A full account of the business cycle analysis to which Geoffrey Moore has contributed (the views of the National Bureau of Economic Research [NBER] of W. C. Mitchell and A. F. Burns vintages) pays close attention to coincident and lagging indicators as well as to the leading indicators. The less thoughtful public, guided by popular economists who look for more sensational recognition, pay special attention to the leaders. The coinciders are less associated with tailored indexes; they are the components of production, national income accounts, industrial output, and sales. They, too, are often index numbers, but not indexes that are designed primarily for their use as cyclical indicators.

Econometric models of the system as a whole generate estimates of such endogenous variables as GNP, components of GNP (both income and product side), employment, unemployment, inflation, interest rates, and in recent years, exchange rates. A number of the coinciding indicators are in this group, and the analysis of their relationship to the cyclical characteristics that are deemed important by Geoffrey Moore and his close colleagues was strikingly displayed in the very important article by Irma and Frank Adelman.[2]

The Adelman study did not investigate the particular correspondences between individual variables of the model and those in the NBER's group of indicators. Their study examined the correspondence between business cycle characteristics of models and the various measures that have been established by the NBER, i.e., cycle length, phase length (upswing and downswing), and cycle diffusion. In a stochastic simulation mode, the Adelmans found striking similarity between cyclical properties of the Klein-Goldberger Model and the NBER's statistical annals of American business cycles. In subsequent studies, other authors have confirmed these findings with other models.

Not only do models generate many of the coincident indicators; they also generate lagging indicators, a number of which correspond to those in the NBER list.

Anticipatory Variables

Among the main cyclical indicators, there are two important leaders that represent a degree of advance commitment, namely building permits and new orders. Less binding commitments in the form of subjective anticipations are also useful variables. In a sense, stock market prices are supposed to represent the discounted value of expected earnings, but the wild gyrations of the market leave me in doubt about the meaningfulness of this assumption. It is hard to believe that the discounted value of expected earnings was markedly different between Friday, October 16, 1987 and Monday, October 19, 1987. But since stock prices are not being considered here as a sensible model variable, the role of this form of anticipation is not to be analyzed.

The most reliable and important reports on anticipatory data for model building are available monthly on only a partial basis in the United States. There are quarterly reports, covering the past 20 to 25 years, only for business investment plans and consumer attitudes (including buying plans for household durables). Shorter time series are available for some consumer anticipations on a monthly basis.

Consumer expenditures, at least for major durable goods, could be replaced in the model by survey reports from quarterly samples. The same would be true of business investment plans and indicators of other business decisions or plans. There are two objections to the straightforward use of such expectations together with the rest of a model for estimating business cycle behavior and forecasts. In the first place, the time horizon over which such stated expectations remain in force is fairly short, certainly less than six months and possibly no more than about three months. Secondly, the replacement of equations for consumer and business investment spending by the survey information changes the response characteristics of the system over several periods, say up to eight quarters.

The technique in model building ought to be to express the anticipatory variables as functions of information that is available at the time of forecast estimation. Business investment anticipations are made a function of output volume, real factor prices, money market conditions, fixed capital stock, and some other cyclical variables. Similarly, consumer expectations measured in sample surveys should be functions of consumer income, wealth, relative prices, and demographic changes. *Realization* functions then relate investment and consumer choices to anticipated values, the observations being from historical cases. In this way, the forward-looking anticipatory variables are made endogenous in the system.

In the United States, the Michigan and Wharton Models have used anticipatory variables in this way in various historical vintages.[3] They are not being so used in models at this moment, but anticipatory variables are being monitored regularly by model builders for their forecasting content. In the Wharton records, the models with endogenous anticipations performed very well and even reduced conventional error statistics; but the latest generation of model builders have not kept up this line of research—not because it failed to be fruitful, but because they have been looking for other ways to maintain and improve their models.

Mixed Frequency Data

For a very long time, Geoffrey Moore and his former colleagues at the NBER relied heavily on monthly data for business cycle studies. They continue to work at this frequency. In this information age, more and more monthly (weekly, daily) data are becoming readily available. While macro model builders still find it difficult to construct monthly models, they still make intensive use of monthly information. This use is not generally formal, i.e., in equation form for model use. A present research interest at Pennsylvania, Michigan, and the Federal Reserve is, however, to combine monthly indicator information in a formal, systematic way with quarterly model information.[4]

The Pennsylvania approach is to collect data on all those monthly indicators that are closely related, when averaged into quarterly values, to GNP and its components of national expenditures and national income. This list of indicators includes many that are in the sensitive list of leaders, coinciders, and laggards, but it includes many others, too. The components of GNP and the totals, as well, are estimated as contemporary and lagged functions of the indicators. The indicators, themselves, are estimated in individual equations by formal time series methods (ARIMA) or in VAR systems; this enables us to extrapolate them for predictive use. The predictions of the indicators for periods up to six months and the corresponding estimates of GNP and components as functions of these indicators enables one to project many components of the GNP for the current quarter and one quarter ahead. A formal macroeconometric model is forced, by "add-factors," to agree "as closely as possible" with the indicator-based estimates for two quarters. The add-factors are then retained in the model for extended solution, by simulation techniques, for another six to ten quarters. In this way, high-frequency monthly indicators are combined with low-frequency quarterly model magnitudes for combined use. At the present time, this provides the closest correspondence between cyclical indicators and macroeconometric models. We have come a long way in several decades toward following Geoffrey Moore's suggestion.

Some Further Thoughts

There has been a strong interest in the use of movements of raw material prices as early warning signals for inflation and exchange rates. At meetings of the International Monetary Fund, American authorities have suggested using such signals to tell about the need and direction for international policy coordination. Also, the Federal Reserve Board released some written statements during 1987 about the close relationship between commodity price movements and *subsequent* inflation. The former are thus regarded as leading indicators of the latter. Also, there is significant interest in commodity price movements during 1988 because of the expected inflationary effects of the serious drought in grain and other feed-producing areas of the United States.

It has already been noted how commodity market models and price projections from them are integrated into the international LINK system of macro models. Supplementary to this combined use of information are commodity prices in the LINK model. I have made a separate statistical investigation of the relationship of monthly commodity price movements as early warning signals for inflation and exchange rate dynamics.

There are significant relationships between U.S. inflation measured by the producer price index of finished goods, on the one hand, and fuel prices, food prices, and exchange rates on the other. Food and fuel price movements were so outstanding during the past 25 years that they "crowd out" the effects of other commodity prices in the statistical correlations. Fuel price changes show definite tendencies to lead inflation by one to two months, but food prices appear to be contemporaneous. The exchange rate effect has, however, a much longer lead of between 12 and 24 months.

The exchange rate, in turn, reflects the movements of the price of gold (inversely) with one to three months' early warning. The exchange rate change is also affected by the U.S. relative inflation rate (relative to Germany's, for example) which, in turn, is affected by food and fuel prices. This, too, has one to three months' lead time for warning.

There is, therefore, significant content to the early warning nature of commodity price movements; however, two very important caveats must be stated. In correlated statistical movements of monthly change, there is much unexplained variation, perhaps more than one half. Commodity price movements matter, but other things do, as well. Secondly, it is not simply a matter of considering commodity price movements alone, apart from an unexplained random residual. There are other significant variables too. These are the typical variables that are related to inflation and exchange rates in macroeconometric models. Inflation depends very significantly on wage rates and productivity growth. Exchange rate changes depend on interest rate spreads and on the merchandise trade balance. These other effects are very important and are part of standard relationships in macroeconometric models. To get the full early warning flavor of commodity price movements, I would recommend that they be combined with macro model information.

Notes

1. See F. G. Adams, "Primary Commodity Markets in a World Model System," in *Stabilizing World Commodity Markets*, edited by F. G. Adams and S. A. Klein (Lexington: D. C. Heath, 1978), pp. 83–104.

2. See Irma and Frank Adelman, "The Dynamic Properties of the Klein-Goldberger Model," *Econometrica* 27 (October 1959): 596–625.

3. See F. G. Adams and L. R. Klein, "Anticipations Variables in Macroeconometric Models," in *Human Behavior in Economic Affairs*, edited by B. Strumpel, J. N. Morgan, and E. Zahn (Amsterdam: Elsevier, 1972), pp. 289–319.

4. Presentations of research results were reported by L. R. Klein (Pennsylvania), E. P. Howrey, S. H. Hymans, and M. R. Donihue (Michigan), and C. Corrado and J. Haltmaier (Federal Reserve Board) in a session entitled "Can Economic Forecasting Be Improved?" at the annual meeting of the American Economic Association, Chicago, December 1987.

IV

THE USEFULNESS OF INDICATORS IN ECONOMIC FORECASTING

8

Forecasting Turning Points in the Stock Market Cycle and Asset Allocation Implications

Michael P. Niemira

The evolution of leading economic indicator methods and empirical business cycle research by Geoffrey Moore naturally leads to specific applications of these techniques to the financial markets. Moore repeatedly has documented the "leading indicator" properties of the stock and bond markets in the unfolding of the business cycle.[1] However, this chapter demonstrates and evaluates whether leading indicators can be used to anticipate stock price activity. The purpose of this chapter is to show that the National Bureau of Economic Research (NBER) methods, which have been extended and refined by Geoffrey Moore, can be applied to specific financial market analysis. The analysis is also extended to demonstrate an analytical system for calling turning points and predicting the likely amplitude change in stock price activity.

The Profile of the "Typical" Stock Market Cycle

The basic pattern of the stock market cycle can be demonstrated using the Mitchell-Burns stages of the cycle. Chart 8.1 shows the unfolding of the typical stock market cycle over a sequence of nine stages. As might be expected, the best gains in the market cycle are in the early stages of a bull market; the gains get increasingly smaller as the bull market ages. When the stock market enters a bear market, stock market losses are relatively small but get increasingly larger until the trough of the cycle is reached. Table 8.1 presents another picture of the stock market cycle since the early 1950s. Of the eleven stock market cycles since 1950, six were associated with business cycles, two were associated with growth cycles, and three (including the 1987 experience) were not associated with any economic slowdown or recession. In one case, 1980, stock prices failed to anticipate the recession. During the average bull market (trough to peak) prices rose nearly 64 percent, while the average bear market decline (peak to trough) was about 20 percent. With respect to duration, bull markets outlive bear markets by a ratio of 2:1 (see Table 8.2). On the other hand, business cycle expansions during the same period outlive recessions by a ratio of almost 4:1, and even excluding the long

Chart 8.1. **Standard & Poor's 500 Stock Price Index.**

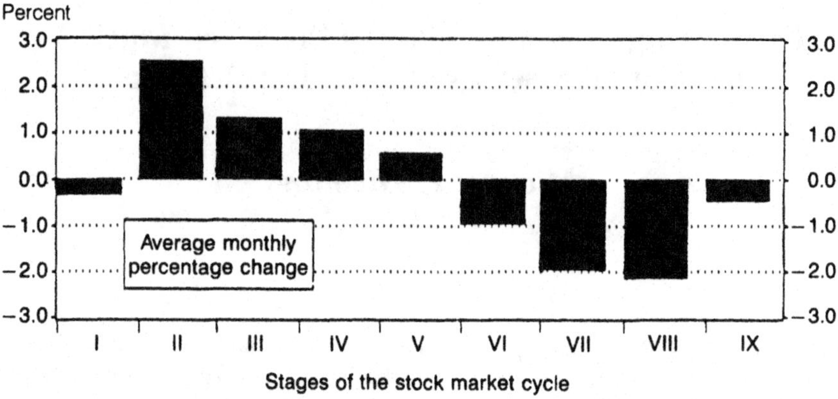

Percent

Stages of the stock market cycle

Note: The average monthly change of the stock market cycles is calculated between 1953 and 1984.

expansion in the 1960s, expansions last 2.5 times the length of recessions. This suggests that using the stage of the business cycle to forecast stock prices will not necessarily work since the stock price cycle often goes its own way.

Shifting the Focus from the Business Cycle

In John le Carré's novel, *Tinker, Tailor, Soldier, Spy*, which is a tale of a high level spy in the British foreign intelligence agency, le Carré poses the problem: Who do you get to spy on the spies? A similar question can be posed in our analysis. Stock prices are a leading indicator of the business cycle and a component of the U.S. Department of Commerce's composite index of leading indicators. As such, stock prices serve as a kind of "spy on the business cycle," but if we shift the focus to the stock market cycle, then which indicators would be useful to "spy on the stock market?"

The answer does not lie with individual stocks or industry groups since as much as 90 percent of the fluctuation in industry stock prices or specific equity issues are determined, or at least strongly influenced, by the overall market swings.[2] This then seems to raise the basic question: "Why does the overall market fluctuate?" One answer is tied to the performance of profits and the economy, but from a cyclical standpoint, overall economic performance lags the stock market while profits may or may not presage moves in stock prices.[3] A second reason is tied to interest rates. The higher the rate of interest—a competing investment—the more likely it is that money will be reallocated from the stock market to the bond market. This second reason, as simple as it is, seems to prevail as a key reason for the cyclical pattern of stock prices.

Based on the role of interest rates, we have found that our leading indicator of

Table 8.1

Turning Points in the Stock Market
(S&P 500 Stock Price Index, 1953–87)

Date of turn		Value at turn		Change	
Peak	Trough	Peak	Trough	Peak	Trough
January 1953*		26.2		—	
	September 1953		23.3		– 11.1%
July 1956*		48.8		+ 109.4%	
	December 1957		40.3		– 17.4
July 1959*		59.7		+ 48.1	
	October 1960		53.7		– 10.1
December 1961		71.7		+ 33.5	
	June 1962		55.6		– 22.5
January 1966		93.3		+ 67.8	
	October 1966		77.1		– 17.4
December 1968*		106.5		+ 38.1	
	June 1970		75.6		– 29.0
January 1973*		118.4		+ 56.6	
	December 1974		67.1		– 43.3
September 1976		105.4		+ 57.1	
	March 1978		88.8		– 15.7
November 1980*		135.6		+ 52.7	
	July 1982		109.4 ·		– 19.3
October 1983		167.6		+ 53.2	
	July 1984		151.1		– 9.8
August 1987		329.4		+ 118.0	
	December 1987		241.0		– 26.8
Average				+ 63.5%	– 20.2%

*=cycle associated with business cycle.

inflation,[4] a composite indicator of seven sensitive barometers of future inflation, also serves as a leading indicator of interest rates and of stock market activity, as shown in Chart 8.2. The logic for the lead is intuitive. An increase in the leading indicator of inflation suggests that inflation and interest rates are likely to increase.

The relationship between actual inflation and stock prices is shown in Table 8.3. The information in this table demonstrates that troughs in the inflation cycle, on average, lead peaks in the stock market by 9 months. While the relationship is not without its failings, it does offer one explanation for stock market peaks. If interest rates are increased because of higher inflation, then this

Table 8.2

Duration of the Stock Market Cycle
(Based on the S&P 500 Price Index)

Peak	Trough	(In months) P→T	T→P	Ratio bull/bear market duration
January 1953				
	September 1953	8		
July 1956			34	4.3
	December 1957	17		
July 1959			19	1.1
	October 1960	15		
December 1961			14	0.9
	June 1962	6		
January 1966			44	7.3
	October 1966	9		
December 1968			26	2.9
	June 1970	18		
January 1973			32	1.8
	December 1974	23		
September 1976			21	0.9
	March 1978	18		
November 1980			33	1.8
	July 1982	20		
October 1983			15	0.8
	July 1984	9		
August 1987			38	4.2
	December 1987	4		
Average		13.4	27.6	2.1
Average excluding 1987		14.3		1.9

lessens the attractiveness of stocks versus bonds.

While this explanation is intuitive, there is one shortcoming. The generally long lead time of this composite leading indicator of inflation (and to a lesser extent inflation itself) over stock price turns may be due to the fact that initially when inflation increases, stock prices—which are the price of financial assets—move with inflation before they move countercyclically. This suggests the possibility of a "money illusion" in financial assets during the early stages of a stock market cycle.

An earlier attempt to find leading indicators of the stock market cycle was undertaken by Beryl W. Sprinkel. He observed, "stocks price trends are particu-

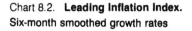

Chart 8.2. **Leading Inflation Index.**
Six-month smoothed growth rates

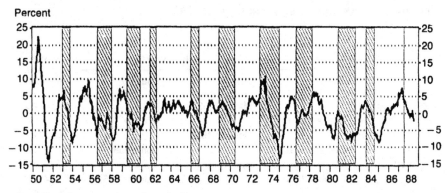

Note: Shaded areas represent bear markets.

larly difficult to predict, since they appear to have no close and simple relation to the general pattern of business and profits. It is true that economic activity and stock prices go in the same direction about two-thirds of the time, but it is the other third that is most interesting and potentially most profitable."[5] Sprinkel concludes that changes in the stock of money or liquidity precede the turns in stock prices. However, Robert D. Auerbach, in a review and update of these findings, concluded that money and stock prices are related but the relationship is weaker than earlier studies claimed.[6] The mixed performance of the money supply as a leading indicator of stock prices can be seen in Chart 8.3.

Still another approach to forecasting the future path of stock prices was undertaken by Geoffrey Moore who relied upon the composite index of lagging indicators.[7] Moore argued that the lagging indicators represented a measure of costs, and that the inverse of that set of indicators would call turning points in the stock market cycle (see Chart 8.4). Other candidates for leading indicators of the stock price cycle include interest rates and inflation (inverted). These two indicators are shown in Charts 8.5 and 8.6. However, their overall forecasting record is mixed. Psychology is an another often cited reason for stock price fluctuations, but this is an illusive concept.

Our cursory review of the typical determinants of stock prices leads us to tentatively conclude: (*i*) no single leading indicator or composite works all of the time and, (*ii*) by visual inspection alone, some of the better leading indicators of stock price activity seem to be the inverse of the composite index of lagging indicators (a measure of costs), the inverse of our leading indicator of inflation (a measure of the future direction of interest rates), and the real money supply (a measure of liquidity). Clearly, while these indicators are not completely unrelated, they each represent factors that influence stock price behavior.

Table 8.3

The Stock Market Cycle vs. Inflation, 1953–1987

Stock market cycle		Inflation cycle		Relation-ship (in months)
Peak	Trough	Trough	Peak	
January 1953		March 1953		+2
	September 1953		October 1953	+1
July 1956		October 1954		−21
	December 1957		April 1958	+4
July 1959		April 1959		−3
	October 1960		October 1959	−12
December 1961		June 1961		−6
	June 1962		NCT	NCT
January 1966		NCT		NCT
	October 1966		October 1966	0
December 1968		May 1967		−19
	June 1970		February 1970	−4
January 1973		June 1972		−7
	December 1974		September 1974	−3
September 1976		June 1976		−3
	March 1978		March 1980	+24
November 1980		NCT		NCT
	July 1982		NCT	NCT
October 1983		NCT		NCT
	July 1984		NCT	NCT
August 1987		April 1986		−16
	December 1987			

Average timing at peaks −9.1
Average timing at troughs +1.4

Notes: Lead time is indicated in months by the minus (−) sign, while the plus (+) sign indicates a lagging relationship.
NCT = No corresponding turn.

Guideposts for Forecasting

On the surface, even if a leading indicator or composite leading indicator worked well historically, there is no guarantee that it will continue to work well in the future; no leading economic indicator is 100 percent reliable. But even more important, the use of leading indicators alone for current monitoring of the cycle is very difficult. The major limitation is that without the benefit of hindsight, it is

Chart 8.3. **Real Money Supply (M2).**
Six-month smoothed growth rates

Percent

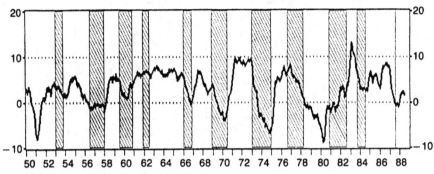

Note: Shaded areas represent bear markets.

Chart 8.4. **Lagging Indicators, Inverted.**
Six-month smoothed growth rates

Percent

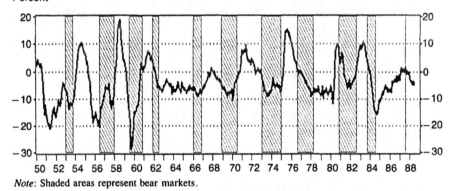

Note: Shaded areas represent bear markets.

unclear whether a decline or an increase in a leading indicator is a "real" signal of a turning point or not.

One general forecasting technique to reduce the recognition time while increasing the reliability of the signal is to use a probability-based turning point signaling system devised by Neftci and known as "sequential analysis."[8] In our application, sequential analysis will evaluate period-to-period change in an economic time series against historical norms and answer the question: "Is the current observation more consistent in a probability sense with a bear or bull stock market?" Once this determination is made statistically, the current information is incorporated into a cumulatively calculated turning point probability. In

Chart 8.5. **Ten-Year Government Bond Yield (Inverted).**
Percent

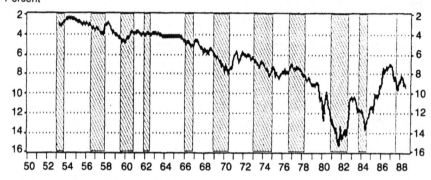

Note: Shaded areas represent bear markets.

Chart 8.6. **Consumer Price Index.**
Inverted, six-month smoothed growth rates
Percent

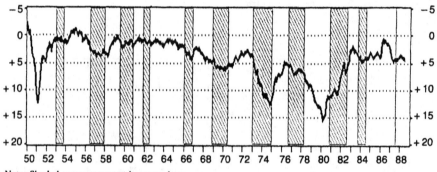

Note: Shaded areas represent bear markets.

this way, the technique builds a picture through time of the type of market environment that is likely to unfold.

Sequential analysis also can be used to derive turning point chronologies in economic time series. However, a cycle chronology of peaks and troughs that is based on this Neftci sequential probability method could differ from one that is derived using "standard" NBER (Burns and Mitchell) rules. Differences in turning point dates between the NBER and Neftci methods can occur since the Neftci method gives more weight to the degree of consistency that the current cycle shares with *patterns* of change from past cyclical expansions or contractions. Thus, the Neftci method weights the amplitude change in an indicator much more heavily than the NBER method would.

In effect, a turning point can be defined using sequential analysis as the time when the probability of a cumulative sequence of period-to-period changes exceeds some pre-set statistical level of confidence (say, 90 percent). When that condition is met, the cycle phase has switched. While this definition clearly differs from the standard NBER concept of a turning point, sequential analysis should be viewed as a supplement to the NBER methods for current monitoring and forecasting of the cycle. The derivation of the Neftci technique and the formulae used for forecasting are described in depth elsewhere.[9]

In this chapter, this Neftci method will be applied to three potential leading indicators of the stock market: (1) our leading indicator of inflation, (2) the inverse of the composite index of lagging indicators, and (3) the real money supply.

Using an Inflation Barometer to Call
Turning Points in Stock Prices

Six-month growth rates of the leading indicator of inflation (inverted) were divided into two subsamples between 1952 and 1980, one represented observations during and prior to bull markets and the other sample represented observations during and prior to bear markets. Chart 8.7 presents the two sample distributions which were fitted to normal probability curves. The buy signal sample had an average monthly growth rate of +3.0 percent, while the sell signal sample had an average growth rate of −1.5 percent.

The sell signals from this indicator had an overall lead time of 13 months when evaluated using a 90 percent statistical confidence level. However, the buy signals occurred nearly simultaneously with stock market troughs. As indicated in Table 8.4, the higher level of statistical confidence one demands from the indicator signaling system, the more recognition time was needed. In this application, in moving from a 90 percent to a 100 percent level of statistical confidence, the average lead time at peaks is reduced by about two months while at troughs the average turning point recognition lag is increased by about three months.

In two cases, 1962 and 1980, the calculated probability of a turning point using this signaling scheme did not increase sufficiently to statistically call a turning point in the stock market cycle, despite the fact that the inflation index itself showed a clear move. In these two cases, the Neftci method screened out too much information at the expense of missing two turning points.

Using the Lagging Indicators (Inverted) to Call
Turning Points in Stock Prices

Six-month growth rates of the U.S composite lagging indicator, on an inverted basis, also were divided into two subsamples between 1952 and 1980; one represented observations during and prior to bull markets, and the other sample represented observations during and prior to bear markets. Chart 8.8 presents the two sample distributions, which were fitted to normal probability curves. The

118

Chart 8.7. **Histogram of LI of Inflation.**
Stock market buy and sell signal samples

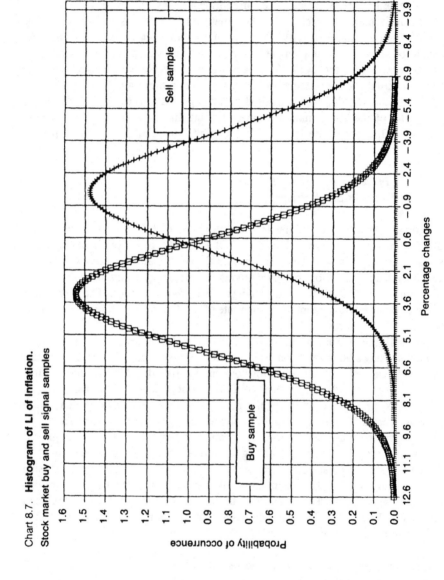

Table 8.4

Turning Point Signals in Stock Market Based on Leading Indicator of Inflation

Stock market cycle dates		Turning point signals in inflation index					
Peak	Trough	90% signal		95% signal		100% signal	
January 1953		September 1952	−4	September 1952	−4	November 1952	−2
	September 1953	November 1953	+2	November 1953	+2	December 1953	+3
July 1956		October 1954	−21	October 1954	−21	November 1954	−20
	December 1957	May 1957	−7	May 1957	−7	November 1957	−1
July 1959		September 1958	−10	September 1958	−10	October 1958	−9
	October 1960	June 1960	−4	July 1960	−3	October 1960	0
December 1961		August 1961	−4	September 1961	−3	October 1961	−2
	June 1962	NCT		NCT		NCT	
January 1966		May 1963	−33	May 63	−33	August 1963	−29
	October 1966	February 1967	+4	February 1967	+4	March 1967	+5
December 1968		December 1967	−12	December 1967	−12	February 1968	−10
	June 1970	May 1970	−1	May 1970	−1	July 1970	+1
January 1973		October 1971	−15	November 1971	−14	January 1972	−12
	December 1974	May 1974	−7	June 1974	−6	July 1974	−5
September 1976		November 1975	−10	December 1975	−9	February 1976	−7
	March 1978	November 1979	+20	November 1979	+20	February 1980	+23
November 1980		NCT		NCT		NCT	
	July 1982	November 1981	−8	December 1981	−7	January 1982	−6
October 1983		June 1983	−4	June 1983	−4	August 1983	−2
	July 1984	August 1984	+1	September 1984	+2	October 1984	+3
August 1987		February 1986	−18	March 1986	−17	July 1986	−13
Average timing							
At peaks			−6.9		−6.5		−4.4
At troughs			−13.1		−12.7		−10.6
Median timing							
At peaks			0.0		+0.4		+2.6
At troughs			−7.0		−6.0		−2.0
At peaks			−11.0		−11.0		−9.5
At troughs			−1.0		−1.0		+1.0
Missed turns			2		2		2
% missed			9.5		9.5		9.5

Notes: Lead time is indicated in months by the minus (−) sign, while the plus (+) sign indicates a lagging relationship.
NCT = No corresponding turn.

120

Chart 8.8. **Histogram of Lagging Index.**

Bear and bull market samples

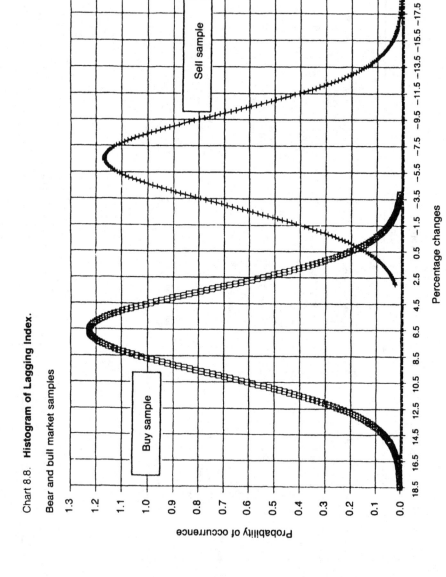

buy signal sample had an average monthly growth rate of +6.6 percent, while the sell signal sample had an average growth rate of −6.8 percent.

The overall results using this indicator to give advanced warning of turning points in the stock market were not very favorable. At a 90 percent level of statistical confidence, the average timing suggested a lagging relationship of about one month (see Table 8.5). While the average timing relationship showed a lead of about three months at peaks, this was quite deceptive since it included a 27-month lead against the 1953 stock market peak. Since 1970, the signals had a median lag of six months. In addition to the lagging property against stock market cycles, the number of missed stock market turns was high—almost one-fifth of all the turns were not called.

Using Real Money Supply to Call Turning Points in Stock Prices

The final series tested using the Neftci criteria is the real money supply (M2) calculated as six-month growth rates.[10] This series, as was the case with the other indicators, was divided into two subsamples between 1950 and 1980. Chart 8.9 presents the two sample distributions, which were fitted to normal probability curves. The buy signal sample had an average monthly growth rate of +5.4 percent, while the sell signal sample had an average growth rate of −0.5 percent.

Real M2 growth performed the worst by far among the three indicators examined. Nearly 10 percent of the signals were false turning points (at both peaks and troughs), while about 30 percent of the actual turning points were not called. Despite the average lead time of nearly two months at a 90 percent confidence level for all turning points, the median timing told a better story. The median timing relationship between real M2 and stock market turning points was four months for all turns, which would classify these real money supply signals as confirming and not warning signals of stock market turning points (see Table 8.6).

Beyond Timing—How Much Change?

One of the perennial problems with cyclical turning point systems, the Neftci method included, is that they do not answer the question of how much amplitude change is expected. To address this question, a different methodology can be used in conjunction with the Neftci probability scheme. A simple amplitude test is how well our leading indicator of stock prices (or more correctly, the leading indicator of inflation) worked in calling the magnitude change in stock prices from the point when a turning point is signaled.

Based on this amplitude test, the rank correlation between the ultimate change in stock prices and the cumulative decline in the leading indicator of inflation was the highest at three months after the Neftci signal of a peak in the stock market

Table 8.5

Turning Point Signals In Stock Market Based on Lagging Indicator (Inverted)

Stock market cycle dates		Turning point signals in lagging indicator					
Peak	Trough	90% signal		95% signal		100% signal	
January 1953	September 1953	October 1950	−27	October 1950	−27	October 1950	−27
July 1956	December 1957	April 1954	+7	April 1954	+7	April 1954	+7
July 1959	October 1960	July 1955	−12	July 1955	−12	August 1955	−11
December 1961	June 1962	March 1958	+3	March 1958	+3	April 1958	+4
January 1966	October 1966	May 1959	−2	May 1959	−2	June 1959	−1
December 1968	June 1970	October 1960	0	October 1960	0	October 1960	0
January 1973	December 1974	May 1962	+5	May 1962	+5	June 1962	+6
September 1976	March 1978	NCT		NCT		NCT	
November 1980	July 1982	March 1965	−10	March 1965	−10	March 1965	−10
October 1983	July 1984	NCT		NCT		NCT	
August 1987		May 1968	−7	June 1968	−6	July 1968	−5
		December 1970	+6	December 1970	+6	January 1971	+7
		February 1973	+1	February 1973	+1	March 1973	+2
		May 1975	+5	May 1975	+5	May 1975	+5
		March 1977	+6	March 1977	+6	May 1977	+8
		July 1980	+28	July 1980	+28	August 1980	+29
		July 1981	+8	July 1981	+8	August 1981	+9
		September 1982	+2	September 1982	+2	October 1982	+3
		March 1984	+6	March 1984	+6	March 1984	+6
		NCT		NCT		NCT	
		NCT		NCT		NCT	
Average timing							
At peaks			+1.1		+1.1		+1.9
At troughs			−3.2		−3.1		−2.3
Median timing							
At peaks			+7.3		+7.3		+7.9
At troughs			+3.0		+3.0		+4.0
At peaks			−0.5		−0.5		−0.5
At troughs			+5.0		+5.0		+5.0
Missed turns			4		4		4
% missed			19.0		19.0		19.0

Notes: Lead time is indicated in months by the minus (−) sign, while the plus (+) sign indicates a lagging relationship. NCT = No corresponding turn.

Chart 8.9. **Histogram of Real M2.**

Bull and bear market samples

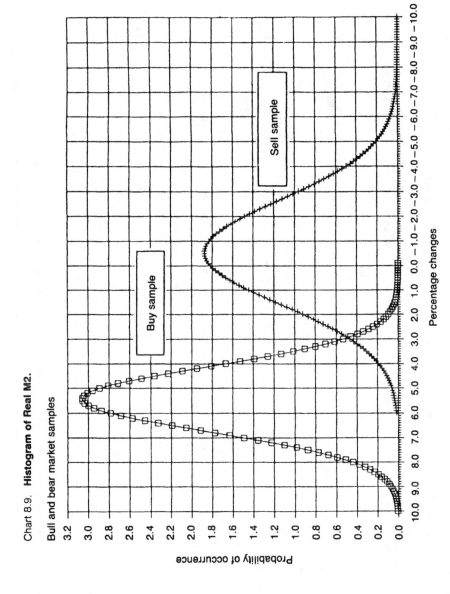

Table 8.6 Turning Point Signals in Stock Market Based on Real Money Supply (M2) Growth

Stock market cycle dates		Turning point signals in real M2		
Peak	Trough	90% signal	95% signal	100% signal
January 1953		August 1950 −29	August 1950 −29	August 1950 −29
	September 1953	January 1953 −8	February 1953 −7	NCT
July 1956		October 1955 −9	October 1955 −9	November 1955 −8
	December 1957	August 1958 +8	August 1958 +8	September 1958 +9
July 1959		November 1959 +4	November 1959 +4	January 1960 +6
	October 1960	January 1961 +3	January 1961 +3	February 1961 +4
December 1961		NCT	NCT	NCT
	June 1962	NCT	NCT	NCT
January 1966		July 1966 +6	August 1966 +7	August 1966 +7
	October 1966	June 1967 +8	June 1967 +8	July 1967 +9
December 1968		August 1968 −4	September 1968 −3	April 1969 +4
	June 1970	February 1971 +8	February 1971 +8	March 1971 +9
January 1973		July 1973 +6	August 1973 +7	August 1973 +7
	December 1974	August 1975 +8	August 1975 +8	August 1975 +8
September 1976		NCT	NCT	NCT
	March 1978	NCT	NCT	NCT
November 1980		March 1978 −32	March 1978 −32	April 1978 −32
	July 1982	December 1982 +5	December 1982 +5	January 1983 +6
October 1983		NCT	NCT	NCT
	July 1984	NCT	NCT	NCT
August 1987		May 1987 −3	May 1987 −3	June 1987 −2
Average timing		−1.9	−1.7	−0.1
At peaks		−7.6	−7.3	−5.9
At troughs		+4.6	+4.7	+7.5
Median timing		+4.0	+4.0	+6.0
At peaks		−3.5	−3.0	+1.0
At troughs		+8.0	+8.0	+8.5
Missed turns		6	6	7
% missed		28.6	28.6	33.3
False turns		2	2	2
% wrong		9.5	9.5	9.5

Notes: Lead time is indicated in months by the minus (−) sign, while the plus (+) sign indicates a lagging relationship.
NCT = No corresponding turn.

Chart 8.10. **Actual and Estimated Decline in Stock Market Cycle.**

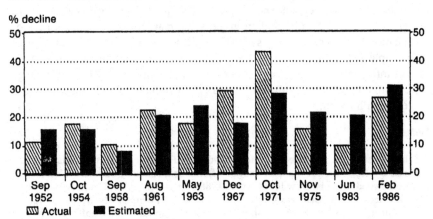

% decline

occurred. This suggested that three months after a signal occurs is the optimum time to forecast the ultimate severity of the stock market decline. But the drawback in reading too much into this relationship is that the statistical regression was not overwhelmingly sound. Nonetheless, this crude relationship worked reasonably well in anticipating the magnitude change in the stock market as shown in Chart 8.10.[11]

Future Work: Extensions to International Markets and Across Assets

Our work suggested that leading indicators of inflation can be a useful indicator of the future direction of stock prices. The clear extension of this work would be to test the same hypothesis in the international markets. Moreover, even domestically, this type of indicator system could be useful to adjust investment portfolios. For example, the same methodology could be applied to forecast turning points in interest rates; linking these two turning point probabilities could suggest when to be invested in stocks and/or bonds, or simply when to hold cash.

Evaluation and Conclusions

In October 1988, there was a news story about Shearson Lehman Hutton's Elaine Garzarelli's stock market timing system and her mutual fund's investment performance based upon it. The news story noted that she relied on 13 market indicators such as interest rates, the money supply, and corporate earnings to presage the direction of the stock market. Historical testing of Garzarelli's market timing system found that if an investment manager followed the buy or sell signals from that system, the return on the investment would have outperformed the S&P 500 by more than 11 percentage points between 1981 and 1987. However, between December 1987 and September 1988, the fund's total return had been down 12 percent versus a 21.6 percent gain in the stock market over that same period.

The moral of this news story is equally applicable to our own results: no single or multiple indicator system will work well all the time; fundamental stock market influences shift importance, but a systematic monitoring of a wide range of economic indicators with a formal statistical framework will pay off over a longer term horizon.

Notes

1. For example, Geoffrey H. Moore and John P. Cullity, "Security Markets and Business Cycles," in *The Financial Analyst's Handbook*, edited by Sumner N. Levine, 2d ed. (Homewood, Illinois: Dow Jones-Irwin, 1988), pp. 45–69. Also, Geoffrey H. Moore, "Stock Prices and the Business Cycle," *The Journal of Portfolio Management*, Vol. 1, No. 3 (Spring 1975), pp. 59–64. A short comment also appeared in: Geoffrey H. Moore and John P. Cullity, "Little-known Facts About Stock Prices and Business Cycles," *Challenge*, March-April 1988, pp. 49–50. Another article highlighting the relationship between stock prices and the economy is: Douglas K. Pearce, "Stock Prices and the Economy," *Economic Review*, Federal Reserve Bank of Kansas City (November 1983), pp. 7–22.

2. This view is echoed by the comment "it has been shown that the single most important determinant of price performance for any individual stock is the trend of the overall market." See Robert W. Colby and Thomas A. Meyers, *The Encyclopedia of Technical Market Indicators* (Homewood, Ill.: Dow Jones-Irwin, 1988), p. iii.

3. This statement is based on the cyclical pattern of the comparable earnings measure to the S&P 500 stock price index. Based on S&P 500 earnings per share (EPS), it is hard to make a convincing argument that earnings generally lead stock prices. This may in fact be because stock analysts are forecasting earnings and their expectations, as a group, get "built" into the stock price faster than do the reported earnings. On the other hand, a four-quarter smoothed growth rate in aftertax profits tends to decelerate at or shortly before the stock market peak, though their are major exceptions, such as in 1987. Even profit margins, as measured by the ratio of economic profits to corporate domestic income, has a mixed record of forecasting the turning points in the stock market—though it performs well in anticipating turns in the general economy.

4. The current composition of our composite leading indicator of inflation includes: (1) the employment-to-population ratio, (2) the National Association of Purchasing Management's survey of purchasing managers paying more, less or about the same for supplies, (3) the Purchasing Management Association of Chicago's survey of how quickly orders are being filled, (4) the Federal Reserve Bank of Dallas' "X-131" exchange rate, (5) the Federal Reserve Board's manufacturing capacity utilization rate, (6) the Journal of Commerce's spot price index, and (7) the U.S. Department of Agriculture's index of agricultural prices received by farmers. A detailed discussion of the methodology and performance is contained in: "Updated PW Leading Indicator of Inflation," PaineWebber, December 26, 1986. Our index differs from the leading indicator of inflation that Geoffrey Moore's Center for International Business Cycle Research compiles but has similar properties. For an earlier discussion of the indicator and comparison with others: see Howard Roth, "Leading Indicators of Inflation," *Economic Review*, Federal Reserve Bank of Kansas City (November 1986), pp. 3–20.

5. *Money and Stock Prices*, (Homewood, Ill.: Richard D. Irwin, Inc., 1964), p.1.

6. "Money and Stock Prices," *Monthly Review*, Federal Reserve Bank of Kansas City (September-October 1976), pp. 3–11.

7. Moore has discussed this point in some unpublished work.

8. Salih Neftci, "Optimal Prediction of Cyclical Downturns," *Journal of Economic Dynamics and Control* (1982), pp. 225–241. Also see Michael P. Niemira, "An International Application of Neftci's Probability Approach for Signalling Growth Recessions and Recoveries Using Turning Point Indicators," in *Leading Economic Indicators: New Approaches and Forecasting Records*, edited by Geoffrey Moore and Kajal Lahari (Cambridge University Press), 1989, forthcoming.

9. Neftci (1982).

10. Friedman has argued that real M2 income velocity leads real stock price fluctuations with an average of three quarters. While we are not testing this variable, a further "test" of the Friedman hypothesis could be subjected to this Neftci criteria. See Milton Friedman, "Money and the Stock Market," *Journal of Political Economy* 96 (2) April 1988, pp. 221–245.

11. The actual estimated relationship is: stk $= -1.225*\text{LII3} - 38.01$ where stk is the cumulative decline in the stock market, LII3 is the cumulative decline in the leading indicator of inflation (inverted, six month growth rates) three months after a turning point signal occurred. The R^2 is 0.388.

9

The Future Lies Ahead

Edgar R. Fiedler

Forecasting is a maddening occupation. It is always fascinating and exciting and rewarding. Yet it is also regularly exasperating and infuriating, occasionally even deranging. And where does all the futility and frustration come from? From the fact that forecasting is simultaneously inescapable and impossible.

Forecasting is inescapable because it is an intrinsic part of every important decision. For such things as Federal Reserve policy, this is an obvious point. And, as Rudy Penner (1988) has observed, the Gramm-Rudman-Hollings law that mandates reduced budget deficits is almost totally dependent on economic forecasts. But it's just as true in other areas—in family decisions, for example. To make or accept a proposal of marriage is a judgment loaded with predictions about human compatibility for (presumably) a lifetime ahead. Similarly, decisions about having children, what job to take, in what part of town to live—each of these difficult choices has innumerable consequences for the future and thus requires many forecasts.

The same holds true for important business decisions. To start a company, to build a plant, to adopt a new technology, to manufacture a new product—none of these issues can be resolved without reaching knotty judgments about the shape of the future: Will there be enough demand for our product? What price will we be able to charge? Will we find enough skilled labor? Buy enough raw materials? Borrow enough capital? In each case, at what cost? What production efficiency can be achieved? Will it all add up to a profit or a loss?

Oliver Wendell Holmes summed this up nicely when he observed that all values depend largely on prophecy. No one would argue his statement as it pertains to a share on the stock exchange, the value of which is usually described as equal to the flow of future dividends appropriately discounted to their present worth. But Holmes' statement is equally, if less obviously, true for a farm or a painting or a postage stamp or anything else one would place a value on.

The prophecies behind these valuations are frequently based on gut instinct rather than careful calculation. Indeed, the valuations are often made with no explicit prophecy at all. In my view, off-hand decision making of this sort is seriously defective. Surely there is a distinct advantage if the forecasts underlying major decisions are considered *explicitly*, rather than being only a subconscious part of the calculation. At the least, explicit projections force a direct consideration of the often unspoken assumptions that underlie the decision.

Some years ago while trying to make that point, I was quoted by the Wall Street Journal as saying, "Bad forecasts are better than none." The quotation was picked up by what seemed like an endless stream of editorial writers who pilloried me for offering such a manifestly absurd idea. I was sorry to have made that remark, but not because of the editorials and not because the idea is balmy. The problem was that I expressed the idea so poorly. Had I said, "Imprecise forecasts are better than none," or "Explicit forecasts are better than implicit forecasts," maybe I could have put the point across.

But is accurate prognostication really impossible? According to mythology, Melampus was the first mortal endowed with prophetic powers. All subsequent experience confirms that he was the only one so endowed. In modern business cycle forecasting, on which this chapter will focus, it is clear that the accuracy of most forecasts falls far short of public expectations.

Back in the early 1960s during the golden age of macroeconomics (golden for the attention and respect afforded to economists, as well as for the stellar performance of the economy), most economists were confident that the business cycle could be forecast with considerable precision. Certainly most felt that the art had been developed sufficiently to justify the "fine tuning" of fiscal and monetary policy. Some went farther, occasionally to the point of arrogance, and in the mid-to-late sixties there was even some loose talk about eliminating the business cycle altogether. In 1967 a conference explored the question, "Is the business cycle obsolete?" The conference proceedings were published under that title (Bronfenbrenner 1969) just in time for the 1970 recession to provide a decisive answer. As this episode suggests, the economics profession, gulled by its own rhetoric, oversold its ability to prognosticate, thus contributing to the public's excessive expectations.

Not everyone shared this naive overconfidence about either the prospect of eliminating the business cycle or our ability to accurately forecast it. Geoffrey Moore was among those who kept a sensible perspective. As the primary developer of the indicator approach to cyclical analysis, he had a vested interest in the idea that forecasting could be accurate—a vested interest that would have predisposed most economists to self-serving hyperbole. Yet Moore always maintained a careful respect for the limitations of forecasting. I recall a statement he made long ago to the effect that the leading indicators tell you where you're going only about the time you get there, although such information is nevertheless very useful because it is an earlier signal than you get from other data. I have always remembered that statement because, in addition to being valid (still valid today in my view), it always seemed to me to be a model of balanced judgment.

In the 1960s, however, the limitations of forecasting were seldom recognized either inside or outside the profession. During the following decades, public expectations have subsided, although not as far or as fast as the repute of the economics profession. Nevertheless, the general public still expects a lot more forecasting accuracy than any of us can consistently deliver.

Why is this so? Why should Americans have developed such grandiose portentions (pun intended, alas!) about our ability to foretell the business cycle? One reason is that too many of us have an overdeveloped faith in "experts." I remember a top bank trust officer who was so frustrated at his failure to get the bank's economist to give him an unqualified forecast that he finally blurted out, "Oh, if I only had a Ph.D. in economics—then I'd *know*!" Not so, as 99 percent of all Ph.D. economists would tell him. He'd be just as baffled—maybe more so—with a doctorate as he was without one in deciding which stocks would be winners. One thing he *would* understand better is why responsible Ph.D. economists don't make many unqualified statements about the future, and why experts in all fields have less faith in experts than does most of the public.

A second important reason behind the excessive expectations about forecasting is the fatalism that many people have about how the world works. Much of what will happen next year or next decade is preordained, they feel, either by God's master plan, or by past scientific discoveries, or for some other reason. In this view the future, or at least a good part of it, is predetermined. The road ahead is all laid out, and to see where we're headed we only need to brush away the clouds that now obscure the road.

The flaw in this idea was expressed two decades ago by Irving Kristol, another individual who did not succumb to the delusion that forecasting has become an exact science. In a highly laudatory review of Peter Drucker's *The Age of Discontinuity* in *Fortune* (February 1969), Kristol explained that

> The beginning of wisdom, for any social analyst or critic, is to know that the future is unknowable. This sounds easy, but it is in fact rare achievement. Recognizing the inscrutability of the future requires an extraordinary degree of humility and intellectual self-discipline. It requires the candid recognition that human history is a discontinuous process, rather than the neat projection of established trends. In a sense, we are all aware of this. . . . But the occasional awareness of our limitations is quickly elbowed aside by our all too human eagerness to define, right now, the shape of things to come.

Accordingly, there is no formula that will guarantee success in forecasting, no magic words that will part the clouds. The real problem, as the old saw puts it, is that the future lies ahead.

The Business Cycle

If precise prognostication is both impossible and inescapable, what are we to do? This question, as another contributor to this volume, Steve McNees, once observed, is similar to the question of the chronic complainer, who in effect is asking, "Isn't life difficult?" The obvious rejoinder is, "Sure, but what's the alternative?" And the single answer to that question, as to the forecasting dilemma, is that the only alternative is just to do the best you can.

Well, how do we go about doing the best we can? A logical first step is to "know thine enemy." If we're going to forecast the business cycle, surely it is a good idea to know the business cycle. Sounds reasonable, but it's not that easy. Like pornography, the business cycle is too untidy and amorphous to be defined simply, even though you always know it when you see it.

What we can say for sure (drawing on a National Bureau of Economic Research definition that is little changed since 1927) is that business cycles are made up of (a) alternating waves of expansions and contractions in aggregate economic activity, (b) that are recurrent but not periodic, (c) that vary greatly in both duration and intensity, with a life-span ranging from 1 to 12 years, (d) that occur in most (but not all) types of business activity simultaneously, and (e) in which developments in each phase of the cycle help to shape the following phase so that the phases merge into one another and the pattern of cycles looks

like this   not like this

That's about as precise as we can be in describing the regularities of the business cycle, which is of course a strong signal that the irregularities are at least as important as the regularities. Solomon Fabricant, former Director of Research at the National Bureau of Economic Research, used to make this point by noting that when you compare one business cycle with another, you find that they share a family resemblance, but it's more like a resemblance among cousins than among siblings—and certainly not the resemblance between twins.

To attain a bit more precision, we can turn to the short-hand definition of a recession, namely, two consecutive quarters of decline in real GNP.[1] For many purposes this short-hand definition turns out to be perfectly valid and all you'll ever need. But any serious student of the business cycle, including those who forecast it, will want to examine the three key dimensions of a recession, known as the "three Ds," duration, depth, and diffusion.

On depth, to qualify as a recession, economic activity must decline in an absolute sense; a mere slowdown in real growth is not enough. The eight recessions we have experienced since World War II have shown an average decline of about 2½ percent in real GNP. During a recession the unemployment rate typically climbs by 3.3 percentage points to a high of 7½ percent. By this measure, the mildest recessions were 1954 and 1970, when unemployment reached a peak of about 6 percent, and the worst was 1982 at 10½ percent.

On duration, the postwar record shows that recessions have lasted 11 months on average, from a minimum of 6 months (1980) to a maximum of 16 months (1973–75 and 1981–82). Cyclical expansions have averaged about 4 years or a bit more, which means that the full cycle, expansion and contraction combined, has an average life span of five years plus.

Diffusion, the third D, is a term that refers to how widespread a business cycle movement becomes, that is, how high a percentage of all industries participate in the recession or expansion. Experience shows that a recession is never the result of just a few large industries dragging the economy down while the others continue to expand. It is, rather, a process in which an overwhelming majority (75 to 90 percent) of industries move in the same direction as the overall economy. The same is true for cyclical expansions.

Thus we see from these figures on the depth, duration, and diffusion of the business cycle that any forecaster who relies solely on past averages when forecasting a recession should be prepared for surprises, because the averages hide a wide range of variance. When forecasting the next recession, one may not be able to do better than to project that it will be of average length and severity, but everyone should realize that actual experience can deviate from the average by as much as 50 or even 100 percent.

Periods of cyclical expansion are subject to even more variability than recessions in both the duration and vigor of growth to the next cyclical peak. One common characteristic that is useful for forecasting, however, is the close correspondence that exists from cycle to cycle in the initial growth rate of the rebound from the recession trough. During the first 18 to 24 months of recovery, GNP growth takes place at a fairly consistent rate of 5 to 6 percent. Subsequently, the growth rate moderates and the expansion proceeds at its own pace—sometimes steadily, sometimes with slow-downs and speed-ups,[2] until it reaches the next business cycle peak. In contrast to the initial period of recovery, however, the pace and pattern of expansion after the first two years is highly individual for each cycle.

The duration of expansions is another example of the individuality of that stage of the cycle. As mentioned, postwar expansions have lasted about 4 years on average. Yet the 1980–81 upswing lasted a mere 12 months, whereas the prolonged expansion of the 1960s endured for almost 9 full years. In fact, after the first year or two, the age of the expansion seems to contain little or no forecasting information. You often hear the thought expressed, e.g., that "this expansion, now approaching its fifth birthday, is old and tired and destined soon to give way to recession." But in contrast to humans, the age of a business cycle expansion is not closely correlated with its remaining life expectancy or (after the first two years) with its vigor. There is no valid geriatric theory of the business cycle. Expansions do not die of old age. The probability of recession in the following year is the same for a three-year-old expansion as it is for a five- or six-year-old expansion.

Causes of the Cycle

If expansions do not die of old age, what do they die of? Although this is not a settled issue within the economics profession, I would classify the reasons into two types: external and internal. The external causes of recession—and at the other end of the cycle, the reasons why recessions are transformed into expansions—are usually the excessive application of governmental economic policy. On rare occasions, there can be other types of external shocks such as the oil embargo of 1973–74, but usually it's fiscal and/or monetary policy that does the damage. The most prominent example is the severe monetary restraint—sometimes referred to as "cold-turkey monetarism"—instituted in 1979 by the Federal Reserve to fight the rampant inflation of that time, and which brought on the recessions of 1980 and 1981–82.

Probably more important are the internal causes of recession. These are the excesses and imbalances and distortions that develop within the structure of the economy itself as the expansion unfolds and cause consumers to cut back on their buying and business executives to cut back on production and employment. These developments would include, for example, an excessive build-up of inventory, an imbalance in price-cost movements that brings on a profits squeeze, and excessive demands for credit that drive rates beyond viable levels.

Frequently, of course, several of these structural imbalances develop simultaneously and reinforce one another in the expansion. Correspondingly, there is no reason why internal and external causes of recession can't develop at the same time. It is easy to imagine, for example, an overexuberant capital goods boom taking place simultaneously with an excessive build-up of inventories and the two together pushing the economy into an overheated condition and provoking an acceleration of inflation. The inflation, in turn, would lead the Federal Reserve to tighten its policies, sending interest rates soaring. Sooner or later that combination of internal and external forces would lead to recessionary cutbacks in production and employment.

A related question, more difficult to answer, is why some business cycles do so much damage while others are almost benign. Specifically, why do some recessions (1953–54, for example, and 1969–70) come and go so routinely that we barely notice them, while others inflict frightful pain in the form of widespread unemployment and bankruptcy? And why do some business cycle expansions develop into inflationary conflagrations, while others do not?

At some risk of oversimplification, I suggest that the usual reason a business cycle turns into a monster is an overdose of government policy. The one exception I can recall was the overriding contribution the oil shocks made to the inflation and recession of both the mid and late 1970s. But usually the reason is too much fiscal or monetary policy not merely causing a cyclical reversal but going beyond that and pushing the economy and the financial markets to extremes and creating a crisis. The best example is the overstimulation generated by the Great Society programs and Vietnam which propelled the economy beyond full employment, thereby setting off the inflationary binge of the late 1960s. On the down side, the obvious example again is the stringent monetary policy that brought on the long, deep recession of 1981–82.

These major policy overdoses are always rationalized in one way or another. President Johnson was told by his economists that he was taking a serious risk of inflation in the 1960s, but he didn't want to give up either the Vietnam War or the Great Society initiatives. In the early 1980s, Federal Reserve officials with support from President Reagan wanted to end double-digit inflation. Whether or not these reasons in fact justify the policy choices that were made is a debatable question. I suspect most people would answer "no" to President Johnson, but "yes" to the Federal Reserve in the early 1980s. In any event, the excessive cyclical consequences of policy overdoses cannot be avoided.

Risk of Catastrophe

This raises the question, what are the chances of a full-fledged business cycle catastrophe? More specifically, what are the chances of a recurrence of the Great Depression, a 3½ year debacle with GNP plunging by 32 percent and unemployment rising to 25 percent? A cyclical convulsion of that magnitude can never be ruled out entirely, but fortunately the odds against it appear to be fairly long.

A rerun of something like the Great Depression seems unlikely for two reasons. First, the structure of the American economy has changed in a far-reaching way. Relatively stable industries such as health care and some other services have become a much larger part of the economy, while cyclically sensitive industries like steel and machine tools carry relatively less weight. Further, within the cyclically sensitive industries, blue-collar workers and others who are subject to short-notice layoff are a smaller part of the workforce. The dramatic rise in dual income households is another structural change that attenuates the business cycle. Second, economic policy is less likely to go awry. A wide range of "built-in stabilizers" have been put in place: unemployment compensation, social security, food stamps, and other programs that help maintain spending power when earnings are curtailed. Deposit insurance keeps bank failures from spreading panic and distress.

In addition to the changes in our economic structure, the federal government has become more sophisticated in its use of discretionary fiscal and monetary policy. Probably the biggest reason the 1929 downturn developed into such a debacle was not (as so often claimed) either the wild speculation in common stocks or a deterioration in credit quality during the late 1920s. Rather, it was the gross policy error of the early 1930s when the Federal Reserve, in an effort to preserve the gold-exchange standard, presided over a contraction of one third of the money supply! Policy makers still make mistakes, of course, but the chances of staying with such a bad error so long seem slim indeed.

Economic developments like these account for the dramatic changes that have taken place in the business cycle in recent decades. Since World War II, cyclical expansions have been longer and recessions much shorter and much milder than between the world wars. Consequently, a modern-day scenario of the Great Depression does not deserve a prominent place in business planning.

What about the other side of the business cycle, the risk of a rerun of the 1970s with another bruising bout of inflation? Is that possibility also remote? No, not remote, because one of the prime lessons of the second half of the twentieth century is that the U.S. economy has a persistent tendency to generate too much rather than too little demand. So it's not difficult to imagine consumers, business-es, and government going on a simultaneous spending spree that would push labor and product markets to capacity and seriously overheat the economy before the Federal Reserve started applying the brakes.

How far the inflation rate could accelerate would depend on how much mo-mentum the cyclical expansion generated and how long the Fed delayed in reacting adequately to it. Starting from the recent inflation rate of about 4 percent, it's easy to picture a flare-up to high single digits. But as long as we remember the lessons of the 1960s and 1970s, it seems unlikely the Federal Reserve will accommodate inflationary pressures generously enough and persis-tently enough to bring back the 1970s. Unless, of course, we experience a supply shock like the oil price hikes of 1973–74 and 1979–80, or unless we disregard those painful earlier lessons. With such events, most anything is possible. With-out them, a return to double-digit inflation, while not as implausible as a repeat of the 1930s, is still a stretch for the imagination.

Forecasting Methods

In a sense, there are as many forecasting methods as there are forecasters. But I would argue that most projections are derived from two major methods: macro-econometric models and eclectic judgment. Macro models are huge systems of equations that until a few years ago taxed the capacity of large computers. But the models are not as overpowering as they often seem to be. Michael Evans de-scribed them in a chapter of *Methods and Techniques of Business Forecasting* (Butler et al., 1974) that takes up just 29 pages (which for Mike Evans is a mere inhalation)!

In fact, I contend that nothing more than a reasonable mastery of a good college statistics course, one that included multiple regression, is needed to understand the essentials of how an econometric model works. One can think of such a model as just a long series of multiple regression equations fitted togeth-er—mostly end to end but with a number of feedback loops. The output is a batch of computer printouts containing an endless list of projections, of which most of the major aggregates for the ensuing year, along with a few of the more detailed forecasts, are respectably accurate by the usual standards.

The eclectic-judgment forecaster, on the other hand, is one who uses every method and every relevant piece of information, whether or not it's quantitative. Despite the absence of big machinery and endless detailed projections, the eclectic-judgment method has more in common with the macro models than might be expected. Both encompass the same basic framework, i.e., the GNP accounts. Most of the same key relationships are considered, except that instead of being in the equations of the model the relationships are synthesized in the mind of the eclectic forecaster. The same key feedback loops are present, too—e.g., comparing the projections for employment and the income side of the GNP accounts with the product side to be sure that such sensitive variables as productivity growth, the personal saving rate, and corporate profits, are moving in a pattern that is consistent with the overall thrust of the forecast. Eclectic forecasters may use these feedback loops in a more flexible way than the econometricians do. The eclectic-judgment approach also uses the same input data, fewer of them in explicit fashion but probably more of them indirectly. Both approaches make use of other valuable forecasting methods such as the cyclical indicators and anticipation surveys, but the eclectic forecasters normally use these other methods more explicitly.

Accordingly, the two forecasting approaches end up being quite similar. Both are based on historical relationships. Both make systematic use of the available quantitative information. The econometric models are forced to use the average relationship for the period on which they are based, none of which they forget, which is both an advantage and disadvantage. The eclectic forecaster can choose to ignore certain periods of history, an advantage, but can also inadvertently forget some experience, a disadvantage. The econometric forecaster can choose to override the model, an advantage or disadvantage depending on the quality of judgment. Which is the superior method? There is no clear choice. Which one you prefer is a matter of style.

The anticipations surveys of business executives and consumers, which in the 1950s and early 1960s were considered so important that major forecasting conferences were scheduled around their release dates, have not lived up to initial expectations. Most disappointing were the surveys of consumer buying plans for homes, cars, appliances and the like, which somehow never did help us figure out how much of their income consumers were going to spend and on what. Why not? Evidently because consumers are less likely to plan their purchases in advance. They tend to be impulse buyers, at least in the sense that they frequently are not able to provide accurate information about their plans for big-ticket purchases in the near future.

Surveys of consumer confidence, however, move in a highly cyclical fashion with some anticipatory content. Thus they are helpful to forecasters. In the survey data from The Conference Board and National Family Opinion, the Consumer Expectations Index, which is calculated from the three questions that ask consumers what economic conditions they expect *six months ahead*, turns out to be a slightly better cyclical indicator than the overall Consumer Confidence Index, which is based on two questions about *current economic conditions* as well as the three expectations questions.

Finally, we still have the "old faithfuls," the surveys of business capital spending intentions. These are more reliable now than in the old days, but today we also have data series such as contracts and orders for plant and equipment that are probably better near-term forecasters of business investment than are the surveys.

The Cyclical Indicators

The "leading indicators" are so widely known and so well regarded that they could easily be classified as an entirely separate methodology. I include them here as part of the eclectic judgment classification because I've never known any able practitioners of that persuasion who didn't use the cyclical indicators as part of their methodology. Nor have I ever known any good students of the indicators who didn't also use other information as part of their forecasting process.

The central idea of the indicator approach is to find a batch of statistical time series that (a) conform well to the business cycle and (b) show a consistent timing pattern as leading or coincident or lagging indicators. Once that empirical classification exercise is completed, it's a simple matter to use the coincident indicators to define the turning points of the cycle and the leading indicators to forecast it. And the lagging indicators? Well, they sort of confirm that the business cycle took place as prescribed.

Such a description of the indicator approach to business cycle analysis is grossly oversimplified, almost a caricature—the sort of thing that led to the accusation that the cyclical indicators are "measurement without theory." In fact, the indicator approach is quite complex both in theory and practice. The theory is too comprehensive to be summarized here. It goes back at least to Wesley Mitchell's *Business Cycles* (1913) and is still being developed and refined. See for example, "When Lagging Indicators Lead: The History of an Idea" (Moore 1983). One key part of the theory already has been mentioned: the structural imbalances and distortions that develop during the late stages of a cyclical expansion and help bring on the first stage of the contraction.

What we're talking about here, really, are the lagging indicators. Many forecasters dismiss them as being inconsequential, but any analyst who does so ignores vital information about the cyclical process. Like some of the leaders, the laggers are measures of the structural imbalances within the business cycle. Inventories rising persistently faster than sales, for example, warn of a dangerous overhang of stocks on sellers' shelves. Rising interest rates suggest a developing credit squeeze. Rising labor costs signal a squeeze on profits. All three of these developments are typical of the ingredients from which recessions are made. The lagging indicators, therefore, can be viewed as measures of cyclical sin, and in this sense are "leaders of the leaders."[3]

In my view, those who fail to find a theory behind the indicator approach simply haven't looked closely. Those who do look, although they may be disappointed because it's not as simple as they would like, should nevertheless be pleasantly surprised at just how rich the theory is.

Selection of the time series that qualify as leading, coincident, and lagging indicators is also considerably more complicated than suggested above. In addition to the two criteria already mentioned—cyclical conformity and consistent timing—a qualifying indicator must meet four other tests:

• Economic significance: Its cyclical timing must be economically logical.

• Statistical adequacy: The data must be collected and processed in a statistically reliable way.

• Smoothness: Its month-to-month movements must not be too erratic.

• Currency: The series must be published on a reasonably prompt schedule, preferably within a month.

By these standards, few individual time series pass muster. No quarterly series qualifies—for lack of currency. Many monthly series lack smoothness. Indeed, when the tests are applied rigorously, there is no single time series that fully qualifies as an *ideal* cyclical indicator. A handful come close, but each is flawed in one respect or another—more often than not because they have too much month-to-month volatility.[4]

In the absence of any ideal indicators, we attempt to surmount their shortcomings by using composite indexes, specifically three separate indexes made up of leading, coincident, and lagging indicators. In the United States, the official composite indexes are calculated from eleven leaders, four coincident indicators and seven laggers—in each case selected from among those indicators that would be in competition for "best of breed."[5] These composites serve as a handy summary measure of the current behavior of the indicators.[6] Even more important, because they are averages, the composites tend to smooth out a good part of the volatility of the individual series and thus give more reliable signals about the direction of the business cycle.

Nevertheless, the composites are not without their limitations. They retain some erratic movements, especially in data for the latest month. (Sometimes the erratic fluctuations are removed by later data revisions, sometimes not.) Thus, often you will hear a rule of thumb that it takes three consecutive (monthly) declines in the composite leading index to signal a recession; that's a bit too pat, but it reminds us that a one-month drop is not a meaningful signal of a cyclical downturn.

From a forecaster's point of view, the composites are also limited by a certain degree of timing irregularity. It's reasonable to expect the composite leader to lead the business cycle, and the laggers to lag, and they do so reliably. It's not reasonable, however—given the imprecise nature of the economy—to expect the leading composite always to precede the turns in the business cycle by a fixed interval (forecasters' heaven) and indeed it does not. At business cycle peaks over the past four decades, the leading composite has led by intervals ranging from 3 to 23 months, and at troughs from 1 to 8 months. The lagging composite trailed cyclical turns by 2 to 11 months after peaks and by 4 to 15 months after troughs. Even the coincident index, the most regular of the three composites, has its off cycles; once in the mid-1950s, it started down six months ahead of the "official" peak month as determined by National Bureau of Economic Research.

In summary, the indicator approach is more complex and more difficult to use than it seems at first glance. Under the best of circumstances, the leads are short. But the effective lead is shorter for a variety of reasons: many series are erratic; some are reported late; others occasionally skip a business cycle altogether or show an extra cycle (e.g., the stock market in 1962 and again, evidently, in 1987); And many series behave indecisively around cyclical turning points—just when you need them most. But the difficulties notwithstanding, as several other essays in this volume point out, the indicator approach is still the best analytical system we have for figuring out where the economy is right now and where it is headed over the coming half year.

When the forecasting horizon is a full year ahead, the cyclical indicator approach is still very useful, but at that range I wouldn't go so far as to claim it is superior to other methods. But near-term, no other system is better.

The Forecasting Record

Well, looking a year ahead, what can we say about the record of professional prognosticators? The main conclusion, as already pointed out, is that everybody makes mistakes. No one can escape the iron rule that once you make a forecast, you know you're going to be wrong; you just don't know when and in which direction!

But thanks to the research of such stalwarts as Geoffrey Moore, Victor Zarnowitz, and Steve McNees, we can make a few additional points about the record of forecasters. (See the essay in this volume by McNees for a more comprehensive and more detailed examination of this topic.) For one thing, looking a year ahead, their errors are likely to be about one percentage point. On one side or the other, whether they are forecasting GNP growth or the inflation rate, they will probably miss the mark on average by about a percentage point.

Is that a good forecast? Well, compared to what? A logical standard is what's known as "naive extrapolation," defined as a forecast made on the assumption that the next 12 months will show the same change as the past 12 months. Against that standard, the inflation forecasts are a near stand-off, but on GNP the forecasters are clearly winners. They do better than the naive model. Furthermore, against this same standard, there is evidence that the accuracy of forecasters has improved over the past three decades. As the London *Economist* once put it, economic forecasters are "better than a blindfold and a pin."

Next question: *Which* forecasters do better? Again, among regular practitioners, no one and everyone. The econometricians do no better than the eclectic-judgment forecasters. Private sector forecasters no better than academic or government forecasters. Keynesians no better than monetarists. For this, it seems to me, there is a simple explanation: All forecasters use the same methodology. All players in the forecasting game, whatever their background, learn all the techniques as they go along and they incorporate the best features of all of them into their own forecasting approach, either explicitly or implicitly. For example, if Data Resources had a good forecasting record when the late Otto Eckstein was Chairman, was it because the firm had a superior macroeconometric model? Most unlikely, I would argue. It was, rather, because he and his associates were highly competent analysts. They knew how to adjust those "add factors" in the models, based on what the leading indicators were telling them, and on what they saw in the anticipation surveys, and on every other piece of information they could lay their minds on. (Otto Eckstein was one smart cookie, as well as being a likable guy, which is why I choose him as an example.) The basic point, I suppose, is that in forecasting, as elsewhere, nobody has a corner on brainpower.

Next important point: there is no indication in the statistical record of any systematic bias among forecasters. Their mistakes are not predominately in the same direction. In other words, they are not guilty of either chronic optimism or chronic pessimism.

While it is not (to my knowledge) in the empirical record, I believe there is one persistent tendency among business cycle forecasters: a timidity bias. This was first brought to my attention by the late Arthur Okun, who said that economic forecasters "catch the minnows but miss the sharks." That is, although they are good at foreseeing a change in direction for the economy, they are bad at sensing its severity, and they tend to be cautious on that part of the forecast. Thus when forecasters make a good case for slowdown, watch out for a steep recession.[7]

Finally: How much are forecasters worth? Like everybody else, they're worth what they contribute to the organization. Some do more than others, i.e., beyond just forecasting and economic analysis, and get paid for it accordingly. Some bring a lot of "show-biz" to their forecasting act, which in moderation is a good thing in this dismal science of ours. Occasionally, however, the substance of the forecaster's message is engulfed by the bombast of the presentation, at which point the show biz has obviously been carried too far.

Within the private sector, although there are many exceptions, the best and highest paid economic forecasters are most often found at investment and commercial banks, probably because those firms and their clients have more at risk to the business cycle and related macroeconomic events and are affected by them more directly and more sensitively than other industries. Thus it's worthwhile for the banks to hire the best. At the other end of the scale, an industry like book publishing would not ordinarily find it useful to hire a high-priced forecaster, since any fool can use a ruler, i.e., forecast industry sales by straight-line extrapolation.

Concluding Remarks

What we come down to, in the end, are three simple lessons: First, since forecasting is both inescapable and impossible, you'd better keep your powder dry. That is, you want to maintain maximum flexibility in your business plan, so that you can shift gears as quickly as possible when the economy performs contrary to your forecast.

Next, you want to stay on the right side of the law. You should be aware, for example, that New York's Code of Criminal Procedure, section 899, provides that anyone "pretending to forecast the future" shall be deemed a disorderly person under subdivision 3, section 901, of the code, and is liable, upon conviction, to a fine not to exceed $250 and/or a prison term of six months. This does not apply, however, to incorporated ecclesiastical bodies acting in good faith and without personal fee.

Finally, to maintain your sanity, keep your sense of humor sharpened. Above all remember the three central laws of forecasting:[8]
1. Forecasting is very difficult, especially if it's about the future!
2. If you must forecast, forecast often!
3. If you're ever right, never let 'em forget it!

Notes

1. Here and through most of this chapter I use the popular word, "recession," rather than the more precise term, "contraction." In popular usage, "recession" often refers to any period of economic weakness, including not only the period when economic activity is declining but also the early stages of recovery—but before economic activity has returned to levels that would be referred to as "prosperity." Here, however, "recession" is used to refer only to the period from business-cycle peak to business-cycle trough, i.e., the months of actual contraction.

2. Sometimes what I refer to here as slow-downs and speed-ups take the form of a "subcycle" (or "cyclical pause," or "growth cycle" or "mini-recession") which is a fluctuation in the economy similar in nature to a business cycle except smaller and shorter. This topic, however, is more esoteric than I wish to explore in this chapter.

3. An indicator based on this line of reasoning is found in the U.S Department of Commerce's monthly publication, *Business Conditions Digest* (BCD), as series #940, the ratio of the coincident index to the lagging index. (I always thought it was more logical the other way around, but (as in sex) who's on top doesn't matter much.)

4. In my view, the best single coincident indicator is nonfarm (payroll) employment (BCD series #41). Among the leading indicators, my favorites are common stock prices (BCD #19), the factory workweek (BCD #1), new housing permits (BCD #29) and the real (M2) money supply (BCD #106). But there is really no need to limit yourself to a handful

of indicators, because it takes only a modest amount of time each month (once you've got the hang of it) to follow all of them. *Business Conditions Digest* provides reasonably current charts and tables covering more than 100 cyclical indicators and also some 150 other useful economic series. BCD is available (curently $4.00 per issue, $44.00 per year, domestic; $5.00 and $55.00, foreign) from the Superintendent of Documents, U.S. Government Printing Office, Washington, D.C. 20402.

5. The composite indexes are also found in *Business Conditions Digest.*The component series that make up the composite indexes are shown in the first group of charts in BCD. The method by which the composites are calculated is summarized in the "Method of Presentation" section near the front of BCD and spelled out in detail in *1984 Handbook of Cyclical Indicators*, also published by the U.S. Department of Commerce.

6. Composite indexes of leading and lagging indicators for ten other major industrial countries are available monthly in *International Economic Scoreboard* published by The Conference Board. The indexes are compiled by the Center for International Business Cycle Research at the Columbia Business School.

7. Perhaps the best illustration of this tendency was the consensus reached in the late summer of 1974, when President Ford's "Summit Conference on Inflation" brought together a bipartisan group of the best forecasters in the country, who agreed that little change was in store for the economy in the year ahead. The differences were all in the range of plus or minus one percent change in real GNP. As it turned out, at that moment the economy was on the precipice of a cyclical downturn that would send GNP plunging 3 percent over the next six months. To my mind, that experience tolled the end of the "golden age" of economics.

8. Part of a collection of one-liners in Edgar R. Fiedler, "The Three Rs of Economic Forecasting—Irrational, Irrelevant and Irreverent," *Across the Board*, The Conference Board Magazine, New York, June 1977.

References

Bronfenbrenner, Martin, ed. 1969. *Is the Business Cycle Obsolete?* New York: Wiley Interscience.

Butler, William F., Robert A. Kavesh, and Robert B. Platt, eds. 1974. *Methods and Techniques of Business Forecasting*. Englewood Cliffs, N.J.: Prentice Hall.

Mitchell, Wesley C. 1913. *Business Cycles*. Berkeley and Los Angeles: University of California Press; and *Business Cycles and Their Causes*. 1941. Berkeley and Los Angeles: University of California Press. (A reprint of Part 3 of *Business Cycles*.)

Moore, Geoffrey H. 1983. *Business Cycles, Inflation and Forecasting*. 2d ed. Cambridge, Mass.: Ballinger.

Penner, Rudolph G. "Economics: A Profession in Trouble?" *Public Opinion*, November/December 1988.

10

The Accuracy of Macroeconomic Forecasts

Stephen K. McNees

This chapter evaluates the accuracy of forecasts of the U.S economy from several perspectives. The first section examines annual forecasts over the past 35 years to address the questions: On the basis of past experience, how accurate can we expect macroeconomic forecasts to be? and, Has forecast accuracy improved over time? The second section examines a richer set of quarterly forecasts over a 12-year period, covering more forecasters, more variables, and multiperiod forecast horizons. These data are used to address the questions of how forecast accuracy differs among variables, across different horizons, and at cyclical turning points. The chapter concludes with remarks on the questions of who is the "best" forecaster and what are the most accurate forecasting techniques.

Annual Forecasts

Chart 10.1 displays the forecasts issued each November since 1952 by the Research Seminar in Quantitative Economics (RSQE) at the University of Michigan for real GNP in the following year. This 35-year history provides the longest consistent set of forecast data available, invaluable for placing recent experience in perspective. Over this period, the average discrepancy between forecast and "actual" outcome, the mean absolute error (MAE), is 1.3 percentage points (Table 10.1). No systematic tendency to overestimate or underestimate appears. The mean error (ME), a mere –0.2 percentage point, is small relative to the root mean squared error (RMSE) of 2.0 percentage points. More often than not (in 54 percent, or 19 of 35 cases) the error was less than 1 percentage point and four times out of five was less than 2 percentage points. The two largest errors were made in 1955 and 1959, first years of recovery from recessions. The next two largest errors reflect failures to anticipate the downturns in 1974 and 1982.

While it is obvious that large errors often occur near business cycle turning points, the forecasts of the 14 years in which a business cycle turn occurred are actually somewhat *more* accurate than those of years in which no turn occurred. This finding can be reconciled with the conventional wisdom by distinguishing

Chart 10.1. **RSQE Forecasts of Real GNP.**

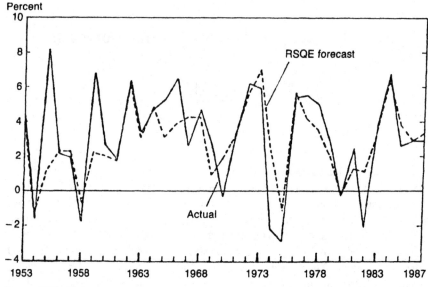

Source: Table 10.1.

carefully between the year when the forecast is made and the year that is being predicted. The forecasts made during years in which turning points occurred (especially 1954, 1958, and 1973) were unusually inaccurate, while earlier forecasts of those turning point years were more accurate than most.

The accuracy of RSQE's real GNP forecasts has clearly improved over time. As Table 10.1 shows, summary error measures are smaller in the second half of the period. In absolute terms, errors so far in the 1980s have been slightly smaller than those in the 1960s, which in turn were much smaller than those in the 1950s. The 1970s were the only decade in which the errors increased in absolute terms. In a relative sense, however, real GNP forecast accuracy has improved steadily in each decade. The traditional standards of comparison have been naive rules of thumb such as, "Next year will be the same as this year" (N1) or "Next year will be the same as the average over the past four years"(N4). Only the results for N4, the more accurate for real GNP, are presented in the table. These simple rules have performed much worse since 1969, so that the RSQE real GNP forecast has steadily improved relative to both of these naive standards of comparison.

Improvement is also evident relative to the more demanding standard of comparison of a constant forecast equal to the average of actual real GNP growth in the forecast period. The variance of a variable in the forecast period can be regarded as the mean squared error of a "forecast that assumes (the log of) real GNP follows a random walk with *known* drift"—i.e., a constant forecast equal to the actual mean growth rate in the forecast period. For example, the average rate of growth of real GNP over this forecast period was 3 percent. A forecaster who had known the actual average in advance, but nothing else, would always have issued the same forecast—real GNP will grow at its 3 percent trend rate. The root mean squared error of this forecast would be equal to the standard deviation of real GNP in the forecast period. If the mean of a variable in the forecast period were as readily available as its historical mean, this would be a reasonable standard of comparison.

However, whenever the mean value in the forecast period is highly uncertain, this criterion seems unrealistically harsh since it is not clear that a more accurate forecast was feasible. The RSQE forecasts have steadily improved relative to a forecast based on perfect knowledge of the *actual trend* rate of real GNP growth in the forecast period but no information on its yearly variations. Such a "random walk with known drift" forecast was nearly as accurate as the RSQE forecasts in the first half of the forecast period, but much less accurate in the second half.

Chart 10.2 shows forecasts of the inflation rate, as measured by the GNP implicit price deflator (IPD) issued early each year since 1962 by the President's Council of Economic Advisers (CEA). The average discrepancy between the forecasts and actual data is 0.9 percentage point. About two-thirds of the errors are less than 1 percentage point, and only two (of the 26) exceed 2 percentage points. The two large errors occurred in 1973 and 1974, the period of the first oil shock and the relaxation of wage and price controls. The widely noted "systematic" tendency to underestimate inflation in the 1960s and 1970s has been followed by a tendency to overestimate inflation in the 1980s; over the entire period, even though these errors are autocorrelated and therefore in some sense inefficient, there is no indication of bias in these inflation forecasts. The CEA inflation rate forecasts have become more accurate in the 13-year period since the two large underestimates in 1973 and 1974 (Table 10.2). In absolute terms, the summary error measures are only slightly smaller in the past 13 years than in the prior 13-year period, despite the fact that the mean and the variance of the inflation rate have increased. Similarly, inflation forecasts have improved relative to the two naive standards of comparison. In the mid-1970s, inflation forecasts seemed only slightly more accurate than the naive "last-change" or N1 forecast (Zarnowitz 1979, 13–15). More recently, the accuracy of such naive forecasts has deteriorated while the accuracy of other forecasts has improved slightly in absolute terms.

Since 1969, the CEA's inflation forecasts have been as accurate as the median forecasts of private forecasters surveyed late each year by the American Statistical Association (ASA) and the National Bureau of Economic Research (NBER) (see Chart 10.2). It is no coincidence that both the government (CEA) and private (ASA/NBER) forecasts of 1974 contain their largest errors for both inflation and real growth. These forecasts were made during the period of relaxation of wage and price controls, shortly after the price of imported oil had quadrupled and OPEC had imposed an embargo on oil shipments. The fact that these extraordinarily large errors were (nearly) equal and of opposite sign is consistent with the

Table 10.1

Accuracy of RSQE Forecasts of Real GNP, 1953–87

Years	RSQE forecast	Actual	Error	Years	RSQE forecast	Actual	Error
1953	3.7	4.4	-0.7	1970	1.9	-0.4	2.3
1954	-1.2	-1.6	0.4	1971	3.3	3.3	0.0
1955	1.2	8.2	-7.0	1972	5.6	6.2	-0.6
1956	2.3	2.1	0.2	1973	7.0	5.9	1.1
1957	2.3	1.9	0.4	1974	2.3	-2.2	4.5
1958	-0.7	-1.8	1.1	1975	-1.1	-2.9	1.8
1959	2.2	6.8	-4.6	1976	5.7	5.4	0.3
				1977	4.2	5.5	-1.3
1960	2.0	2.6	-0.6	1978	3.5	5.0	-1.5
1961	1.7	1.8	-0.1	1979	2.0	2.8	-0.8
1962	6.1	6.4	-0.3	1980	-0.2	-0.3	0.1
1963	3.0	3.4	-0.4	1981	1.3	2.5	-1.2
1964	4.9	4.7	0.2	1982	1.1	-2.1	3.2
1965	3.1	5.3	-2.2	1983	3.4	3.7	-0.3

1966	3.9	6.5	−2.6	1984	6.5	6.8	−0.3
1967	4.3	2.6	1.7	1985	3.8	2.6	1.2
1968	4.3	4.7	−0.4	1986	2.9	2.9	0.0
1969	0.9	2.7	−1.8	1987	3.4	2.9	0.5

Years	ME	MAE	MAE/N4	RMSE	RMSE/SD actual
All	−0.2	1.3	0.48	2.0	0.70
1953–69	−1.0	1.5	0.63	2.3	0.87
1970–86	0.5	1.2	0.38	1.6	0.55
1950s	−1.5	2.1	0.58	3.2	0.90
1960s	−0.7	1.0	0.70	1.4	0.85
1970s	0.6	1.4	0.41	1.9	0.57
1980s	0.4	0.8	0.33	1.3	0.52

Sources: Forecasts: Research Seminar in Quantitative Economics, University of Michigan *The Economic Outlook for 1988.* Table 1, p. 3. Actual data: 1953–64, *Economic Report of the President*, 1965. 1966–74, *Economic Report of the President*, 1975. 1976–84, *Economic Report of the President*, 1985. 1965, 1975 and 1985, *Survey of Current Business*, November issue, plus estimate of fourth quarter. 1986–87, *Survey of Current Business*, March 1988.

Notes: ME = Mean Error, MAE = Mean Absolute Error, RMSE = Root Mean Squared Error, N4 = naive "same as four year average" forecast, SD Actual = standard deviation of actuals in forecast period.

Chart 10.2. **CEA Forecasts of GNP Deflator.**

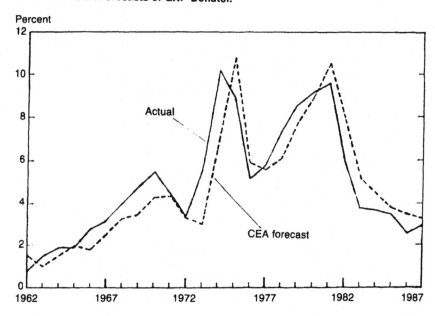

GNP Deflator: Forecast Errors.

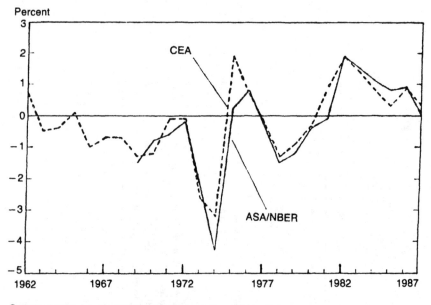

Sources: Actual data for GNP implicit price deflator, Table 10.1; CEA forecast, *Budget of the U.S. Government*: ASA/NBER forecast, *NBER Reporter.*

Table 10.2

CEA Forecast Accuracy Relative to Naive Models and ASA/NBER Forecast

Forecast	1962–87	1962–74	1975–87
Real GNP			
Mean Error (ME)	0.3	0.6	−0.1
Mean Absolute Error (MAE)	1.0	1.1	0.9
MAE/N4	0.39	0.46	0.32
MAE/ASA-NBER			1.10[a]
Root Mean Squared			
Error (RMSE)	1.3	1.4	1.2
RMSE/N4	0.39	0.47	0.33
RMSE/ASA			1.08[a]
RMSE/SD Actual	0.47	0.55	0.43
Implicit price deflator			
ME	−0.2	−0.8	0.5
MAE	0.9	1.0	0.9
MAE/N1	0.79	0.89	0.70
MAE/ASA-NBER			1.00[a]
RMSE	1.2	1.3	1.1
RMSE/N1	0.73	0.85	0.61
RMSE/ASA-NBER			0.93[a]
RMSE/SD actual	0.46	0.55	0.45
Nominal GNP			
ME	0.0	−0.3	0.4
MAE	1.2	1.0	1.3
MAE/N4	0.50	0.52	0.48
MAE/ASA-NBER			0.79[a]
RMSE	1.5	1.3	1.6
RMSE/N4	0.53	0.57	0.52
RMSE/ASA-NBER			0.82[a]
RMSE/SD actual	0.59	0.69	0.54

Notes: N4 = naive "same as four year average" forecast.

N1 = naive "same as last year" forecast.

ASA/NBER = median forecast of survey late each year by the American Statistical Association and the National Bureau of Economic Research.

SD Actual: standard deviation of actuals in forecast period = RMSE of "random walk with known trend" forecast.

As in Table 10.1, actual data are latest actuals prior to benchmark revisions.

CEA forecasts prior to 1969 taken from Moore 1983, pp. 442–49.

[a]19 years from 1969 through 1987.

designation of this period as a "supply shock." Given aggregate demand, a disturbance to aggregate supply will reduce real GNP and increase inflation. Its impact on nominal GNP will be secondary, depending on the exact elasticity of aggregate demand.

This interpretation of 1974 is borne out by Chart 10.3, which displays the errors of the nominal GNP forecasts by the CEA and the ASA/NBER survey. The large real GNP and inflation errors were not only of opposite sign but of roughly equal magnitude: the huge overestimate of real growth offset the huge underestimate of inflation, so that the nominal GNP forecast in 1974 was extremely accurate.

Forecasters might console themselves by arguing that a supply shock is inherently "unpredictable" and thus does not call into question their understanding of aggregate demand. In fact, while oil price swings have remained volatile, their consequences have become easier to anticipate; neither the positive shock that followed the Iranian Revolution in late 1978, nor the 1986 collapse in oil prices, nor the subsequent sharp rebound produced extraordinarily large errors in forecasts of inflation in the economy as a whole.

In sharp contrast, the conviction that the determinants of aggregate demand could be predicted accurately was shattered in 1982. Government and private forecasts overestimated both the rate of inflation and the rate of real growth, producing the largest error in estimating nominal GNP of the period—roughly double those observed before or since. Only time will tell whether the 1982 experience was an aberration or a warning that our understanding of aggregate demand is superficial. In any event, it is difficult to make a case that nominal GNP forecasts have become more accurate over time. Summary error measures have increased somewhat in absolute terms, and they have held fairly steady relative to the naive standards of comparison. Only when the error measures are compared with the actual volatility of movements in GNP, which increased considerably, is there any ground to argue that nominal GNP forecasts have improved.

Quarterly Forecasts

Based on the evidence from 1976:II through 1987:IV, this section examines the accuracy of 10 forecast sets:

1. American Statistical Association and National Bureau of Economic Research survey of regular forecasts, median (ASA/NBER)
2. U.S. Bureau of Economic Analysis (BEA)
3. Benchmark forecast (BMARK), formerly Charles R. Nelson Associates, Inc.
4. Chase Econometrics (CHASE)
5. Data Resources, Inc. (DRI)
6. Economic Forecasting Project, Georgia State University (GSU)

Chart 10.3. **CEA Forecasts of Nominal GNP.**

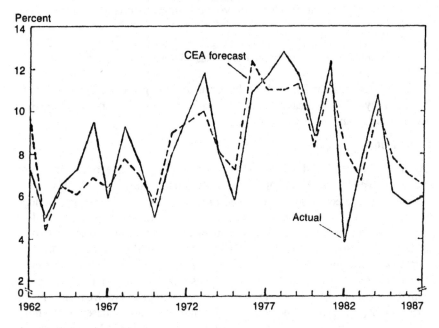

Nominal GNP: Forecast Errors.

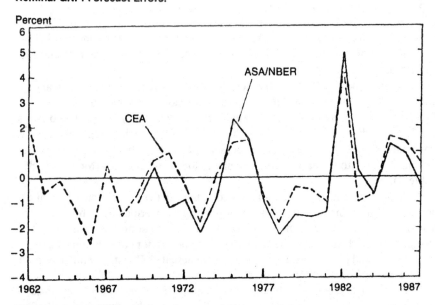

Sources: Actual data for growth rate of nominal GNP, *Survey of Current Business*, July 1988. CEA and ASA/NBER forecasts, see Chart 10.2.

7. Kent Economic and Development Institute (KEDI)
8. Research Seminar in Quantitative Economics, University of Michigan (RSQE)
9. University of California at Los Angeles, School of Business (UCLA)
10. Wharton Econometric Forecasting Associates, Inc. (WEFA)

The actual data against which these forecasts are compared are explained next. The accuracy of the forecasts is then evaluated by forecast horizon, at cyclical turning points, and by forecaster.

Actual Data

Several different official estimates of actual GNP are made over time. The appropriate version of actual data to use for evaluating forecasts depends on the interests of the forecast user. Participants in financial markets, for example, hope to capitalize on the markets' reaction to "news." Financial markets tend to respond more to the initial estimate than to the revised estimates issued well after the fact. Wall Streeters are less interested in the verdict of history than in tomorrow's headlines. These initial estimates are, however, relatively imprecise, being based on incomplete information plus estimates of unavailable data. Later estimates are more reliable, being based on more complete low-frequency information such as tax returns and censuses. The most recent data based on the most complete information are our best measure of what actually happened in the economy. Using any other actual data to compare forecasters runs the risk of penalizing the best prediction of what actually occurred in favor of the best estimate of what initially but mistakenly was thought to have happened. Moreover, historical data, not preliminary estimates, are used to construct and test models and theories of the economy.

Table 10.3 shows that these distinctions among various versions of actual data are of little practical importance for the summary error measures of annual forecasts, even though they can greatly affect a particular year. (See also Artis 1987, Appendix B.) Previous research has shown that such distinctions can be important, however, for *quarterly* forecasts: specifically, that quarterly forecasts are much closer to the early estimates than to the revised actuals (McNees 1986, Table 3).

In late 1985, the U.S. Bureau of Economic Analysis completed one of its periodic changes in its procedures for estimating the National Income and Product Accounts (henceforth, the GNP accounts). The most notable feature of this change was the shift from a 1972 to a 1982 base period for constructing constant-dollar series and price indexes. All subsequent actual GNP data conform to these new "post-benchmark" procedures.

This change presents a problem for evaluating "pre-benchmark" forecasts—those made prior to the accounting change—of the post-benchmark period. The comprehensive revision involved several definitional changes in addition to such

Table 10.3

Forecast Accuracy Relative to Different Estimates of Actual Data, 1969–86

	Preliminary[a]	Revised[b]	Last pre-benchmark[c]	Latest available[d]
Real GNP				
ME	0.3	0.2	0.3	0.4
MAE	1.0	0.9	1.1	0.9
RMSE	1.3	1.2	1.4	1.1
Implicit price deflator				
ME	−0.2	−0.3	−0.3	−0.7
MAE	1.1	1.1	1.1	1.3
RMSE	1.5	1.4	1.5	1.6

[a]Data typically released in January of year $t+1$ for year t.
[b]Data released in late January of year $t+2$ for year t.
[c]See sources of actual data in Table 10.1.
[d]Data available as of 7/1/88.

usual statistical changes as the incorporation of additional information from tax returns and census data. How can forecasts in 1972 dollars be assessed when the only actual data are in 1982 dollars and from a different definitional accounting framework?

Without actual data for 1986–87 under the pre-benchmark procedures, the post-benchmark data must be adjusted to be as comparable as possible with pre-benchmark accounting procedures. The approach employed here rests on two assumptions: (*i*) it is assumed that the definitional and classification changes affected the levels but not the percentage changes in current dollar GNP; (*ii*) it is assumed that the rebasing affected the levels but not the rates of change of the deflators of the major components of GNP, although the rebasing clearly does affect the levels and growth rates of the implicit price deflator for total GNP (IPD). Both real GNP and IPD are obtained by the standard accounting identities. This assumption has been employed in previous research (Grimm and Hirsch 1983, 337–38). With these two assumptions, a set of actual 1972 dollar data was constructed to evaluate the pre-benchmark forecasts.

Accuracy and Forecast Horizon

The accuracy of a forecast tends to increase as the horizon of the forecast decreases. Initially, the improvement is quite gradual and summary error measures are virtually constant as the forecast horizon decreases. We know little more today about what will happen in a given quarter a year from now than we do about a quarter two years from now. For quarterly data like GNP, the improvement in accuracy becomes quite sharp during the quarter that is being predicted. This improvement reflects not so much better forecasting but rather the fact that as a quarter progresses more and more of the higher-frequency (monthly, weekly, or daily) actual data become available. Current-quarter forecasting, in other words, is a mixture of predictions of the future and social accounting of the past. As a quarter progresses, "forecasting" essentially replicates the procedures national income accountants use to produce initial estimates of the "actual" outcome. The sharp improvement in accuracy that occurs during a quarter is the reason why the release date of a forecast is so important in forecast comparisons. The improvement resulting from only one month's additional data is often large relative to the differences in accuracy among forecasters. For this reason, the forecast sets studied here are divided into those prepared in the first (early quarter), second (mid-quarter), and last (late quarter) month of each quarter.

While a forecast's accuracy naturally deteriorates as its horizon increases, it is less widely appreciated that, for many variables, longer time spans can be predicted more accurately than short time spans. For example, forecasts of real GNP growth over the next four quarters are typically 1.5 to 2 percentage points off the mark, while forecasts of the next quarter's annual rate of growth err by 2.5 to 3 percentage points. This tendency appears for many components of both nominal and real GNP. However, this is not a necessary result, and it does not hold for all variables. Forecasts of the inflation rate, for example, show no tendency to improve over longer time spans. This difference reflects the tendencies of the variables toward error offsetting versus error buildup. Often, a surprise in real GNP growth in one quarter portends another surprise in the opposite direction in the next quarter. Recall, for example, the unexpected declines in real GNP in the second quarters of both 1979 (energy shortage) and 1980 (credit controls). In each case, the unexpected weakness was followed by unexpected strength in the subsequent quarter. Forecasts of the half-year time span that included both quarters were more accurate than those of either quarter alone, thanks to errors of opposite signs in the quarterly pattern.

The phenomenon of offsetting errors is not uncommon in GNP forecasts, reflecting temporary disruptions to either supply (a strike or an energy shortage) or demand (credit controls or temporary auto price incentive programs). In contrast, inflation rate forecasts exhibit a tendency toward error accumulation—a surprise in next quarter's inflation rate tends to be followed by surprises in the same direction in subsequent periods. Forecasters consistently underestimated inflation in the 1970s and consistently overestimated it in the 1980s. (See McNees and Ries [1983, 7–8] for an analysis of forecast deterioration for other variables.)

One way to appreciate differing tendencies toward forecast error accumulation is to consider the implications of forecast errors for forecast revisions. Suppose a forecaster has overestimated last quarter's real GNP. Does this imply

Table 10.4

Forecast Accuracy and Previous Forecast Error, 1970:III to 1987:IV

$(F_{t+m,t} - A_{t+m,t}) = a + \beta(F_{t,t-1} - A_t'),$

where $F_{t+m,t}$ = Forecasted rate of growth from quarter t to quarter t + m, issued just after advance estimate of quarter t (A_t'),

$A_{t+m,t}$ = Revised actual rate of growth from quarter t to quarter t + m, and

A_t' = Advance estimate of rate of growth in quarter t, available in first month of quarter t + 1.

Forecast horizon (quarters)	β	s.e. of β	$\bar{R}^2$
Real GNP			
1	−0.14	0.15	0.0
4	−0.08	0.10	−0.01
8	−0.14	0.08	0.03
GNP implicit price deflator			
1	0.30	0.12	0.08
4	0.51	0.15	0.14
8	0.61	0.21	0.11

Note: Data calculated using median early-quarter forecasts from the following groups: BEA, DRI, CHASE, and WEFA, and the forecast of ASA/NBER.

that, other things equal, the next forecast should be reduced? Without further information on the reasons for the error, the answer is no; last quarter's error contains no information useful for revising the previous forecast. Table 10.4 illustrates that last quarter's real GNP error bears no systematic relationship to the one-, four-, or eight-quarter-ahead real GNP forecast error. The bottom panel of the table, in contrast, suggests that inflation forecast errors do provide useful information for revising inflation forecasts. Inflation forecast errors have been associated with errors of the same sign in subsequent one-, four-, and eight-quarter-ahead inflation rate forecasts. In contrast to real GNP forecasts, where either past errors contain no useful information or that information already has been incorporated into subsequent forecasts, forecasters did not exploit the information in past inflation errors in formulating their subsequent forecasts. Whether the in-sample correlation of observed inflation errors is sufficiently stable to be exploited to improve inflation forecasts or constitutes evidence of "inefficiency" is not clear.

Turning Points

Many economic decision makers attach special importance to whether the economy is in an expansion or a recession. This concern about the stage of the business cycle is both a cause and an effect of the pioneering work by the National Bureau of Economic Research in identifying and dating cyclical turning points.

The origin of this effort predates the development of the National Income and Product GNP Accounts and thus predates the development of macroeconometric models of GNP. While the designation of cyclical turning points derives from analyses of monthly data, the quarterly GNP accounts are the language of most macroeconomic models and forecasts. This presents a problem for assessing how well cyclical turning points have been predicted. Most forecasts do not provide an explicit statement of when the economy will change from one phase to the next, and any attempt to assess their accuracy must first select the configuration of macroeconomic forecast data that can be taken as an indication that a cyclical turning point will occur. Assessment, in other words, is contingent on the procedure used to translate a forecast into a statement about turning points.

The most straightforward macroeconomic criteria for identifying and dating turning points do not conform closely to the official chronology of business cycle turning points. For example, a recession (expansion) is a period in which the level of aggregate economic activity is declining (rising). It would be a mistake, however, simply to identify recessions (expansions) with quarters in which the level of real GNP declined (rose). Changes in the real GNP have not been closely associated with the official National Bureau of Economic Research (NBER) business cycle chronology. For example, over the past 40 years, real GNP has declined in 11 quarters classified as expansions and has risen in five quarters during recessions. Even this count excludes the quarters in which cyclical turns have occurred. In quarters classified as cyclical peaks, real GNP has increased six times and declined twice. In quarters classified as cyclical troughs, real GNP has increased four times and fallen four times. Clearly, the task of identifying cyclical turning points cannot be reduced to simply observing the direction of change of real GNP.

A common rule of thumb has developed, classifying recessions as periods of two consecutive quarterly declines in real GNP. This popular rule of thumb also bears little resemblance to the officially designated recession periods. Since 1947, real GNP has declined in two or more consecutive quarters only six times. Neither the 1960–61 recession nor the 1980 recession had that feature. Moreover, these six periods do not conform closely to the official recessions. The popular rule of thumb, thus, does not provide a very accurate criterion for establishing recession periods. The main moral of these examples is that magnitudes matter. One cannot reliably infer recessions and expansions by merely observing the direction of changes in real GNP.

Defining a recession as a half-year (i.e., two-quarter) period in which real GNP has declined is more promising. As illustrated in Table 10.5, this criterion conforms more closely to the officially designated recession and expansion periods. Specifically, this criterion identifies all postwar recessions but also intro-

Table 10.5

Alternative Criteria for Defining Cyclical Turning Points

Official NBER turning point	First half-year change in real GNP[a]	Consecutive "sizable" increases in the unemployment rate[b]
Peaks		
1948:IV	1948:IV	1948:IV
1953:II[c]	1953:III	1953:III
1957:III	1957:III	1957:III
1960:II	1960:II	1960:II
1969:IV	1969:IV	1969:IV
1973:IV	1974:I[d]	1974:II
1980:I	1980:I	1979:IV
1981:III	1981:III[e]	1981:III
False Signal	1979:I	None
Troughs		
1949:IV	1949:IV	1949:IV
1954:II	1954:II	1954:II
1958:II	1958:II	1958:II
1961:I	1960:IV	1961:I
1970:IV	1970:II	1970:IV
1975:I	1975:II	1975:II
1980:III	1980:III	1980:III
1982:IV	1982:IV	1982:IV
False Signal	1949:II	None

[a]Peak (trough) occurs in the first quarter of the first half-year decline (increase) in real GNP.
[b]Peak (trough) occurs in the quarter prior to two consecutive increases in the quarterly average unemployment rate of (less than) 0.3 or more percentage points.
[c]Trough month was in 1953:III (July).
[d]Based on preliminary data, peak was in 1973:IV.
[e]Based on preliminary data, peak was in 1981:II.

duces two false signals, a false trough in 1949 and a false peak in 1979. Nonetheless, the timing of recessions implied by this definition is far closer to official recessions than the criteria previously considered. All but two cyclical peaks occurred in the first quarter of the first half-year decline in real GNP. In the only two exceptions to this tendency, in 1953 and 1973, the cyclical peak occurred in the quarter preceding the half-year decline.

A half-year increase is a somewhat less reliable criterion for the timing of cyclical troughs. Five of eight cyclical troughs occurred in the first quarter of the first half-year increase in real GNP. However, the 1975:I trough occurred one quarter earlier, the 1961:I trough one quarter later, and the 1970:IV trough two quarters later than this general tendency suggests.

Thus, the criterion of defining half-year declines (increases) in real GNP as recessions (expansions) conforms to the official NBER designations somewhat better than the more commonly employed rules of thumb based on quarterly changes in real GNP. Even so, this criterion provides two false signals (from 1949:I to 1949:III and from 1978:IV to 1979:II) and can vary in timing from its normal relationship to cyclical turning points by as much as two quarters. It appears that no simple rule is sufficient to translate two quarterly real GNP changes into official cyclical turning points.

Changes in the quarterly average unemployment rate have conformed quite closely to official turning points, especially recession troughs. With minor exceptions, all postwar cyclical turning points have occurred in the quarter prior to "sizable" changes in the behavior of the unemployment rate. More precisely, cyclical peaks have tended to occur in the quarter *prior* to an increase of 0.3 percentage point or more in the unemployment rate, and cyclical troughs in the quarter *prior* to the first change of less than 0.3 percentage point in the unemployment rate. In the three exceptions to this tendency (the 1953 peak, the 1975 trough, and the 1980 peak), the turning point occurred within a month of the quarter implied. These exceptions are minor given that it is not generally possible to establish timing on a monthly basis with quarterly data, the most common frequency for forecasted data. Alternatively, one need only qualify the observed tendency by modifying "prior quarter" with the phrase "plus or minus one month."

While sizable (henceforth taken to mean 0.3 percentage point or more) increases in the unemployment rate have been a necessary condition for peaks and the absence of sizable increases for troughs, this criterion has not been a sufficient one—the simple rule would produce false peaks in 1959:IV and 1963:I and a false trough in 1974:I. These instances further illustrate what was previously noted for real GNP—turning points cannot be identified from data for one quarter in isolation. The rule could be easily modified arbitrarily to omit all false signals. The simplest modification, requiring two consecutive sizable increases for peaks and their absence for troughs, suffices to eliminate all false signals but only by greatly displacing the dating of the 1973 peak.

The following analysis is, therefore, based on the following criteria: A cyclical peak is expected to occur in the first quarter of a half-year decline in real GNP and a cyclical trough in the quarter prior to two consecutive changes in the quarterly average unemployment rate of less than 0.3 percentage point. These criteria will be applied to available forecasts of three prominent forecasting organizations and one well-known survey-based consensus forecast to assess how well cyclical turning points have been predicted. An alternative consensus forecast and a fourth forecaster are also included when data are available.

The traditional approach to evaluating turning point forecasts focuses on the difference between the time a signal of a turning point at some *unspecified* future date is issued and the time that a turning point actually occurs. Within this approach, the *variability* of this lead (lag) is probably even more important than the average lead (lag) time itself. For example, a forecaster could easily achieve very long lead times by calling the next peak as soon as a recession ends, so long as the date of the peak was unspecified. To account for such uninformative behavior, great attention must be placed on the variability of lead (lag) times of such turning point forecasts with unspecified dates. An alternative approach is followed here, one that stresses the importance of timing in forecasting turning points. Here a turning point signal is considered to have two components: a statement that a turning point will occur and a statement of *when* it will occur. A turning point signal is regarded as a false signal if it does not date the turning point correctly.

This is a harsher standard than the traditional one in that it introduces more false signals. In the traditional approach, false signals are relatively rare: a false peak signal would occur only if a peak call were issued and later rescinded; a false trough signal would occur only if a recession were expected to persist indefinitely. This methodological difference has a major impact on the interpretation of the results; what are called here false signals of the 1980 peak would be regarded as long lead times in the traditional approach. The variability of the lead (lag) time of the correct peak signal is less critical here than it is in following the traditional approach.

Tables 10.6, 10.7, and 10.8 are organized as follows: The first three columns follow the traditional approach, showing the date the first peak call was issued along with the predicted peak and trough dates; the next two columns show the date the first correct peak call was made and the trough date of that forecast; the final two columns show the date of the first correct trough call and, because the date the trough was expected was frequently changed, the date that the correct trough was first consistently identified.

The 1973–75 Recession

The poor performance in forecasting the severity of the 1973–75 recession has been described elsewhere (McNees 1976). The focus here will be on forecasting the timing of the turning points rather than the magnitudes of the changes as such. As discussed above, the criterion used to identify the peak will be the first predicted half-year decline in real GNP. For all data prior to the December 1985 benchmark revision, this criterion conforms to the official designation of 1973:IV (November) as the cyclical peak. Specifically, before that revision, it appeared that the level of real GNP in 1974:I was lower than in 1973:III. Based on prior experience, this suggests a peak occurred in 1973:IV. The criterion used to identify the trough will be the quarter prior to two consecutive quarters of expected increases in the unemployment rate of less than 0.3 percentage point.

Specifically, the quarterly average unemployment rate fell 0.4 and 0.2 percentage point in 1975:III and 1975:IV, respectively, after rising 0.6 percentage point in 1975:II. Based on postwar experience, this would suggest the trough occurred in 1975:II. To ensure that a perfect unemployment rate forecast would be regarded as having correctly identified the turning point, this date, rather than the March 1975 official date, is employed below. The criterion of the first half-year increase in real GNP would also place the trough in 1975:II.

Although muted murmurs of a 1974 recession could be heard as early as mid-1973, none of the forecasters examined here clearly signaled a recession. Even in their October forecasts, after the war in the Middle East had led to a 70 percent increase in the posted price of imported oil, the prevailing view continued to be one of sustained expansion. As shown in Table 10.6, it was not until November, the peak month, that two of these forecasters signaled a cyclical peak. One forecaster correctly signaled the peak was at hand (see columns 1 and 2). The other forecaster expected only a one-quarter recession starting in 1974:I, that is, that the first and only half-year decline in real GNP would occur 1973:IV to 1974:II. While this forecast is consistent with the most recent revised data, it is not consistent with any of the real GNP data prior to the 1985 rebenchmarking to 1982 dollars or with the official designation of 1973:IV as the peak; thus, it can be regarded as a false signal in terms of timing. It was not until the January forecast that this forecaster recognized 1973:IV as the peak (compare columns 1 and 4). In December, a third forecaster correctly recognized 1973:IV as the peak, but this forecaster was also expecting a very brief recession. Further evidence of the difficulty of calling the peak is the fact that the consensus forecast released in December did not show a recession. Thus, although none of these forecasters anticipated the 1973 peak, two correctly recognized it in the quarter in which it occurred, while most forecasters did not recognize the peak until after it had occurred.

The trough of this recession proved much more elusive. In the spring of 1974, after the oil embargo had ended, most forecasters reached the view that the recession was over. The June consensus forecast, for example, showed no large increases in the unemployment rate after 1974:II. This overly optimistic view of the recession as a mere "energy spasm" seemed to be confirmed by the actual path of the unemployment rate, which held essentially flat through May. The 0.3 percent increase in June was dismissed by most as an aberration related to seasonal adjustment difficulties in the month when students enter the labor force.

In July, however, after GNP revisions revealed a massive inventory buildup, one forecaster predicted the recession would last into 1975. The September consensus forecast, however, showed 1974:IV as the last large increase in the unemployment rate and it was not until October that a different forecaster first correctly called the trough quarter. By the end of the year, all forecasters agreed that an upturn would occur in mid-1975. Only one forecaster, however, held consistently to the correct trough date. In early 1975, the others became more

Table 10.6

Forecasting Cyclical Turning Points: 1973–75 Recession

	(1) First called peak	(2) Peak date called	(3) Corre- sponding trough	(4) First called correct peak	(5) Corre- sponding trough	(6) First called correct trough	(7) Final call of correct trough
Consensus A[a]	March 1974	1973:IV	1974:III	March 1974	1974:III	December 1974	June 1975
Forecaster 1	November 1973	1974:I	1974:II[b]	January 1974	1974:II	December 1974	December 1974
Forecaster 2	December 1973	1973:IV	1974:II	December 1973	1974:II	October 1974	July 1975
Forecaster 3	November 1973	1973:IV	1974:I	November 1973	1974:I	January 1975	July 1975

Notes: Dates are approximate because monthly forecasts are not available from all forecasters.

[a]Consensus A is the ASA/NBER consensus forecast.
[b]Based on real GNP criterion because unemployment data unavailable from November 1973 forecast.

pessimistic, moving the onset of the expansion back to 1975:III. It was not until June that the consensus forecast consistently recognized that the large increases in unemployment would end in 1975:II.

Thus, in contrast to the peak which was not anticipated but which was unequivocally recognized with a fairly short lag, prediction of the end of the recession was characterized by numerous false signals, predictions of troughs that never occurred. The early expectation was that the recession would be brief. This error was compounded in the spring of 1974 when all but one forecaster became even more optimistic. It was not until July that the first forecaster consistently indicated that the recession would last into 1975 and not until October that a forecaster first called the correct trough date. In December 1974, another forecaster correctly and consistently called the trough. All other forecasters became more pessimistic in early 1975 and did not finally settle consistently on the correct trough date until the expansion was already underway.

The 1980 Recession

The 1975–80 expansion was the longest peacetime expansion in more than one hundred years. It is perhaps not surprising, therefore, that premature forecasts of the end of the expansion were issued as early as October 1978. As shown in Table 10.7, these early recession forecasts envisioned a brief recession in 1979. This view was not widely shared—neither of the two consensus forecasts at the end of 1978 showed a recession. This changed in early 1979 after the revolution in Iran had disrupted the world oil market. By March, both of the consensus forecasts concurred with the two individual forecasters who had, since late in 1978, been expecting a brief recession in 1979. The third individual forecaster saw no recession until the June forecast, which correctly anticipated that real GNP in 1979:II would be lower than it was in 1978:IV.

All previous half-year declines in real GNP had been associated with a cyclical peak. When actual data released in July confirmed the expected half-year decline in real GNP, it seemed to confirm that a cyclical peak had occurred in early 1979. With hindsight, we now realize that this was a false signal—the only half-year decline in real GNP not associated with a recession. It seems a bit odd, however, to criticize forecasts for accurately predicting the drop in real GNP. The problem in this instance is less in the forecasts than in the use of the criterion of a half-year decline in real GNP to infer a recession signal from the forecasts. Nevertheless, it seems fair to say that the false expectation of an imminent recession followed from the accurate real GNP forecast. In September, even before the sharp increase in interest rates in October 1979, all these forecasters were anticipating large increases in the unemployment rate for three or four consecutive quarters. In fact, despite the decline in real GNP in early 1979, the unemployment rate inched up slowly in late 1979. The failure of these forecasts, in other words, was the failure to anticipate that the unemployment rate would

Table 10.7

Forecasting Cyclical Turning Points: 1980 Recession

	(1) First called peak	(2) Peak date called	(3) Corresponding trough	(4) First called correct peak	(5) Corresponding trough	(6) First called correct trough	(7) Final call of correct trough
Consensus A	March 1979	1979:III	1979:IV	March 1980	1980:III	March 1980	December 1980
Consensus B[a]	March 1979	1979:II	1979:IV[b]	February 1980	1980:III	November 1979[b]	November 1980
Forecaster 1	November 1978	1979:I	1979:IV	February 1980	1980:IV	October 1979	February 1981
Forecaster 2	October 1978	1979:II	1979:III[c]	January 1980	1980:IV	September 1979	October 1980
Forecaster 3	June 1979	1979:I	1980:II	March 1980	1980:IV	November 1979	October 1980

Notes: Dates are approximate because monthly forecasts are not available from all forecasters.

[a]Consensus B is the Blue Chip consensus forecast.
[b]Based on real GNP criterion because unemployment data unavailable before February 1980.
[c]Based on real GNP criterion as the peak was not confirmed by the unemployment criterion.

hold stable in the wake of declines in output, reflecting a collapse in labor productivity.

Although their peak predictions proved premature, none of these forecasters abandoned their recession forecasts. In December 1979, all were still expecting that a recession was already underway: all the individual forecasters had correctly identified 1979:IV as the peak quarter by the unemployment rate criterion. In their January or February forecasts, two individual forecasters and one consensus forecast first correctly identified 1980:I as the cyclical peak by the real GNP criterion.

The problems in predicting the peak of the 1980 recession illustrate that any assessment of turning point forecasts must be a joint evaluation of the criteria chosen to translate the forecast into a binary (expansion or recession) statement as well as the predictive content of the forecast. The failure of the fall 1979 forecasts was less a failure in forecasting real GNP than a failure of the criterion of a half-year decline in real GNP. A false recession signal also emerges when the unemployment rate criterion is employed but only to the extent that this criterion would date the peak in 1979:IV rather than the official date of 1980:I. By any criterion, forecasters had clearly given advance warning of the 1980 recession. The problem was that using either criterion, a series of premature false signals had been made for several months, undermining the credibility of the correct calls that were made at about the time of the peak.

The trough of the 1980 recession proved equally difficult to predict. The problem was not in the criterion adopted, as both criteria correctly identify 1980:III as the trough. Rather, the problem was that a long sequence of false trough calls, corresponding to the series of false peak calls, had been made in 1978 and 1979. The correct trough had, in fact, been identified in late 1979 by the individual forecasters and in early 1980 by the consensus forecasts. In 1980, after the recession had been correctly predicted and was underway, all forecasters became overly pessimistic about its duration. The 1980 recession is the shortest on record, and forecasters were either unable or unwilling to predict such an unprecedented event. The Consensus A forecasts in March and June of 1980 correctly called the 1980:III trough. At the same time, Consensus B and three individual forecasters were expecting a trough in 1980:IV. In September, the Consensus A forecast mistakenly joined the more pessimistic majority. It was not until October 1980 that two individual forecasters consistently called the correct 1980:III trough. It was not until late in 1980 that the two consensus forecasts correctly perceived that the string of large increases in the unemployment rate had ended in 1980:III. The problem of overestimating the length of the 1980 recession was most dramatically illustrated by one forecaster who continued to forecast large increases in the unemployment rate until February 1981, more than a half-year after the 1980 trough and less than six months before the next official peak.

Table 10.8

Forecasting Cyclical Turning Points: 1981–82 Recession

	(1) First called peak	(2) Peak date called[a]	(3) Corresponding trough	(4) First called correct peak	(5) Corresponding trough	(6) First called correct trough	(7) Final call of correct trough
Consensus A	September 1981	1981:II	1981:IV	March 1982	1982:II	December 1982	December 1982
Consensus B	July 1981	1981:II	1981:III[b]	December 1981	1982:I	November 1982	November 1982
Forecaster 1	April 1981	1981:II	1981:III[b]	September 1981	1982:I	October 1982	February 1983
Forecaster 2	June 1981	1981:II	1981:III[b]	October 1981	1982:I	October 1982	February 1983
Forecaster 3	June 1981	1981:II	1981:III[b]	September 1981	1982:I	October 1982	October 1982
Forecaster 4	July 1981	1981:II	1981:III	November 1981	1982:II	October 1982	January 1983

Notes: Columns 1 through 3 are based on the real GNP criterion. By that criterion and preliminary GNP data, the peak occurred in 1981:II so there were no false signals. Columns 4 and 5 are based on the unemployment rate criterion, which accords with the officially designated peak in 1981:III. By this criterion there were also no false signals. Dates for Consensus A are approximate because monthly forecasts do not exist.

[a]Based on preliminary real GNP data, the real GNP criterion places the peak in 1981:II.
[b]Based on real GNP criterion as the peak signal was not confirmed by unemployment rate criterion.

The 1981–82 Recession

In sharp contrast to the previous peak, which had been prematurely advertised well before it occurred, the 1981 peak was not widely anticipated. This may reflect the fact that the 1980–81 expansion was the shortest since 1919–20. Like the 1973 peak, the exact dating of the 1981 peak by the real GNP criterion depends on whether preliminary or revised data are used. Unlike the earlier experience, when the preliminary data suggested the officially designated peak date and the revised data did not, the preliminary real GNP data suggested a somewhat different peak date in 1981. One of the earliest recession signs was issued in April but was largely ignored because (*i*) it predicted only a one-quarter recession; (*ii*) it came from the same pessimistic forecaster who a few months earlier had been questioning whether the 1980 recession had ended; and (*iii*) this recession call was rescinded the next month. Two forecasters again showed one-quarter recessions in June (see Table 10.8). These hesitant recession calls were not confirmed by the unemployment criterion but were reinforced in July when the preliminary estimates showed real GNP had declined 1.9 percentage points in the second quarter.

The four individual forecasters and Consensus B all expected smaller gains in the third quarter and thus, by the real GNP criterion, issued a one-quarter recession call in their July forecasts. The same conclusion appeared in the Consensus A September forecast. Unlike the current revised data, the preliminary data released in October confirmed their expectation that real GNP in 1981:III would fall below 1981:I. On the basis of prior experience, this suggested a peak near 1981:II. In their October forecasts, all of the individual forecasters expected a three-quarter recession starting in 1981:II and ending in 1982:I. Thus, on the basis of the real GNP criterion and preliminary estimates of real GNP, the peak occurred in 1981:II, was first predicted in April, but was not widely recognized until July or September.

The unemployment rate criterion, like the revised real GNP data, correctly dates the peak in 1981:III, as large increases in the unemployment rate occurred in 1981:IV and 1982:I. By this criterion, two individual forecasters first recognized the peak in their September forecasts. By the end of 1981, all individual forecasters and Consensus B agreed on the correct peak. However, Consensus A did not call the correct peak until March 1982. Thus, while there were no premature false signals of the 1981 peak, there was also no significant prior anticipation. The best that can be said is that many forecasters recognized the peak rather quickly as it was occurring, but that it was not widely acknowledged until several months after it occurred. This optimistic bias may have reflected either support for the incoming President's economic program or disbelief that the 1980–81 expansion would last only a year.

Once recognized, the 1981 recession was generally expected to be brief. In December, views of the trough date ranged from 1981:IV to 1982:II. The view that the recession would last less than a year persisted until July. The first forecasts that the trough would not come until 1982:IV were made in October. By the end of the year, both consensus forecasts shared the view that 1982:IV would be the trough. Unfortunately, as the quarter evolved, three of the four individual forecasts incorrectly extended the recession into 1983:I. It was not until February 1983 that all forecasters consistently agreed that a large increase in the unemployment rate would not occur in 1983:I, the view that only one forecaster had espoused consistently since October 1982.

Thus, despite a belated, unwarranted wave of pessimism that engulfed some but not most forecasters, a pattern of undue optimism characterized forecasts of the 1981–82 recession. The recession was a year old before it was first suggested that the recession would match the 1974–75 recession in duration, and this view did not become widespread until the month of the trough. Whether this overly optimistic assessment was due to a misjudging of the stimulative effects of the 1981 tax cuts relative to the impact of monetary restraint or simply to the fact that real GNP increased in 1982:II is not clear.

Evaluation of Forecasters

Consistent with earlier studies, none of these forecasters dominates the others for all, or even most, variables. Virtually every forecaster excels for some variable(s). For example, among the early-quarter forecasts, BEA excels for IPD and real state and local government purchases; Chase for personal consumption expenditures for nondurable goods and services, and current dollar federal government purchases; DRI for real nonresidential fixed investment and nominal GNP; GSU for the CPI, real federal government purchases, and current dollar change in business inventories; RSQE for real residential fixed investment and the 90-day Treasury bill rate; and WEFA for personal consumption of durable goods, real net exports, the federal government deficit, household employment and the unemployment rate for longer horizons. (Tables of mean absolute errors for 21 variables during the period from 1976:II through 1987:IV are available upon request from the author.) Consequently, evaluation of forecasters depends greatly on which variables are of most interest to the forecast user.

Even for a specific variable, however, it is often impossible to identify a best forecaster without being quite specific about what forecast horizon is of most interest. Consider, for example, the MAEs of real GNP forecasts shown in Table 10.9. At least three different forecasters could plausibly claim to have been the most accurate for at least one forecast horizon. Even for a specific variable and horizon, it can be difficult to generalize about the best forecaster. The differences in summary error statistics between the best forecaster and second best, or often even between the best and worst, are commonly too small to be regarded as reliable indicators of future performance. This conclusion does not imply that "anyone's forecast is as good as anyone else's" but only that the past perfor-

Table 10.9

Real GNP Forecasts
Mean Absolute Errors 1976:II to 1987:IV
Percentage Points, Annual Rates of Growth

Forecast Horizon	Q1	Q2	Q3	Q4	Q5	Q6	Q7	Q8
				Early-quarter forecasters				
BEA	2.9	2.2	2.0	1.7	1.5	1.4	1.3	1.2
BMARK	3.3	2.6	2.4	2.0				
CHASE	3.0	2.2	2.0	1.8	1.6	1.5	1.4	1.3
DRI	2.8	2.0	1.7	1.5	1.4	1.3	1.3	1.3
GSU	2.4	2.0	1.8	1.6	1.4	1.3	1.1	1.1
RSQE	2.2	2.0	1.8	1.6	1.3	1.3		
WEFA	2.9	2.2	1.9	1.6	1.5	1.3	1.2	1.2
				Mid-quarter forecasters				
ASA/NBER	2.5	2.1	1.8	1.5	1.3			
KEDI	2.7	2.1	1.8	1.6	1.4	1.5	1.6	1.6
UCLA	2.3	1.9	1.7	1.5	1.5			
WEFA	2.3	1.9	1.6	1.5	1.3	1.2	1.1	1.1
				Late-quarter forecaster				
DRI	1.8	1.8	1.6	1.4	1.2	1.2	1.3	1.2

mances of this group of prominent forecasts are, on average, often quite similar.

How good are these forecasts? Clearly, there have been times like 1974 and 1982 when the errors have been extremely large. But forecasts are bound to be wrong in an absolute sense. The real issue is whether more accurate forecasts could realistically have been made: if not, dissatisfaction with their accuracy is simply a dissatisfaction with the inevitable uncertainty of the future; if so, criticism of the forecasts is well deserved.

Since 1976, Charles Nelson has issued forecasts based on a simple, low-cost extrapolative ARIMA model to be used as a benchmark for evaluating macroeconomic forecasts. These forecasts are generated mechanically, without any adjustments even when they appear to the forecaster highly likely to be incorrect. The other six early-quarter forecasters are measured against the Benchmark forecast in Table 10.10. Clearly, one can either regard the glass as half full or half empty. On the one hand, with only one exception (Chase's IPD forecasts), the BMARK forecasts are distinctly less accurate than the others. On average, the margin of superiority is fairly large (about 20 percent) for real GNP and nominal GNP and much smaller (less than 10 percent) for IPD. On the other hand, it is also clear that considerable effort, expense, and expertise is required to shave a few tenths

Table 10.10

Evaluation of BMARK Forecast Percentage Reduction in MAE[a]

		Horizon (quarters)						
		Cumulative changes			One-quarter change			
Variable		2Q	3Q	4Q	1Q	2Q	3Q	4Q
Real GNP	High	23	29	25	27	3	0	3
	Mean	19	22	18	18	0	−6	−4
	Low	15	17	10	9	−7	−13	−9
IPD	High	33	25	23	23	29	25	21
	Mean	10	6	3	14	7	0	5
	Low	0	−9	−15	0	−14	−19	−11
Real GNP	High	28	28	30	29	11	0	3
	Mean	24	20	19	18	2	−6	−2
	Low	13	3	0	8	−14	−24	−10

[a]Percentage reduction in MAE $= 1 - \dfrac{MAE_i}{MAE \, (BMARK)} \cdot 100$

where MAE_i = Mean absolute error of forecaster i

MAE (BMARK) = Mean absolute error of BMARK forecast

Mean is the average for the six early-quarter forecasters: BEA, CHASE, DRI, GSU, RSQE, and WEFA.

of a percentage point off summary error statistics. For those who do not place much value on this extra precision, a simple, low-cost alternative forecasting procedure is available.

These conclusions are based on the accuracy of forecasts of *cumulative* changes over one-quarter, half-year, three-quarter, and one-year time spans. It is worth noting that, beyond the first quarter, BMARK forecasts are as accurate as the other forecasts of quarterly changes. This result suggests that forecasters know little about the future *quarterly pattern* of these macroeconomic variables beyond the information that can be extracted from their own past history. Nevertheless, macroeconomic forecasts are apparently able to anticipate sustained periods of deviation from the extrapolative trends. This is consistent with the view that there is little to be gained from scrutinizing differences among forecasts of any particular future quarter. The informational content of the forecasts is in the future levels, or cumulative changes from the present, not in the quarterly patterns by which the predicted level will be reached.

Summary and Conclusions

Forecasting errors exhibit great variability over time. For example, based on the CEA's yearly forecasts from 1962 through 1987, errors are usually "small"— more than half are less than 1 percentage point—and almost always "tolerable"— 90 percent were less than 2 percentage points. Nevertheless, huge outliers do occasionally appear, such as the rates of real growth and inflation in 1974 and nominal GNP in 1982. Large improvements in forecasting accuracy seem more likely to come from reducing these egregious errors rather than from shaving a few tenths off the normal-sized errors.

Within this wide variation, annual forecasts of real GNP and the inflation rate have improved over time. Summary error measures have declined slightly in absolute terms but even more relative to either naive standards of comparison or the variability of the actual outcomes. Improvement is not clear, however, for nominal GNP forecasts. Those errors have increased somewhat in absolute terms but have declined relative to the common standards of comparison.

The evidence does not suggest that private forecasts, as represented by the median of the ASA/NBER survey, have been more accurate than the government forecasts made by the CEA. Over the past 19 years, the government forecasts of nominal GNP were slightly more accurate, the private survey of forecasts of real GNP slightly more accurate, and the inflation rate forecasts about equally accurate. Neither of the forecasts exhibits "bias," a systematic tendency to either over- or underestimate. The pervasive tendency to underestimate the inflation rate in the 1970s was largely offset by a tendency to overestimate inflation in the 1980s.

Generalizations about the accuracy of quarterly forecasts since 1976 are elusive not only because of variability over time but also because of differences across time horizons and among variables. For example, even though the accuracy of a forecast of any given time span tends to decrease as a forecast horizon increases, for some variables longer time spans are easier to forecast than shorter time spans. Errors of forecasts of next quarter's real GNP growth rate (about 2¼ to 3 percentage points at annual rates) are larger than those of forecasts one year ahead (about 1½ to 1¾ percentage points) or two years ahead (only about 1¼ percentage points at an annual rate).

Real growth rates over longer time spans are less variable and therefore easier to forecast. This does not hold for all variables. Errors in forecasts of next quarter's CPI growth rate (1 to 1½ percentage points) are smaller than those for one year ahead (1½ to 2 percentage points) or two years ahead (2½ to 2¾ percentage points). These results reflect differing tendencies for error accumulation versus error offset. Because inflation forecast errors are so strongly serially correlated, last period's error could be used to improve future forecasts. Because real GNP forecast errors do not exhibit stable serial correlations, last period's real GNP forecast error does not seem useful for improving current forecasts.

As previous studies have also shown, no one forecaster dominates all others in terms of accuracy. Each of the most prominent forecasters excels for some variable over some horizon, or even one variable over all horizons, but no one for all, or even most, variables and horizons. Even when a superior forecaster can be identified, the margin of superiority is typically so small that it is far from certain it will be sustained in the future. Thus, a determination of the "best" forecast must rest upon which variables and horizons are of most interest to the forecast user.

With one exception, all of the forecasts considered in this study were generated with the help of large-scale, "structural" econometric models. At the same time that skepticism about the value of such models has grown, especially in the academic community, the use of these models in business and government has proliferated worldwide (Klein 1988). Since 1976, univariate, statistical equations—ARIMA models—developed by Charles Nelson have been used mechanically to generate forecasts of nominal GNP and IPD and thus, implicitly, of real GNP. The MAEs of the conventional forecasters were, on average, about 20 percent smaller than BMARK's for nominal and real GNP and less than 10 percent for IPD. The only forecasts inferior to BMARK were one forecaster's IPD forecasts. In contrast to the results frequently obtained for financial market variables (such as interest rates, exchange rates, or stock prices), the evidence suggests that "experts" do predict important nonfinancial macroeconomic variables (like real GNP growth and the inflation rate) more accurately than extrapolative statistical models (such as the "random walk" or ARIMA models).

The most obvious conclusion to be drawn from the experience in forecasting the three most recent business cycles is the broad similarity between the performances in the two major recessions (1973–75 and 1981–82) and the differences between those experiences and the brief 1980 recession. In both 1973 and 1981, forecasters recognized the peak at about the time that it was occurring. There were few clear prior warnings but also fairly quick, widespread recognition that a recession period had begun. In particular, forecasters gave few false peak signals, early warnings of an earlier or later cyclical peak.

The 1980 experience was exactly the opposite. Warnings of a recession in 1979 were issued as early as late 1978, but it was not until their forecasts in January 1980, the officially designated peak, that most forecasters pinpointed the exact date of the peak. The tradeoff between timeliness and accuracy is striking. These forecasts provided no clear advance warnings of the two major recessions but also few false Cassandras. No one could say there were no advance warnings of the 1980 recession. The difficulty in that instance was that the warnings had been so imprecise in dating the peak that they seemed to have been largely ignored.

References

Artis, M. J. 1987. "How Accurate is the World Economic Outlook? A Post Mortem on Short-Term Forecasting at the International Monetary Fund." *World Economic Outlook: Staff Studies*. International Monetary Fund. December 18. Mimeo.

Burns, Sir Terence. 1986. "The interpretation and use of economic predictions." *Proceedings of the Royal Society of London*, vol. 407, pp. 103–125.

Daub, Mervin. 1987. *Canadian Economic Forecasting*. Kingston and Montreal: McGill-Queen's University Press.

Fair, Ray, and Robert Shiller. 1987. "The Information Content of Ex Ante Forecasts." Presented at American Economic Association Annual Meeting, Chicago, Ill., December.

Grimm, Bruce T., and Albert A. Hirsch. 1983. "The Impact of the 1976 NIPA Benchmark Revision on the Structure and Predictive Accuracy of the BEA Quarterly Econometric Model." In *The U.S. National Income and Product Accounts: Selected Topics*. Edited by Murray F. Foss. National Bureau of Economic Research. Chicago: University of Chicago Press.

Klein, Lawrence R. 1988. "Past, Present, and Possible Future of Macroeconometric Models and Their Uses." Mimeo.

McNees, Stephen K. 1976. "The Forecasting Performance in the 1970s." *New England Economic Review* (July/August): 29–40.

———. 1986. "Estimating GNP: The Trade-Off between Timeliness and Accuracy." *New England Economic Review* (January/February): 3–10.

———. 1987. "Forecasting Cyclical Turning Points: The Record in the Past Three Recessions." *New England Economic Review* (March/April): 31–40.

———. 1988. "How Accurate are Macroeconomic Forecasts?" *New England Economic Review* (July/August): 15–36.

McNees, Stephen K., and John Ries. 1983. "The Track Record of Macroeconomic Forecasts." *New England Economic Review* (November/December): 5–18.

Moore, Geoffrey H. 1983. *Business Cycles, Inflation, and Forecasting*. 2d ed. National Bureau of Economic Research Studies in Business Cycles, No. 24, especially chapter 26, pp. 433–51.

———. 1985. "Forecasting Unemployment with the Leading Employment Index." *Economic Forecasts* 2 (12).

Neftci, Salih N. 1982. "Optimal Predictions of Cyclical Downturns." *Journal of Economic Dynamics* 4 (3).

Nelson, Charles R. 1984. "A Benchmark for the Accuracy of Econometric Forecasts of GNP." *Business Economics*. April, pp. 52–58.

Palash, Carl J., and Lawrence J. Radecki. 1985. "Using Monetary and Financial Variables to Predict Cyclical Downturns." *Federal Reserve Bank of New York Quarterly Review* (Summer): 36–45.

Zarnowitz, Victor. 1979. "An Analysis of Annual and Multiperiod Quarterly Forecasts of Aggregate Income, Output, and the Price Level." *The Journal of Business* 52 (January): 1–33.

Zarnowitz, Victor, and Geoffrey H. Moore. 1986. "Forecasting Recessions Under the Gramm-Rudman-Hollings Law." NBER Working Paper No. 2066.

V

CYCLICAL INDICATORS AND THEIR APPLICATIONS: CURRENT METHODOLOGICAL ISSUES

11

Major Macroeconomic Variables and Leading Indexes: Some Estimates of Their Interrelations

Victor Zarnowitz and Phillip Braun

Background and Objectives

How the economy moves over time depends on its structure, institutions, and policies, all of which are subject to large historical changes. It would be surprising if the character of the business cycle did *not* change in response to such far-reaching developments as the great contraction of the 1930s and the post-depression reforms, the expansion of government and private service industries, the development of fiscal and other built-in stabilizers, and the increased use and role of discretionary macroeconomic policies. It is consistent with our priors that the data for the United States and other developed market-oriented countries generally support the hypothesis that business contractions were less frequent, shorter, and milder after World War II than before (Gordon 1986; Zarnowitz 1989).

Although business cycles have moderated, they retain a high degree of continuity, which shows up most clearly in the comovements and timing sequences among the main cyclical processes.[1] An important aspect of this continuity is the role of the variables that tend to move ahead of aggregate output and employment in the course of the business cycle. The composite index of leading indicators combines the main series representing these variables. Several studies point to the existence of a relatively close and stable relationship between prior changes in this index and changes in macroeconomic activity (Vaccara and Zarnowitz 1977; Auerbach 1982; Zarnowitz and Moore 1982; Diebold and Rudebusch 1987). Yet, the currently popular, small reduced-form macro models make little or no use of the leading indicators.[2] We suspect that the reason is lack of familiarity. The role of the indicators is probably often misperceived as being purely symptomatic. Heterogeneous combinations of such series resist easy theoretical applications. On a deeper level, the notion that the private market economy is inherently stable led to an emphasis on the role of the monetary and fiscal disturbances. Interest in the potential of stabilization policies had a similar effect in that it stimulated work on models dominated by factors considered to be amenable to government control.

This orientation is understandably appealing but can easily become one-sided and error-prone, both theoretically and statistically. For example, a simple vector autoregressive (VAR) model in log differences of real GNP, money, and government expenditures suggests the presence of strong lagged monetary and fiscal effects on output.[3] However, it is easy to show that these relationships are definitely misspecified. One way to demonstrate this is by adding changes in a leading index that excludes monetary and financial components so as not to overlap any of the other variables. In this expanded model, the dominant effects on output come from the past movements of the leading index, while the roles of the other variables (including the lagged values of output growth itself) are greatly reduced (see Results section below). In general, omitting relevant variables in a VAR will cause the standard exogeneity tests, impulse responses, and variance decompositions to be biased, as shown in Lütkepohl (1982) and Braun and Mittnik (1985).

The first objective of this paper is to examine the lead-lag interactions within larger sets of important macroeconomic variables, including interest and inflation rates along with output, monetary and fiscal variables, and a nonduplicative leading index. The rationale for including this index is twofold: (1) The changes in the leading index can be interpreted broadly as representing the early collective outcomes of investment and production (also, less directly, consumption) decisions. As such, they presumably reflect the dynamic forces that shape the basic processes within the private economy and account for the continuity of business cycles. Both aggregate demand and aggregate supply shifts are involved, but the demand effects may be stronger in the short run. (2) The addition of the leading index helps us overcome the omitted variables bias. The index stands for a number of important factors that would otherwise be omitted. It would not be practical to include the several individual series to represent these variables.

We work with equations that include up to six variables plus constant terms and time trends. They are estimated on quarterly series, each taken with four lags, which means using up large numbers of degrees of freedom. Given the size of the available data samples, it is not possible for such models to accommodate more variables and still retain a chance to produce estimates of parameters in which one could have some confidence. It is, of course, easy to think of additional, possibly important variables whose omission might cause some serious misspecifications. All vector autoregressive (VAR) models face this dilemma, but the only way to avoid it is by assuming a full structural model which could be still more deficient. We seek some partial remedies in alternative specifications guided by economic theory and history as well as comparisons with related results in the literature.

Although the format adopted is that of a VAR model, the implied system-wide dynamics, i.e., impulse response functions and variance decompositions, are beyond the scope of this study. These statistics seek to describe behavior in reaction to innovations, require longer series of consistent data than are actually available,[4] and are probably often very imprecise even for smaller systems (cf. Zellner 1985 and Runkle 1987 with discussion). In contrast, there is sufficient information to estimate the individual equations well, even with more lagged terms. We find that much can be learned from attention to the quality and implications of these estimates, which are logically prior to inferences on overall dynamics but carry no commitment to the particular interpretations of a VAR model.

The second and related objective is to extend the analysis to the periods between the two world wars and earlier in another effort to study the continuity and change in U.S. business cycles. To evaluate any persistent shifts or the secular evolution in the patterns of macroeconomic fluctuation, it is of course necessary to cover long stretches of varied historical experience. Estimates of the interrelations among the selected variables are calculated from quarterly seasonally adjusted data for three periods: 1886–1914, 1919–40, and 1949–82. Generally, we look for the similarities and differences within the three periods which are suggested by this exercise.

Historical data are scanty and deficient, which inevitably creates some difficult choices and problems. The next part of this chapter discusses this and lists the variables and series used. The following section discusses the applied methods and presents tests that determine what transformations must be used on any of the series to validate our statistical procedures. Then the results are examined, focusing on simple exogeneity and neutrality tests for a succession of models as well as on interperiod comparisons. The final section sums up our conclusions and views on the need for further work.

Data

The Selected Variables and Their Representations

Table 11.1 serves as a summary of the information on the data used in this study. It defines the variables and identifies the time series by title, period, symbol, and source. Some notes on the derivation of the underlying data are included as well.

The table includes 11 different variables and 23 segments of the corresponding series, counting one per time period (columns 2 and 3). No equation contains more than six variables. Some variables have different representations across the three periods covered because consistent data are not available for them. Further, unit root tests indicate that, in some cases, levels of a series ought to be used in one period and differences in another. (These tests and the required transformations are discussed in the next section which covers the statistical framework). As shown in column 4, natural logarithms are taken of all series except the commercial paper rate. Federal expenditures in 1886–1914, the fiscal index in 1949–82, and the interest rate in both of these periods are level series; in all other cases first difference series are used.

Table 11.1

List of Variables, Symbols, and Sources of Data

Number (1)	Variable[a] (2)	Periods[b] (3)	Form[c] (4)	Symbol[d] (5)	Source[e] (6)	Notes on derivation[f] (7)
1	Real GNP (1972 dol.)	1,2,3	$\Delta\ln$	q	B&G	Annual data from F&S (1982) and Kuznets (1961) and Commerce NIPA (1981 ff. since 1889), interpolated quarterly by Chow-Lin (1971) method using the Persons (1931) index of industrial production and trade.
2	Implicit price deflator	1,2,3	$\Delta\ln$	p	B&G	(nominal GNP/real GNP) x 100
3	Monetary base	1,2,3	$\Delta\ln$	b	B&G	Based on data in F&S (1970, 1963) through 1914 and Gordon and Veitch 1986 for 1949–82.
4	Money supply, M1	2,3	$\Delta\ln$	m_1	B&G	1919–46: Gordon and Veitch 1986; 1947–58: old M1, FRB. 1958–82: new M1, FRB.
5	Money supply, M2	1,2,3	$\Delta\ln$	m_2	B&G	1886–1907: F&S 1970; 1907–1914: 1919–80: Gordon 1982; 1980–82: FRB.
6	Commercial paper rate	1,3	In level	l	B&G	1886–89: in New York City, from Macaulay 1938; 1890–1914, 1919–80: 4–6 month prime. From Gordon 1982. 1981–82: 6 month, from FRB.
7	do.	2	Δ	i	B&G	do.
8	Federal expenditures	1	In level	GX	Firestone	Based on Daily Treasury Statements of the United States (see Firestone 1960, app, pp. 76–86, and data, seasonally adjusted. pp. 97–111).

9	do.	2	Δln	gx	Firestone	do.
10	Fiscal index	3	level	G	Blanchard	From Blanchard 1985 and Blanchard and Watson 1986, app. 2.2. Based on data for government spending, debt, and taxes.
11	Diffussion index, 75 leading series	1	Δln	ℓdc	Moore	Analyzed in Moore 1961, vol. I, ch. 7. Based on specific cycle phases. Data from Moore 1961, vol. 2, p. 172.
12	Amplitude-adjusted (composite) index, six leading series	2	Δln	ℓd	Shiskin	Analyzed in Shiskin 1961, pp. 43–55. Data from NBER files.
13	Composite index of leading indicators	3	Δln	ℓ	Commerce	The composite index of 12 leading indicators minus three components: M2 in constant dollars, change in business and consumer credit outstanding, and the index of stock prices, from BCD.

[a] All variables are used as quarterly series.

[b] Period 1: 1886–1914; period 2: 1919–40; period 3: 1949–82.

[c] Δln: first difference in natural logarithm; Δ: first difference.

[d] Small letters are used for rates of change or absolute changes; capital letters are used for levels of the series.

[e] B&G: Balke, Nathan S. and Robert J. Gordon 1986, Appendix B, Historical Data. Firestone: Firestone, John M. 1960, Appendix Tables. Blanchard: Blanchard, Olivier J. and Mark W. Watson, 1986, Appendix 2.2. Moore: Moore, Geoffrey, H. 1961. Shiskin: Shiskin, Julius 1961. Commerce: U.S. Department of Commerce, Bureau of Economic Analysis.

[f] F&S: Friedman, Milton and Anna J. Schwartz, 1970.
NIPA: National Income and Product Accounts.
FRB: Federal Reserve Bulletin.
NBER: National Bureau of Economic Research.
BCD: Business Conditions Digest (U.S. Department of Commerce).

Lowercase letters serve as symbols for variables cast in form of first differences, capital letters for those cast in levels (Table 11.1, column 5). The series relating to output (q), prices (p), the alternative monetary aggregates (b, m_1, m_2), and interest (I or i) are staple ingredients of small reduced-form or VAR models. They appear numbered in the table on lines 1–7. Of the additional series, three represent fiscal variables (8–10). For the postwar period, there is an index combining federal spending, debt, and taxes (G). For the interwar and prewar periods, there are two segments of the federal expenditures series (gx and GX, respectively).

Finally, there are three different indexes of leading indicators (11–13). The only such series presently available for 1886–1914 is a diffusion index based on specific cycles in individual indicators (ℓdc). The composite indexes for 1919–40 and, particularly, for 1949–82 (ℓd and ℓ, respectively) are much more satisfactory.

Data Sources and Problems

The "standard" historical estimates of GNP before World War II, based mainly on the work of Kuznets, Kendrick, and Gallman, are annual at most. We use the new quarterly series for real GNP and the implicit price deflator from Balke and Gordon (1986).[5] These data are constructed from the standard series by means of quarterly interpolators which include the Persons 1931 index of industrial production and trade before 1930, the FRB industrial production index for 1930–40, constant terms, and linear time trends. The use of interpolations based on series with narrower coverage than GNP is a source of unavoidable error if the unit period is to be shorter than a year.[6]

The historical annual estimates of U.S. income and output leave much to be desired, but it is difficult to improve on them because the required information simply does not exist. The series have been recently reevaluated, leading to new estimates by Romer (1986 and 1987) and Balke and Gordon (1988). Romer's method imposes certain structural characteristics of the U.S. economy in the post-World War II period on the pre-World War I data. This produces results that contradict the evidence of postwar moderation of the business cycle by prejudging the issue (Lebergott 1986; Weir 1986; Balke and Gordon 1988). It is mainly for this reason that we do not use Romer's data. The basic source of historical monetary statistics (monthly since May 1907, biennial earlier) is Friedman and Schwartz 1970. Here, too, interpolations based on related series are applied in early years. The data for money (like those for income, output, and prices) improve over time but are never without serious problems. The interwar and postwar series are produced by the Federal Reserve Board (FRB).

Market interest rates are more easily and much better measured than the macroeconomic aggregates and indexes on our list. The commercial paper rate series (Macaulay 1938 and FRB) is of good quality, at least in a comparative sense.

The Blanchard fiscal index is designed to measure "the effect of fiscal policy on aggregate demand at given interest rates" (Blanchard and Watson 1986, 149). This series moves countercyclically most of the time, hence presumably retains in large measure elements of built-in tax-and-transfer stabilizers. For the earlier periods, no comparable comprehensive index is available, and we use the series on federal expenditures from Firestone (1960).

From the Commerce Department's leading index for 1949–82, we exclude real money balances (M2 deflated by the consumer price index) and change in business and consumer credit outstanding. This is done to avoid overlaps or conflicts with the monetary variables covered in our equations. The stock price component (Standard & Poor's index of 500 common stocks) may be strongly affected by monetary and fiscal developments and, adopting a conservative bias, we remove it as well. This newly adjusted composite index consists of nine series representing primarily the early stages of fixed capital investment, inventory investment, and marginal adjustments of employment and production.[7]

The only composite index of leading indicators available in the literature for the interwar period covers six series: average workweek, new orders for durable manufacturers, nonfarm housing starts, commercial and industrial construction contracts, new business incorporations, and Standard and Poor's index of stock prices. The index is presented and discussed in Shiskin (1961). Its method of construction is very similar to that used presently for the Commerce index.[8] The coverage of the Shiskin index, though narrower, also resembles that of the postwar index, particularly when the money and credit components are deleted from the latter. The one major difference is that the interwar index is based on changes in the component series over five-month spans, whereas the postwar index is based on month-to-month changes.[9]

Unfortunately, no composite index of leading indicators exists for the pre-World War I period. To compute such an index from historical data would certainly be worth while but also laborious; the project must be reserved for the future. In the meantime, we report on some experimental work with the only available series that summarizes the early cyclical behavior of a set of individual leading indicators. The set consists of 75 individual indicators whose turning points have usually led at business cycle peaks and troughs. It covers such diverse areas as business profits and failures, financial market transactions and asset prices, bank clearings, loans and deposits, sensitive materials prices, inventory investment, new orders for capital goods, construction contracts, and the average workweek. Moore (1961) presents a diffusion index showing the percentage of these series expanding in each month from 1885 to 1940. The index is based on cyclical turns in each of its components: a series is simply counted as rising during each month of a specific cycle expansion (and declining otherwise). Clearly, the type of smoothing implicit in this index construction is ill-suited for our purposes as it was designed for a very different task of historical timing analysis. Nevertheless, for lack of any other measure, we use this diffusion index by cumulating its deviations from 50 and taking log differences of the results.

The Statistical Framework

Method of Estimation

Conflicting macromodels draw support not only from different theoretical rationalizations of economic behavior but also, when implemented econometrically, from different empirical priors imposed on the data. Dissatisfaction with the "incredible identification" of existing large-scale simultaneous equation systems led to the recent popularity of vector autoregressions, which treat all variables as endogenous and shun unfounded *a priori* restrictions. The method has been used in attempts to discriminate among alternative explanations of money-income causality (cf. Sims 1980).

This paper examines the interactions within a larger set of macroeconomic variables than that considered in the money-income causality studies. The particular statistics that interest us in this context are exogeneity and neutrality tests for the selected macrovariables within the different time periods.

Define $x^i_{s,t}$ as a generic variable with s denoting the time series $(q,p,b...)$ and i denoting the time frame (prewar, interwar, postwar). For each series and time frame, we estimate ordinary least squares regressions of the form (the superscript i is hencefore omitted for simplicity):

(1)
$$x_{s,t} = \alpha_s + \beta_s t + \sum_{r=1}^{R} \sum_{j=1}^{J} \gamma_{r,j} x_{r,t-j} + e_t$$

where $R = 3, \ldots$ up to 6 series and $J = 4$ quarterly lags. The neutrality test is a t-statistic which tests the null hypothesis

(2)
$$H_o: \sum_{j=1}^{J} \gamma_{s,j} = 0$$

against the alternative that the sum is not equal to zero. The exogeneity test is an F-statistic which tests

(3)
$$H_o: \gamma_{s,1} = \ldots = \gamma_{s,k} = 0$$

against the alternative that not all γ are equal to zero.

Unit Roots and Transformations

Since the work of Nelson and Plosser (1982), much interest has been paid to the existence of unit roots in macroeconomic time series. The magnitudes of the secular and cyclical components of these series receive primary attention in the work of Cochrane (1988) and Campbell and Mankiw (1987). Sims, Stock, and Watson (1986) also consider the role unit roots play in hypothesis testing with VARs. They show that, to interpret correctly exogeneity and neutrality tests using standard asymptotic theory, it is necessary to transform the data to zero-mean stationary series. Moreover, Stock and Watson (1987) shed new light on the long debated problem of money-income causality by taking nonstationarities into account. Therefore, because of both an explicit interest in the results and also the necessity of having stationary series to employ standard asymptotic theory, we calculate a set of unit root tests.

We test the null hypothesis

$$(4) \qquad x_{s,t} = \sum_{j=1}^{J} p_{s,j} x_{s,t} + e_t,$$

against the general alternative

$$(5) \qquad x_{s,t} = \mu_s + \psi_s t + \sum_{j=1}^{J} p_{s,j} x_{s,t} + e_t$$

with $\sum p_{s,i} < 1$ and, depending on the test, with and without ψ_s restricted to be zero. Rejection of the null hypothesis implies that the series does not contain a unit root and is stationary either around its mean, when ψ_s is restricted to be zero, or around a time trend, when ψ_s is not so restricted.

The unit root tests are presented in Tables 11.2, 11.3, and 11.4 for the postwar, interwar, and prewar sample periods, respectively. Part A of each table includes the tests for a single unit root for each series, calculated by using levels. Part B contains tests for a second unit root calculated by using first differences.

Because there does not exist a uniformly most powerful test for unit roots, we use two different sets of test statistics. To test the hypothesis that a series is stationary around its mean, we estimate the Dickey-Fuller $\hat{\tau}_\mu$ statistic (column 2 in Tables 11.2, 11.3, and 11.4) and the Stock-Watson q^μ_f statistic (column 3). These statistics restrict ψ_s in the alternative hypothesis (eq. 5) to be zero. To test the hypothesis that a series is stationary around a linear time trend, we estimate the Dickey-Fuller $\hat{\tau}_T$ statistic (column 4) and the Stock-Watson q^T_f statistic (column 5).

Table 11.2

Univariate Tests for Unit Roots and Time Trends
Postwar Sample: Quarterly Data, 1949:1–1982:4

A. Tests on levels[b]

Series[a]	Unit root test statistics[c]				t-statistics[d]	
	$\hat{\tau}_\mu$	q^μ_f	$\hat{\tau}_\tau$	q^τ_f	Time	Constant
Q	−1.92	−0.61	−1.90	−7.82	2.17+	2.04+
M1	4.21	1.39	0.53	0.44	0.71	−3.23*
M2	2.22	0.41	−1.56	−2.92	2.09+	−1.74°
B	3.12	0.58	−1.45	−0.74	2.81*	−2.64*
G	−2.90+	−15.56+	−4.76*	−36.21**	−3.34**	−2.81*
L	−1.54	−1.48	−3.38°	−17.83°	4.51*	1.72
I	−1.78	−7.00	−3.73+	−24.96+	3.17*	1.89°
P	3.16	−0.13	0.68	−0.08	0.89	−1.89°

B. Tests on differences[b]

Series[a]	$\hat{\tau}_\mu$	q^μ_f	$\hat{\tau}_\tau$	q^τ_f	Time	Constant
q	−5.09*	−85.86**	−5.41**	−88.41**	−1.72ℓ	4.52**
m₁	−2.67°	−54.56**	−4.21*	−89.71**	4.20**	3.51**
m₂	−2.84°	−24.10°	−4.07*	−48.73**	3.21*	3.24*
b	−3.29+	−37.60**	−4.73*	−65.18**	4.37**	3.08*
g	−6.28*	−114.65**	−6.24*	−114.63**	0.50	−0.33
ℓ	−7.26*	−87.91**	−7.39*	−88.68**	−1.19	3.79**
i	−3.42+	−115.49**	−3.30*	−115.48**	−0.06	0.64
p	−3.30+	−39.14**	−4.20*	−67.00**	2.94*	3.05*

[a] On the definitions of the variables, see Table 11.1. Capital letters denote levels (in logs, except for I). Lowercase letters denote first differences (in logs, except for i).

[b] Significance level at the ⅒ of 1% level is denoted by ** (except for the Dickey-Fuller tests for which 0.001 significance levels are not tabulated); at the 1% level, by *; 5% level, by +; and at the 10% level by °.

[c] $\hat{\tau}_\mu$ denotes the Dickey-Fuller (1979) statistic computed using a regression with four lags. q^μ_f is the Stock-Watson (1986) statistic, also from a regression with four lags. $\hat{\tau}_\mu$ and q^τ_f are again, respectively, the Dickey-Fuller and Stock-Watson statistics calculated using a time trend.

[d] t-statistics for the time and constant coefficient estimated from a regression of the variable on four own lags with time trend and without.

Table 11.3

Univariate Tests for Unit Roots and Time Trends Interwar Sample: Quarterly Data, 1919:1–1940:1

A. Tests on levels[b]

Series[a]	Unit root test statistics[c]				t-statistics[d]	
	τ_μ	q^μ_f	τ_τ	q^τ_f	Time	Constant
Q	−1.21	−8.74**	−1.90	−11.33	1.71°	1.60
M1	0.29	1.05	−0.87	−3.15	2.17+	0.05
M2	−0.94	−2.55	−1.63	−5.71	1.78°	1.18
B	3.06	3.14	0.48	−1.49	2.17+	−2.28+
GX	0.06	−1.36	−3.07	−13.65	3.33*	0.04
LD	−1.53	−4.99	−1.78	−7.04	−1.23	2.33+
I	−1.42	−4.26*	−3.38*	−16.68	−2.93*	0.66
P	−3.38*	−8.74**	−3.11	−11.33	−1.26	3.28**
			B. Tests on differences[b]			
q	−3.33*	−35.18**	−3.22+	−35.64**	0.59	0.96
m_1	−2.67°	−21.32**	−3.05	−23.96**	1.80°	1.08
m_2	−3.33*	−21.02**	−2.58	−20.41**	0.89	0.89
b	−2.25	−58.90**	−4.30*	−76.41**	3.76**	1.79°
gx	−5.85*	−90.52**	−6.72*	−99.09**	2.20+	0.90
ℓd	−4.80*	−57.41**	−4.77*	−54.29**	0.16	0.00
i	−5.43*	−49.00**	−5.38*	−48.95**	0.33	−1.21
p	−5.64*	−35.18**	−6.10*	−35.65**	−2.07	−1.26

[a]On the definitions of the variables, see Table 11.1. Capital letters denote levels (in logs, except for I). Lowercase letters denote first differences (in logs, except for i).

[b]Significance level at the $\frac{1}{10}$ of 1% level is denoted by ** (except for the Dickey-Fuller tests for which 0.001 significance levels are not tabulated); at the 1% level, by *; 5% level, by +; and at the 10% level by °.

[c]τ_μ denotes the Dickey-Fuller (1979) statistic computed using a regression with four lags. q^μ_f is the Stock-Watson (1986) statistic, also from a regression with four lags. τ_μ and q^τ_f are again, respectively, the Dickey-Fuller and Stock-Watson statistics calculated using a time trend.

[d]t-statistics for the time and constant coefficient estimated from a regression of the variable on four own lags with time trend and without.

Table 11.4

Univariate Tests for Unit Roots and Time Trends
Prewar Sample: Quarterly Data, 1886:1–1914:4

A. Tests on levels[b]

Series[a]	Unit root test statistics[c]				t-statistics[d]	
	$\hat{\tau}_\mu$	q^μ_f	$\hat{\tau}_\tau$	q^τ_f	Time	Constant
Q	−0.93	−0.93	−2.24	−15.22	3.11*	1.20
M2	0.00	−0.45	−2.04	−6.50	1.85°	1.31
B	0.17	−0.10	−1.94	−19.77	2.11+	2.28+
GX	−1.17	−2.23	−3.64*	−43.42**	4.04**	1.52
LDC	−2.84°	−5.66	−4.24*	−21.90+	2.66*	2.15+
I	−5.10*	−49.94*	−6.30**	−56.93**	−2.68*	4.59**
P	0.45	0.91	−1.35	−2.74	2.35+	−0.15

B. Tests on differences[b]

Series[a]	$\hat{\tau}_\mu$	q^μ_f	$\hat{\tau}_\tau$	q^τ_f	Time	Constant
q	−5.18*	−70.48**	−5.18*	−70.77**	−0.68	3.19*
m2	−4.09*	−161.64**	−8.04*	−39.39**	0.38	3.17*
b	−5.88*	−161.65**	−5.88*	−161.86**	0.60	3.87**
gx	−6.60*	−150.58**	−6.58*	−150.58**	−0.40	1.80°
ℓdc	−7.45*	−68.23**	−7.71*	−63.13**	−1.40	2.02+
i	−6.98*	−123.60**	−6.95*	−123.59**	−0.18	0.09
p	−5.72*	−113.51**	−6.15*	−117.50**	2.11+	1.30

[a]On the definitions of the variables, see Table 11.1. Capital letters denote levels (in logs, except for I). Lowercase letters denote first differences (in logs, except for i).
[b]Significance level at the ½₀ of 1% level is denoted by ** (except for the Dickey-Fuller tests for which 0.001 significance levels are not tabulated); at the 1% level, by *; 5% level, by +; and at the 10% level by °.
[c]$\hat{\tau}_\mu$ denotes the Dickey-Fuller (1979) statistic computed using a regression with four lags. q^μ_f is the Stock-Watson (1986) statistic, also from a regression with four lags. $\hat{\tau}_\tau$ and q^τ_f are again, respectively, the Dickey-Fuller and Stock-Watson statistics calculated using a time trend.
[d]t-statistics for the time and constant coefficient estimated from a regression of the variable on four own lags with time trend and without.

The Dickey-Fuller statistics are calculated by estimating via OLS the following transformation of equation 5

(6)
$$x_{s,t} = \mu_s + \psi_s t + \phi_{s,1} x_{s,t} + \sum_{j=2}^{J} \phi_{s,j}(x_{s,j+1} - x_{s,t-j})$$

and calculating the adjusted t-statistic for $\phi_{s,t}$ as

(7)
$$\hat{\tau}_\mu = \frac{\phi_{s,1} - 1.00}{SE(\phi_{s,1})}$$

with and without ψ_s restricted to be zero. $SE(\phi_{s,1})$ is the typically reported standard error of $\phi_{s,}$. The critical values for these statistics are tabulated in Fuller (1976).

The Stock-Watson test statistics we use are based on the more general Stock-Watson $q_f(k,m)$ test for common trends in a vector of time series variables. The statistic is simply

(8)
$$q_f(k,m) = T [Re(\hat{\lambda}) - 1]$$

where $\hat{\lambda}$ is the largest real (Re) root of the sample autocorrelation matrix and T is the number of observations. The $q_f(k,m)$ statistic tests the hypothesis of k versus m unit roots for an n-vector time series ($m < k \leq n$). For the univariate tests used here, the null hypothesis (eq. 4) is one unit root, $k=1$, against the alternative (eq. 5) of no unit root, $m=0$. The critical values for the q^μ_f and q^τ_f statistics are tabulated in Stock and Watson (1986).

We also test for the order of any deterministic components in these series. We regressed the level and first difference of each series against a constant, time, and four of its own lags. Column 6 reports the t-statistic for the time coefficients. Likewise we tested for significant drift terms by replicating this estimation without a time trend. Column 7 reports the t-ratio on the constant term.

Looking at the results for the postwar sample (Table 11.2), only the fiscal index is stationary in levels around its mean as well as around a time trend. The leading index and the commercial paper rate are stationary in levels around a time trend only. All postwar series are stationary in first differences, with significant time trends occuring for all three money series and prices. We infer from this that it is necessary to take first differences of real GNP, money, and prices.

Although the tests indicate the leading index is stationary in levels around a time trend, we decided to perform our subsequent analysis using first differences. This is because the leading index has a built-in nonstationary component constructed from the trend of the coincident index (see U.S. Department of Commerce 1984, 65–69). Because this nonstationary component is implicitly related to the trend rate of growth of GNP and we take first differences of GNP, we also take first differences of the leading index. According to Sims, Stock, and Watson (1986), the presence of significant trends in the series of money and price changes makes it necessary to include a time trend in our equations to permit us to use standard asymptotic theory to interpret the exogeneity and neutrality tests.

For the interwar period (Table 11.3), the unit root tests are more difficult to interpret because of the small sample size (87 observations). For levels (Part A), the Dickey-Fuller tests indicate that the interest rate is stationary around a time trend and the price level is stationary around its mean. The Stock-Watson tests contradict these particular results, however, bringing into question the power of these tests (see Dickey and Fuller 1979 for power calculations of $\hat{\tau}_\mu$). Looking at the tests on differences (Part B), the tests indicate that all of the interwar series are stationary, except for the Dickey-Fuller tests for m_1 and m_2 around a trend and the monetary base around its mean. However, these particular tests again contradict the Stock-Watson tests. Because of these results, we act conservatively and use first differences of all of the interwar series. Moreover, following the arguments for the postwar sample, a time trend is also necessitated by the significant t-ratios for m_1, b, and g on the trend coefficients.

Finally, for the prewar sample (Table 11.4) it is sufficient to take first differences only of real GNP, the monetary base, $M2$, and the implicit price deflator while the series on government expenditures and the interest rate can be left in levels. Again, although the tests indicate the leading diffusion index is stationary in levels around a trend, we instead use first differences of this series in our subsequent analysis. This is because the trend is artificially induced via the accumulation of the original series. A time trend is also included because of the significant trend coefficient for inflation.

The Results

Factors Influencing Changes in Real GNP: A Stepwise Approach

1949–1982

Table 11.5 is based on regressions of real GNP growth on its own past ($q_{t-i}, i=1, \ldots, 4$) and the lagged values of from 2 to 5 other selected series, plus a constant term and time. Each variable has the form shown in Table 11.1, column 4, as indicated by the tests discussed previously. The calculations proceed by successively expanding the set of explanatory variables, in four steps. First, only the lagged terms of q are used along with the corresponding values of a fiscal and a monetary variable. The inflation group is added next, and then the interest rate group. The last step includes the leading index terms as well.

This table and those that follow are standardized to show the F-statistics for conventional tests of exogeneity and, underneath these entries, the t-statistics for the neutrality tests, i.e., for the *sums* of the regression coefficients of the same groups of lagged terms for each variable. The estimated individual coefficients are too numerous to report and their behavior is difficult to describe in the frequent cases where their successive values oscillate with mixed signs. It seems advisable, however, to show at least the summary t-ratios in each equation. When sufficiently large, these statistics suggest that the individual terms in each group are not all weak or not all transitory, that is, that they do not offset each other across the different lags.

In the 1949–82 equations with three variables only, the lagged q terms are always significant at least at the 5% level; each of the monetary alternatives makes a contribution (m_2 is particularly strong); and the fiscal index G is relatively weak, except when used along with the monetary base b (Table 11.5, part A, equations 1–3). Adding inflation p is of little help in explaining q, but on balance the coefficients of p are negative and some may matter (eq. 4–6). When the commercial paper rate I is entered, it acquires a dominant role at the expense of the other (especially the monetary) variables (eq. 7–9).[10] Finally, equations 10–12 show that, of all the variables considered, the rate of change in the leading index exerts the statistically most significant influence on q. Five of the test statistics for ℓ are significant at the $\frac{1}{10}$ of one percent level, one at the 1% level. The level of interest rates represented by I retains its strong net inverse effect on q. The direct contributions of m_1, m_2, and G to the determination of real GNP growth are much fewer and weaker, those of b and p are altogether difficult to detect.[11]

Alternative calculations show that when ℓ is added to the equations with the monetary and fiscal variables only, the effects of these variables on q are again drastically reduced. Had we retained the money, credit, and stock price components in the leading index, the role of the index in these equations would have been even stronger, and that of the other regressors generally weaker.[12] In any event, the evidence indicates that the quarterly movements of the economy's output in 1949–82 depended much more on recent changes in leading indicators and interest rates than on recent changes in output itself, money, the fiscal factor, or inflation.

Conceivably, longer lags could produce different results, so we checked to see what happens when eight instead of four lags are used. These tests suggest some gains in power for the lagged q and G terms, but the leading index and the interest rate still have consistently strong effects. However, we do not report these statistics because the restriction to lags of 1–4 quarters is dictated by the limitations of the available data. With eight lags, for example, the number of degrees of freedom is reduced from 109 to 81 for the six-variable equations.

Table 11.5

Rate of Change in Real GNP (q) Regressed on Its Own Lagged Values and Those of Other Selected Variables: Tests of Exogeneity and Significance, Quarterly Data for Three Periods Between 1886 and 1982

A. 1949–1982[a]

Equation no.	df[b]	Lagged explanatory variables[c]	Test statistics[d] for							$\bar{R}^2$
			q (1)	b,m₁,m₂ (2)	G (3)	p (4)	l,i (5)	ℓ,ℓd,ℓdc (6)	t (7)	(8)
1	121	q,b,G	4.2*	3.4*	3.1+					0.26
			1.6	-0.7	2.7*				1.3	
2	121	q,m₁,G	2.9+	3.1+	1.6					0.26
			1.1	1.1	1.6°				-0.3	
3	121	q,m₂,G	3.1+	5.3**	1.3					0.30
			0.8	2.7*	0.9				-1.5	
4	117	q,b,G,p	3.5*	3.2+	2.1°	0.8				0.26
			1.2	0.1	2.2+	-1.6			1.4	
5	117	q,m₁,G,p	2.1°	3.5+	1.1	1.3				0.27
			0.6	1.7°	0.9	-1.8°			-0.3	
6	117	q,m₂,G,p	2.3°	5.2**	1.0	0.9				0.30
			0.8	2.4+	0.8	-0.8			-1.0	
7	113	q,b,G,l	2.0°	2.4+	0.9	0.3	4.7**			0.34
			0.4	-1.2	0.7	0.4	-3.2*		3.0*	
8	113	q,m₁,G,p,l	2.3°	2.0°	0.7	0.4	4.0*			0.34
			-0.7	2.3+	-0.8	-0.6	-3.2**		0.5	
9	113	q,m₂,G,p,l	2.0	2.3°	1.0	0.8	2.8+			0.34
			0.2	1.0	0.7	0.1	-2.4+		0.5	
10	109	q,b,G,p,l,ℓ	1.3	1.3	1.7	0.7	3.7*	4.4*		0.41
			-1.9	-0.1	-0.6	1.3	-3.3**	3.7**	1.1	

#	Variables								R²
11	q,m₁,G,p,l,ℓ	2.7+ / -3.1*	2.4° / 2.2*	2.5+ / -1.8°	0.4 / 0.9	4.6* / -3.8**	6.0** / 4.7**	-0.5	0.44
12	q,m₂,G,p,l,ℓ	1.7 / -2.3	2.1° / 0.6	2.4+ / -1.0	0.9 / 1.5	3.2+ / -3.1*	5.3** / 4.4**	0.2	0.43

B. 1919–1940[e]

#	Variables								R²
13	q,b,gx	7.0** / 3.0*	5.2** / 1.4	6.7** / -1.4				-0.7	0.44
14	q,m₁,gx	2.6 / 0.7+	3.9* / 2.0+	5.3** / -1.3				-0.5	0.40
15	q,m₂,gx	4.6* / 1.7°	4.0* / 0.9	5.2* / -1.5				0.4	0.41
16	q,b,gx,p	5.2** / 3.0*	5.3** / 1.4	5.6** / -1.5	0.9 / -0.8			-0.4	0.43
17	q,m₁,gx,p	1.1 / 0.8	5.0* / 2.7*	3.9* / -0.8	1.7 / -2.0+			-0.4	0.43
18	q,m₂,gx,p	2.4+ / 1.6	4.6* / 1.6	3.6* / -1.0	1.2 / -1.7°			0.8	0.42
19	q,b,gx,p,i	4.8* / 2.9*	4.4* / 1.5	5.3** / -1.4	0.8 / -0.6	0.2 / -0.5		-0.5	0.41
20	q,m₁,gx,p,i	0.8 / 0.6	4.2* / 2.7*	3.6* / -0.8	1.8 / -2.1+	0.3 / 0.5		-0.5	0.40
21	q,m₂,gx,p,i	2.1° / 1.2	3.9* / 1.7°	3.6* / -1.0	1.4 / -1.7°	0.3 / 0.3		0.8	0.39
22	q,b,gx,p,i,ℓd	1.4 / -0.6	4.1* / 1.3	3.0+ / -1.0	1.3 / -0.1	0.2 / -0.2	3.9* / 2.6*	-0.7	0.50
23	q,m₁,gx,p,i,ℓd	2.0 / -1.4	3.5* / 2.4+	1.9 / -0.7	1.9 / -1.4	0.2 / 0.7	3.5* / 2.3+	-0.7	0.49
24	q,m₂,gx,p,i,ℓd	1.9 / -0.8	3.7* / 1.5	1.7 / -0.5	1.2 / -1.2	0.6 / 0.4	4.0* / 2.2**	0.4	0.49

Table 11.5 (continued)

C. 1886–1914[f]

	df	Variables	1	2	3	4	5	6	7	$\bar{R}^2$
25	101	q,b,G,x	8.9**	0.2	0.7				−1.2	0.21
			0.9	0.3	1.1					
26	101	q,m₂,GX	3.0+	5.3**	0.2				−0.6	0.34
			−0.5	2.2+	0.3					
27	97	q,b,GX,p	7.2**	0.2	0.8	1.7			−1.4	0.23
			1.3	0.4	1.4	−1.7*				
28	97	q,m₂,GX,p	3.0*	5.0**	0.2	1.6			−0.4	0.36
			−0.6	2.6*	0.3	−1.8°				
29	93	q,b,GX,p,l	4.0*	0.3	0.3	1.7	3.3*		−1.0	0.30
			0.0	0.7	0.6	−1.7°	−2.4+			
30	93	q,m₂,GX,p,l	2.4+	3.0+	0.2	1.6	1.6		−0.4	0.37
			−0.8	2.2+	0.1	−1.7°	−1.4			
31	89	q,b,GX,p,l,ℓdc	4.0*	0.3	0.1	1.5	3.7*	0.7	−1.1	0.29
			−0.3	0.7	0.5	−1.4	−2.4+	−0.7		
32	89	q,m₂,GX,p,l,ℓdc	2.6+	3.5*	0.1	1.6	2.3°	1.2	−0.4	0.38
			−1.1	2.2*	−0.4	−1.5	−1.8°	−1.2		

[a]Sample period: 1949:2–1982:4.
[b]Degrees of freedom.
[c]See Table 11.1 for definitions of the variables and sources of the data.
[d]The first line for each equation lists the F-statistics for groups of lagged values of each variable covered (columns 1–6) and squared correlation coefficients adjusted for the degrees of freedom (column 8). The second line lists the t-statistics for the sums of regression coefficients of the same groups (columns 1–6) and for the time trend (column 7). Significance at the $\frac{1}{10}$ of 1% level is denoted by **; at the 1% level, by **; at the 5% level, by *; at the 10% level, by +; and at the 10% level by °.
[e]Sample period: 1920:4–1940:4.
[f]Sample period: 1886:2–1914:4.

1919–1940

In the equations for the interwar period, all variables appear in form of first differences. In the first subset (Table 11.5, part B, eq. 13–15), q depends positively on its own lagged values and those of the monetary variables, inversely on the recent values of federal expenditures gx. All the F-statistics are significant, most highly so. On the other hand, inflation contributes but little to these regressions, as shown by the results for equations 16–18 (only two t-tests indicate significance and none of the F-tests). Further, no gains at all result from the inclusion of the change in the commercial paper rate (eq. 19–21).

In contrast, there is strong evidence in our estimates for 1919–40 that the lagged rates of change in the index of six leading indicators (ℓd) had a large net positive influence on q. Four of the corresponding test statistics are significant at the 1% level, two at the 5% level (part B, column 6). In these equations (22–24), ℓd shows the strongest effects, followed by the monetary variables; gx is significant only in one case; and the tests for lagged q, p, and i terms are all negative.

On the whole, the monetary series appear to play a somewhat stronger role in the interwar than in the postwar equations, while the leading series appear to play a somewhat weaker role. It should be recalled, however, that ℓ is a more comprehensive index than ℓd and is based on better data. Even for the series that are more comparable across the two periods, the quality of the postwar data is probably significantly higher. Further, the reliability of the results for 1919–40 suffers from the small sample problem: the number of observations per parameter to be estimated here is little more than half the number available for 1949–82.

In light of these considerations, it seems important to note that the interwar results resemble broadly the postwar results in most respects and look rather reasonable, at least in the overall qualitative sense. The leading indexes are highly effective in the regressions for both periods. The main difference between the two sets of estimates is that the commercial paper rate contributes strongly to the statistical explanation of q in 1949–82 but the change in that rate does not help in the 1919–40 regressions (cf. column 5 in parts A and B of Table 11.5). We checked whether interest levels (I) would have performed significantly better than interest changes (i) in the interwar equations, and the answer is no.

1886–1914

For the pre-World War I period, the equations with three variables indicate strong effects on q of its own lagged values and those of m_2, but no significant contributions of either the monetary base or government expenditures (Table 11.5, part C, eq. 25–26). The inflation terms add only a weak negative influence, as shown in the summary t-statistics for equations 27–28.

The recent values of the commercial paper rate have substantial inverse effects on the current rate of change in real GNP, particularly in the equations with the base and after the change in diffusion index of leading indicators (ℓdc) is added (eq. 29–32). The ℓdc index itself appears to be ineffective. In light of the major importance of the leading indexes in the postwar and interwar equations, this negative result is probably attributable mainly to the way ℓdc is constructed. (Recall from a previous discussion that this index uses only the historical information on specific-cycle turning points in a set of 75 individual indicators.)

Test Statistics for Six-Variable Equations

1949–1982

Each of the monetary variables (b, m_1, m_2) depends strongly on its own lagged values and those of the interest rate I, as shown by the corresponding F-values in Table 11.6, equations 1–3. The I terms have coefficients whose signs vary and their t-statistics are on balance small, though mostly negative. The fiscal index G appears to have a strong positive effect on m_1, and the time trends in column 7 are important. The effects of the other variables are sporadic and weak.

G is more strongly autoregressive yet. It also depends positively on b and m_2 and inversely on I, the change in the leading index ℓ, and time (equations 4–6).

Inflation p also depends mainly on its own lagged values, according to equations 7–9. A few relatively weak signs of influence appear for b, I, and G. The time trends are significant. These results are consistent with a view of the price level as a predetermined variable adjusting but slowly with considerable inertia. Monetary influences on p involve much longer lags than are allowed here.

The interest rate depends most heavily on its own recent levels, as is immediately evident from equations 10–12. Still, some significant inputs into the determination of I (which yields R^2 as high as 0.95) are also made by other factors, notably m_1 and ℓ.

As for ℓ, it is not strongly influenced by either its own recent past or that of the other variables. The largest F-values here are associated with the interest rate in equations 13 and 14 and with inflation in equation 15.

The corresponding tests for real GNP (q) equations have already been discussed in the previous section (relating to the estimates in the last six lines of Table 11.5, part A). It is interesting to note that very few significant F or t statistics are associated with the lagged q terms according to our tests (Table 11.6, column 1).

1919–1940

Tests based on the interwar monetary regressions indicate high serial dependence for m_1 and m_2 but not b (Table 11.7, eq. 1–3). The base is influenced strongly by recent changes in output q, moderately by those in the leading index ℓd. There are signs of some effects on m_2 of ℓd and p, but no measurable outside influences on m_1.

Table 11.6 **Tests of Exogeneity and Significance, Six-Variable Equations: Quarterly, 1949–82**

Equation no.[a]	Dependent variable[b]	Test statistics[c] for							$\bar{R}^2$
		q (1)	b,m_1,m_2 (2)	G (3)	p (4)	— (5)	ℓ (6)	t (7)	(8)
1	b	1.7	10.5**	1.2	1.5	3.4*	2.9+	2.6*	0.71
		1.8°	3.2**	-0.2	0.1	-0.9	1.7°		
2	m_1	1.1	3.3*	3.3*	1.3	8.0**	0.4	3.3*	0.54
		0.6	1.5	2.0+	0.7	-0.4	1.2		
3	m_2	0.7	7.3**	0.8	0.4	10.6**	0.4	2.9*	0.76
		0.4	3.7**	0.3	-0.2	-1.6°	0.3		
4	G	1.1	2.4+	36.0**	0.7	3.5*	0.1	-2.9*	0.87
		-0.8	2.4+	9.7**	-0.7	-0.1	-0.2		
5	G	0.7	1.3	28.3**	1.0	3.6*	0.1	-2.3+	0.86
		-0.6	1.6	8.6**	-1.7°	-0.9	0.1		
6	G	0.7	2.4+	34.8**	1.1	2.6+	0.4	-2.7*	0.87
		-0.4	1.8°	9.6**	-1.9°	0.1	1.2		
7	p	1.1	2.5+	2.3°	0.5	2.8+	9.1**	3.0*	0.63
		0.7	-1.8°	2.6*	-1.1	0.7	4.6**		
8	p	1.0	0.8	1.1	-0.3	1.7	8.7**	1.2	0.61
		-0.4	0.9	1.5	-0.3	1.0	4.0**		
9	p	1.0	1.6	2.1°	0.2	1.6	8.4**	3.0*	0.62
		0.5	-1.9+	2.5*	-0.8	0.2	4.1**		
10	l	1.8	1.3	0.2	4.1*	81.0**	3.0+	0.9	0.94
		1.1	-0.4	-0.5	0.5	13.1**	1.7°		
11	l	2.8+	6.6**	-0.2	1.6	98.1**	1.9	0.9	0.95
		0.7	0.2	-0.1	0.5	14.8**	1.6		
12	l	1.8	2.1°	0.2	3.4*	68.0**	2.4+	1.5	0.95
		1.5	-0.8	-0.0	0.3	12.5**	1.2		
13	ℓ	1.2	1.1	1.9	1.8	3.8*	-1.3	3.6**	0.45
		0.1	-1.8°	2.2+	0.2	-1.4	-1.3		
14	ℓ	1.2	1.6	1.6	2.2°	4.0*	2.5+	2.3+	0.46
		-1.0	0.6	1.6°	1.0	-1.1	-2.4+		
15	ℓ	-1.0	1.2	1.7	2.1°	1.2	2.5+	2.3+	0.45
		-0.4	-0.5	2.1+	0.9	-1.1	-2.5*		

[a] Sample period: 1949:2–1982:4. Degrees of freedom: 109.
[b] See Table 11.1 for definitions of the variables and sources of the data.
[c] F-statistics on the first line, t-statistics on the second line for each equation. Significance at the $\frac{1}{10}$ of 1% level is denoted by ***; at the 1% level, by **; at the 5% level, by +; and at the 10% level by °.

Table 11.7 **Tests of Exogeneity and Significance, Six-Variable Equations: Quarterly, 1919–40**

Equation no.[a]	Dependent variable[b]	Test statistics[c] for							$\bar{R}^2$
		q (1)	b1,m₁,m₂ (2)	g (3)	ℓ (4)	i (5)	p (6)	t (7)	(8)
1	b	3.5*	0.1	1.4	2.6+	0.7	0.7	3.7**	0.40
		2.8**	-0.3	1.3	-1.7°	-1.4	-0.7		
2	m₁	-0.3	8.2**	-1.4	0.9	-0.1	1.3	1.5	0.55
		-0.1	3.3*	-1.7°	-0.3	-0.2	0.7		
3	m₂	0.6	4.6*	1.7	2.1°	0.7	2.2°	1.1	0.60
		0.3	2.8*	-2.4+	0.7	-0.3	1.6		
4	gx	1.9	1.1	2.7+	1.4	1.5	0.8	2.1+	0.36
		-1.8	-1.2	-2.0+	1.4	0.4	1.5		
5	gx	-1.6	1.2	2.2+	1.5	1.0	0.7	1.5	0.36
		-1.9	-0.4	-1.8°	1.7	0.4	1.5		
6	gx	-1.3	1.2	3.3+	1.2	0.9	0.9	1.7	0.36
		-1.5	-1.4	-2.3+	1.5	0.3	1.9°		
7	p	0.7	-0.2	1.0	1.7	1.7	5.1*	1.1	0.54
		0.5	-0.2	1.4	1.4	-2.1+	1.9°		
8	p	1.2	2.2°	1.5	2.1+	-1.4	6.2**	1.4	0.60
		0.2	-0.5	1.2	2.0+	-1.4	2.0+		
9	p	1.4	1.4	1.2	2.3+	2.0	5.7**	1.6	0.58
		0.7	-1.3	0.7	1.6	-1.6	2.2+		
10	i	0.6	0.7	0.5	1.3	2.7+	0.3	-0.7	0.14
		-0.6	0.9	0.9	1.1	0.9	0.8		
11	i	0.5	0.1	0.4	1.0	2.7+	0.3	-0.0	0.10
		-0.1	0.1	1.0	0.7	0.7	0.6		
12	i	0.6	0.9	0.7	1.3	2.6+	0.3	-0.1	0.15
		-0.4	0.8	1.5	0.9	0.7	0.2		
13	ℓd	1.1	4.7*	2.2°	3.0+	0.8	1.4	-1.4	0.39
		-1.1	2.4+	-1.4	2.2+	-0.6	-0.1		
14	ℓd	1.3	4.6*	1.5	2.0°	0.5	1.8+	-0.7	0.39
		-1.8°	3.0*	-1.1	1.7+	0.6	-1.7		
15	ℓd	1.3	7.4**	2.0°	2.7+	1.5	1.5	0.7	0.47
		-1.2	2.1+	-1.0	1.9°	0.5	1.6°		

[a] Sample period: 1920:4–1940:4. Degrees of freedom: 55.

[b] See Table 11.1 for definitions of the variables and sources of the data.

[c] F-statistics on the first line, t-statistics on the second line for each equation. Significance at the $\frac{1}{10}$ of 1% level is denoted by **; at the 1% level, by *; at the 5% level, by +; and at the 10% level by °.

Equations 4–6 for the rate of change in government expenditures gx produce F-statistics that are generally low and significant only for the lagged values of the dependent variable. The same applies to the equations 10–12 for the change in the interest rate i.

The rate of inflation p depends heavily on its own lagged values, too (eq. 7–9). Some of the test statistics suggest that m_1, ℓd, and perhaps i, may influence p slightly over the course of a year.

Interestingly, according to equations 13–15, ℓd is affected much more strongly by the recent monetary changes than by its own lagged values. There are also some signs of influence of gx on ℓd. This raises the possibility that monetary and fiscal changes, including those due to policy actions, may affect real GNP with long lags through the mediating role of the leading indicators (ℓd). But note that this is only suggested by the estimates for the interwar period, not those for the postwar era.[13]

Comparing Tables 11.6 and 11.7 and drawing also on Table 11.5 (parts A and B, equations 10–12 and 22–24), we observe that q depends strongly on the leading indexes (ℓ, ℓd) in both periods and on the monetary factors in the interwar period. The autoregressive elements are weak in q, ℓ, and ℓd and strong (as a rule dominant) in the other variables according to the interwar as well as the postwar estimates. The effects of q on the other factors are generally weak or nonexistent.

1886–1914

The F-statistics for the own-lag terms are significant in all the pre-World War I equations, highly so (at the 0.1% level) for the monetary, fiscal, leading, and interest series, less so for q and p (see Table 11.8 and Table 11.5, C, equations 30–32). The leading index ℓdc for 1886–1914 is very strongly autocorrelated, in contrast to the indexes ℓd for 1919–40 and ℓ for 1949–82. This reflects the construction of the prewar index, which assumes smooth cyclical movements in the index components (cf. section on data sources and problems).

Prewar changes in the monetary base are poorly "explained," mainly by own lags and those of government expenditures GX and the commercial paper rate I. The corresponding changes in the stock of money m_2 are fit much better by lagged values of m_2 itself, I, and p. And as much as 94% of the variance of GX is explained statistically, mainly by lagged GX terms and the time trend. (See Table 11.8, eqs. 1–4.)

The estimates for inflation p are problematic. They suggest that p was influenced positively by lagged money changes but also inversely by its own lagged values and those of I and ℓdc. The R^2 coefficients are of the order of 0.2 to 0.3 (eq. 5–6).

The equations for the interest rate (7–8), besides being dominated by autoregressive elements, indicate some short-term effects of q (with plus signs) and m_2 (minus). These results seem generally reasonable.

Table 11.8

Tests of Exogeneity and Significance, Six-Variable Equations: Quarterly, 1886–1914

Equa-tion no.[a]	Dependent variable[b]	Test statistics[c] for							$\bar{R}^2$
		q (1)	$b1,m_2$ (2)	GX (3)	p (4)	l (5)	ℓdc (6)	t (7)	(8)
1	b	0.7	7.3**	2.0°	0.3	2.8+	0.9		0.14
		1.4	-3.7**	1.7*	0.1	2.8*	0.6	-1.1	
2	m_2	1.1	20.8**	0.5	1.7	2.8+	4.2*		0.59
		-1.8	5.2**	-0.2	-1.4	-2.0+	0.6	-0.2	
3	GX	0.9	0.4	10.8**	0.2	0.9	0.3		0.94
		-0.4	0.9	5.1**	-0.4	-1.4	0.5	3.7**	
4	GX	1.6	0.9	9.2**	0.3	0.4	0.1		0.94
		-1.0	1.1	4.6**	0.2	-0.9	0.4	3.7**	
5	p	1.4	1.2°	1.5	3.3*	3.7*	1.8		0.23
		-0.3	2.0+	-0.3	-2.7*	-2.6+	-1.6°	0.1	
6	p	2.3*	2.8+	2.1°	3.3*	2.7+	2.5+		0.28
		-1.8°	3.2*	-1.0	-3.1*	1.4	-2.3*	1.1	
7	l	2.6+	1.9	0.7	2.3*	11.4**	1.5+		0.49
		2.8*	-2.5*	0.1	1.2	4.6**	2.3+	-0.4	
8	l	1.9	2.3°	0.7	1.7	8.1**	0.8		0.51
		2.3+	-1.2	-0.5	1.2	3.5**	1.3	0.1	
9	ℓdc	1.8	0.3	1.9	55.6**	2.2	2.0°		0.72
		2.3+	0.4	-0.5	6.6**	-1.7*	0.4	-0.2	
10	ℓdc	1.3	0.3	1.9	56.3**	2.2	2.1°		0.72
		-1.8°	0.3	-0.5	6.7**	-1.5	0.1	-0.1	

[a] Sample period: 1886:2–1914:4. Degrees of freedom: 89.
[b] See Table 11.1 for definitions of the variables and sources of the data.
[c] F-statistics on the first line, t-statistics on the second line for each equation. Significance at the $\frac{1}{10}$ of 1% level is denoted by **; at the 1% level, by *; at the 5% level, by +; and at the 10% level by °.

The leading diffusion index ℓdc (eq. 9–10) depends primarily on own lags, with traces of positive effects of q and p and negative effects of I. In view of the probable measurement errors involved (mainly in the ℓdc series), the serviceability of these estimates is uncertain.

Conclusions and Further Steps

The following list of our principal findings begins with a point of particular importance, which receives clear support from the better quality of the data available for the postwar and interwar periods.

1. Output depends strongly on leading indexes in equations which also include the monetary, fiscal, inflation, and interest variables (all taken in stationary form, with four quarterly lags in each variable). Hence, models that omit the principal leading indicators are probably seriously misspecified.

2. Short-term nominal interest rates had a strong inverse influence on output (specifically, the rate of change in real GNP) during the 1949–82 period. When interest is included, the effects of the monetary and fiscal series are reduced (this resembles the results of some earlier studies; cf. Sims 1980). When the leading index is also included, most of the monetary effects are further diminished.

3. In the interwar period, the role of money appears greater, while the fiscal and interest effects tend to wane. In the prewar (1886–1914) equations, output is influenced mainly by its own lagged values and those of the money stock and the interest rate. The other factors, including a diffusion index based on specific cycles in a large set of individual leading series, have no significant effects. However, this probably reflects errors in the data, especially the weakness of the available leading index.

4. The monetary, fiscal, and interest variables depend more on their own lagged values than on any of the other factors, and the same is true of inflation, except in 1886–1914. The opposite applies to the rates of change in output and (again, except in 1886–1914) the leading indexes. None of the variables in question can be considered exogenous.

5. The reported unit root tests are consistent with earlier findings that most macroeconomic time series are difference-stationary (see Nelson and Plosser 1982 on annual interwar and postwar data, and Stock and Watson 1987 on monthly postwar data). The major exceptions to this are the prewar and postwar fiscal and interest series.

Our work offers some suggestions for further research. The following steps at least should be considered:

(a) Construct a satisfactory composite index of leading indicators for the periods before World War II from the best available historical data.

(b) Compute variance decompositions and impulse response functions for alternative subsets of up to four variables represented by the quarterly series used in this paper.

(c) Do the same computations for larger sets of six variables by using monthly data. This would complement the results obtained here for individual equations in the same sets; further, it would permit comparisons with some recent smaller VAR models estimated on monthly data. The main problem with this approach is that no suitable monthly proxies for GNP may be found.

(d) Update the postwar series and check on predictions beyond the sample period, e.g., for 1983–88.

(e) Try to find out where the explanatory or predictive power of the leading index is coming from by testing important subindexes relating to investment commitments, profitability, etc.

(f) Compare the implications of this paper with those of the most recent and ongoing studies of leading indicators (de Leeuw 1988, 1989; Stock and Watson 1988a, 1988b).

Notes

1. For assessments and references concerning the U.S. record, see Moore (1983, chaps. 10 and 24), and Zarnowitz and Moore (1986).

2. Large econometric models incorporate some individual indicators but probably suboptimally and not in a comprehensive and systematic way.

3. This recalls the old St. Louis Fed model with its reliance on "policy variables" only.

4. With $m = 6$ variables and $k = 4$ lags, $km^2 = 144$. For the sample period 1949:2–1982:4 covered by our postwar series, the number of degrees of freedom is 109.

5. New annual estimates of nominal GNP, the implicit price deflator (1982 = 100), and real GNP for 1869–1929 are presented in Balke and Gordon (1988). This study develops some additional sources for direct measurement of nonmanufacturing output and the deflator. It concludes that real GNP was on the average about as volatile as the traditional Kuznets-Kendrick series indicate, but that the GNP deflator was significantly less volatile. These estimates appeared too late to be taken into account in this paper.

6. The Persons index consists of a varying assortment of weighted and spliced series on bank clearings outside New York City, production of pig iron and electric power, construction contracts, railroad car loadings and net ton-miles of freight, indexes of volume of manufacturing and mining, etc. The compilation is spotty and uneven, particularly before 1903. A few other historical indexes of business activity are available but they have similar limitations (Zarnowitz 1981).

7. These indicators are: average workweek, manufacturing; average weekly initial claims for unemployment insurance; vendor performance (percent of companies receiving slower deliveries); change in sensitive materials prices; manufacturers' orders in constant dollars, consumer goods and materials industries; contracts and orders for plant and equipment in constant dollars; index of net business formation; building permits for new private housing units; change in manufacturing and trade inventories on hand and on order in constant dollars.

8. Percent changes in each component series (computed so as to insure symmetrical treatment of rises and declines) are standardized, i.e., expressed as ratios to their own long-run mean, without regard to sign. The resulting changes are averaged across the series for each month and then cumulated into an index. Simple averages are used by Shiskin, weighted averages by Commerce, but this makes little difference since the Commerce weights, based on performance scores of the selected indicators, are nearly

equal. Also, the Commerce index has a trend adjusted to equal the trend in the index of coincident indicators (which is close to the trend in real GNP), whereas the Shiskin index has no such adjustment. (Cf. Shiskin 1961, pp. 43–47 and 123–125; U.S. Department of Commerce 1984, pp. 65–70.)

9. Except for the inventory and price components which are weighted 4-month moving averages, trailing.

10. The addition of I reduces further the statistics for p. The simple correlation between I and p in 1949–82 is about 0.7. During the latter part of the postwar era, inflation spread and accelerated and financial markets became increasingly sensitive to it. Since I depends on the real interest rate R and expected inflation (i.e., forecasts of p, probably based in part on p_{t-i}), our results suggest an independent role for R in codetermining q.

11. These results are not inconsistent with b influencing q with longer lags via changes in m_1 or m_2 or I, or with a negative effect of inflation uncertainty on output, which is found in some studies that work with higher moments or forecasts of inflation (see also, Makin 1982; Litterman and Weiss 1985; Zarnowitz and Lambros 1987).

12. It should be noted that the index is robust in the sense of not being critically dependent on any of its individual components or their weights. Thus, any large subset of these indicators can produce a fair approximation to the total index under the adopted construction and standardization procedures. Some of the components are known to have good predictive records of their own (e.g., stock prices, as shown in Fischer and Merton 1984), but the leading index outperforms any of them on the average over time. The reductions in coverage and diversity detract from the forecasting potential of the index but, up to a point, only moderately. And, as in the present case, they may often be advisable for analytical purposes.

13. The difference could be related to the fact that the interwar index includes, while the postwar index excludes, the stock price series. Financial asset prices and returns are probably subject to stronger monetary and fiscal influences than other leading indicators are.

References

Auerbach, A. 1982. The Index of Leading Economic Indicators: " 'Measurement without Theory,' Thirty-Five Years Later." *Review of Economics and Statistics* 64: 589–95.

Balke, N. S., and R. J. Gordon. 1986. *Historical Data*. In *The American Business Cycle: Continuity and Change*, pp. 781–850. Edited by R. J. Gordon. Chicago: University of Chicago Press for NBER.

————. 1988. *The Estimation of Prewar GNP: Methodology and New Evidence*. NBER Working Paper no. 2674.

Blanchard, O. J. 1985. "Debt, Deficits, and Finite Horizons." *Journal of Political Economy* 93: 223–47.

Blanchard, O. J., and M. W. Watson. 1986. "Are Business Cycles All Alike?" In *The American Business Cycle: Continuity and Change*, pp. 123–56 and 178–79. Edited by R. J. Gordon. Chicago: University of Chicago Press for NBER.

Braun, P., and S. Mittnik. 1985. "Structural Analysis with Vector Autoregressive Models: Some Experimental Evidence." Washington University in St. Louis Working Paper no. 84.

Campbell, J. Y., and N. G. Mankiw. 1987. "Permanent and Transitory Components in Macroeconomc Fluctuations." *American Economic Review* 77: 111–117.

Chow, G. C., and A. Lin. 1971."Best Linear Unbiased Interpolation, Distribution, and Extrapolation of Time Series by Related Series." *Review of Economics and Statistics* 53: 372–76.

Cochrane, J. H. 1988."How Big is the Random Walk in GNP?" *Journal of Political Economy* 96: 893–920.

de Leeuw, F. 1988. "Prime Movers as Leading Indicators." Bureau of Economic Analysis Discussion Paper no. 37.

———. 1989. "Toward a Theory of Leading Indicators." In *Leading Economic Indicators: New Approaches and Forecasting Methods*. Edited by K. Lahiri and G. Moore. Forthcoming.

Dickey, D. A., and W. A. Fuller. 1979. "Distribution of the Estimators for Autoregressive Time Series with a Unit Root." *Journal of the American Statistical Society* 74: 1057–1072.

Diebold, F. X., and G. P. Rudebusch. 1987. Scoring the Leading Indicators. Division of Research and Statistics, Federal Reserve Board. Manuscript.

Firestone, J. M. 1960. *Federal Receipts and Expenditures During Business Cycles, 1879–1958*. Princeton: Princeton University Press for NBER.

Fischer, S., and R. C. Merton. 1984. "Macroeconomics and Finance: The Role of the Stock Market." *Carnegie-Rochester Conference on Public Policy* 21: 57–108.

Friedman, M., and A. J. Schwartz. 1963. *A Monetary History of the United States, 1867–1960*. Princeton: Princeton University Press for NBER.

———. 1970. *Monetary Statistics of the United States: Estimates, Sources, and Methods*. New York: National Bureau of Economic Research.

———. 1982. *Monetary Trends in the United States and the United Kingdom: Their Relation to Income, Prices and Interest Rates, 1867–1975*. Chicago: University of Chicago Press for NBER.

Fuller, W. A. 1976. *Introduction to Statistical Time Series*. New York: Wiley.

Gordon, R. J. 1982. "Price Inertia and Policy Ineffectiveness in the United States, 1890–1980." *Journal of Political Economy* 90: 854–71.

———. 1986. *The American Business Cycle: Continuity and Change*. Chicago: University of Chicago Press for NBER.

Gordon, R. J., and J. M. Veitch. 1986. "Fixed Investment in the American Business Cycle, 1919–83." In *The American Business Cycle: Continuity and Change*, pp. 267–335 and 352–57. Edited by R.J. Gordon. Chicago: University of Chicago Press for NBER.

Kuznets, S. 1961. *Capital in the American Economy: Its Formation and Financing*. Princeton: Princeton Univerity Press for NBER.

Lebergott, S. 1986. Discussion. *Journal of Economic History* 46: 367–371.

Litterman, R. B., and L. M. Weiss. 1985. "Money, Real Interest Rates, and Output: A Reinterpretation of Postwar U.S. Data." *Econometrica* 53: 129–53.

Lütkepohl, H. 1982. "Non-Causality Due to Omitted Variables." *Journal of Econometrics* 19: 307–378.

Macaulay, F. C. 1938. *The Movements of Interest Rates, Bond Yields, and Stock Prices in the United States Since 1856*. New York: National Bureau of Economic Research.

Makin, J. K. 1982. "Anticipated Money, Inflation, Uncertainty and Real Economic Activity." *Review of Economics and Statistics* 64: 126–35.

Moore, G. H., ed. 1961. *Business Cycle Indicators*. Princeton: Princeton University Press for NBER.

———. 1983. *Business Cycles, Inflation, and Forecasting*. Cambridge, Mass.: Ballinger for NBER.

Nelson, C. R., and C. I. Plosser. 1982. "Trends and Random Walks in Macroeconomic Time Series: Some Evidence and Implications." *Journal of Monetary Economics* 10: 139–62.

Persons, W. M. 1931. *Forecasting Business Cycles*. New York: Wiley.

Romer, C. 1986. "The Prewar Business Cycle Reconsidered: New Estimates of Gross

National Product, 1869-1918." NBER Working Paper no. 1969.
————. 1987. "Gross National Product, 1909-1928: Existing Estimates, New Estimates and New Interpretations of World War I and Its Aftermath." NBER Working Paper no. 2187.
Runkle, D. E. 1987. "Vector Autoregressions and Reality." *Journal of Business and Economic Statistics* 5: 437-42.
Shiskin, J. 1961. *Signals of Recession and Recovery: An Experiment with Monthly Reporting*. New York: National Bureau of Economic Research.
Sims, C. A. 1980. "Comparison of Interwar and Postwar Business Cycles: Monetarism Reconsidered." *American Economic Review* 70: 250-57.
Sims, C. A., J. H. Stock, and M. W. Watson. 1986. Inference in Linear Time Series Models with Some Unit Roots. Stanford University. Manuscript.
Stock, J. H., and M. W. Watson. 1986. Testing for Common Trends. Harvard University. Manuscript.
————. 1987. Interpreting the Evidence on Money-Income Causality. Harvard University. Manuscript.
————. 1988a. A New Approach to the Leading Economic Indicators. Harvard University. Manuscript.
————. 1988b. A Probability Model of the Coincident Economic Indicators. Harvard University. Manuscript.
U.S. Department of Commerce. 1984. *Handbook of Cyclical Indicators*. Washington, D.C.: Government Printing Office.
Vaccara, B. N., and V. Zarnowitz. 1978. "Forecasting with the Index of Leading Indicators." NBER Working Paper no. 244.
Weir, D. 1986. "The Reliability of Historical Macroeconomic Data for Comparing Cyclical Stability." *Journal of Economic History* 46: 353-65.
Zarnowitz, V. 1981. "Business Cycles and Growth: Some Reflections and Measures." In *Wirtschaftstheorie und Wirtschaftspolitik: Gedenkschrift für Erich Preiser*. Edited by W. J. Mückl and A. E. Ott. Passau: Passavia Universitätsverlag.
Zarnowitz, V. 1989. "Facts and Factors in the Recent Evolution of Business Cycles in the United States." NBER Working Paper no. 2865 (February).
Zarnowitz, V., and L. A. Lambros. 1987. "Consensus and Uncertainty in Economic Prediction." *Journal of Political Economy* 95: 591-621.
Zarnowitz, V., and G. H. Moore. 1982. "Sequential Signals of Recession and Recovery." *Journal of Business* 55: 57-85.
————. 1986. "Major Changes in Cyclical Behavior." In *The American Business Cycle: Continuity and Change*, pp. 519-72 and 579-82. Edited by R. J. Gordon. Chicago: University of Chicago Press for NBER.
Zellner, A. 1985. "Bayesian Econometrics." *Econometrica* 53: 253-69.

12

A Reassessment of Composite Indexes

Charlotte Boschan and Anirvan Banerji

In the three decades since composite indexes of cyclical economic activity were first used, they have evolved into various forms, each with strengths and weaknesses. Despite criticism, they have endured as important tools for tracking cyclical economic activity. With greater availability of economic data around the globe, the use of composite indexes is becoming increasingly widespread. This is an appropriate time, therefore, to review their evolution, compare the different methods for their construction, and suggest eclectic syntheses of these variants.

This chapter begins by tracing the evolution of the composite index from the older diffusion index. The two indexes are shown to differ only in the way they treat the magnitude of movements, with amplitude standardization lying at the heart of composite index construction. The different approaches to amplitude standardization are critically examined in light of their purpose, their implicit and explicit assumptions, and their adequacy, and suggestions are made for improvements. The best features of each method are then combined into an improved procedure leading to a more consistent, eclectic approach to composite index construction. Finally, the relevant issues involved in weighting the components of a composite index are discussed.

History

In 1927, Wesley C. Mitchell defined the concept of business cycles by summarizing their characteristics (Mitchell 1927, 468). In 1948, "with modifications suggested by experience in using [the definition]" he and Arthur F. Burns formulated a widely accepted definition of business cycles that contained the following description:

The authors wish to thank Debashis Guha, Lorene Hiris, Allan Layton, and Robyn Patterson for all their insights, help, and encouragement throughout the preparation of this paper. While the paper has benefited considerably from these inputs, any remaining errors are entirely the responsibility of the authors.

A cycle consists of expansions occurring at about the same time in many economic activities, followed by similarly general recessions, contractions and revivals which merge into the expansion phase of the next cycle . . . (Mitchell 1927, 468).

The definition refers not only to aggregate activity, but also to the widespread movements in many individual activities. It was, therefore, "necessary to have some measure of the scope of the fluctuations being considered. For this purpose diffusion indexes [were] constructed" (Moore 1982).

Diffusion indexes measure the proportion of indicators of activity, in the overall economy or within some group of industries, that are experiencing expansion over a given span of time. By constructing diffusion indexes for those groups of economic activities that typically turn early in the cyclical process, those that coincide and those that turn late, one can determine the extent of diffusion of an expansion or contraction through the economy.

Cyclically sensitive time series are combined into groups to yield diffusion indexes because some series would "prove more useful in one set of conditions, others in a different set. To increase the chances of getting true signals and reduce those of getting false ones, it is advisable to rely on all such potentially useful (series) as a group" (Zarnowitz and Boschan 1975).

However, diffusion indexes do not take into account the magnitudes of movements; they reflect neither the depth of a contraction nor the vigor of a recovery. A method was needed to combine the movements of a number of heterogeneous time series that cannot be combined by quantity, price, or any other weights, as they are in the usual index number construction.

The advent of computers facilitated the development of all kinds of measures related to time series analysis in general and to business cycle analysis in particular. One such measure was the composite index.

The first composite indexes were developed by Geoffrey H. Moore and Julius Shiskin. In 1958, Moore developed and used a method of combining cyclical indicators to forecast industrial production (Moore 1958). He was concerned with the problem that once magnitudes were considered in addition to mere counts of changes, time series which typically moved in wide swings had a much larger influence on the movement of the combined index than those which typically moved in narrow swings. He solved this problem by adjusting the amplitudes of each of the components by the relationship between its own historical volatility and that of a target series, which in this case was industrial production. He then combined the amplitude-adjusted changes. Later, Shiskin generalized this procedure by standardizing each component according to its own volatility, without regard to a target series (Shiskin 1961).

Since this initial work, various methodologies for constructing composite indexes were devised for different purposes. However, all currently established composite indexes use essentially the same idea for combining time series.

In the 1960s two developments occurred which had a strong influence on business cycle analysis and on composite indexes: First, it seemed that business cycles in the U.S. had become so mild that actual contractions had been replaced by declines in the rate of growth. Second, it became feasible through better data collection and the use of computers to analyze the economies of developing and rapidly growing countries where steep trends dominated the economy and precluded actual declines.

In general, it may not be possible to apply a methodology which has been designed for the analysis of economic conditions in a mature economy with relatively long cyclical swings *pari passu* to the conditions in developing or other countries with fast growing economies or even to rapidly growing segments of a mature economy. However, even in such conditions, there are cyclical retardations in growth that must be tracked and analyzed.

In order to analyze and measure retardations in an economy, new definitions of cycles in terms of deviations from trend (Deviation Cycles) or in terms of declines in the rate of growth (Growth Cycles) became prevalent (Mintz 1969).

Although economic conditions in the United States have, at least for the present, reverted to "classical cycles" with actual declines, and economic growth of some fast growing countries is slowing down, it may still be appropriate in some cases to use the concept of the Deviation Cycle. The extent to which this new definition of cycles affects the construction and use of composite indexes will be discussed later in this essay.

Standardization

The issue of amplitude standardization (i.e., expressing a cyclical indicator in terms of its own historical amplitude) is central to the construction of composite indexes because it arises from the key difference between diffusion indexes and composite indexes. This issue also lies at the heart of the differences between the various methods of constructing composite indexes. Table 12.1 provides a synopsis of the various standardization procedures and their different features. They will be described and discussed in detail in the following section.

Standardization Procedures and Their Problems

The development of composite indexes is often identified with Julius Shiskin, who also pioneered the development of X-11, the well-known computerized seasonal adjustment method. Shiskin's composite index is essentially a diffusion index that takes magnitudes into account. This becomes obvious when one considers the method of index construction, including the standardization procedure.

In Shiskin's method (Shiskin 1961), the month-to-month changes of each of the components are divided by the component's own standardization factor, which is defined as the average of its absolute month-to-month changes over a specified time period.[1] The standardized changés may then be explicitly weighted and added together, and the resulting sum of changes is cumulated to yield a composite index. Finally, this index may be trend and amplitude adjusted to match a target series. This standardization method insures that, if every month-to-month change for each series happens to be equal in magnitude to the series' standardization factor, the composite index will be identical to the diffusion index. In other words, Shiskin's composite index differs from the diffusion index only to the extent that the magnitudes of the month-to-month changes differ from the standardization factors of the series. Traditionally, Shiskin's composite index has been calculated for changes over a one-month span, but it may be possible, as in diffusion indexes, to use longer spans to get smoother indexes with less irregular movement.

The Statistics Canada Method (Rhoades 1982) differs from the Shiskin method essentially in two respects: The standardization factor used is the standard deviation of the month-to-month changes rather than their absolute average; and the composite index is smoothed with minimum phase-shift filters to minimize false signals.

Although standardization is generally understood to be a form of amplitude adjustment which "equalizes the average cyclical amplitude of the series . . ." (Moore 1961, 649), Shiskin's method, as well as the Canadian method, standardizes for month-to-month changes, which include the cyclical, the trend, and the irregular movements. Of two series with identical cyclical amplitudes, the one with a larger trend (and/or irregular) component has a much larger standardization factor, and its cyclical movement may therefore be eclipsed after standardization. This is one reason the British Central Statistical Office (CSO) prefers to use the mean absolute deviation from trend as the standardization factor (Central Statistical Office 1976), while the Organization for Economic Co-operation and Development (OECD) uses average absolute deviations of the detrended series from its mean (OECD 1987, 39).[2] In the OECD and British methods, the detrended series are divided by the standardization factor and aggregated to yield a composite index. Like the Shiskin index, this index may be trend and amplitude adjusted to match a target series.

While the OECD and CSO methods mitigate the Shiskin and Canadian methods' problem of possible dominance of the trend or irregular movement over the cyclical movement, they create new problems in the process. One problem stems from the artificial nature of the trend, which must be repeatedly re-estimated, particularly near the end. For the trend, the CSO uses a centered 5-year moving average, extended by regression lines for 2½ years at each end. Therefore, the CSO continually re-estimates the trend for the last 2½ years of the series which results in extra revisions of current data; this is a problem with all centered moving averages. The Phase-Average Trend used by the OECD has similar problems, but the resultant changes are likely to be smaller than those for trends based on moving averages, except in the vicinity of a new turning point.

Table 12.1

Standardization Procedures

	Shiskin (U.S. Dept. of Commerce and CIBCR)	Statistics Canada	OECD	CSO (U.K.)	Haywood (static)	Haywood (dynamic)	EPA (Japan)	Ecumenical
1. Series Standardized:								
Month-to-month changes*	X							
Deviations from:								
a) Centered 75-month moving average, extended by projecting average rate of change (% deviation) smoothed by 5 mo. mov. avg.		X						
b) Centered 60-month moving average, extended by regression lines				X	X	X		
Deviations of month-to-month changes* from their 60-month trailing average							X	
Ratio of series to its PAT, minus mean of this ratio			X					
Amplitude-Stationary time series								X

2. *Standardization factor:*

Average, over fixed time span, of absolute:

a) Month-to-month changes*   X

b) Deviations from centered 60-month moving average   X

c) Deviations of ratio of series to its PAT, from the mean of this ratio   X

Standard deviation of:

a) Month-to-month changes,* calculated over:

  i) Fixed time span   X

  ii) 60-month moving time span   X

b) Deviations from 75-month moving average, calculated over:

  i) Fixed time span   X

  ii) 75-month moving time span   X

c) Deviations of smoothed series from PAT, calculated over fixed time span   X

Notes: Deviations, wherever mentioned, mean differences, not ratios.

*These are symmetric percent changes, or straight period-to-period changes, depending on the series. For quarterly composite indexes, these are quarter-to-quarter changes; for weekly composite indexes, week-to-week changes, and so on.

The other problem is that removal of a trend from individual series is likely to shift turning points: If the trend is upward, then the peaks are usually shifted to an earlier date and the troughs may occur later.[3] Furthermore, if the trend is not linear, the magnitude of the shifts will vary. But these shifts are only a symptom of the basic problem that the removal of a trend from individual series creates—it is inconsistent with the classical Mitchellian "cycle of experience" (Burns and Mitchell 1946, 37–40).

The term "cycle of experience" refers to the actual configuration of the cyclical processes to which each economic activity is subject. It includes cyclical timing, amplitudes, asymmetric expansions and contractions, different patterns at peaks and at troughs, mid-expansion retardations and, in particular, intracyclical trends. As Mitchell pointed out, trends and cycles are inseparable, one influencing the other. Further, "Cyclical fluctuations are so closely interwoven with . . . secular changes in economic life that important clues to the understanding of the former may be lost by mechanically eliminating the latter" (Burns and Mitchell 1946, 270). After experimenting with trend adjustment, Burns and Mitchell concluded, "We have seen that cyclical measures of different series, as well as cyclical measures of the same series, tend to be more alike when made from trend-adjusted data than when made from unadjusted data. To us that is a disadvantage of trend adjustment. The variations of cyclical behavior among and within series count in the interplay of forces that produce the business cycle of experience, and we therefore wish to preserve them" (Burns and Mitchell 1946, 307). It is clear, therefore, that removing an artificially calculated trend destroys the integrity of the classical cycle of experience, even though it may be consistent with a "deviation cycle of experience."

Of course, the deviation cycle is not as well established a concept as the classical cycle, not only because it has a shorter history of empirical and theoretical analysis to establish its validity, but also because its nature depends so critically on the trend elimination procedure. However, the deviation cycle, first introduced by Mintz (1969), has been used for composite index construction not only by the OECD and the CSO but in Australia (Haywood 1973) as well; the Economic Planning Agency (EPA) in Japan (EPA 1988) also uses a variation of deviation cycles.

Haywood developed two alternative approaches—the static deviation cycle and the dynamic deviation cycle. In the first method, the deviations from a 75-month moving average trend are divided by the standard deviation (calculated over a fixed span) of the detrended series; the second approach is similar, except that the standardization factor is the standard deviation calculated over a moving 75-month span. It is worth noting that the use of a 75-month moving average was first suggested by Mintz (1969). However, Mintz experimented with 50- to 75-month moving averages and decided to use the 75-month moving average. Subsequently, the Phase-Average Trend (Boschan and Ebanks 1978) was developed to replace moving average trends and, as Klein and Moore testify, it produces better results than the 75-month moving average, which was "noticeably affected by the shorter cycles in the data" (Klein and Moore 1985).

In fact, while Mintz's 75-month average was the best option available at the time, it suffers from serious shortcomings. The OECD (OECD 1987, 33), therefore, uses the Phase-Average Trend in preference to the 75-month moving average, and this choice clearly affects the standardization factor.

In the Japanese EPA's new method, the deviations of the month-to-month changes from their 60-month trailing average are divided by the standard deviation of these deviations calculated over the moving 60-month period. This method is likely to share with Haywood's dynamic method the shortcomings of a fixed-span moving average mentioned above. There are other problems with moving standard deviations that will be mentioned later.

In any case, the composites created by these methods may be consistent only with deviation cycles of various kinds, but not with the classical cycle. However, the classical business cycle has not yet been rendered obsolete, as the U.S. experience of the 1970s proves. Furthermore, as fast-growing economies mature their rates of growth typically decline—Japan's experience in the 1980s is a case in point. It is therefore more judicious to construct composite indexes in a way that is consistent with both the classical cycle and the deviation or growth cycle. This may be accomplished by combining series into a composite without eliminating the trend from the components, and then detrending the resultant composite index. Incidently, the Center for International Business Cycle Research (CIBCR) maintains its International Economic Indicator system using the Shiskin standardization procedure (Klein and Moore 1985) but, as we have already noted, large trends distort the standardization factors in this procedure.

Stationarity of Cyclical Amplitude[4]

A major problem with all the methods described above concerns the process of standardization whereby, in most cases, an entire time series is divided by a single number that represents the cyclical amplitude of that series. This procedure is meaningful only if the cyclical amplitude remains more or less constant over time, that is, if the amplitudes of successive cycles are not significantly different. These amplitudes may be measured in terms of average absolute changes, or standard deviations of changes, or standard deviations of detrended series—calculated separately for each successive cycle.

The Shiskin procedure of taking symmetric percentage changes may induce such amplitude-stationarity in many cases, and growth rates are also often inherently stationary. The Canadian method is similar. The OECD method of dividing each series by its trend may also result in some kind of stationarity. However, no systematic attempt is made in these procedures to insure that each series is amplitude-stationary, and in cases where they are not, the purpose of standardization may not be achieved.

The British CSO method, on the other hand, contains no procedure to induce such stationarity for indicators whose amplitudes are inherently likely to be non-stationary, perhaps changing at different rates over time. There is a serious question, therefore, about the efficacy of the standardization procedure carried out by the CSO.

Haywood's procedure based on static deviation cycles has similar problems, and his procedure based on dynamic deviation cycles was meant to overcome these problems. In this latter method, the deviations from a moving average are standardized using a moving standard deviation, rather than a single number. While this results in stationarity of a sort because the standard deviation tends to increase when the cyclical amplitude is higher, it also results in moving standard-ization factors and makes the index inconsistent over time. Once again, the cycle of experience is undermined.

If every cycle were of equal length, say 75 months, then standard deviations of ratios to a 75-month moving average would measure the amplitudes correctly and stationarity might be achieved. Cycles, however, vary greatly in length. If a cycle is longer than 75 months, part of it would be cut off by using a 75-month span, and the amplitude might be overestimated. If a cycle is much shorter than 75 months, some cyclical phases might occur more than once and bias the measurement of the amplitude.

The new Japanese Economic Planning Agency (EPA) method, like Haywood's dynamic method, aims to compensate for the changes in cyclical amplitude that may be occurring constantly over time. At least part of the time, however, the natural asymmetry of the cycle, with the well-known sharp troughs and gently rounded peaks, creates a problem of bias in amplitude measurement.

But the real issue is whether such a procedure is necessary to achieve ampli-tude stationarity in the first place. If there is an obvious trend in the change of amplitude over time, then the series can be transformed explicitly to make it stationary before standardization. On the other hand, the change of amplitude may be illusory. A case in point is the Australian experience, where an apparent decrease in cyclical amplitude had prompted the use of the dynamic deviation cycle; Boehm, who had earlier used the dynamic deviation cycle, abandoned it after witnessing "the increasing amplitude and shorter duration of cyclical fluc-tuations during the 1970s" (Boehm 1977). Thus the major problem with a moving standard deviation is that it may be unduly sensitive to apparent changes of cyclical amplitudes which may be a purely temporary phenomenon. Given all these problems, it is questionable whether amplitude stationarity can be achieved at all by using a constant-span moving average.

The Problem of Statistical Tractability

There is a problem of tractability with many of the standardization procedures we have examined. The Shiskin method, the OECD method, and the British CSO method all use the absolute average of changes (or deviation from trend) as a measure of amplitude. Such an absolute average measure does not have the useful statistical properties possessed by variance or standard deviation which has been used by Statistics Canada (1982) and by Haywood (1973).

This is a critically important issue when it is necessary to derive equivalent standardization factors for an indicator which is available at a lower frequency (say, quarterly) in earlier years and at a higher frequency (say, monthly) in more recent years. If the absolute average measure is used as a standardization factor instead of the standard deviation, there is no easy way to derive higher frequency standardization factors statistically equivalent to the lower frequency ones.

This is an important issue for some developing countries for which monthly or even quarterly data are just beginning to become available, though data collected at a lower frequency may be available much further back in time. In industrialized countries as well, data previously published only quarterly are now available monthly, and some monthly data are now available weekly. If the lower frequency historical data are not to be dispensed with when more frequently available data are used, there needs to be a way to derive statistically equivalent standardization factors.

This is relatively easy when the standard deviation is used as a measure of amplitude because the variance of the lower frequency series can be derived from the variance of the higher frequency series using an estimate of the autocorrelation in higher frequency data. The absolute average measure, on the other hand, does not possess such convenient statistical properties and has been used mainly for historical reasons. In fact, even Shiskin himself acknowledged that "other methods of standardizing series might give equally good or even better results; for example, the . . . observations . . . might be expressed in units of their standard deviation . . ." (Shiskin 1961, 124, footnote 2).

As shown in this one instance, the statistical properties of standard deviation may be critically important, and the use of a standardization factor with such properties is likely to facilitate statistical analysis in other instances. However, it should be noted that, though the new EPA method uses standard deviations, it may still be difficult to derive equivalent standardization factors. The problem stems from the fact that the deviations are measured from a moving average, whose cyclical amplitudes may change with the frequency of available data, and complicate the statistical relationships.

An Ecumenical Approach

We have reviewed the existing standardization procedures, and weighed the advantages and disadvantages of each. Ideally, there should be a way of retaining the advantages of various standardization procedures while surmounting the disadvantages of each. (Table 12.2 summarizes some advantages and disadvantages of different methods of composite index construction.) A procedure that

Table 12.2

An Evaluation of the Different Approaches

	Shiskin (U.S. Dept. of Commerce)	Statistics Canada	OECD	CSO (U.K.)	Haywood (static)	Haywood (dynamic)	EPA (Japan)	Ecumenical
Series standardized:								
Amplitude-Stationarity ensured	U	U	U	N	N	U	U	Y
Cycle of experience preserved	Y	Y	N	N	N	N	N	Y
Detrending procedure appropriate (undistorted by varying cycle length)	NA	NA	Y	U	U	U	U	NA
Standardization factor:								
Measures cyclical amplitude, undistorted by trend	N	N	Y	Y	Y	Y	Y	Y
Measures cyclical amplitude, undistorted by irregular movements	N	U	N	N	U	U	N	Y
Easily converted for different frequencies	N	Y	N	N	N	N	N	Y
Composite index:								
Can be analyzed using business cycle of experience	Y	Y	N	N	N	N	N	Y
Can be analyzed using deviation cycle of experience	Y	Y	Y	Y	Y	U	U	Y
Insensitive to problems with trend estimation	Y	Y	N	N	N	N	N	Y
Smoothed to reduce false signals	N	Y	N	N	N	N	N	Y

Note: Y means "Yes," the criterion is met in large measure.
U means that the fulfillment of the criterion is uncertain.
NA means "not applicable."
N implies that the criterion is not met.

comes close to achieving this objective will now be presented.

Since the object of standardization is to adjust for cyclical amplitudes, it is important that the trend and irregular movements do not significantly distort the estimate of the standardization factor. A good solution is that adopted by the OECD, the British CSO, Haywood and the Japanese EPA. In effect, they use deviations from trend as the basis for calculating the standardization factor. The trend to be used is a matter of preference, but we, like the OECD, favor the Phase-Average Trend (PAT) because it captures the trend through the cyclical average better than any moving average and is a more appropriate base from which to measure cyclical amplitude. The substantial revisions of the PAT after each turning point do not affect the standardization factor, which is calculated over a predetermined earlier time span.

This still leaves the problem of irregular movements distorting the standardization factor. Haywood uses a 5-month moving average (Haywood 1973) in order to prevent irregular movements from distorting the standardization factor. Another possibility would be to use the Whittaker-Henderson trend (Hodrick and Prescott 1980; Lucas 1977) with appropriate parameters to smooth the series.[5] In any case, ideally, a smoothed, detrended series should be used for calculating the standardization factor.

As previously discussed, there are some compelling reasons of tractability for using standard deviation rather than an absolute average measure as the standardization factor. Also, to measure cyclical amplitudes undistorted by trend and irregular components, the underlying series must be detrended and smoothed. In the suggested procedure, the standard deviation of the smoothed, detrended series would be used as the standardization factor.

An ancillary benefit that may result from using such a measure of amplitude is that it may facilitate probabilistic inferences under certain circumstances. When Haywood (1973) introduced the deviation cycle he may have made such an implicit assumption, since he proposed a turning point selection procedure based on amplitude criteria. In his words, ''One method would be to calculate the standard deviation of the deviation series and then select a value such as perhaps one standard deviation as the minimum amplitude level for the identification of a new phase.'' This point of view may have some appeal because the amplitude of deviations from trend depends on a large number of individual factors which drive the movement of any statistical indicator. Given that there exists a long-term trend in the indicator, the magnitude of deviation from this trend can well be imagined as being probabilistically determined, since there is some uncertainty involved in each of the myriad factors driving the indicator. Of course, this does not by any means preclude the conception of the pattern of cyclical movements being determined temporally by the dynamic interaction of cyclical forces.

The emphasis until now has been on the best way to estimate the standardization factor for each series. The other major issue concerns the series to be standardized.

The first consideration is that of amplitude-stationarity. The unstated assumption behind amplitude adjustment, effected by dividing each series by a single number, is that the cyclical amplitude of the series remains roughly the same over time. It is important, therefore, that the series used to calculate the standardization factor is amplitude-stationary and that the series into which the standardization factor is divided is also stationary in amplitude. Since different series have different patterns of nonstationarity, no mechanical procedure will invariably achieve such stationarity. Every series that is standardized must, therefore, be first examined individually and be transformed as appropriate in each particular case.

The second consideration is whether the series to be standardized should be trend adjusted, smoothed, or transformed in any way before division by the standardization factor. When the standardization factors are derived from deviations from trend, the factors themselves are sensitive to the trend being used. However, if the series being standardized are also the deviations from trend, the index becomes critically dependent on the nature of the artificial separation between trend and cycle.

While it is necessary to compute the cyclical amplitude from smoothed, detrended series to minimize distortion caused by trend and irregular movements, there is no such compelling reason to detrend the series to be standardized. If we keep in mind the historical objections to the artificial separation of trend and cycle (Burns and Mitchell 1946) and consider the somewhat arbitrary shift in turning points caused by such detrending, it becomes increasingly reasonable not to detrend the series to be standardized. This is one of the important virtues of the Shiskin method that should be retained.

The fact that standardizing a series without detrending can change the existing trend is of little account because in every case the final composite index can be transformed to match any target trend. What is important is that there is no need to distort the natural leads and lags and the integrity of the classical cycle of experience, on the basis of which many of the indicators might have been chosen in the first place. For similar reasons, we might prefer not to smooth the components before they are combined into a composite index—the final index can be smoothed if necessary, as in the Canadian method.

If growth cycle analysis or deviation cycle analysis is more appropriate than classical business cycle analysis in any given situation, such analyses can be done by removing the trend from the composite index itself (Klein and Moore 1985), so that the lead-lag relationship among the components of the index is not distorted in the process of constructing the index.

Growth cycle analysis and business cycle analysis are not substitutes for one another but complementary tools, the usefulness of which may change with time, across countries and across sectors of the economy within a country. It is, therefore, reasonable to construct composite indexes which can be used for either kind of analysis by simply adding or removing a trend rather than forcing a choice between classical business cycle analysis and growth cycle analysis.

The recommendations outlined above have been incorporated in an ecumenical procedure for constructing composite indexes. A computer program to perform the calculations has also been developed. In this procedure, the first objective is to ensure that each indicator included in the composite is amplitude-stationary. For this purpose, we take the logarithms of indicators whose cyclical amplitudes are likely to be proportional to their levels; other indicators, like growth rates, which are likely to be stationary to begin with are used directly.[6] If obvious regime changes have occurred, the series are split. Each amplitude stationary indicator is now divided by its standardization factor, which is the standard deviation of the detrended stationary series. The standardized indicators are then weighted and added together to yield the composite index. Finally, this composite may be smoothed, trend and amplitude adjusted, and rebased to match a target series. If deviation or growth cycle analysis needs to be conducted, the deviations of the index from trend can be calculated (this is tantamount to targeting a zero trend) or the growth rates of the index can be calculated.

This procedure is being tested extensively on different composite indexes and initial results are quite encouraging. The new procedure is described in detail in Banerji and Boschan (1989).

Weighting

The Purpose of Weighting

One purpose of constructing composite indexes is to increase the chances of getting true signals and decrease the chances of getting false ones. The motivation behind weighting is to insure this same purpose.

Of course, standardization itself is a form of weighting, which equalizes the volatility of the components. This may or, as has been discussed, may not give equal weight to the signals produced by each component. If any component is thought to deserve more weight because of greater importance, longer leads, higher reliability, or any other reason, one may resort to explicit weighting in addition to standardization. A good example is the "scoring system" used in the BEA composite indexes (Moore and Shiskin 1967; Zarnowitz and Boschan 1975). While this kind of weighting constitutes an attempt at using some kind of optimal weighting, it is not clear that such fine tuning produces significantly better results than standardization alone. Therefore, most composite indexes, like the OECD Index, use an equal weighting scheme after standardization, once the components have been selected. (There is reason to believe, however, that such scoring systems are useful in choosing the indicators to be included in the composite index.)

Now, while weights changing over time may have certain advantages, they are generally not used in composite indexes because of the added complications. It is important to mention that the problem of incomplete time series with observations missing either at the beginning or at the end of the series may lead to just such a system of changing weights. In fact, such incomplete series create problems of abrupt changes in both the level and the amplitude of the index. Depending on the assumptions made and on whether the weights of the remaining series are adjusted to compensate for the lack of a series, the level and amplitude may need to be adjusted explicitly to ensure that the index level and amplitude stay the same on both sides of such discontinuities. This problem is discussed further in the Appendix.

Validity, Reliability, and Optimal Weighting

Reliability and validity are important considerations whenever composites are used in the social sciences.

Validity of a composite index is concerned with the extent to which the index is related to whatever it is supposed to measure (i.e., turning points in cyclical economic activity or in a time series that leads or lags it). A composite index has a high degree of validity if, for example, the probability forecast of turning points, constructed from the composite index (Neftci 1982) in itself or with a lag or lead, is highly correlated with the actual occurrence of turning points. It is obvious that components should be selected to maximize the validity of the composite index.

In the discussion of reliability that follows, the words "composite index" or "indicators" or "components of the index" are used to mean the probability estimates of turning points generated from them.

Reliability refers to the consistency with which the composite index measures the same situation. Thus, when the composite index has high reliability, the individual components correlate highly with the index itself. When, however, the composite index is driven by indicators not highly correlated with each other and with the index, the index lacks consistency and has low reliability. For high reliability, therefore, one should give higher weights to those indicators which correlate highly with each other and the resultant composite index. In fact, one can use principal component analysis to choose optimal weights that would maximize the reliability of the composite index. However, such a procedure would minimize the impact of indicators which do not move with the other indicators, and this may defeat one of the purposes of the construction of the composite index, i.e., "to increase the chances of getting true signals . . . [if] . . . some indicators prove most useful in one set of conditions, others in a different set" (Zarnowitz and Boschan 1975).

It is perhaps precisely for this reason that optimal weighting systems may not work very well in the context of composite indexes of cyclical indicators. Even in forecasts of levels of specific economic variables (e.g., GNP), a simple average of forecasts often outperforms most optimal weighting systems (Winkler 1982; Makridakis and Winkler 1983; Figlewski and Urich 1983; Clemen and Winkler

1986). Among the explanations of this phenomenon is the instability of the variance-covariance matrix of the forecasts. This is consistent with the presumption that different indicators, like different models, perform better in different sets of situations.

Of course, any kind of optimal weighting scheme should be used instead of, not in addition to, standardization. But it is not clear that it results in any improvement over traditional standardization.

Conclusions

In tracing the history of the composite index, we have seen how the idea of standardizing the components arose from an attempt to incorporate magnitudes of changes into diffusion indexes which track the spread or diffusion of cyclical changes through some or all sectors of the economy. As a result, all composite indexes of cyclical indicators incorporate some kind of standardization procedure, and they differ primarily in the way standardization is achieved. The different procedures have their advantages and disadvantages, and they may or may not satisfy certain desirable criteria. The extent to which each procedure does so is summarized in Table 12.2.

Starting with Shiskin's original composite index, different methods have evolved because of attempts to address the special problems that became prominent in different applications of the method. The divergence between the OECD method and the Shiskin method is a case in point. As a result, today we have an array of different procedures leading to composites which are not comparable to each other.

Yet this is a time when the use of cyclical analysis is spreading to cover more and more countries and different sectors of the economy as more data become available. It is desirable that, even when different stages of development or the nature of available data give rise to different problems, a unified approach, flexible enough to meet the demands of each such situation, be used. It is imperative that such an approach be utilized, in the interest of comparability across countries, across sectors of the economy, and over stages of development—and as demonstrated, an ecumenical approach can achieve this objective.

At the same time, there is increasing emphasis on the use of probabalistic forecasts and more sophisticated statistical techniques for data analysis. Under these circumstances, it is reasonable to incorporate approaches into composite index construction that would make them more amenable to statistical analysis and consistent with accepted principles of cyclical analysis. For example, the amplitude of a composite index derived from lower frequency historical data needs to be statistically equivalent to the amplitude of the index derived from higher frequency current data when probability estimates of downturns or upturns are based on historical patterns of movements of the index.

In sum, three decades after the composite index was first introduced for cyclical analysis, its very success has led to many modifications of the original concept and encouraged expanding bodies of research. In the process, some degree of comparability has been lost. With the benefit of thirty-odd years of experience, it is clear that it is desirable and possible to unify the divergent approaches to enhance comparability across countries, across stages of development, and across traditions of research.

Appendix on Incomplete Series

Inclusion or exclusion of any component at a particular point in time causes lack of comparability of the index in terms of both level and volatility. To the extent, therefore, that one is interested in levels and amplitudes of the index and not just the turning points, the index should not be computed unless all the components are available. Even if one is interested only in turning points, one needs to ensure that the discontinuities do not result in abrupt changes of level that could be mistaken for turning points. This is attempted both in our procedure and in the Shiskin method by taking first differences and then cumulating to get the final index. Even this procedure, however, may not be very effective when the additional series have slopes (or changes, for "change" series) which are sharply different from the average for the other series. A problem which is not even addressed by the traditional procedure is that the inclusion of an additional component may result in a significant change in the amplitude of the index, even when all the components are standardized. A simple example can illustrate the problem. Suppose we have a two-component index, in which one component starts in January and the other in July. Let the two (standardized) components, each with a weight of 50 percent, vary in the following fashion:

```
Component 1:  -1  -1  +1  +1  -1  -1  +1  +1  -1  -1  +1  +1  -1  -1
Component 2:                  -1  +1  -1  +1  -1  +1  -1  +1
Index      :  -1  -1  +1  +1  -1  -1   0  +1  -1   0   0  +1  -1   0
```

Clearly, before the second component is added, the average absolute month-to-month change in the index is 1; after the second component is added, it is only 0.5. Hence, the amplitude of the index has changed. In our procedure, in terms of standard deviations of the detrended series, a similar shift is evident—it shifts from about 0.75 before the second series is added to about 0.33 afterwards. What is important in the context of our procedure is that there is a relatively easy way to address this issue. It is known that the variance of the index, including the additional component, equals the variance of the index without this component, plus the variance of this component, plus twice the covariance of the component and the index without it. Assuming that the unknown covariance of the index with the additional component (before it was available) is the same as the known covariance after it became available, this tells us what the variance of the index would have been, had the component been available. Since the relationship between the amplitudes of the index (with and without the extra component) is now known, one can adjust the amplitudes to make them comparable.

Notes

1. Changes are computed as symmetric percent changes except when the indicator contains nonpositive observations or is itself a ratio or percentage. In such cases, changes are computed as first differences. Incidentally, the idea of average absolute month-to-month change is one of the key concepts used in the X–11 procedure.

2. The standardization factor used by the CSO is

$$\frac{\sum_{i=1}^{n} \mid Y_i - M_i \mid}{n}$$

that for the OECD is

$$\frac{\sum_{i=1}^{n} \mid Y_i/T_i - \dfrac{\sum_{i=1}^{n} (Y_i/T_i)}{n} \mid}{n}$$

where Y = original time series
       T = Trend (PAT)
       M = Trend (centered 60-month moving average)
and   n = number of observations

3. For example, if employment has a strong upward trend and the average work week a horizontal or downward trend, then detrending would obscure the lead of the adjustments in hours over those in employment, which is likely to exist as an institutional managerial practice.

4. "Strict stationarity" is achieved when the underlying joint probability distribution (and therefore, all moments of this distribution) remain invariant with respect to time. A weaker form, "covariance stationarity," requires that the first two moments (that is, the mean, variance and covariances) of the series are invariant with respect to time. (For a complete definition, see Box and Jenkins 1978.)

The amplitude of a cyclical time series can be measured in different ways. In electrical engineering, for example, one may measure "peak-to-peak"(really, peak-to-trough) amplitude, or more commonly, the "root-mean-square"(RMS) amplitude of an alternating current or voltage. The main voltage in U.S. households, for example, is around 120V, RMS.

If the measure of amplitude is the standard deviation of the detrended series, it is equivalent to the RMS measure of amplitude. Stationarity of cyclical amplitude would then be defined with respect to the variance of the detrended series, i.e., the variance of the series about its trend line. In that case, "stationarity of cyclical amplitude" would be achieved if the variance of the series about its trend line, measured separately for each cycle, remains invariant from cycle to cycle. This differs from the definition of "covariance stationarity'' in the sense that the variances are measured specifically over complete cycles, instead of over arbitrary time-spans.

If other measures of amplitude are used, amplitude-stationarity would require invariance of cyclical amplitude measured analogously, over complete cycles.

5. The Whittaker-Henderson Type A curve is computed by minimizing the sum of squared deviations of the curve from the data, subject to a constraint on the maximum rate of change of the slope of the curve. It has been used to compute long term trends but, with less stringent constraints on the rate of change of the slope, it may provide a useful method of smoothing. Further work on this subject is currently being done by Debashis Guha at the CIBCR.

6. In constructing an index to gauge the cyclical movements across an economy, we believe it is inconsistent to combine levels and growth rates. However, this is done in several existing composite indexes—mainly to increase the leads at turning points.

References

Banerji, Anirvan, and Charlotte Boschan. 1989. "Constructing a Time-Consistent Composite Index: An Eclectic Approach." CIBCR Working Paper, Center for International Business Cycle Research, Columbia University, New York.

Boehm, Ernst A. 1977. "Recurring Periods of Plateau Slumps and Sluggish Recoveries in the Australian Economy: 1950-1976." *The Australian Economic Review* (1st Quarter): 53-60.

Boschan, Charlotte, and Walter W. Ebanks. 1978. "The Phase-Average Trend: A New Way of Measuring Economic Growth." Proceedings of the Business and Economics Statistics Section, American Statistical Association.

Box, G. E. P., and G. M. Jenkins. 1976. *Time Series Analysis: Forecasting and Control.* Rev. ed. San Francisco: Holden-Day.

Bry, Gerhard, and Charlotte Boschan. 1971. *Cyclical Analysis of Time Series: Selected Procedures and Computer Programs.* Technical Paper 20. New York: National Bureau of Economic Research.

Burns, Arthur F. and Wesley C. Mitchell. 1946. *Measuring Business Cycles.* New York: National Bureau of Economic Research.

Central Statistical Office. 1976. "Changes to the Cyclical Indicator System." *Economic Trends* (May) 271: 67-69.

Clemen, Robert T., and Robert L. Winkler. 1986. "Combining Economic Forecasts." *Journal of Business and Economic Statistics* 4: 39-46.

Economic Planning Agency. 1988. Personal communication from Mr. Ichiro Fujimoto, Business Statistics Research Division.

Figlewski, Stephen, and Thomas Urich. 1983. "Optimal Aggregation of Money Supply Forecasts: Accuracy, Profitability and Market Efficiency." *The Journal of Finance* 28: 695-710.

Haywood, Eric. 1973. "The Deviation Cycle: A New Index of the Australian Business Cycle 1950-1973." *The Australian Economic Review* (4th Quarter): 31-39.

Hodrick, R. J., and E. C. Prescott. 1980. "Post-War U.S. Business Cycles: An Empirical Investigation." Carnegie-Mellon University working paper no. 451, revised, November.

Klein, Philip A., and Geoffrey H. Moore. 1985. *Monitoring Growth Cycles in Market-Oriented Countries: Developing and Using International Economic Indicators.* NBER Studies in Business Cycles No. 26. Cambridge, Mass.: Ballinger.

Lucas, R. E., Jr. 1977. "Understanding Business Cycles." In *Stabilization of the Domestic and International Economy.* Edited by Karl Brunner and Allan H. Metzler. Amsterdam: North-Holland.

Makridakis, Spyros, and Robert L. Winkler. 1983. "Averages of Forecasts: Some Empirical Results." *Management Science* 29: 987-996.

Mintz, Ilse. 1969. *Dating Postwar Business Cycles, Methods and Their Application to Western Germany, 1950-67.* Occasional Paper 107. New York: National Bureau of Economic Research.

Mitchell, Wesley. 1927. *Business Cycles: The Problem and Its Setting.* New York: National Bureau of Economic Research.

Moore, Geoffrey H. 1958. "Forecasting Industrial Production—A Comment." *Journal of Political Economy* (February).

————. 1961. "An Amplitude Adjustment for the Leading Indicators." In *Business Cycle Indicators*, Vol. 1, pp. 645ff. Edited by Geoffrey H. Moore. Princeton, N.J.: Princeton University Press for NBER.

Geoffrey H., and Julius Shiskin. 1967. *Indicators of Business Expansions and Contractions.* Occasional Paper 103. New York: National Bureau of Economic Research.

Neftci, Salih N. 1982. "Optimal Prediction of Cyclical Downturns." *Journal of Economic Dynamics and Control* 4: 225-241.

OECD Department of Economics and Statistics. 1987. *OECD Leading Indicators and Business Cycles in Member Countries 1960-1985.* Sources and Methods 39. Paris: OECD.

Rhoades, Darryl. 1980. "Minimum Phase-Shift Filtering of Economic Time Series." *Canadian Statistical Review* (February).

————. 1982. "Statistics Canada's Leading Indicator System." *Current Economic Analysis* (May).

Shiskin, Julius. 1961. "Signals of Recession and Recovery." Occasional Paper 77. New York: National Bureau of Economic Research.

Winkler, Robert L. 1982. "Combining Forecasts." In *Major Time Series Methods and Their Relative Accuracy.* Edited by Spyros Makridakis et al. New York: Wiley.

Zarnowitz, Victor, and Charlotte Boschan. 1975. "Cyclical Indicators: An Evaluation and New Leading Indexes." In *Handbook of Cyclical Indicators.* Washington, D.C.: Government Printing Office.

13

Long-Leading Index, 1919–1988

Chantal Dubrin and Jean Maltz

We wish to extend our best wishes to Dr. Moore on his 75th birthday and to join in honoring him. We feel we can make no better contribution than submitting a small sample representative of the work we have done at the CIBCR—the kind of work we know is close to his heart.

A long-leading index beginning in January 1948 was developed in the summer of 1987 with the cooperation of the Bureau of Economic Analysis, Department of Commerce. In October 1988, we constructed an equivalent long-leading index which starts in 1919 and continues through 1950. The components for the post World War II period are:
—Dow Jones Average Bond Price, 20 Bonds
—Ratio, Price to Unit Labor Cost, Manufacturing
—Money Supply (M2) (Deflated)
—New Building Permits, Housing.
The equivalent components for the earlier period are:
—Yield on Corporate Bonds, Highest Rating, (Inverted)
—Ratio, Price to Unit Labor Cost, Manufacturing
—Demand and Time Deposits + Currency, (Deflated)
—Contracts, Residential Buildings, Floor Space.
The two segments are combined into a continuous long-leading index by linking them in January 1948. This index, along with its turning points and the Business Cycle Chronology, is shown in Chart 13.1. The six-month smoothed growth rate of this index is shown in Chart 13.2. The growth rate is based on the ratio of the current month's index to the average index over the preceding twelve months and is expressed as a compound annual rate. Table 13.1 shows the timing relationship of the index and its growth rate to the Business Cycle Chronology.

The long-leading index is the only leading index we know of that spans almost the whole of the twentieth century and even predicts the great depression. We think, therefore, that this is perhaps a fitting tribute to someone who takes the truly long-term perspective in focusing on the unbroken threads that run through the economic ups and downs in this world of ours.

Chart 13.1. **United States Long-leading Index, 1919–1988.**

1967 = 100

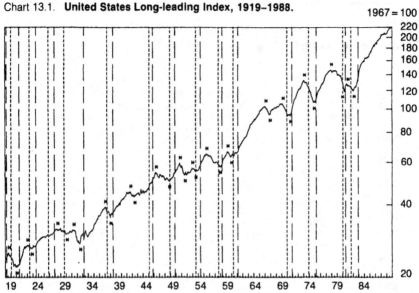

Notes: Vertical lines are peaks (- - - -) and troughs (— — —) in the business cycle chronology.
* indicates peaks and troughs.

Chart 13.2. **Growth Rate in United States Long-leading Index, 1919–1988.**

Six-month smoothed percentage change at annual rate

Percent

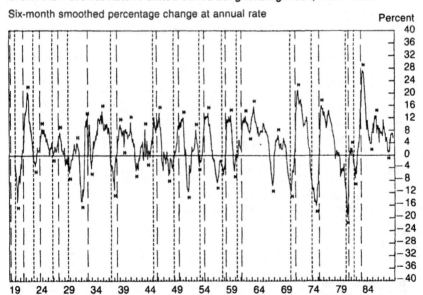

Notes: Vertical lines are peaks (- - - -) and troughs (— — —) in the business cycle chronology.
* indicates peaks and troughs.

Table 13.1

Cyclical Timing, Long-leading Index, 1919–1988

Business cycles chronology		Long-leading index leads (−) or lags (+) in months		Long-leading index growth rate leads (−) or lags (+) in months	
troughs	peaks	troughs	peaks	troughs	peaks
3/19		—		—	
	1/20		−6		—
7/21		−7		−13	
	5/23		−5		−13
7/24		−10		−10	
	10/26		N.C.		−23
11/27		N.C.		−11	
	8/29		−15		−18
3/33		−9		−13	
	5/37		−5		−19
6/38		−6		−6	
	2/45		N.C.		−18
10/45		N.C.		−20	
	11/48		−31		−31
10/49		−13		−22	
	7/53		−8		−8
5/54		−11		−11	
	8/57		−27		−30
4/58		−5		−19	
	4/60		−13		−13
2/61		−15		−15	
	12/69		−10		−27
11/70		−4		−9	
	11/73		−10		−30
3/75		−5		−6	
	1/80		−26		−53
7/80		−2		−3	
	7/81		−10		−5
11/82		−10		−13	
Median leads or lags		−8	−10	−12	−19
Mean leads or lags		−8	−14	−12	−22
All turns					
Median leads or lags		−10		−13	
Mean leads or lags		−11		−17	
Number of extra cycles		4		7	
Number of skipped cycles		2		0	

Note: "N.C." means no timing comparisons can be made.

VI
RECENT BUSINESS CYCLE RESEARCH: IMPLICATIONS FOR THEORY AND POLICY

14

The Long-Run Efficacy of Efforts to Mitigate Downturns

Alfred L. Malabre, Jr.

The business cycle, like death and taxes, will always be with us. If this is true, as I believe to be the case, there follow distinct advantages, at least for those of us so foolhardy as to try to make sense out of the economic world around us. Indeed, it's wonderfully comforting to know that there's at least one constant on the ever-shifting economic landscape.

Fiscalism or monetarism or even the so-called supply-side notion may come and go, enjoying their respective days in the sun and then slowly fading along with their various champions, whether Maynard Keynes or Milton Friedman or Arthur Laffer. There can be no such disillusionment, however, for those of us whose natural skepticism, perhaps, has dictated a less definite approach, one whose main compass is nothing more elaborate than what we have come to call the business cycle.

A View on the Business Cycle

As commonly defined, the business cycle provides a reference point for appraisals of the ever-changing outlook. It constitutes a guidepost much less likely to mislead over the long term than, say, the size and direction of the federal budget deficit or the growth rate of a particular monetary aggregate, be it M1 or M2 or M-whatever, or the level of the top tax rate, be it 50 percent or 40 percent or 30 percent.

Because of its notable constancy, the business cycle proves a difficult subject for new and illuminating discussion. Much of what follows, I must therefore stress, is drawn from a range of earlier work, including my own two recent books dealing extensively with the subject—*Beyond Our Means* and *Understanding the New Economy*—as well as the seminal essays of such stalwarts as Geoffrey H. Moore, both while he was at the National Bureau of Economic Research (NBER) and later at Columbia University's appropriately named Center for International Business Cycle Research (CIBCR).

231

First off, let me recall that the ups and downs of the business cycle—from trough to ensuing expansion peak to ensuing recession or, as economists call it, contraction—have been tracked by NBER and Commerce Department economists as far back as 1854, more precisely to December of that year, which is deemed a trough month in *Business Conditions Digest*, the official record book. Since that time the NBER, using a variety of economic statistics including Gross National Product data, has recorded thirty expansions through the 1980-81 upswing and an equal number of contractions through the severe 1981-82 slump.

The up phases, happily, have proved a good deal longer, on the average, than the down phases. Indeed, this is how the American economy has grown over the decades, in a sort of two-steps-forward, one-step-back fashion. The expansions, trough to peak, work out to an average duration of 33 months. The contractions, peak to trough, average 18 months. The longest of the expansions occurred from 1961 to 1969, lasting 106 months, and the shortest ran from the spring of 1919 to early 1920, only 10 months. The longest contraction began all the way back in 1873 and lasted into 1879—quite obviously a very large backward step that spanned 65 months. The shortest took place relatively recently, in early 1980, and lasted only 6 months. To this day some analysts, including myself but not (he tells me) Geoffrey Moore, believe that for once the NBER erred in its determination and that the 1980 episode by itself did not constitute a bona fide recession—but that is another story, of little concern in this discussion.

NBER analysts have subdivided their business-cycle data into three narrower time frames—from 1854 to 1919, an interval encompassing sixteen cyclical ups and downs; from 1919 to 1945, which spans six cyclical swings; and from 1945 onward, a period encompassing eleven cycles up to the expansion that coincided with Ronald Reagan's first Presidential victory in November 1980.

Viewed along chronological lines, this breakdown pinpoints some significant patterns. Expansions have been growing progressively longer. In the 1854-1919 stretch, the cyclical upturns averaged 27 months. In 1919-45 period, the average expansion increased to 35 months. And in the latest period, it reached 45 months, a full year and a half longer than in the pre-World War I decades. Recessions, by the same token, have been slowly diminishing in length. Between 1854-1919, contraction phases of the cycle averaged 22 months; during 1919-45, the average was 18 months; and since 1945, only 11 months.

In the main, the longest expansion periods have coincided partly or wholly with wars. The long 1961-69 upturn roughly coincided with the Vietnam War. The second longest expansion was also largely a wartime affair, the 80-month 1938-45 upswing. At the same time, the longest contractions have tended to occur in peacetime. The long 1873-79 slump is an illustration. Better known and more painful was the 43 months during 1929-33. Its March 1933 trough is generally regarded as the Great Depression's low point.

Patterns of Business Cycle Severity

Sturdy, long-running expansions often follow in the wake of severe recessions. By the same token, weak, short-lived upturns often occur after short, mild recessions.

The longest peacetime expansion—previous to the latest upswing, which began in November 1982—was a 58-month rise from early 1975 to the beginning of 1980, and it is noteworthy that it followed one of the most severe recessions of the postwar era, the 16-month slump of 1973–75. The weak upturn of 1980–81, the shortest on record after the 1919–1920 expansion, followed on the heels of the record-short recession of 1980. The expansion that began in 1982, of course, followed the very harsh slump of 1981–82, the first contraction of the postwar period in which the unemployment rate, for example, climbed into double-digit territory. None of these patterns is happenstance, and all are exceedingly useful to bear in mind in any effort to assess the economic scene, whether now or a dozen years hence.

Enduring expansions naturally tend to follow severe recessions because such slumps, almost by definition, serve to cleanse the economy of the strains and distortions that normally mark a peak in the business cycle. These range from intense inflationary pressure and soaring interest rates to worsening shortages of material and labor, widening bottlenecks in production, and later and later delivery schedules. In similar fashion, weak expansions tend to follow mild recessions precisely because such recessions fail to provide the necessary cleaning out. They fail to lay the groundwork for renewed, vigorous economic growth. In such circumstances, inflation and other boom-time problems rapidly re-emerge as business activity begins to move up from the business-cycle trough. As these problems intensify, further economic gains grow increasingly difficult. The upshot is a subpar, abbreviated expansion.

The tendency of expansions to lengthen and recessions to shorten in recent decades isn't happenstance, either. Particularly since World War II, transfer payments have acted to blunt recessions. Ever more generous programs of unemployment relief have served to shore up consumer buying power even as joblessness has spread. Thanks to transfer payments, consumer spending kept right on rising through the otherwise severe recession of 1981–82, which as noted was the first postwar slump in which joblessness reached double-digit territory. As recessions have shortened, so, naturally, have expansions grown longer. As business activity has moved up from troughs, the rise in transfer income has slowed but by no means halted. Superimposed on reviving activity within the economy's private sector, this climb in transfers has further spurred expansion.

Nor is it coincidental that the most enduring upturns have tended to occur in wartime and the longest contractions in peacetime. Like transfer payments, military spending tends to pump up consumers' purchasing power—albeit in a highly inflationary manner since, for example, bomb factories do nothing to enlarge the supply of goods or services available for purchase in the marketplace. When military outlays are generally on the increase, as during the long expansion of 1961–69, the boost to buying power serves as a powerful economic stimulant. The effect is directly opposite when these outlays diminish. After spending for the Vietnam War began to decline, the economy sustained two recessions, both relatively severe, within a short five years. Why does cyclical instability endure? These various patterns, as important as they may be, hardly explain why the business cycle exists in the first place or why the economy, over so many decades, has shown this tendency to expand-contract, expand-contract. In brief, why is the business cycle, like death and taxes, always with us?

Perhaps the simplest and best explanation that I've come across wasn't in any economic textbook or scholarly journal, but in a letter that I once received from a *Wall Street Journal* reader by the name of Russell M. Fowler. Responding to an article that I had written for the newspaper in November 1984, Fowler, who served at the time as the administrator of the Wayne Economic Development Corporation in Lyons, New York, put it this way, "Maybe the reason the business cycle endures is the economy is solidly based on human nature. When things are going good, some human reactions occur: overconfidence, complacency, poor workmanship, greed, overexpansion, mistakes; all bad and leading to [a] downturn. Then when things are going bad, there is a tendency to shape up and turn things around. Maybe that's all there is to it."

Amen. It's as clear and accurate an explanation of the why of the cycle as I have encountered; as a description of the national mood during the upswing of the middle 1980s, for instance, it could hardly be better. It's a good deal clearer, in fact, than anything I've managed to extract over the years from an array of eminent business people who should know better. I've even heard prominent economists profess—though not recently—that the cycle, which existed once upon a time, has been eliminated with the advent of a new era of enlightened policy-making in Washington.

One such one-time believer was the late Otto Eckstein, an economic adviser to President Lyndon Johnson. Professor Eckstein was fortunate to fill that role just when the longest upswing in business cycle history was in progress. Before his untimely death in 1984, the Harvard economist, who also headed the highly successful economic consulting firm of Data Resources Inc., had become convinced of the cycle's inevitability. But back in the mid–1960s, he was among the brave new economists who sincerely supposed that they could guide business activity comfortably along a path without end of recession-free expansion. Fine-tuning the economy was the catchword. This conviction occasionally was stretched to ludicrous extremes, as when Eckstein and his colleagues in Washington decided that the name of the Commerce Department's premier statistical publication was no longer appropriate. The monthly publication for years had been called *Business Cycle Developments*, a to-the-point appellation in that the periodical not only reported all sorts of business data but took the extra step of relating the various numbers back over the decades to the ups and downs of the business cycle. The title—in accordance with the prevailing notion that the cycle had been eliminated forever through more enlightened policy-making—was ordered changed to *Business Conditions Digest*. Notwithstanding the name change, the economy, as perverse as ever, soon entered a particularly nasty slump. So much for new eras of recession-free growth. The new name has stuck, with only the *BCD* acronym unchanged. The business cycle has stuck as well.

As Russell Fowler understood, contractions of business activity occur and will continue to occur because of an immutable constant—human nature. Planners, be they public or private, make mistakes. When things are going along in fine fashion, planners tend to neglect the sometimes painful belt-tightening that in the long run might help to keep business on the upswing. They tend to overestimate prospects for further economic gains, inventories begin to pile up, workers finally must be laid off, and an expansion transforms into a recession. And when it's all too evident that the economy is finally on the skids, planners begin believing that the depressed conditions will keep worsening. Inventories are worked down, perhaps too far. Eventually, customer demand for goods and services begins to outstrip supply. Businesses scramble to catch up, production is stepped up, and the economy starts recovering once again.

This recurring tendency to overestimate and underestimate will subside as soon as human nature changes, I submit, and not a moment sooner. It's particularly pronounced in economies, such as the major industrial ones, where manufacturing plays a prominent role. Manufacturing, of course, spans such important industries as automobiles, appliances, and heavy machinery, plus sundry smaller businesses. Such products must be fashioned in factories, using basic materials like steel, copper, coal, aluminum, and plastics, and then be distributed and sold to customers at home and abroad. If factory operations are precisely geared to demand so as not to overproduce or underproduce particular items, the economy generally should prosper and expand without nasty surprises. After all, the U.S. population continues to grow, though somewhat more slowly than in decades past. Moreover, technological advances keep coming that enhance the nation's productive efficiency; this, too, serves to prolong economic expansion.

It should be added that outside factors, as well as the fallibility of planners in and out of Washington, occasionally contribute to the economy's cyclical behavior. An example is the oil squeeze that the Arab countries imposed on the United States and other major oil-using countries in late 1973. It is generally agreed that the U.S. economy was still in an expansion mode, which started in 1970, when the oil squeeze developed. How much longer that expansion phase would have lasted had the Arabs not cut the oil supply is a matter of conjecture. To be sure, forces were already at work in the fall of 1973—for example, an excessive accumulation of inventories in many businesses—that would have led sooner or later to an expansion peak and a subsequent contraction of the cycle. But there is little question that the jolting reduction in Middle Eastern oil supplies, with the long lines at gasoline pumps and the occasional restriction of output at fuel-starved factories, hastened and deepened the new slump.

Coping with Enduring Instability

If the business cycle is inevitable, as experience and common sense suggest, what does this portend for the economy? Are we simply to sit back and suffer through the inevitable down phases of the cycle, with their spreading joblessness and sinking profits, and hope that recovery time won't prove too far over the horizon? Or should we strive to minimize, perhaps even aim to eliminate, the contraction periods and perpetuate the expansions?

The latter course, not surprisingly, has long been a primary goal of Washington's policy-makers. The record of recent decades is marked by a succession of noble efforts to bring incipient recessions to a rapid end and get the economy moving again. A major engine of this economic stimulation has been the Federal Reserve Board which, through its so-called Open Market Committee, has repeatedly moved, when the outlook seemed dark, to spur monetary growth far faster than the economy's own long-term ability to advance.

A second source of stimulation has been the government's proclivity, thanks mainly to the Congress, to spend far more each year than is taken in by the tax man. Whatever else can be said about the resulting budgetary deficits, they have acted on balance to spur business activity. If nothing else, federal outlays tend, at least in the shortest term, to create jobs and spur demand for all sorts of goods and services, and there can be no doubt that monetary and fiscal stimulation has helped prolong expansions and limit contractions.

So far, this stimulation has worked reasonably well, with the upturns lengthening and the recessions, until recently, becoming milder and shorter. But in this forced-draft effort to alter the economy's natural patterns—its tendency to slump, cleanse itself, and recover with renewed vigor—a rigidity has developed that transcends the business cycle. With each new up-and-down of the cycle in the post-World War II decades, a degree of natural resiliency has drained from the economy.

With this increasing brittleness, the business cycle takes on a dangerous new aspect. With each new contraction phase, the possibility of a real collapse grows larger. Because we have lived so far beyond our means for so long, the economy has come to require ever greater doses of adrenaline to recover. The doses, to be sure, have been supplied quickly and in massive quantity—as when the Federal Reserve explosively expanded the money supply in 1982, and the feared collapse didn't materialize. But the treatment gets riskier and trickier the longer it's applied. In brief, the decades-long effort to modify the business cycle has led to the institutional crises that now confront us. In this regard, consider the condition of the Federal Savings and Loan Insurance Corporation.

With the brittleness, the expansions also require more attention. Unemployment proves stickier, generally settling in at higher and higher levels with each new business cycle peak. Corporate balance sheets stay shakier for a longer period. The rate of bankruptcies subsides less readily. Inflationary dislocations— shortages, delivery delays, labor-cost increases, stagnant productivity, price increases—tend to redevelop at lower and lower levels of capacity utilization. In the process, the economy requires larger and larger doses of medication to avert a relapse. These have been amply applied by the various successions of authorities in Washington, be they Republican or Democrat. But again, the game grows trickier.

A few statistics help to illustrate the general pattern. Near the trough of the 1981–82 recession, the unemployment rate was about 11 percent, compared to 9 percent near the trough of the severe 1973–75 slump and only about 6 percent near the trough of the 1969–70 recession. There has been a similar worsening in the amount of current liabilities outstanding from business failures. During the 1981–82 recession, the total reached a monthly rate of some $1.8 billion, up from about $350 million in 1973–75 and just under $200 million in 1969–70.

Conclusion

If only the business cycle could be made to fade away, but this eventuality is as likely as an overnight transformation of New York City's subway system into the safest, cleanest mass-transit operation in the world. It's not about to happen. And so the danger mounts that with each new contraction of the cycle an increasingly brittle economy will crack, and not simply creak and groan once again in another of the string of postwar recessions.

Fiscal and monetary stimulation implemented to prolong expansions and shorten recessions works in essence like a drug, masking symptoms that should be attended to directly. The economic system never gets cleansed during recessions of excesses—for instance, excessive borrowing—that accumulated during periods of general economic growth. In the process, larger and larger doses of stimulation are necessary to induce a given amount of growth.

Example: Despite repeated income-tax cuts, more liberal tax treatment of corporate investments, and an exceptionally swift rise in the money supply during the early Reagan years, overall economic growth was largely subpar for an expansion, averaging only 3 percent or less annually through much of the period.

15

Diminished Unit Labor Cost Pressures: Importance for Methuselah Expansion

John P. Cullity

Meteorologists attach names to the hurricanes they study. If business cycle experts did the same for economic expansions, the 1982–1988 economic upswing in the United States would surely be called Methuselah. It is our longest peacetime expansion. Many economists attribute this longevity to the adoption of appropriate fiscal and monetary policies during crucial phases of the upswing. Some subscribing to this viewpoint belong to the "supply-side school" of economics. They stress an intellectual breakthrough occurred in economic policy. Before the 1980s, economic policy makers failed to adequately understand how high marginal tax rates were blunting incentives to work and produce. We now know better as a result of tax cuts in the 1980s; henceforth, we can expect a better economic performance by reducing tax rates further and at the same time hold federal spending in check and apply appropriate monetary policies. Many students of Keynesian economics also find the cause of the long upswing obvious. Their analysis emphasizes the stimulative effect of the gargantuan federal deficits in keeping the economy in a quasi boom.

The objective of this chapter is not to critically evaluate fiscal, monetary, supply-side, or any other policy which seeks to improve U.S. economic performance. Its aim is to emphasize that a fundamental condition responsible for the strong economic performance in the 1980s was a more favorable relationship between changes in hourly compensation and productivity. The improved relationship eliminated much of the upward pressure on prices from the cost side. Thus, the impact of the federal government's reduced tax rates and stimulative fiscal actions along with the Federal Reserve's more accommodative policies had a minimal inflationary impact and a strong effect on jobs, hours of work, and output.

Students of the business cycle research of Mitchell, Burns, Hultgren, Moore, and others at the National Bureau of Economic Research will not be surprised by this speculation. Price-cost-profit relationships once received considerable attention in the Bureau's business cycle section.

The first section of this chapter presents facts about changes in the price-cost variables during the 1982–88 expansion and during preceding periods. Next, structural changes in the economy which may account for the price-cost changes are discussed. This is followed by an examination of some of the policy implications of the new environment in labor markets. And, after six years of expansion, the economic situation is evaluated.

Facts About Recent Developments in U.S. Unit Labor Costs in the 1980s

Statistics on productivity, hourly compensation, and price developments are available in many government publications. One convenient source is the *Annual Report of the President's Council of Economic Advisers*. Table 15.1, based on data from the 1988 report, shows that from 1982 to 1988 output per hour in the nonfarm business sector rose on average close to two percent annually, while compensation per hour increased annually by about four percent. Obviously these growth rates weren't in perfect balance, but compared with earlier changes, this was a respectable performance. The difference between productivity improvements and hourly compensation advances is an important gap from an analytical point of view. If no gap exists, there is an absence of cost pressure on business managers tending to induce them to raise prices.

During the early part of the expansion of the 1980s, the gap was largest between 1984 and 1985 when productivity rose 1.4 percent, hourly compensation increased 4.2 percent, and unit labor costs advanced 2.8 percent. The gross national product deflator rose by 3.0 percent. For a while, it looked like cost inflation was making a comeback. From 1985 to 1986, however, the gap narrowed. This was mainly the result of a speedup of productivity gains. The annual increases in the GNP deflator also slowed somewhat.

A comparison of 1982–87 price-cost developments with those of the preceding quinquennium reveals some dramatic changes occurred in the economic environment. Table 15.2 shows the average yearly change in output per hour from 1977 to 1982 was –0.2 percent while hourly compensation was climbing 9.1 percent per year. Labor costs per unit of output, of course, obeying the laws of arithmetic, skyrocketed close to 9.5 percent annually. There was also a sharp advance in costs from 1972 to 1977, although the run up was not as rapid.

In other words, the economic consequences of annual productivity gains which were below compensation advances were sharp increases in labor costs per unit of output during the 1970s and early 1980s. These unit labor cost rises slackened during the 1981–1982 recession as the gap was reduced. By 1983, during the first year of economic recovery, unit costs rose only 1.0 percent.

The large increases in unit labor costs in the late 1960s, the 1970s, and the early 1980s had a serious effect on prices. (To be sure, causality also worked in the opposite direction as well.) Excluding food and energy costs, the producer price index for consumer goods rose about 8 percent yearly from 1977 to 1982. The increase in the 1982–87 period was 2.7 percent. The consumer price index

Table 15.1

Changes in Wages, Productivity, and Unit Labor Costs in Nonfarm Business and Price Changes, 1982–1988

	Compensation per hour	Output per hour	Unit labor costs	Implicit price deflator
	Annual percent changes			
1982–1983	4.3	3.3	1.0	3.5
1983–1984	3.9	2.1	1.8	3.0
1984–1985	4.2	1.4	2.8	3.0
1985–1986	4.2	2.0	2.2	2.4
1986–1987	3.8	0.8	3.1	2.8
1987–1988	4.7	1.5	3.2	3.3

Source: Economic Report of the President, 1989, U.S. Government Printing Office, Washington, 1989, p. 361.

Table 15.2

Changes in Wages, Productivity, and Unit Labor Costs in Nonfarm Business and Price Changes, 1972–1987

	Compensation per hour	Output per hour	Unit labor costs	Implicit price deflator
	Annual percent changes			
1972–1977	8.7	1.1	7.5	7.7
1977–1982	9.1	−0.2	9.5	8.2
1982–1987	3.8	1.8	2.0	3.3

Source: Economic Report of the President, 1988, U.S. Government Printing Office, Washington, 1988, p. 301.

increased about 10.5 percent annually from 1977 to 1982. The average yearly advance from 1982 to 1987 was about 1.7 percent. Table 15.2 shows the close connection between these changes in unit labor costs and prices.

These cost-price developments made an impact on the investment side of the economy. Corporate profits after taxes with inventory valuation adjustments and capital consumption allowances were 24 percent lower in 1982 than at their peak in 1978. In 1987, they were 93 percent higher than in 1982. From 1979 to 1982, despite the drop in economic profits, the Standard and Poor's 500 stock price index rose 16 percent. However, from 1982 to 1987, this index shot up 140 percent.

These important developments merit more detailed analysis. Chart 15.1 shows the quarterly movements of the growth rate in hourly compensation during the 1980s expansion. The growth rate is a 2-quarter smoothed change calculated by dividing the current quarter by an average of the 4 preceding quarters and expressing the result at an annual rate. The chart compares the 1982–88 movements with changes during the comparable phases of another long expansion, i.e., 1961–69. The 1980s expansion started in the fourth quarter 1982. The chart shows the expansion of hourly compensation growth through the 21st quarter (1988.1). Through the early part of 1988, the cost situation in the U.S. was very good. In the first quarter of 1988, the 21st quarter, hourly compensation grew at a 3.5 percent annual rate. Twenty-one quarters after the start of the 1961–69 expansion, hourly pay grew at a 6.8 percent rate. The comparable statistic for the 1975–80 long expansion was 11.1 percent.

Productivity growth in the 21st quarter of the 1980s expansion was 2.1 percent. The relevant statistics for the 1961–69 and 1975–80 expansions were 1.5 percent and −1.1 percent, respectively.

The results of these growth rates in hourly compensation and productivity show up on the chart in growth in unit labor costs. In the first quarter 1988 (the 21st quarter), cost growth was 1.4 percent. This was well below the 5.1 percent growth in unit costs in the second quarter 1967 and considerably less than the 12.4 percent rate in the second quarter 1980. From the end of World War II until 1961, there weren't any business cycle expansions which lasted 21 quarters; however, by the time the four business cycle expansions during this interval came to a close, they typically had growth rates in unit labor costs much higher than 1.4 percent. Furthermore, factory data show that by the end of the 1933–37 expansion, unit costs were advancing at a rate of 11.4 percent, well in excess of the relevant 1980s statistic. During the 1920s, the average growth rate of unit labor costs in manufacturing at the three business cycle peaks was 1.4 percent, the same as the early 1988 rate.

The statistics on differences in growth rates in these variables are startling. Twenty one quarters into the expansion, the growth rate in hourly compensation was 3.0 percentage points *below* its growth at the start of the expansion. This is considerably different from its behavior in the two earlier long expansions. The early 1988 growth rate of unit labor costs is 3.9 percentage points *below* its rate at the start of the upswing. This is also different than its behavior during the earlier long expansions. Statistics which stretch back in time to the early 1930s suggest that the behavior of unit labor costs during the 1982–88 expansion was exceptional in modern business cycle history. Something new (or perhaps very old) happened during the 1980s. We examine in a later section how some of this progress was unraveled in 1988–89.

A New Environment in Labor Markets

In his mid-1988 report on the economy, Federal Reserve Chairman Alan Green-

Chart 15.1. **Productivity, Wages, Costs.**

Output per hour, growth rate

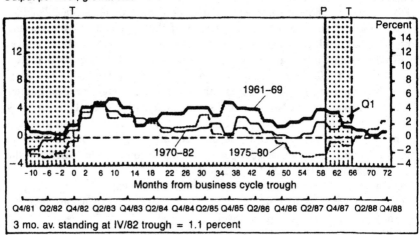

3 mo. av. standing at IV/82 trough = 1.1 percent

Unit labor costs, growth rate

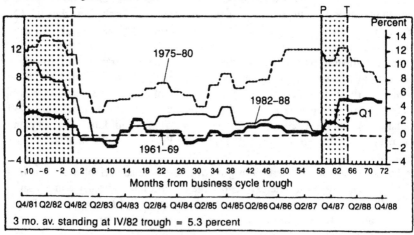

3 mo. av. standing at IV/82 trough = 5.3 percent

Hourly Compensation, Growth Rate

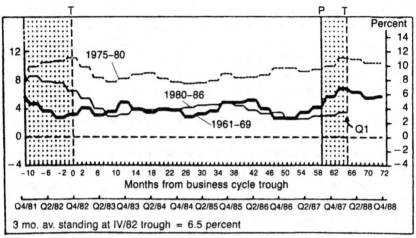

Q4/81 Q2/82 Q4/82 Q2/83 Q4/83 Q2/84 Q4/84 Q2/85 Q4/85 Q2/86 Q4/86 Q2/87 Q4/87 Q2/88 Q4/88

3 mo. av. standing at IV/82 trough = 6.5 percent

span noted that restraint on the part of business and labor in their price and wage decisions had contributed to a better environment for economic growth. Furthermore, he suggested government had made a contribution through deregulation and through the absence of major initiatives that would involve higher business costs.[1]

The previous section on costs showed this restraint in pricing and wage arrangements. The important analytical question is: Why? One might expect restraint if there was a lot of slack in labor markets. However, the jobless rate in mid-1988 was at its lowest level in almost fifteen years, the insured unemployment rate was at levels it achieved only in the boom periods of the 1950s and 1960s, and the employment ratio had hardly ever been higher.

The commentaries in successive *Economic Report of the President* publications disclose a sharp contrast between the analysis of President Reagan's advisers and those of earlier administrations. President Eisenhower's professional staff from 1957 to 1961 continually expressed concern about upward pressure on costs and prices.[2] President Kennedy's advisers lost no time in promulgating wage-price guidelines in the annual reports of 1962 and 1963.[3] President Nixon, a long-time foe of governmental regulations, was so concerned he imposed wage-price controls in 1971. Presidents Ford and Carter also directed considerable attention to these matters. Yet these reports from 1983 to 1988 scarcely mention upward pressure of costs on prices. Something happened!

A new environment was slowly evolving during the period of greatest concern, and developments during the 1980s hastened this evolution. Let us briefly sketch some aspects of this change. First, international competition kept getting stronger from the mid-1950s to the late 1980s. As early as the mid-1950s, German and Japanese producers, their plants rebuilt after wartime destruction, began competing in American markets. For example, their growing competitiveness in steel was already starting to alarm domestic steelmakers.[4] This competition expanded in the 1960s and 1970s. At the same time, Japanese, German, Italian, Swedish, and other automakers began capturing significant portions of U.S. markets through the production of quality goods at competitive prices. Sales of television sets, VCRs, and other electronic equipment quickened. Textile imports, largely from the Pacific Basin, dominated the American market. Computers and their components also became big import items.

In the 1980s, much more intense international competition made its impact on domestic factories. The relative price of foreign manufactured goods sold here fell sharply from 1980 to 1985. The strong appreciation of the U.S. dollar during this period was largely responsible for the decline in import prices. The heightened international competition put pressure on U.S. firms to keep their costs and prices down by limiting wage and profit growth and making productivity improvements.

In 1979, more than one-third of the wage and salary workers in American factories were union members. In the 1970s, it was customary for collective bargaining agreements to include wage increases which reflected productivity improvements and inflation rates. During the 1970s, the differences between the earnings of workers in unionized and nonunionized firms widened. This meant higher relative costs for the unionized firms. The combination of higher relative costs and greater international pressure reduced the competitiveness of many industries, particularly manufacturing.

Onerous adjustments were necessary. Some workers lost their jobs, others suffered a decline in real wages, and profits fell. One result of these changes was a reduction in the percentage of unionized wage and salary workers in manufacturing to 25 percent. Furthermore, the earnings of private nonfarm union workers has grown more slowly than for nonunion workers. The percentage of collective bargaining agreements which called for no wage increase amounted to 22 percent from 1982 to 1987. For manufacturing, the percentage was 29 percent.[5]

Second, trade union membership as a fraction of nonfarm employment peaked in 1953 at 32.5 percent. At first, the decline was gradual, but the drop quickened in the 1980s. Most people are aware that the ''rust belt'' industries experienced trouble in the 1980s. These industries were densely unionized, and in the early post–World War II decades they wielded enormous economic and political power. However, employment dropped sharply in this unionized sector. Few are aware that trade union membership in the private sector as a percentage of total private employment was less than 13 percent in 1988.[6] The last time union membership's relative strength in the private sector was this low was in 1929, 60 years ago. Figures that low were characteristic of the 1920s, years before the passage of favorable union legislation during the New Deal. Overall union membership in

1988 was about 16 percent, down from the all-time high of 32.5 percent in 1953. In general, the private sector unions have gone through a bleak period.

Third, goods employment fell sharply relative to total employment in recent decades. At the same time, service employment was rising rapidly. In the mid-1950s, private service employment was 29 percent of nonfarm employment. By 1988, it was 60 percent, public employment was 16 percent, and goods producing 24 percent. The service sector has traditionally been a nonunion sector. True, there has been a significant increase in membership in some service unions. Nonetheless, the ratio of service union members to total service employment still remains low, about one of every fourteen in 1984.

Fourth, although union membership became a larger fraction of public employment, upward wage pressures were partially blunted in the 1980s. Public employment is, of course, a significant fraction of nonfarm employment. However, changing philosophical and political attitudes worked to contain wage increases in the public sector. On the federal level, the Administration took stern action against public employees engaged in an illegal strike in the airlines industry. Furthermore, the Administration was supportive of restrictive Federal Reserve actions early in the 1980s to deal with the inflation problem. As a consequence, the jobless rate then rose to a high level, and in soft labor markets, wage demands became more moderate. Moreover, large deficits at the federal level somewhat stiffened the resistance of authorities to demands for higher compensation. Not only that, on the state and local government levels, increasing taxpayer resistance to higher rates tended to restrict the growth of receipts needed to fund higher wages and salaries for public employees.

Fifth, more and more firms have cut costs where the competition focuses at the product line level, adopted two-tier wage systems (which pay new workers less than more experienced workers, even when they perform the same job), provided lump sum payments to workers once a year instead of building pay hikes into the wage base, used techniques that tie compensation to output, productivity, and profits, and hired a growing variety of temporary, part-time or contingent workers who are employed only when needed.

All of these forces tended to restrict the growth of union and nonunion wage increases in the 1980s. These fundamental shifts in human resource management practices are not temporary. They will not be reversed. They add to our understanding of some of the fundamental changes in the economic environment of the period.

Policy Implications
of the New Economic Environment

Let us discuss the policy implications of these structural, philosophical, and political developments in a context where the goal of economic policy is to achieve prosperity without inflation. Economic policy, however, would require only minor reformulation if the goal was the achievement of prosperity with a stable but low inflation rate. The achievement of prosperity with high inflation rates is a vastly different matter.

The policy implications of an economic environment within which labor costs per unit of output are rising, as compared with a situation in which they are either stable or falling, are plain.[7] When unit labor costs are rising there is upward pressure on prices, and at some point economic policy will resist this trend. Fiscal and monetary expansion can be excessive even when cost conditions are favorable, but it is a recipe for disaster when they are unfavorable. For fiscal and monetary actions to encourage the upward trend of costs and prices is to invite more inflation and ultimately a serious economic setback. In this environment, an appropriate macroeconomic policy is a restrictive one.

The simple point is: an imbalance between labor cost increases and productivity improvements and the consequent push of unit production costs on prices is not a viable condition for prosperity *without inflation*. In many instances, selling prices cannot be raised, and here and there profit margins will narrow. The "squeeze" on profits tends to become more widespread since all firms do not have the same power to raise prices. Some are prevented or limited by custom, trademarks, govermental regulations, or international competition. These developments spread doubts or financial pressures to other firms whose profits are still rising and, in time, lead some to cancel or postpone their investment plans. These are crucial developments and often turn economic expansion into recession.

Thus, imbalances of this sort eventually have to be corrected. From the mid-1960s to the early 1980s, these imbalances were chronic in the U.S. The consequences were disheartening. At first they led to quickening inflation, and then later to stagflation, a combination of high and rising inflation and high unemployment.

This study cannot offer a full explanation of the forces at work which led to these imbalances. The persistence in the application of aggressive macroeconomic actions in the late 1960s despite the emergence of cost pressures is part of the story. Still another aspect of the condition were the aftereffects of wage-price controls and the oil shocks in 1974 and 1979. The latter surely affected production costs. The sharp growth in entitlement and other public programs also influenced total spending, prices, and costs. In any event, there were numerous imbalances in the U.S. economy in the 1970s. The argument that all that was needed to get the economy moving ahead was a sharp reduction in tax rates neglects the impact of these imbalances and their subsequent corrections. Sure, the tax reductions provided additional incentives for individuals and businesses to work and to invest. These were good things to do. However, account must be taken of the changing cost environment to achieve a fuller understanding of the forces sustaining the expansion. It is important to recognize that a balanced relationship between employment cost increases and productivity gains was also essential for reasonable price stability and vigorous economic growth.

Fortunately, restrictive monetary actions in the early 1980s helped to eliminate some of the persistent imbalances of the earlier period. By early 1983, the basis for a strong upswing had been established. In this new environment, stimulative fiscal and monetary actions could be taken with minimal fear of unleashing inflation and the maximum impact of employment and output. Later that year, the Federal Reserve Board slowed monetary growth to contain what was perceived to be economic overheating. However, a subsequent slowing of aggregate activity led them to reverse course and to sharply expand the money supply in 1985 and 1986. Could such steps have been taken successfully in an environment in which cost inflation was widely diffused?

There are, of course, limits to how long and to what degree an aggressive policy can be pursued. The expansionary policies can sometimes be pushed too far even in a broadly favorable environment. Furthermore, in an economic context when the federal government is running large budgetary deficits, a strong economic performance in the United States accompanied by sluggish growth overseas can lead to large trade imbalances. The large trade deficits eventually lead to deterioration in the value of the dollar. The latter could be serious if foreign investors are large purchasers of U.S. government debt. A reduction in their demand for these securities could lead to higher interest rates and endanger the expansion, or it could lead to an expansion of the money stock by the central banking system with serious consequences in the battle against inflation. This is, of course, one of the serious problems the Federal Reserve endeavors to cope with.

The Changing Situation in 1988–1989

In August 1989, the expansion became the second longest in terms of the NBER's monthly chronology, which goes back to 1854. Stock price indexes were higher than their levels of October 1987, the month of the stock market crash. The much predicted recession, which many believed the crash would cause, did not occur. The Commerce Department's leading composite was showing signs that economic growth was slowing down. The close approximation to balance between hourly compensation increases and productivity improvements of late 1987, discussed above, had disappeared. Instead hourly pay increases were much higher than productivity gains in early 1989. This was worrisome.

Prices moved up after early 1986. The rate of increase of the consumer price index was 5.3 percent in June 1988 (six-month smoothed). The price advance was considerably above the 0.6 percent growth measured in April 1986. That figure was greatly affected by the sharp drop in oil prices associated with OPEC disputes.

The growth of unit labor costs at a 4.7 percent rate in early 1989 was well above the 2 percent advance from 1986 to 1987. As discussed above, these inflationary pressures need to be reduced if an ongoing economic expansion is to be sustained. Monetary policy turned restrictive in 1988 in an effort to reduce the inflationary pressures, and this continued in the first half of 1989. There were signs that the inflation rate might decline while more moderate growth in employment and output continued.

Notes

1. Alan Greenspan, "Testimony before Committee on Banking, Finance, and Urban Affairs," *Federal Reserve Bulletin*, Board of Governors of the Federal Reserve System, Washington, April 1988, p. 231.

2. Cf. *Economic Report of the President*, 1957, p. 44 and *Economic Report of the President*, 1959, pp. 5–6, U.S. Government Printing Office, Washington.

3. For an extensive review, see Arthur F. Burns, "Wages and Prices by Formula," *Harvard Business Review* (March-April) 1965.

4. For an early presentation expressing concern, see Arthur F. Burns, "World Competition and the American Economy," American Iron and Steel Institute, New York, May 1961.

5. For details, see *Economic Report of the President*, 1988, pp. 77–79.

6. Cf. Leo Troy and Neil Sheflin, *Union Sourcebook* (West Orange, N.J.: Industrial Relations Data Information Services, 1987).

7. An implication of the discussion is that wage-push inflation was of some significance in earlier decades. Monetarist criticism of this idea emphasizes that the price and wage increases by monopolies (or oligopolies) are strictly one-shot affairs. They happen when the monopoly is first created or when its power is augmented. One prominent monetarist, the late Harry Johnson, argued that "wage push cannot explain a general upward movement of wages and prices without a subsidiary assumption that the political process will not tolerate and live with the resulting unemployment," that governments will try to reduce unemployment "by inflationary policies to which the monopolist will react by again raising wages and prices." Many who believe in wage-push would accept this formulation. However, the monetarists were clearly suggesting more than this. Their position was that the joblessness which would result from monopolies, if the money supply was not expanded, would be moderate. Whether that was true in the earlier post–World war II period when trade union membership as a fraction of nonfarm employment was greater could easily trigger debate. However, with the sharp decline in union strength more recently their argument may have more substance. For a fuller discussion of these matters, see Gottfried Haberler, *Economic Growth and Stability* (Los Angeles: Nash Publishing, 1974).

16

The 1987 Stock Market Crash and the Wealth Effect

Phillip Cagan

In October 1987 the stock market crashed, reducing the value of the public's equity holdings by about a half trillion dollars. This sudden decline reduced the market value of the public's wealth significantly. According to a long literature developing the economics of consumption, such a large decline in wealth could be expected to reduce consumer expenditures. This literature views wealth as one of the important variables in addition to income determining consumption. Indeed, past studies cited below typically estimated the effect of wealth on consumption to be around 5 percent, which implied that in the aftermath of the market crash consumer expenditures would drop by $25 billion ($500 billion times 5%). With multiplier repercussions of (say) two, this implied a sizable $50 billion decline in GNP. In fact, though, consumption and GNP continued a moderate upward trend in the fourth quarter of 1987 and (at the time of writing) through at least 1988. Thus no wealth effect could be detected, though initially it led many forecasters to predict a slowing or even a decline in economic activity.

What explains the apparent nonexistence of this wealth effect? There are several possible answers. First, other forces such as stimulative fiscal and monetary policies might have countered it. However, no such forces seemed at the time sufficient. Second, the crash took stock values down to their approximate level at the end of 1986. Neither the capital appreciation during 1987 nor the depreciation in October appeared to have had an effect, possibly because wealth takes time to affect consumption, and the up-and-down movements during 1987 simply cancelled each other out. Yet much of the wealth analysis in the literature claims to find effects either concurrently or with a short lag. Finally, the 1987 episode may indicate that previous findings of wealth effects were wrong, that changes in wealth even as large as a half trillion dollars have minuscule effects on consumption. This third possibility is argued in this paper.

The Literature

The widely accepted theory of life-cycle consumption posits that consumption depends mainly on expected life-cycle income.[1] Income derives from labor and capital, so that changes in (nonhuman) wealth can affect expected life-cycle income. Changes in wealth can result from changes in interest rates by which future income streams are discounted to the present, by changes in accumulated capital through saving, and in the short-run mainly by changes in the market value of capital. Many empirical studies have related consumer expenditures to measures of labor income and wealth. Wealth represents income from capital as well as capital gains and losses. Consumer expenditures in these studies are defined as in the national income accounts, but sometimes expenditures for durable goods are excluded on the grounds that these represent capital and only their services should be included.

Representative equations of this type, estimated in Table 16.1, are carried through third-quarter 1987 just prior to the stock market crash. They are quarterly and begin in second-quarter 1952. Estimates of services from durable goods are of controversial accuracy and have not been used. Results are presented for both total consumption and for nondurable goods and services (excluding durables entirely). Income is labor income (with no adjustment to exclude taxes) including noncorporate income which is largely salary of owners. Wealth is measured by household net worth in the flow of funds accounts of the Federal Reserve System. Stocks are an average of Standard and Poor's (S&P) daily index of 500 companies for the last month of each quarter. The variables are divided by the implicit deflator for consumer expenditures to convert to real terms and, except for the stock index, also by total population to convert to per capita. Although other variables or refinements used in the literature have not been incorporated here, these simple equations show the wealth effects typically reported in the literature.[2]

Revisions in the data and coverage of later years through 1987 do not change the basic results of past studies. In regression (1) of Table 16.1, end-of-quarter wealth of the preceding quarter is highly significant with an effect of 8.6 percent.[3] This implies a major effect on consumption in first-quarter 1988. The relevant lagged wealth variable, namely for fourth-quarter 1987, declined $378 billion, and 8.6 percent of this is $32.5 billion. But aggregate consumption for first-quarter 1988 actually increased $46 billion in current dollars.

A problem with equations like (1) in Table 16.1 is that total wealth variables are not exogenous but include accumulated saving from the past, thus standing in for past consumption and income. There is no reason, however, why past decisions to save should directly influence concurrent saving. In theory, saving reflects a life-cycle decision, and wealth represents the outcome of that decision and not a determinant of it. Only unanticipated changes in wealth—capital gains and losses—should influence the saving decision, as much of the literature acknowledges but does not uniformly follow.[4] In regression (1) the wealth variable is probably capturing some of the long-run effect of income, which would explain why the coefficient of income is so low.

Unanticipated changes in wealth for the most part reflect changes in the

Table 16.1

Consumption Regressions 1952-1987

Dependent variable:	Constant	Real labor income per capita	Real wealth per capita W_{1Q}	Change in deflated stock prices $S - S_{1Q}$	$S_{1Q} - S_{2Q}$	$\bar{R}^2$ / DW	Std. error
Real total consumption per capita			Period: 1952QII-1987QIII				
(1)	−0.006(10.2)	0.633(23.0)	0.086(14.0)			0.992 / 0.18	$149
(2)	−0.004(4.9)	1.003(86.6)			0.006(4.2)	0.982 / 0.24	$218
(3)	−0.005(5.3)	1.005(90.1)		0.005(3.7)	0.005(3.5)	0.983 / 0.25	$210
		Lagged dependent variable C_{1Q}					
(4)	−0.000(0.0)	1.005(364.5)			0.002(4.9)	0.999 / 01.7	$52
(5)	−0.000(0.0)	1.005(364.2)		0.002(4.6)	0.000(0.9)	0.999 / 01.6	$52
Real consumption per capita excluding durables			Period: 1968QI-1987QIII				
(6)	0.000(0.3)	1.005(513.9)			0.001(2.8)	0.999+ / 1.6	$32
(7)	0.000(0.2)	1.005(525.6)		0.001(2.7)	0.001(2.4)	0.999+ / 1.6	$31
(8)	0.001(1.4)	0.998(197.4)			0.001(2.5)	0.998 / 1.6	$35
(9)	0.001(2.0)	0.995(199.8)		0.001(2.7)	0.001(2.3)	0.998 / 1.4	$34

Notes: W is end-of-quarter value. S is daily average of final month of quarter. Subscripts denote length of lags. Source of data given in text.

market value of equity, and the other regressions in Table 16.1 use the change in the S&P stock market index to capture these changes. In regressions (2) and (3), the stock changes for the current quarter and the previous quarter are significant. Note, however, that the size of their coefficients cannot be compared with that for wealth in regression (1) because the units of measurement differ. (The coefficient of labor income slightly above unity in these equations implies a marginal propensity to consume out of *total* income that is below unity as it should be.)

The significantly low Durbin-Watson (DW) statistics for these and the other regressions in Table 16.1 indicate the absence of other variables that would account for the short-run fluctuations in consumption. Previous studies include a variety of other variables that largely correct this problem. The results are mixed on the significance of changes in the stock index, but in many studies it remains significant.

A major innovation in the theory of the consumption function was introduced by Hall (1978), who argued that the life-cycle theory could be interpreted to mean that lagged consumption contained all available information relevant to current consumption decisions. Therefore, consumer expenditures should correlate with lagged consumption and no other lagged variables, though of course concurrent variables could correlate because they contain new information relevant to consumption decisions. Hall reported that the lagged change in stock prices did correlate with consumption in a regression including lagged consumption, and lagged stock prices was the only such variable he found. (Hall excluded durables from consumer expenditures, which we may follow in reproducing his form of the function.) Stocks might be interpreted as reflecting unanticipated changes in wealth that affect consumption not immediately but over several quarters. Such equations are presented in Table 16.1.

The significant change in stock prices for the concurrent quarter in regression (3) in Table 16.1 and others can be attributed to new information about expected future income that affects consumption. The significance of the change for the preceding quarter, however, shows an effect not already captured by lagged consumption, which might be interpreted as a lagged response of consumption to unanticipated changes in wealth. This effect remains the same when the period since 1968 is treated separately in regressions (8) and (9). According to the Hall formulation, omitted variables should pose no problem. The DW statistics for such regressions (4)-(9) in Table 16.1 are still a little low, which might be attributed to a small liquidity effect. According to subsequent studies[5] some consumers (perhaps about a fifth) lack sufficient liquidity to maintain desired life-cycle consumption in the face of a temporary but sizable shortfall in income.

Implications of the Equations
for the Stock Market Crash

The regressions of Table 16.1 summarize the kind of evidence on a wealth effect reported by past studies. What does this evidence imply about the stock market crash of 1987? Tables 16.2 and 16.3 show the predicted and actual changes in consumption of these regressions. Those with lagged variables for wealth and stock changes delay the effect of the crash until first-quarter 1988. Table 16.2 compares the predicted and actual values for this and the preceding quarter. Regressions with current *and* lagged stock changes imply a crash effect in both fourth-quarter 1987 and first-quarter 1988. Table 16.3 compares changes in the predicted and actual values for these quarters.

In Table 16.2, the differences between predicted and actual values of the regressions, shown in columns 3 and 5, are mostly within twice the standard errors, even in first-quarter 1988 when the effect of the crash should occur. The exceptions are equations (2) and (4), which have residual errors over three times the standard error.

But minor residual errors which imply no serious discrepancy are misleading because of their serial correlation. A more relevant indicator is given in the remaining columns for changes in the predicted and actual values. All the regressions miss the direction of change appreciably. The predicted values decline between the two quarters while the actual values increase, and the difference between predicted and actual changes is sizable. The changes are translated into current dollar aggregate consumption[6] in column 8 and into a percentage of total consumption in column 9. This percentage varies from over 1 to almost 5. That is, consumption grew by that much more than was predicted, which does suggest something amiss with most of these predictions.

Table 16.3, which gives summary measures for the regressions with current and lagged stock changes, tells the same story though less dramatically. Actual consumption increased while predicted values declined appreciably in first-quarter 1988. Here the lagged change in the stock index for fourth-quarter 1987 accounts for the decline in predicted values. In the preceding quarter the predicted decline, which then reflected the concurrent change in the stock index, was partially offset by the lagged increase of the index in third-quarter 1987.

Doubts about a Wealth Effect

What explains the prediction errors? Other offsetting developments? It is hard to see what they could have been. The stock market crash produced adverse expectations about the economy which reinforced a negative wealth effect and did not offset it. The episode strongly suggests that the equations are misleading and that changes in the market value of wealth as measured by household net worth or stock prices, whether unanticipated or not, do not have the alleged effect on consumption. There are reasons why stock market declines may not have much effect. Stock ownership is largely limited to a selection of upper-income groups or to pension funds whose worker beneficiaries are promised defined benefits

Table 16.2

Actual and Predicted Consumption, 1987QIV-1988QI

Regression no. and variables	SE of reg. (1)	1987QIV Actual / Predicted (2)	1987QIV Predicted − actual (3)	1988QI Actual / Predicted (4)	1988QI Predicted − actual (5)	Change in: Actual / Predicted (6)	Change for total population Current $ billions Actual / Predicted (7)	Error: Predicted − Actual (8)	Per cent of 1988 QI total consumption (9)
		1982 dollars per capita					Current $ billions		
(1) a Total consumption, b labor income, c wealth: c lagged stocks $S_{1Q}-S_{2Q}$:	149	10232 / 10402	+170	10306 / 10283	−23	+74 / −119	+46 / −11	−57	1.9
(2) c lagged stocks $S_{1Q}-S_{2Q}$:	218	10232 / 10012	−220	10306 / 9590	−716	+74 / −422	+46 / −102	−148	4.8
(4) b dependent var. C_{-1Q} c lagged stocks $S_{1Q}-S_{2Q}$:	52	10232 / 10396	+164	10306 / 10168	−138	+74 / −228	+46 / −44	−90	3.0
(6) a Consumption excl. durables. b dependent var. C_{-1Q} c lagged stocks $S_{1Q}-S_{2Q}$:	32	8834 / 8876	+42	8886 / 8836	−50	+52 / −40	+36 / −9	−45	1.5
(8) Same as (6) for later period	35	8834 / 8869	+35	8886 / 8817	−69	+52 / −52	+36 / −5	−41	1.3

Note: Regression numbers pertain to Table 16.1.

Table 16.3

Changes in Actual and Predicted Consumption 1987QIII-1988QI

Regression no. and variables	SE of reg. (1)	1987QIII-1987QIV Change in: Predicted '82 dollars per capita (2) Actual	Predicted	Change for total population Current dollars billions (3) Actual	Predicted	Error: predicted − actual (4)	Percent of 1987QIV total consumption (5)	1987QIV-1988QI Change in: Predicted '82 dollars per capita (6) Actual	Predicted	Change for total population Current dollars billions (7) Actual	Predicted	Error: predicted − actual (8)	Percent of 1988QI total consumption (9)
a Total consumption, b labor income, c lagged stocks $S-S_{1Q}$; $S_{1Q}-S_{2Q}$: (3)	210	−90	−279	−12	−46	−34	1.1	+74	+143	+46	+65	+19	N.C.
b dependent var. C_{-1Q} c lagged stocks $S-S_{1Q}$; $S_{1Q}-S_{2Q}$: (5)	52	−90	+91	−12	+65	+77	N.C.	+74	−196	+46	−34	−80	2.6
a Real consumption per capita excluding durables, b dependent var. C_{-1Q} c lagged stocks $S-S_{1Q}$; $S_{1Q}-S_{2Q}$: (7)	31	+9	−16	+35	−28	−63	2.4	+52	+18	+36	+26	−10	0.4
Same as (7) for later period (9)	34	+9	−30	+35	−24	−59	2.3	+52	+23	+36	+27	−9	0.3

Notes: Regression numbers pertain to Table 16.1. N.C. = not computed because of plus sign in preceding column.

Table 16.4

Consumption Regressions with Changes in Stock and Leading Indexes 1952QII-1987QIII

Dependent variable: real consumption per capita excluding durables	Constant (1)	Dependent variable lagged 1Q (2)	Regression coefficients (and t values)		Change in leading index $L-L_{1Q}$ (5)	$\bar{R}^2$
			Change in deflated stock prices			DW (6)
			$S-S_{1Q}$ (3)	$S_{1Q}-S_{2Q}$ (4)		
(1)	0.00002 (0.1)	1.00467 (548.9)	0.00042 (1.96)		0.00006 (4.3)	0.999 + 1.7
(2)	0.00002 (0.1)	1.00467 (542.3)		0.00015 (0.6)	0.00006 (4.1)	0.999 + 1.8
(3)	0.00001 (0.1)	1.00467 (547.6)	0.00041 (1.93)	0.00013 (0.6)	0.00005 (3.6)	0.999 + 1.7

Notes: $\bar{R}^2$ between $S-S_{1Q}$ and $L-L_{1Q}$ is 0.19.
S is daily average of index for final month of quarter. L is composite leading index of 11 items (excluding stock prices), trend adjusted, for final month of quarter. Subscripts denote length of lags.

Chart 16.1. **Quarterly Changes in Indexes of Leading Indicators and Deflated Stocks, 1952Q2–1988Q1.**

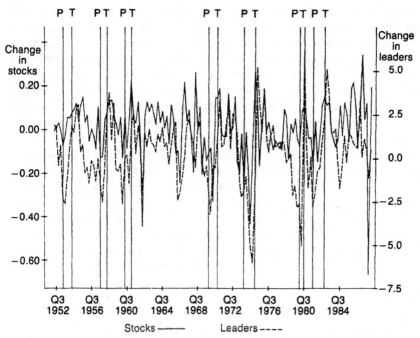

Note: NBER reference cycle peaks and troughs.

unrelated to the value of the funds except indirectly should they be greatly underfunded. Upper-income groups can enjoy stable consumption streams even though their wealth fluctuates, certainly for all but very prolonged changes that appear permanent.[7]

Short-run changes may be largely ignored, therefore, so that concurrent effects are offset by lagged effects over a long period. Thus, if the wealth effect exists for long-run changes only, it would not show up in 1987 or 1988 because the crash erased the increases during 1987, and wealth at the end of 1987 was close to its level a year earlier. It might then show up in a debacle like 1929–33, though even then it would be difficult to distinguish it from the sharp decline in total income and economic activity generally.

These reasons imply that the regressions are picking up, not the effect of current changes in wealth, but regular cyclical fluctuations that affect all economic variables. The stock index is a good leading indicator of cyclical fluctuations, though it is not infallible. Its performance as a leading indicator may forecast general economic conditions rather than a wealth effect. If a sudden large change in stock prices is out of line with general economic conditions, no wealth effect may exist to produce a correlation with consumption.

Evidence on the Absence of a Wealth Effect

We may test this interpretation of the stock variable as a cyclical indicator in the regressions by including a better indicator, the composite index of leading indicators. Although it includes the stock index, the composite performs much better than any of its components. Table 16.4 shows the Hall-type equations including also changes in a composite index of leading indicators. To avoid a confusing overlap with stock changes we may use a revised composite index of leading indicators that omits the stock index.[8] Although changes in the revised leading and stock indexes are only marginally correlated ($R^2 = 0.19$), inclusion of the former generally pushes the stock index into insignificance. Only the concurrent stock change is barely significant (regression 1) with the leading index included. Chart 16.1 presents a plot of changes in the two series.

It is unlikely that the concurrent stock change is acting as a wealth effect rather than a supplementary indicator of new economic developments. When the one-quarter lagged stock change is also included with the concurrent changes in the stock and leading indexes, the lagged stock change is insignificant. Therefore, any possible wealth effect appears to last only one quarter, which is unlikely, to say the least. Moreover, even the significant coefficient of the concurrent stock change when the leading index is included has little economic importance. It implies a wealth effect on consumption in fourth-quarter 1987 of only $-\$8$ billion or 0.3 percent of total consumption.

The evidence is consistent with a role of stock changes in the consumption function as a proxy for cyclical fluctuations in the economy, not as an effect of capital gains and losses except perhaps only marginally.

Notes

1. The basic reference is Modigliani and Brumberg (1954).
2. See Ando and Modigliani (1963), Arena (1964), Zellner et al. (1965), Projector (1968), de Leeuw and Gramlich (1969), Stone (1970), Landsberger (1970), Deaton (1972), Bhatia (1972), Rasche (1972), McElroy and Poindexter (1975), Bosworth (1975), Mishkin (1977), Brayton and Mauskopf (1987), and Boskin and Lau (1988, Table 4.6). Friend and Lieberman (1975), however, find wealth to be insignificant, as does Evans (1967) except for a regression including the 1930s, when the wealth variable was affected by large capital losses.

With both total wealth and capital gains (in some form) included as separate variables along with income, McElroy and Poindexter (1975) report a significant wealth variable while Friend and Lieberman (1975) and Peek (1983) find it to be insignificant. Elliott (1980) reports results that show a stronger effect of price variations in stocks and bonds than of a measure of wealth excluding those variations. Arena (1965), however, finds that the stock market has no effect on consumption.

For general surveys see Mayer (1972, chaps. 8 and 9) and Ferber (1973). For a precursor of the stock market effect, see Silverberg (1963).

3. The effect is smaller when durables are excluded from consumption, which suggests not unreasonably that changes in wealth have their major effect, if any, in postponing purchases of consumer durables.

4. "Higher assets do not necessarily affect saving; they do so only if, on account of unexpected variations, assets turn out to be out of line with income and age: it is only an excess (or shortage) of assets that affects the saving ratio" say Modigliani and Brumberg (1954, 427). See also Spiro (1962).

It is crucial for the long-run effects of government budget deficits whether consumption depends on total wealth or only unanticipated changes in wealth (see Cagan 1984).

5. See Flavin (1985).

6. The values of real per capita consumption in each quarter are multiplied by the deflator and U.S. population in the quarter to convert to aggregate consumption in current $billions. The conversion factors for 1987Q3 to 1988Q1 are, respectively, 0.29172, 0.29541, and 0.29773.

7. Juster (1987-88) and Garner (1988, Table 1).

8. This version of the composite leading indicators was computed with the program of the Center for International Business Cycle Research, Columbia University, using the trend adjusted option, weights of unity, and standardization of components based on 1948-88. It includes all the series except stock prices included in the *Business Conditions Digest* version prior to April 1988 (when *BCD* excluded new businesses). I am indebted to M. Guha for supervising the computations.

References

Ando, Albert, and Franco Modigliani. 1963. "The 'Life Cycle' Hypothesis of Saving: Aggregate Implications and Tests." *American Economic Review* 53 (March): 55-84.

Arena, John J. 1964. "Capital Gains and the 'Life Cycle' Hypothesis of Saving." *American Economic Review* 54 (March): 107-111.

―――. 1965. "Postwar Stock Market Changes and Consumer Spending." *Review of Economics and Statistics* 47 (November): 379-91.

Bhatia, Kul B. 1972. "Capital Gains and the Aggregate Consumption Function." *American Economic Review* 62 (December): 866-79.

Boskin, Michael, and Lawrence J. Lau. 1988. *An Analysis of Postwar Consumption and Saving: Part II Empirical Results.* NBER Working Paper 2606 (June).

Bosworth, Barry. 1975. "The Stock Market and the Economy." *Brookings Papers on Economic Activity* no. 2: 257-90.

Brayton, Flint, and Eileen Mauskopf. 1987. "Structure and Uses of the MPS Quarterly Econometric Model of the United States." *Federal Reserve Bulletin* 73 (February): 93-109.

Cagan, Phillip. 1984. *Deficits and the Wealth Effect on Consumption.* American Enterprise Institute Occasional Papers (November).

Deaton, A.S. 1972. "Wealth Effects on Consumption in a Modified Life-Cycle Model." *Review of Economic Studies* 39 (October): 443-53.

Elliott, J. Walter. 1980. "Wealth and Wealth Proxies in a Permanent Income Model." *Quarterly Journal of Economics* 95 (November): 509-35.

Evans, Michael K. 1967. "The Importance of Wealth in the Consumption Function." *Journal of Political Economy* 75 (August, pt. 1): 335-51.

Ferber, Robert. 1973. "Consumer Economics, a Survey." *Journal of Economic Literature* 11 (December): 1303-42, esp. 1312-14.

Flavin, Marjorie A. 1985. "Excess Sensitivity of Consumption to Current Income: Liquidity Constraints or Myopia?" *Canadian Journal of Economics* 18 (February): 117-36.

Friend, Irwin, and Charles Lieberman. 1975. "Short-Run Asset Effects on Household Saving and Consumption: The Cross-Section Evidence." *American Economic Review* 65 (September): 624-33.

Garner, C. Alan. 1988. "Has the Stock Market Crash Reduced Consumer Spending?" *Federal Reserve Bank of Kansas City Economic Review* (April): 3–16.

Hall, Robert E. 1978. "Stochastic Implications of the Life Cycle-Permanent Income Hypothesis: Theory and Evidence." *Journal of Political Economy* 86 (December): 971–87.

Juster, F. Thomas. 1987–88. "Stock Prices and Consumer Spending: an Appraisal of the Great Crash." *Economic Outlook USA* 14 (winter): 16–19.

Landsberger, Michael. 1970. "The Life-Cycle Hypothesis: A Reinterpretation and Empirical Test." *American Economic Review* 60 (March): 175–83.

de Leeuw, Frank, and Edward M. Gramlich. 1969. "The Channels of Monetary Policy." *Federal Reserve Bulletin* 55 (June): 472–91, esp. 481–82.

Mayer, Thomas 1972. *Permanent Income, Wealth, and Consumption*. Berkeley: University of California Press.

McElroy, Michael B., and J. C. Poindexter. 1975. "Capital Gains and the Aggregate Consumption Function: Comment." *American Economic Review* 65 (September): 700–703.

Mishkin, Frederic S. 1977. "What Depressed the Consumer? The Household Balance Sheet and the 1973–75 Recession." *Brookings Papers on Economic Activity* no. 1: 123–64.

Modigliani, Franco, and Richard Brumberg. 1954. "Utility Analysis and the Consumption Function: An Interpretation of Cross-Section Data." In *Post Keynesian Economics*. Edited by Kenneth K. Kurihara. New Brunswick, N.J.: Rutgers University Press.

Peek, Joe. 1983. "Capital Gains and Personal Saving Behavior." *Journal of Money, Credit and Banking* 15 (February): 1–23.

Projector, Dorothy S. 1968. *Survey of Changes in Family Finances*. Washington, D.C.: Board of Governors of the Federal Reserve System, November, esp. p. 36.

Rasche, Robert H. 1972. "Impact of the Stock Market on Private Demand." *American Economic Review* 62 (May): 220–28.

Silverberg, Stanley. 1963. "Wealth, Stock Prices, and Consumer Behavior." *Western Economic Journal* 1 (Summer): 218–25.

Spiro, Alan. 1962. "Wealth and the Consumption Function." *Journal of Political Economy* 70 (August): 339–54.

Stone, Richard. 1970. "Spending and Saving in Relation to Income and Wealth." In *Mathematical Models of the Economy and Other Essays*, chap. 10, pp. 121–44. Edited by Stone. London: Chapman and Hall.

Zellner, A., and D. S. Huang, and L. C. Chau. 1965. "Further Analysis of the Short-Run Consumption Function with Emphasis on the Role of Liquid Assets." *Econometrica* 33 (July): 571–81.

17

Entrepreneurial Confidence and Money Illusion

Philip A. Klein

The notion that economic agents suffer from "money illusion" has been around at least since 1928. In that year Irving Fisher published his book, *Money Illusion*, which he there defined as "the failure to perceive that the dollar, or any other unit of money, expands or shrinks in value" (Fisher 1928, 4). By the time Don Patinkin wrote his famous *Money, Interest, and Prices* in 1955, the definition of money illusion, like many other things in economics, had become considerably more complicated. "An individual will be said to be suffering from such an illusion if his excess-demand functions for commodities . . . do not depend solely on relative prices and real wealth, inclusive of initial real balances. . . . It follows that if an illusion-free individual were confronted with an equiproportionate change in all accounting prices—including that of paper money—none of his amounts demanded of commodities would thereby be affected: for such a change would affect neither the array of relative prices confronting him, nor the level of his real wealth" (Patinkin 1965, 22).

As inflation became a major macroeconomic problem in the 1970s, economists increasingly came to pay much attention to distinctions between real and nominal magnitudes, techniques of adjusting for inflation became highly sophisticated, and all agents in the economy were assumed to be aware of the purchasing power of nominal magnitudes, that is, they were assumed to distinguish nominal from real and thus to be free of "money illusion."

In the area of labor, the first cost of living adjustment (COLA) clause was inaugurated in 1948 in a United Auto Workers-General Motors collective bargaining agreement. COLA agreements are customarily linked to the consumer price index (CPI) and may provide for full or partial adjustment in wages to cover the change in the CPI. From the start in 1948, COLAs have spread so that now

The author wishes to thank Phillip Cagan, Franz-Joseph Klein, and Geoffrey H. Moore for helpful comments on earlier drafts of this paper. Computations were done at the Columbia Center for International Business Cycle Research by Philip Chen, and at Penn State by Ngina Mugo. An earlier version of this paper was presented at the Eighth International Symposium on Forecasting, Amsterdam, June 1984.

they cover perhaps half of all union contracts (Wachtel 1984, 397). They may have even declined slightly recently, but in any case, never approached coverage of all organized workers because many businesses objected to tying wages to a general price index rather than their own market prices. Nevertheless, the development of COLA agreements, also known as "escalator clauses," indicates that organized labor has given some evidence of escaping from money illusion at least since 1948. Today, workers are generally regarded as being as much aware of their real wages as of their nominal wages (Hammermesh and Rees 1988, 334).[1]

The result of these changes is that workers in general, and unionized workers in particular, are no longer necessarily seen as victims of money illusion and are more likely charged with contributing to inflationary pressures by attempting to maintain or even raise their real wage rates. This must be evaluated against the evidence that the percent of the labor force covered by COLAs is still relatively small. They are rare in contracts in non-union firms, for example (Flanagan et al. 1984, 527–528). However, any increase in real wages in inflationary periods will clearly increase inflationary pressures. This line of reasoning was a principal thread in the "wage-price spiral" explanation of inflation which was very popular in the late 1950s and 1960s. In the environment of the 1970s, attention shifted to other factors (e.g., the OPEC oil price increases) and so less attention was focussed on the wage-price spiral as an explanation, but in principle its potential for explaining inflation has never been rejected.

Somewhat lost in the discussion was the potential contribution of entrepreneurs to the "wage-price spiral" explanation. While "wage-push" inflation was sometimes referred to as "cost-push" inflation, the presumption was often that it was other nonlabor productive factors rather than profits that contributed to the inflationary pressure. (The term "profit-push" inflation was introduced but was never regarded as a significant part of the cost-push explanation of inflation.) A significant thread to this analysis would appear to be the observation that COLAs ratify past increases in the consumer price index without necessarily increasing such pressures further. Entrepreneurs cannot insure themselves against past increases in a parallel fashion but can only react to uncertainty by anticipating inflation in setting prices for the future. Realized real profits will depend on the extent to which they guess correctly. In logic, workers who insist on anticipating price increases by obtaining wage increases which produce inflationary consequences should affect the direction of inflation rates precisely as entrepreneurs who raise prices in anticipation of cost increases would. Whether entrepreneurs are quick to spot the consequences of their action by lowering prices, or whether like wage increases that are locked into contracts, "incorrect" anticipations produce changes which are self-fulfilling is a difficult but interesting question to pose.

In terms of our ability to forecast future economic activity, all this is relevant because the expectations and anticipations of economic agents (including importantly both wage earners and entrepreneurs) has long been recognized as a critical element in forecasting. Clearly, they have expectations (accurate or inaccurate) regarding inflation as well as expectations regarding real changes.

Entrepreneurs' role in the inflationary process involves, therefore, two related questions. The first is to consider whether or not entrepreneurs can anticipate inflation with reasonable and independent accuracy, and the second is to consider whether they are subject to money illusion. Is their attitude toward the future affected by nominal changes or by real changes? The changes we have in mind are the changes triggering their investment and related decisions which will significantly determine the course of economic activity in the immediate future.

In earlier work, Geoffrey H. Moore and I have considered the ability of entrepreneurs to anticipate inflation. In the United States, Dun and Bradstreet has long included a question about expected manufacturers' wholesale and retail prices in their entrepreneurial surveys. In Europe, the EEC has asked entrepreneurs about expected changes in their own prices (which presumably would move with the consumer price index). Moore and I considered the degree to which these surveys could track price changes and concluded:

"In general we may say that the surveys of the views of economic agents concerning price changes are useful in the sense that they frequently anticipate the major cyclical changes in inflation by a quarter or two. However, there are a number of instances when the expected lead fails to materialize. Simple correlation analysis suggests that the surveys of expectations often can monitor the broad cyclical phases, but they cannot, by any means, track the more detailed movements in prices reflected in monthly or quarterly changes in inflation rates. The inherent advantages of surveys of anticipated price changes are often offset, at least in some degree, by their tendency to lag the movements shown by retrospective surveys" (Klein and Moore 1985, 97; cf. also Moore 1986).

This last comment is particularly relevant in the present context. We have frequently found that surveys of entrepreneurs' expectations are not any more helpful in forecasting than entrepreneurs' reports on what has happened in the immediate past, because what entrepreneurs expect in the coming months is often what has in fact been happening to them in the recent past.

From this we have concluded that entrepreneurs' ability to forecast inflation is limited and that they tend to expect inflation when they have been experiencing it. This answers the first question but not the more complicated question of whether or not the entrepreneurs take inflation explicitly into account in setting their policies. It is this question to which the present study is directed. Without a clear answer to this question, the likelihood that improving the entrepreneurs' forecasting ability would lead to noninflationary policies would not be easy to establish.

A Note on Data and Methodology

To consider the degree to which entrepreneurs may be subject to money illusion, data from Dun and Bradstreet for the United States and from the European

Economic Commission (EEC) for the United Kingdom, France, Italy, and West Germany are used. In each case we present the results of net balances of replies to questions concerning industrial confidence. In the case of Dun and Bradstreet, we have based industrial confidence on a question concerning sales expectations. If the "net balance" (i.e., the percentage of respondents expecting sales increases minus the percentage of respondents expecting sales decreases) goes up from the "net balance" for the preceding quarter, we regard this as indicating an increase in entrepreneurial confidence. These net balances are, in effect, first differences, and therefore reflect the rate of change in confidence from quarter to quarter. (They are based on expected changes in sales.)

In the correlation analysis employed, we have searched from minus four quarters to plus four quarters from the current quarter for the highest correlation between the net balances in the survey series and the growth rate in quarterly GNP figures. The surveys are available in the quarter after the quarter to which they pertain. If the surveys are to be useful in forecasting, therefore, they would have to anticipate changes in GNP by more than one quarter. (If they anticipated GNP changes by two quarters, they would have an effective lead of one quarter at the time they become available.)

In the case of the EEC surveys, the industrial confidence indicator consists of the arithmetic mean of the net balances relative to (*i*) a question asking about *production* expectations in the months ahead (increase or decrease), (*ii*) a question concerning orderbooks (above or below normal), and (*iii*) a question on stocks (above or below normal) with the sign on the latter inverted. Unlike the Dun and Bradstreet data, the EEC data are available monthly but have been converted to quarterly series to correspond with the GNP data which are available only quarterly. Because the first question asks about increases and decreases in production, it is, in effect, a question asking about the rate of change in production and hence ought to be related to the rate of change in GNP. We assume it pertains to the quarter following the quarter in which the data are reported.

The major problem arises because the second and third components of the EEC Industrial Confidence Indicator are based on the notion of "above or below normal" and, hence, do not pertain directly to a rate of change. We have decided to treat the confidence index as a rate of change and correlate it with the growth rate in GNP, as we have done with the Dun and Bradstreet series.

These problems are serious, but we have utilized the surveys nonetheless to provide a rough indication of the answer to the question posed: are entrepreneurs' basic attitudes, including their confidence about the future, free of money illusion or not? We propose to investigate this question by correlating entrepreneurs' expectations first with the rate of change in nominal GNP and then with the rate of change in real GNP. We shall look for the lead or lag (in quarters) of the surveys vis à vis the change in GNP which gives the highest correlation. This should tell us something about how well entrepreneurs' expectations monitor changes in GNP. We shall check the timing conclusions by relating the turning points in the surveys to turns in the two GNP series. The GNP rates of change that we use are equivalent to six-month smoothed rates, obtained by taking the ratio of the current quarter's GNP to the average for the preceding four quarters, and raising this to the 1.6 power to obtain an annual rate.

The Findings

Charts 17.1–17.10 show the rates of change in real GNP or nominal GNP, and the Business Confidence Index in the United States, the United Kingdom, France, West Germany, and Italy. Not surprisingly, the tremendous inflation of the period from the late 1960s to the early 1980s in the U.S. shows clearly in the growth of nominal GNP. In the United States, there is clear evidence of a rising trend in nominal GNP, perhaps reversed in the 1980s when inflation declined. There is no evidence of rising trend in the expected sales change (our confidence measure for the United States).

Inasmuch as the cyclical patterns for the two measures of GNP are very similar, the differential trend may account for a part of the explanation of the differences in correlation found for the United States. Table 17.1 summarizes the results of correlation for all five countries. In each case, we examined the timing between the survey and each measure of GNP beginning four quarters before the current quarter and extending four quarters into the future. Over this two year span, we searched for the lead or lag of the surveys with respect to the GNP figures which produced the highest correlation. Table 17.1 presents the maximum correlations as well as the timing to which each pertains for the association of the surveys with real and nominal GNP, respectively, for each of the five countries.

The findings are clear. In every country, the correlations are higher with real than with nominal GNP. Businesses' confidence, as here measured, is based primarily on the changes in real economic activity in the recent past. Entrepreneurs appear to be aware of the relationship between the change in nominal activity and the underlying inflation rate. In effect, they "deflate" the nominal results before responding to them attitudinally. This is perhaps not surprising. Not only do the workers see beyond nominal wages to real wages, but entrepreneurs also are able to differentiate real growth from nominal growth.

The ability of the entrepreneurs to differentiate real from nominal changes does not, however, mean that the surveys help one to forecast real GNP. To our earlier finding that entrepreneurs tend to expect the inflation rate for the immediate future that they have seen in the immediate past, we may now add the observation that their confidence tends to improve when real activity has improved in the immediate past. As crude as our timing comparisons must be, there is no evidence that entrepreneurs correctly anticipate improved growth in real activity in advance. The maximum correlations are reached when the survey net balances lag behind the actual changes in real GNP by one quarter. Inclusion of

Chart 17.1. **United States: Expected Sales and Change in Nominal GNP,***
1959–1986.

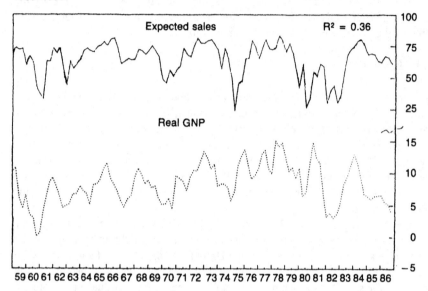

*6-month smoothed rate of change.

Chart 17.2. **United States: Expected Sales and Change in Real GNP,*** **1959–1986.**

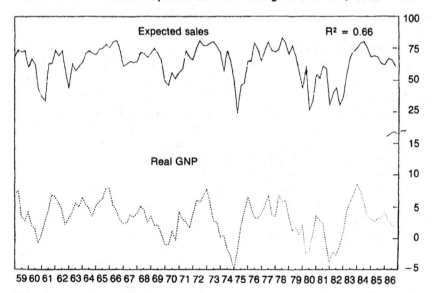

*6-month smoothed rate of change.

Chart 17.3. **West Germany: Industrial Confidence Index and Change in Nominal GNP,* 1969–1985.**

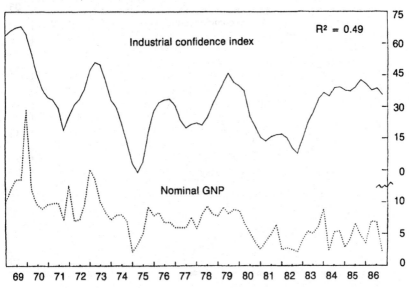

*6-month smoothed rate of change.

Chart 17.4. **West Germany: Industrial Confidence Index and Change in Real GNP,* 1969–1985.**

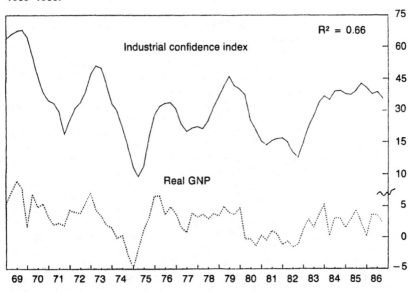

*6-month smoothed rate of change.

Chart 17.5. **France: Industrial Confidence Index and Change in Nominal GNP,***
1976–1986.

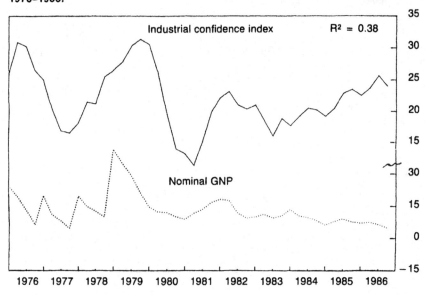

*6-month smoothed rate of change.

Chart 17.6. **France: Industrial Confidence Index and Change in Real GNP,***
1976–1986.

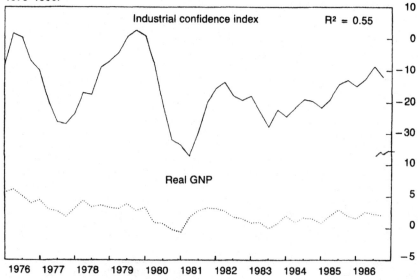

*6-month smoothed rate of change.

Chart 17.7. **Italy: Industrial Confidence Index and Change in Nominal GNP,**[*] **1976–1986.**

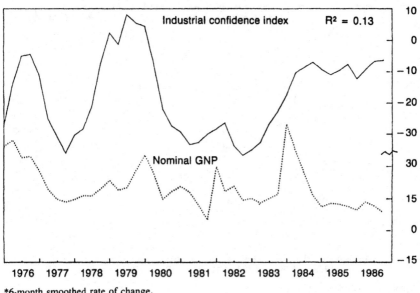

*6-month smoothed rate of change.

Chart 17.8. **Italy: Industrial Confidence Index and Change in Real GNP,**[*] **1976–1986.**

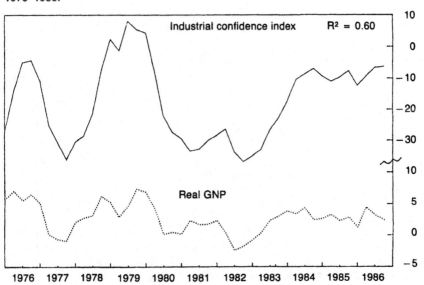

*6-month smoothed rate of change.

Chart 17.9. **United Kingdom: Industrial Confidence Index and Change in Nominal GNP,* 1977–1986.**

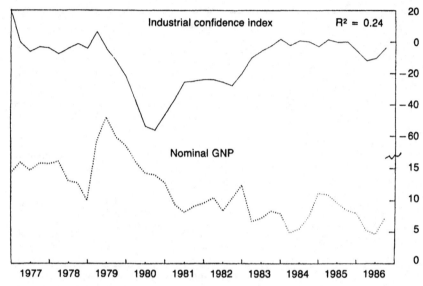

*6-month smoothed rate of change.

Chart 17.10. **United Kingdom: Industrial Confidence Index and Change in Real GNP,* 1977–1986.**

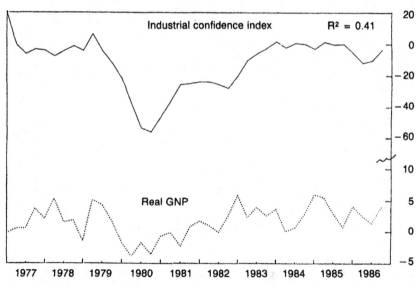

*6-month smoothed rate of change.

these survey results into an indicator system might improve its ability to track cyclical changes in real activity, but it would not improve forecasts perceptibly.

We have tested the consistency of the timing comparisons revealed in the correlation analysis by looking at the timing of the individual turning points in the surveys vis à vis the turns in the growth rates of real and nominal GNP for all five countries. The results are summarized in Table 17.2. While there are some variations, it is clear in general that the search for the lag or lead exhibiting the highest correlation has managed to capture the timing at a majority of the individual turning points as well. (Only in the United Kingdom do we encounter really divergent behavior, and it shows up in both tests. The number of U.K. timing comparisons is so few, however—the table shows 2 for real, 3 for nominal—that little significance can be placed in the results in any case.) In general, it is fair to say that the evidence on timing at individual turning points summarized in Table 17.2 confirms the conclusion of Table 17.1; there is a clear tendency for the survey results to lag one quarter behind the growth rates in GNP, both nominal and real, but the association is closer in the case of real GNP.

Conclusion

It is clear that by the 1980s, all the market-oriented economies studied here had had enough experience with recent high inflation rates that entrepreneurs could scarcely be accused of falling victim to "money illusion."

The consistency with which entrepreneurial confidence was more highly correlated with movements in the growth rates in real rather than nominal GNP in all five countries is impressive. If the tendency of labor unions to push for COLA agreements in the years since 1948 attests to the sensitivity of workers to the potential inroads of inflation on the purchasing power of their wages, the results of this study suggest that entrepreneurs are equally sensitive.

We have seen that this greater sensitivity of entrepreneurs to real changes is not matched by any special ability to anticipate such changes. Indeed, the typical one quarter lag in entrepreneurial reaction, confirmed both by the correlation analysis and the examination of the timing at individual turning points, suggests that entrepreneurial confidence is largely a reaction to changes in the immediate past.

In addition to the lag in entrepreneurial reactions, we have noted that entrepreneurs, sensitive though they clearly are to the impact of inflation, are not very good at forecasting inflation (though the study alluded to earlier[2] suggests they are at least as good as economists). The entrepreneurial surveys of expected selling prices, previously referred to, give us insight into entrepreneurial thinking about future inflation which is unmatched by any comparable surveys of workers expected nominal wages. There are no country surveys of workers' "expected wages in the months ahead," either real or nominal wages. The evidence suggests

Table 17.1

Maximum Correlations, Business Surveys vs. Nominal and Real GNP, Five Countries, 1959–1986

Country	Lead(−) or lag (+), in quarters	Correlation (r)	(r²)	F ratio	Durbin-Watson
	Nominal GNP vs. business surveys				
United States	+1	+0.596	+0.355	56.148	0.480457
West Germany	0	+0.698	+0.487	62.739	1.09619
France	+1	+0.614	+0.377	23.047	1.3411
Italy	+1	+0.363	+0.132	5.754	0.8452
United Kingdom	−4	+0.488	+0.239	10.652	0.499797
	Real GNP vs. business surveys				
United States	+1	+0.810	+0.656	195.113	1.049
West Germany	+1	+0.815	+0.664	130.331	1.43573
France	+1	+0.743	+0.552	46.789	0.76679
Italy	+1	+0.778	+0.605	58.351	1.02121
United Kingdom	+1	+0.638	+0.407	23.295	1.65526

Notes: The correlation coefficient for the U.K. surveys lagged one quarter behind changes in nominal GNP is −0.499. For West Germany the one-quarter lag gives a correlation result of 0.656.

that both entrepreneurs and workers may react to prior changes in real economic activity by pushing for both wage and price adjustments which will "guarantee" growing real returns to both. In so doing they may well both exacerbate rather than mitigate inflationary tendencies.

Peter Howitt recently commented, ". . . the attitude of economists to the assumption of money illusion can best be described as equivocal. The assumption is frequently invoked and frequently resisted" (Howitt 1988, 519). He went on to note that two conflicting beliefs dear to the hearts of most economists are involved: rationality, which suggests paying attention to real magnitudes; and the critical nature of money, which suggests the importance of nominal magnitudes. Our study suggests a certain rationality in the sense that economic agents, here entrepreneurs, surely are aware of the impact of inflation. But the problem is the difficulty in anticipating or allowing in advance for it with any accuracy, which may make the results of entrepreneurial decisions look as though inflation had not been taken into account.

Table 17.2

Average Timing of Turning Points in Business Confidence vs. Nominal and Real GNP, Five Countries, Average Lead (−) or Lag (+) in Quarters

Country	Survey net balance vs. growth rates in real GNP	Survey net balance vs. growth rates in nominal GNP
Number of comparisons—16		
U.S., 1959–86		
Peaks	+1.1	+0.8
Troughs	+1.1	+0.8
Peaks and troughs	+1.1	+0.8
Number of comparisons—9		
West Germany, 1969–86		
Peaks	+1.2	+1.6
Troughs	+0.8	+1.2
Peaks and troughs	+1.0	+1.4
Number of comparisons—7 (real), 6 (nominal)		
France, 1976–86		
Peaks	+0.8	−0.7
Troughs	−0.3	+0.7
Peaks and troughs	+1.0	0.0
Number of comparisons—7 (real), 5 (nominal)		
Italy, 1976–86		
Peaks	0.0	0.0
Troughs	+1.0	−0.5
Peaks and troughs	+0.4	+0.2
Number of comparisons—2 (real), 3 (nominal)		
United Kingdom, 1976–86		
Peaks	+4.0	−3.5
Troughs	+2.0	−3.0
Peaks and troughs	+3.0	−3.3
Mean timing, five countries		
Peaks	+1.4	+1.1
Troughs	+1.2	+2.4
Peaks and troughs	+1.3	+1.9
Median timing, five countries		
Peaks	+0.8	+0.8
Troughs	+1.0	+0.8
Peaks and troughs	+0.9	+0.8

Notes

1. There is some evidence that workers are not only escaping from money illusion, but also from uncertainty. A recent study indicates that between 1967 and 1982 workers covered by COLA agreements settled for wages about 2 percent below those agreed to by workers in agreements without COLA clauses but in otherwise identical bargaining situations. (Cf. Daniel S. Hammermesh and Albert Rees 1988 for a summary of the studies pertaining to this conclusion.)

2. Moore (1986) concludes that business managers do a better job of forecasting inflation than the concensus forecasts of economists.

References

Fisher, Irving. 1928. *The Money Illusion*. New York: Adelphi Publishers.

Flanagan, Robert J., Robert S. Smith, and Ronald G. Ehrenberg. 1984. *Labor Economics and Labor Relations*. Glenview, Ill.: Scott, Foresman and Company.

Howitt, Peter. 1988. "Money Illusion." In *The New Palgrave Dictionary of Economics*. Edited by John Eatwell, Murray Milgate, and Peter Newman. New York: Stockton Press.

Klein, Philip A., and Geoffrey H. Moore. 1985. "How Well Do Surveys Anticipate Inflation Rate Changes?" In *Business Cycle Surveys in the Assessment of Economic Activity*, p. 97. Papers presented at the 17th CIRET Conference Proceedings, Vienna. Edited by Karl H. Oppenländer and Gunter Poser. Aldershot, England: Gower Publishing Company Ltd. 1986.

Moore, Geoffrey H. 1986. "Inflation Forecasts: Businessmen vs. Economists." In *IFO Studien, Zeitschrift für Empirische Wirtschaftsforschung* No. 33, 1986-1-3, pp. 229-38. Boston: Duncher and Hamerbolt.

Patinkin, Don. 1955. *Money, Interest, and Prices*. New York: Harper & Row, Publishers. Second edition 1965.

Wachtel, Howard M. 1984. *Labor and the Economy*. New York: Academic Press, Inc.

18

Cyclical Effects of International Transmission of Real and Monetary Disturbances

Anna J. Schwartz and Michael D. Bordo

Three types of evidence are available on cyclical behavior in response to the transmission of external influences. One type is the set of business cycle studies that accepts the NBER reference cycle chronology or post-World War II growth-cycle chronology. Another type is more recent econometric work. The third type of evidence is historical accounts of individual cycles. The paper summarizes this evidence. It is not fully satisfactory because some of it does not distinguish foreign from domestic disturbances, money from real shocks, or the prevailing exchange rate arrangements. Moreover, the evidence, such as it is, intertwines the disturbance and the propagation mechanism within an economy.

The world economy since the 19th century has been characterized by varying degrees of interdependence. In the pre-World War I world, individual economies to a great extent were exposed to economic events in the rest of the world. Countries were linked together through trade in goods and services, flows of human, financial, and physical capital, and information transfers. World War I fundamentally contracted each of these links. That process accelerated during the interwar period, when countries sought to insulate themselves from what they perceived to be negative impulses transmitted from abroad. One of the hallmarks of the Bretton Woods years, in reaction to the interwar experience, was a drive to liberate trade and immigration flows while preserving barriers to capital flows. Although the record is mixed because of actual steps and threats of further ones to restrict the channels of transmission, a distinctive feature of the period of floating exchange rates since 1973 is said to be a high and rising degree of interdependence.

Theoretical channels of transmission differ under alternative exchange rate arrangements as well as in an open world economy, as compared with a world economy in which restrictions on international trade and capital controls are

This paper was originally prepared for the McGill Macroeconomics Conference: Approaches to the Business Cycle, March 1988.

mandated. The types of theory economists have constructed reflect the differences in conditions that have arisen in the world economy, possibly in response to their doctrines.[1] One objective of this paper is to relate the changing content of the theory of transmission to these differences.

Another objective is to examine the implications for business cycles of the transmission of disturbances in one country that impinge upon the levels of output, national income, and economic well-being of other countries. It is generally accepted that disturbances, which may be either monetary or real in nature, are transmitted by the current account or the capital account of the balance of payments of the affected countries. The effects of balance of payments changes are not, however, exclusively cyclical. The effects may be very short-term, for example, on daily domestic interest rates, or very long-term, on domestic investment. The literature particularly on the latter aspect of international transmission is not the focus of this paper.

Three types of evidence are available on cyclical behavior in response to the transmission of external influences. One type is the set of business cycle studies that accepts the NBER reference cycle chronology or post-World War II growth-cycle chronology. Another type is more recent econometric work. Examples are the identification of residuals as the innovation, or shock, or disturbance in estimated equations of an economic aggregate, and tests of Granger causality. Another example is the investigation of the simulation properties of a macroeconomic model. The third type of evidence is historical accounts of individual cycles. This chapter summarizes this evidence. It is not fully satisfactory because some of it does not distinguish foreign from domestic disturbances, money from real shocks, or the prevailing exchange rate arrangements. Moreover, the evidence, such as it is, intertwines the disturbance and the propagation mechanism within an economy.

In a concluding section we reflect on the evidence. International transmission may affect inflation rates or real variables, such as relative prices, real output, real exchange rates, and real interest rates. Under fixed exchange rates, the impact of international transmission is on inflation rates, real output, and relative prices. Under floating exchange rates, the impact is on all four real variables.

Changes in relative prices impose competitive pressures on firms in the affected industries. Relative price changes in response to international transmission usually enforce shifts between traded and nontraded goods industries. Competitive pressures, however, also arise on account of dynamic changes within a country affecting costs, prices, and employment of particular firms and industries.

Under floating exchange rates in an open world economy, real exchange rate changes influence the profitability of producers of traded goods, and real interest rates influence asset yields and capital flows.

The adjustments required to meet competitive pressures, wherever they originate, are structural. They may be aggravated or mitigated by cyclical forces with their own periodicity. Under fixed exchange rates in the past, monetary contraction in response to a current account deficit was not unusual. In that regime, it may be that international transmission played an important role in cyclical developments.[2] Under floating exchange rates, neither current account deficits nor surpluses are necessarily tied to cyclical developments.

Does the cyclical propagation mechanism differ depending on the source of the disturbance? One aspect of interdependence that we highlight is that our knowledge of the quantitative impact of foreign vs. domestic disturbances is limited. Yet emphasis in policy analyses of the role of foreign disturbances in leading to undesired cyclical developments often promotes xenophobia. Interference with the conduct of international commerce and international borrowing and lending is advocated with no calculation of the losses in efficiency such recommendations enforce. In interpreting the national accounts, theory also encourages the drift to protectionism. The notion of a multiplier effect of foreign purchases of home goods that leads to an increase in output and employment expresses an orientation that treats trade deficits as harmful. Measures to close an economy become thinkable.

Theoretical Channels of Transmission in an Open vs. a Closed World Economy

This section describes the operation of channels of transmission under fixed and floating exchange rates, according to two standard approaches: (*i*) a traditional one of long standing designed for an open world economy, and (*ii*) the other derived from Keynesian thinking influenced by a closed world outlook associated with the interwar period. The Keynesian approach has undergone significant change since the advent of floating exchange rates.

Traditional Approach in an Open World Economy

Under the conditions of the fixed exchange rate specie standard which (in one form or another) characterized an open world for most of the two centuries preceding World War I, both monetary and real shocks were transmitted through the balance of payments, affecting domestic money supplies, expenditure, price levels, and real income. The adjustment mechanism worked through the current account supplemented by the capital account.

An example of a monetary disturbance is the case of a large country on a specie standard, which temporarily issues fiat money to finance a war. Under fixed exchange rates, the increase in the money supply raises domestic expenditures, nominal income, and ultimately, the price level. The rise in the domestic price level leads to an improvement in the terms of trade, but a balance of trade deficit results. In its trading partners, the same forces produce a balance of trade surplus.

The deficit is financed by a specie outflow from the inflating country to its trading partners, reducing the monetary gold stock in the former and raising it in the latter. As a consequence in the trading partners, money supply increases, raising domestic expenditure, nominal income, and ultimately the price level. Depending on the relative share of the inflating country's monetary gold stock in the world total, world prices and income rise. The initial effects of monetary change may fall on real output, reflecting possible rigidities, but ultimately the full effect is on the price level.

An alternative channel is price arbitrage. To the extent the law of one price holds, traded goods prices are continuously equated across the world, without the need for relative prices of exports and imports to adjust. However, relative prices of traded and nontraded goods are altered.

Since the initial effects of money supply increases tend to lower interest rates, capital flows abroad are also a channel of transmission. A short-term capital inflow, however, may provide temporary financing of the current account deficit.

An example of a real disturbance is a new technology that exploits an existing resource, raising the expected real rate of return in the home country. Investors in other countries, with a lower real rate of interest, purchase securities issued by the home country. Under fixed exchange rates, the capital flow is financed by a specie flow from the foreign countries to the home country. The specie inflow raises the home country's money supply and price level, in turn raising the price of exports relative to the price of imports. The demand for imports in the home country rises, with a resulting transfer of real resources from the foreign to the home country.

In the long run, whether the disturbances are monetary or real, the balance of payments under fixed exchange rates returns to equilibrium. In the case of a monetary disturbance, the rise in the price level of the inflating country is reversed as its money supply contracts with a falling monetary gold stock. Specie is redistributed from the inflating country to the recipient countries. In the case of a real disturbance, short-term capital flows from the home country to foreign countries, reverse specie flows consequent upon the higher price level in the former, and interest payments to service the capital imports restore equilibrium.

Under floating rates, the issue of fiat money, if it continues beyond the point where all monetary gold is displaced, will force the country off the specie standard. The consequent rise in the domestic price level will manifest itself in a depreciating currency (Taussig 1917; Graham 1922). In the case of a real disturbance, capital inflows to the home country in response to the new technology will appreciate the country's currency. A negative supply shock will depreciate the country's currency, with contractionary effects on the rest of the world's goods, specie, and capital.

The Keynesian Approach to Transmission
in a Closed World Economy

A more recent and widespread view of how transmission works is the Keynesian approach developed by Meade (1951), Mundell (1968), and Fleming (1962), which was designed for inward-looking countries of the world economy of the interwar years that were expected to behave so post-World War II. Based on the IS-LM framework, the Mundell-Fleming model in its original version assumed Keynesian unemployment, demand-determined output short of feasible capacity utilization, rigid wages and prices. Domestic wages determined in domestic labor markets determined domestic prices. Commodity arbitrage was neglected, and changes in exchange rates had little effect on domestic prices. Private capital outflows were held to be insufficient to finance current account imbalances. National monetary systems were assumed to be insulated. Short-term interest rates were controlled by domestic monetary authorities and were not influenced by foreign interest rates or exchange rate expectations (Kenen 1985). The model was consistent with recommendations to policymakers to restrict capital flows in the post-World War II period, based on the difference between transmission in the presence and in the absence of capital mobility that was featured.

Under fixed exchange rates, a monetary disturbance is exemplified by an increase in the money supply in one country that lowers interest rates and raises real expenditure, including the purchase of imports. That leads to a current account deficit at home, financed by decumulation of official reserves, and a surplus abroad, financed by accumulation of official reserves. Real income rises both at home and abroad, the extent of its rise determined by a multiplier, which in turn depends on the relative sizes of the marginal propensities to import and save. The home country increases its consumption of domestic plus imported goods. The output of the foreign country responds to the increased demand from abroad by an amount that exceeds the initial increase in demand. This is transmission in the absence of capital mobility. In its presence, the fall in interest rates at home leads to a capital outflow, which in turn reduces official reserves. This forces a contraction of the money supply, which offsets the effects on income of the initial monetary expansion. The foreign country's surplus is increased by the capital outflow from the home country, so its income is raised even more than is the case in the absence of capital mobility.

Under fixed exchange rates a real disturbance is exemplified by an increase in government expenditure in one country that raises real expenditure and income, including the demand for imports, leading to a balance of trade deficit at home and a surplus abroad. Real income rises in both countries through the multiplier. In both cases, the balance of payments disequilibrium cannot be sustained. The decline in reserves in the deficit country (rise in the surplus country) will cause the domestic money supply to fall (rise), reversing the process. This is the case in the absence of capital mobility. With perfect capital mobility, the rise in real government expenditure raises the domestic interest rate, which induces a capital inflow, which in turn enhances the rise in income at home but offsets the rise in income abroad. Thus capital mobility under fixed exchange rates enhances the transmission abroad of a domestic monetary disturbance and offsets the transmission abroad of a domestic real disturbance.

Under floating exchange rates, insulation against both monetary and real shocks results, provided capital mobility is absent. An increase in the domestic money supply lowers interest rates, raises real expenditure including the demand for imports, leading to an incipient balance of payments deficit at home, and surplus abroad. The home currency depreciates, which lowers the price of domestic goods relative to the domestic price of foreign goods. Demand shifts from foreign to domestic goods, offsetting the increase in foreign income induced through the current account. Similarly, an increase in government expenditure in one country raises real expenditure including the demand for imports, thus depreciating the exchange rates. Demand shifts from foreign to domestic goods, offsetting the increase in foreign income.

However, under floating exchange rates with perfect capital mobility, although a rise in the domestic money supply creates an incipient balance of payments deficit at home and surplus abroad leading to a depreciation of the home currency, the concomitant decline in interest rates induces a capital outflow which further depreciates the home currency. Demand for the home country's goods is thereby stimulated and demand for the foreign country's goods is reduced, raising income at home and reducing it abroad. With capital mobility, monetary expansion at home leads to a recession abroad.

Under floating exchange rates, an increase in government expenditure in one country raises real expenditure including the demand for imports, hence depreciating the exchange rate. With capital mobility, however, the rise in interest rates induced by the increase in government expenditure leads to a capital inflow, which offsets the effect of the current account imbalance on the exchange rate. At the same time, the capital outflow from the foreign country depreciates its exchange rate, stimulating the demand for its goods. Hence, real output abroad rises. Thus under floating exchange rates with perfect capital mobility, in contrast to the traditional approach, the Mundell-Fleming model predicts perverse effects on foreign countries' income from monetary disturbances in the home country and positive effects from real aggregate demand disturbances in the home country. Insulation no longer prevails.

The Mundell-Fleming Model 25 Years Later

In recent years, the Mundell-Fleming model has been modified in an attempt to correct its shortcomings (Frenkel and Razin 1987a, 1987b). The shortcomings include the failure of the model to base the money demand function and savings, investment, and the trade balance on intertemporal optimizing behavior. Expectations in the model are static. It does not take into account country size, which is an important determinant of the effectiveness of monetary and fiscal policies. The results of a model in which capital flows alter capital stocks are different from one in which flow equilibrium alone is examined. In addition, the model ignores not only the distribution of assets and money across countries but also wealth effects. The rigid price and wage assumptions of the model have been relaxed, and the treatment of government expenditures has been broadened to distinguish financing of expenditures by taxation rather than bonds.

The original Mundell-Fleming model accordingly has been the inspiration for a host of recent models that vary some or many of its conditions. One direction of change has been to incorporate rational expectations and uncertainty in two-country general equilibrium approaches with full employment and flexible prices (Lucas 1982; Svensson 1985; Stockman and Svensson 1985). Another direction retains the assumption of sticky goods prices and demand-determined output but with proper microeconomic foundations, derived from optimizing behavior in a rational expectations context (Svensson and van Wynbergen 1986). Some models assume wages that are temporarily fixed due to contract lags or wage indexation (Flood and Marion 1982). Models vary according to the degree of substitutability assumed between domestic and foreign goods and between domestic and foreign money and assets denominated in different currencies.

In addition to the choice of model assumptions, the results obtained depend on the elaboration of the character of the disturbances: anticipated or unanticipated, temporary or permanent, current or future. Does the monetary disturbance originate on the supply or on the demand side? Is it a domestic or foreign disturbance? Is the real disturbance created by a supply rather than a demand disruption (Fischer 1976)?

With such an array of variables, it is no simple task to summarize the effects on transmission under fixed or floating exchange rates. The current state of the art reflects the ingenuity of the investigator in ringing changes on the original or modified versions already reported.

How complicated the analysis becomes, even when limited to two effects of transmission, may be illustrated by the question of whether a foreign country is benefited or harmed by high interest rates in the United States (Corden 1985). The answer depends in part on whether the foreign country is a net creditor or debtor, which must be considered in relation to a terms of trade effect. Terms of trade might deteriorate for the period during which additional capital flows from the foreign country to the United States—the channel of transmission that generates a current account surplus. Although worsened terms of trade would be adverse, the gain to the foreign country as a net creditor at a variable interest rate thanks to its capital exports would be offsetting. The total effect of transmission is thus not easy to determine even in theory.

In addition to the modifications of the Mundell-Fleming model in the recent literature, analyses of floating exchange rates have proposed at least two channels of transmission that have not been recognized in that literature. One channel is possible interdependence of money demand through direct currency substitution (Miles 1978; Brittain 1981) and indirect currency substitution—the substitution of foreign and domestic assets which in turn are close money substitutes (McKinnon 1982). The other channel is interdependence of money supply through policy reaction functions that incorporate exchange rates and foreign interest rates (McKinnon 1982) or through buffer stock effects (Bordo, Choudhri, and Schwartz 1987).

Direct transmission of real disturbances under floating rates has also been proposed (Swoboda 1979). Examples are a fall in expected rates of return on investment in an important foreign country as well as at home, an increase in uncertainty at home and abroad, and changes in prospective profitability for a large industrial sector at home and abroad. Direct transmission is also possible in this view when international capital flows are interrupted for domestic reasons from the countries of outflows.

Whether the theoretical effect of international transmission is positive or negative is thus ambiguous. The results obtained appear to reflect the model-builders' priors.

Types of Evidence on Cyclical Effects of Transmission of Disturbances

The preceding survey of theories of transmission cannot be matched with a collection of references to studies testing the empirical validity of the different versions. Tested knowledge of cyclical effects of transmission is exceedingly sketchy. The distinctions crucial to theories—an open or closed world economy, fixed or floating exchange rates, real or monetary disturbances—are not the guidelines that have been used regularly in empirical work. The best that can be done in summary of the available evidence is to distinguish three different types of evidence: (1) business-cycle studies, (2) econometric studies, (3) historical studies.

Evidence from Business-Cycle Studies

Business cycle studies that accept the NBER reference-cycle chronology provide several sorts of evidence on the transmission of external influences. One offers evidence on the degree of synchronization of cycles across countries (Klein 1976; Huffman and Lothian 1984; Moore and Zarnowitz 1986). A related study combines roughly coincident trend-adjusted economic indicators for selected market-oriented countries to form an international growth-cycle chronology (Klein and Moore 1985). Another study examines fluctuations in exports, imports, and the balance of trade in the United States and the United Kingdom (Mintz 1959, 1961,

1967). Still another study presents tests of interest rate arbitrage and correlation coefficients among short-term interest rates in London, New York, Paris, and Berlin (Morgenstern 1959).

Matching of 60 percent of the turning points in the NBER reference-cycle chronologies for a sample of four countries for 1854–1938 supports the idea of an international business cycle (Moore and Zarnowitz 1986). Since World War II chronologies designating peaks and troughs in growth cycles (deviations from trend; not absolute rises and declines in cyclical indicators) are available for a broader sample of countries, again roughly synchronized. In one study, a difference has been noted in the association between U.S. and U.K. cycles before 1932 (Huffman and Lothian 1984). It was weaker when either the United States or the United Kingdom was off the gold standard. A finding in another study is that U.S. peaks and troughs tended to precede the corresponding turns in the United Kingdom and Germany before 1938; since World War II, the relationship has persisted at troughs but has been reversed at peaks (Klein 1976).

An international growth-cycle chronology for the post-World War II period, based on roughly coincident trend-adjusted indicators for selected countries, serves to mark years in which there is an international consensus of high growth rates or low growth rates in real GNP, industrial production, imports and exports (Klein and Moore 1985). Growth swings appear to be widespread and synchronous among industrial countries. Nearly every turn in the international growth cycle is matched by a turn in each of the countries represented in the international combination. In addition, very few countries exhibit extra cycles, or do so infrequently. No country leads the other countries invariably into a recession, but the United States was one of the first countries to turn at four of six troughs. The United States thus tends to lead other countries out of recession. At peaks, the leading role shifts from country to country, seemingly at random. An examination of the ordering of turns from leading to lagging indicators at the international cycle turning points suggests, however, that no country regularly acts as the bellwether in leading industrial economies into or out of recession. Since cyclical instability can be transmitted through trade flows, leading indicators prove useful in forecasting growth cycles and trade flows.

Links across countries from international trade have also been suggested by studies of the volume, prices, and value of U.S. trade. Before World War II, fluctuations in foreign demand for U.S. exports drove the trade balance over the cycle. Prices rose in response to the increase in foreign demand for U.S. exports, improving the terms of trade and moving the trade balance into surplus (Mintz 1959). Since World War II, fluctuations in domestic demand for imports have driven the trade balance over the cycle (according to Eichengreen 1987, whose analysis is not based on NBER reference dates). Increased domestic demand for imports and reduced availability of exports has raised U.S. export prices, improving the terms of trade and moving the trade balance into deficit.

Tests of capital markets integration under the gold standard are available. One study produced results that challenged the view that arbitrage ensured uniformity of interest-rate differentials to exchange rate risk (measured by the difference of the exchange rate from the gold points) (Morgenstern 1959). An interest rate differential on ninety-day bills between London and New York under the gold standard was calculated to be 3.73 percent. The commercial paper rate in New York was on average 2.17 percent higher than the corresponding rate in London (1876–1914), with considerable variability in the interest rate differential. A later study compared the variability of the difference between U.S. and U.K. treasury bill rates (1974–83) and found the floating rate period variability substantially higher (Dornbusch and Fischer 1986). During the interwar years, the differential and variability of the London–New York rates were comparable to their magnitudes under fixed exchange rates in 1964–71 (Dornbusch and Fischer 1986). The correlation coefficients among different pairs of short-term interest rates (1876–1914) in London, New York, Paris, and Berlin varied from 0.36 (New York–Paris) to 0.73 (London–Berlin). The variation (1925–38) was between 0.13 (Berlin–Paris) and 0.84 (London–Berlin), comparable at the high end to the 0.794 correlation between monthly U.S. and U.K. treasury bill rates (1964–71). Interdependence from these results appears not to have increased over time.

Evidence from Econometric Studies

Granger-Sims autoregressive causality tests with respect to transmission between the United States and the United Kingdom for the combined period 1837–59 and 1882–1914 report relationships between annual U.S. income and price variables and U.K. income and price variables (Huffman and Lothian 1984). These tests show U.S. real income growth Granger-caused by U.K. monetary variables (gold, Bank rate, and high-powered money) but not by U.S. gold nor U.K. income. In turn, U.K. income growth is Granger-caused by U.S. high-powered money, prices, and interest rates, but not by U.K. prices or Bank rate.

Disturbances or shocks are discussed in econometric work. Estimates of equations that relate an economic aggregate to its own lagged values and also to lagged values of other economic aggregates (vector autoregressions) identify the residual in such equations as the innovation or shock (Blanchard and Watson 1986). Time series of the shocks make it possible to link them with particular historical events, but the quantitative contribution of an external event to a given shock cannot be determined.

Another approach to examining the role of shocks is to investigate simulation properties of a macroeconomic model usually built on the income-expenditure framework. Simulations for a given number of quarters (years) over the forecast period report the responses of the model to selected domestic or foreign shocks, retaining other variables on their actual historical paths. Fischer (1987), for example, based on simulations for a number of multicountry econometric models, shows that fiscal shocks in the United States have positive and lasting effect on real income in U.S. major trading partners, although the reverse effect from foreign fiscal shocks on the U.S. is negligible. Indeed, spillover effects are not overwhelming. Moreover, there is great diversity of views among the individual empirical models. One finds that a bond-financed increase in U.S. government expenditures leads to a small negative effect on output at home and abroad, while another obtains strong positive effects (Minford 1985; Oudiz and Sachs 1985).

There is even greater diversity of views among individual model simulations with respect to the effects of monetary expansion than with respect to the effects of fiscal expansion. Expansionary U.S. monetary policy leads to worsened current accounts of the U.S. and OECD countries, and presumably improved current accounts of non-OECD countries, according to Fischer's summary of simulations of twelve models. Again, one model reports strong positive spillover effects of monetary expansion in the United States, the other small negative effects.

Simulations based on the OECD INTERLINK model, run over the period 1982 to 1987, also indicate limited spillovers from U.S. policy to the rest of the world (Chouraqui, Clinton, and Montador 1987).

A different conclusion about the size of spillover effects is based on simulations of an 8-country model over the period 1955 to 1976 (Darby, Lothian et al. 1983). According to this study, U.S. monetary policy transmitted inflationary shocks from country to country through changes in relative prices and capital flows. Other channels including currency substitution and direct income effects were negligible. Though the dominant impulse originated in the United States, the seven other countries maintained some short-run control over domestic policy by sterilization.

Evidence from Historical Studies

The evidence from historical studies is mainly qualitative but also includes econometric estimates of single equations. We summarize the evidence for selected subperiods.

Classical gold standard. The 19th-century gold discoveries in California and Australia were examples of monetary shocks that Cairnes and Jevons studied. They demonstrated how the increased gold output was transmitted to other countries through the balance of payments, altering money supplies, expenditures, and prices (Bordo 1975; Laidler 1982; for a counterview, see Glasner 1985). Stock market crashes and bank runs that occurred simultaneously in a number of countries also suggest international financial linkages (Bordo 1986).

Another kind of monetary shock is exemplified by an increase in Bank rate by the Bank of England to stem a drain of its gold reserves at various times in the 19th century. As a consequence capital outflows were reduced, causing financial stringency and on occasion panic in countries that were previously recipients of the outflow (Levy-Leboyer 1982; Kindleberger 1984). These consequences of a halt in inflows were mitigated in the case of Canada, which had been a substantial importer of British and American capital from 1900 to 1912. The capital inflows were accompanied by a specie inflow that raised the reserves of the Canadian banking system. The increase in the money supply, domestic price level, and terms of trade that followed produced a balance of trade deficit allowing a real transfer of goods (Viner 1924). Debate continues over the question whether the rise in prices was related to the investment boom the capital inflow financed rather than the increase in bank reserves (Ingram 1957; Rich 1989; Dick and Floyd 1987). In 1913, the capital inflow dried up. Canada experienced a short, severe recession in 1914 that cut imports sharply but was accompanied by growth in exports. The increased supply of exports was made possible by capacity increases as investment projects came on stream, and the outbreak of war in Europe stimulated foreign demand (Eichengreen 1987).

U.S. greenback period. From 1862 through 1878, the U.S. greenback dollar floated against the British pound and other European currencies that were on a specie standard. Historical studies have examined the relationship of heavy capital inflows into the United States (1863–73) and their curtailment (1873–79) to the extent of the depreciation of the dollar and the movement of the terms of trade in each subperiod (Graham 1922; Friedman and Schwartz 1963). Studies of the cyclical record during the greenback era tend to concentrate on domestic developments without fully integrating the effects of capital flows on the three expansions and two contractions during the first subperiod and the long contraction during the second subperiod (Fels 1959; Friedman and Schwartz 1963).

Gold exchange standard, interwar years. Fisher (1935) first clearly stated the case that the Great Depression was transmitted from the United States to the rest of the world by the gold standard and gave evidence of insulation from declining income and prices in countries not linked to gold. Confirmation for a number of European countries of Fisher's insight is found in Choudhri and Kochin (1980). The depression was transmitted through relative price and income effects. The gold exchange standard did not survive the gold hoarding policies of the United States and France and misaligned exchange rates (an overvalued pound and an undervalued French franc). Universal sterilization (Nurske 1944) exacerbated the effects of inappropriate policies in the United States and France (Eichengreen 1987).

The cyclical experience of Japan during the 1920s has been studied initially in relation to the worldwide postwar boom and slump that affected foreign demand for Japanese raw materials and subsequently in relation to a domestic supply shock (the Kanto earthquake). No conclusions are reached with respect to the relative importance of each disturbance.

Bretton Woods. The transmission of monetary shocks from abroad under the adjustable pegged-rate post-World War II system has been documented in studies of balance of payments crises in countries other than the United States. All sorts of expedients were resorted to and were aimed at blocking unwanted effects of inflows of capital into countries that resisted appreciation of their currencies, and of outflows of capital by countries that resisted depreciation of their currencies. The cyclical effects were generally limited to fluctuations in growth rates of the real economy. Sorting out the contribution of foreign developments to the net outcome has not been attempted. One study has estimated the effect of a shift in foreign demand for the home country's output to assess transmission of real shocks. With the possible exception of the United Kingdom and Canada, the finding is that distributed-lag coefficients on real export shocks in a real income equation are insignificant (Darby, Lothian et al. 1983 in a sample of eight countries).

Canada's experience under floating exchange rates, 1950-62. To avoid the inflationary consequences of a massive capital inflow, Canada shifted to a floating exchange rate in 1950. The evidence on insulation in this episode is mixed. Wonnacott (1965, 78-79) reports a decline in the average amplitude of cycles relative to U.S. cycles in the 1950s compared to the interwar period (1946-54 vs. 1929-39). He provides limited evidence of monetary independence in the trends of short-term interest rates. However, he concludes that Canada's success at stabilization policy during the floating rate period may have stemmed from following conservative monetary and fiscal policies not dissimilar to those in the United States. Using spectral analysis, on the other hand, Bonomo and Tanner (1972) find little evidence of reduced Canadian cyclical sensitivity to U.S. cycles in the 1950s.[3]

Floating rate since 1973. Since the advent of general floating in 1973, evidence exists of increased independence of monetary policy and a tendency for long-run independence in the movements of nominal magnitudes (interest rates and price levels) (Darby and Lothian 1989), but also evidence of increased short-run interdependence of nominal and real magnitudes manifested in widespread common cyclical downturns in 1973-75 and 1980-83.[4]

Among the factors accounting for the high degree of short-run interdependence are the reaction to common real shocks, such as the oil price shocks of 1974 and 1979, increased capital mobility (Fischer 1987), and the presence of foreign variables in policy reaction functions in different countries (Hodgman 1983). Interdependence has been related to changes in world commodity supplies: oil in 1974 and 1979, sugar in 1973-74, and grain in 1972-73 (Cooper 1986).

The international money multiplier—the response of foreign money growth to U.S. money growth—has been cited as contributing to interdependence (McKinnon 1982): world depression results when the exchange value of the dollar appreciates and growth in world money contracts, and world inflation results when the exchange value of the dollar depreciates and world money increases.

Likewise, with an increase in the dollar exchange rate, debt-service payments in dollars of debtor countries become more burdensome and the reverse for a decrease in the dollar exchange rate.

Fiscal policy interdependence, as predicted by the Mundell-Fleming model, is generally taken for granted. U.S. fiscal expansion since 1982 is implicated in producing an increase in real interest rates that attracted foreign capital and created a demand for dollar securities. The capital inflow caused a dollar appreciation and, by drawing capital out of foreign economies, raised interest rates abroad too. High real U.S. interest rates and a high real interest rate differential between the United States and the rest of the world produced the dollar appreciation. The evidence is an annual regression of the dollar-DM exchange rate (1973–84) on a five-year forward-looking measure of the U.S. budget deficit and other variables including money growth and inflation forecasts. The budget deficit in this regression has the most explanatory power (Feldstein 1986).

Several problems with this mainstream view that cast doubt on the fiscal channel may be noted. The domestic link between fiscal deficits and real interest rates has not been established (Evans 1986; Mascaro and Meltzer 1983). In any event, the rate of interest is not set by the market for the flow of new debt but for the existing stock of debt. Through early 1985, dollar investment opportunities were more advantageous than foreign investments thanks to favorable tax provisions and, combined with declining U.S. inflation, they stimulated the rise in foreign demand for dollars. The U.S. experience from 1982 to 1985 is not an exception to the historical inverse relationship between fiscal deficits and the external strength of a currency. The depreciation of the dollar since early 1985 is inconsistent with the commonly held view that high budget deficits drive up the U.S. dollar. The depreciation since 1985 reflects a lower foreign demand for dollars in view of weaker U.S. real growth and less favorable tax provisions.

The fiscal deficit approach ignores effects related to the stock of government debt, the influence of government spending and tax policies on the use of resources for consumption or investment, and effects of increased monetary uncertainty that accompanied the growth in the fiscal deficit.

Reflections on Evidence of Transmission

The evidence on transmission has been accumulating for different states of the world. The pre–1914 world was characterized by a relatively free international flow of factors and goods. At the time, countries did not believe that they had the leeway to resist the adjustments required to maintain gold convertibility. Higher priority was assigned to maintenance of external balance than to stabilizing the internal level of prices and income. In the gold exchange regime and the Bretton Woods system that followed, intervention was widely accepted as needed to achieve domestic economic objectives. That concern has carried over into the current floating regime.

In the past, under fixed exchange rates, the effects of foreign disturbances were mainly on inflation rates, real output, and relative prices. Cyclical changes appeared to be associated with these effects. Deficit country money supplies, domestic demand, real output, and prices fell while real interest rates rose, and surplus country money supplies, domestic demand, real output, and prices rose while real interest rates fell. Investment declined in deficit countries and rose in surplus countries. None of these influences on domestic demand were expected to occur if imbalances in international payments on current account were corrected by movements in exchange rates.

Under the current managed floating rate system, countries have experienced real effects of changes in relative prices, real exchange rates, and real interest rates. Economists do not agree on the links among variables domestically or on the extent of spillover of these connections to the rest of the world. The empirical evidence is hardly systematic. There is no consensus on the relative roles of domestic versus foreign disturbances in contributing to cyclical change, nor is it known whether the propagation mechanism varies if the disturbance is one kind rather than the other.

If in a dynamic economy firms in an industry are periodically subject to competitive pressure from other firms in that industry or firms in other industries, does it matter whether that pressure comes from domestic or foreign competitors? It surely matters if economists encourage policy makers to intervene to block transmission in goods and capital markets because the source of the competition is beyond national boundaries. Cyclical developments occur over and above these continuing structural competitive stresses. An understanding of these complex forces is not yet within the grasp of the profession.

Notes

1. Keynes, for example, advocated a gold exchange standard with limited intervention early in his career, but by the 1940s proposed extensive intervention and made the case for exchange and capital controls. See Keynes 1913, 1941 [1971, 1980].

2. Backus and Kehoe (1988) present correlations of detrended output for pairs of ten countries, prewar, interwar, and postwar. The postwar correlations are consistently higher. They suggest the results support increasing integration and not measurement error in the early data. We are dubious that the detrending procedures used isolate cyclical behavior. We also question the finding that the quality of the data for Australia, Canada, and the United Kingdom is unimpeachable.

3. Baxter and Stockman (1988) find little evidence of changes in the variability of the trade balance when the Canadian exchange rate system changed. In addition, there was no similarity in the variability of the trade balance between the Canadian float from 1951 to 1962 and post-1973.

4. In a study of statistical properties of economic aggregates under the Bretton Woods system and the subsequent period of floating exchange rates, Baxter and Stockman report that these properties are not related in a systematic way to the exchange rate system, although this finding depends critically on the detrending procedure employed (Baxter and Stockman 1988).

References

Backus, David K., and Patrick J. Kehoe. 1988. "International Evidence on the Historical Properties of Business Cycles." Paper presented at McGill Macroeconomics Conference, March 25.

Baxter, Marianne, and Alan C. Stockman. 1988. "Business Cycles and the Exchange Rate System: Some International Evidence." NBER Working Paper No. 2689.

Blanchard, Olivier J., and Mark Watson. 1986. "Are Business Cycles All Alike?" In *The American Business Cycle: Continuity and Change*, pp. 123–79. Edited by R. J. Gordon. Chicago: University of Chicago Press.

Bonomo, Vittorio, and J. Ernest Tanner. 1972. "Canadian Sensitivity to Economic Cycles in the United States." *Review of Economics and Statistics* 54 (February): 1–8.

Bordo, Michael D. 1975. "John E. Cairnes on the Effects of the Australian Gold Discoveries, 1851–73: An Early Application of the Methodology of Positive Economics." *History of Political Economy* 7 (Fall): 337–59.

————. 1986. "Financial Crises, Banking Crises, Stock Market Crashes and the Money Supply: Some International Evidence, 1870–1933." In *Financial Crises and the World Banking System*, pp. 190–248. Edited by F. Capie and G. E. Wood. London: Macmillan.

Bordo, Michael D., Ehsan U. Choudhri, and Anna J. Schwartz. 1987. "The Behavior of Money Stock Under Interest Rate Control." *Journal of Money, Credit, and Banking* 19 (May): 181–97.

Brittain, Bruce. 1981. "International Currency Substitution and the Apparent Instability of Velocity in Some Western European Economies and the United States." *Journal of Money, Credit and Banking* 13 (May): 135–55.

Choudhri, Ehsan, and Levis A. Kochin. 1980. "The Exchange Rate and the International Transmission of Business Cycle Disturbances." *Journal of Money, Credit, and Banking* 12, pt. 1 (November): 565–74.

Chouraqui, J-C., K. Clinton, and R. B. Montador. 1987. "The Medium-Term Macroeconomic Strategy Revisited." OECD Department of Economics and Statistics, Working Paper No. 48 (December).

Cooper, Richard N. 1986. "The United States as an Open Economy." In *How Open Is the U.S. Economy?* pp. 3–24. Edited by R. W. Hafer. Lexington: Heath.

Corden, W. Max. 1985. "On Transmission and Coordination under Flexible Exchange Rates." In *International Economic Policy Coordination*, pp. 8–24. Edited by W. H. Buiter and R. C. Marston. Cambridge: Cambridge University Press.

Darby, Michael R., and James R. Lothian. 1989. "International Transmission Afloat." In *Money, History and International Finance: Essays in Honor of Anna J. Schwartz*. Chicago: University of Chicago Press.

Darby, Michael R., James R. Lothian, et al. 1983. *The International Transmission of Inflation*. Chicago: University of Chicago Press.

Dick, Trevor J. O., and John E. Floyd. 1987. "Canada and the Gold Standard, 1871–1913." Toronto (July). Mimeo.

Dornbusch, Rudiger, and Stanley Fischer. 1986. "The Open Economy: Implications for Monetary and Fiscal Policy." In *The American Business Cycle: Continuity and Change*, pp. 459–516. Edited by R. J. Gordon. Chicago: University of Chicago Press.

Eichengreen, Barry. 1989. "Trade Deficits in the Long Run." In *U.S. Trade Deficit: Causes, Consequences and Cures* pp. 239–78. Edited by A. E. Burger. Boston: Kluwer.

Evans, Paul. 1986. "Is the Dollar High Because of Large Budget Deficits?" *Journal of Monetary Economics* 18 (November): 227–49.

Feldstein, Martin. 1986. "The Budget Deficit and the Dollar." In *NBER Macroeconomics*

Annual 1986, pp. 355–92. Cambridge, Mass.: MIT Press.

Fels, Rendigs. 1959. *American Business Cycles, 1865–1897*. Chapel Hill: University of North Carolina Press.

Fischer, Stanley. 1976. "Comment on R. Dornbusch." *Scandinavian Journal of Economics* 78 (No. 2): 276–79.

———. 1987. "International Macroeconomic Policy Coordination." NBER Working Paper No. 2244 (May).

Fisher, Irving. 1935. "Are Booms and Depressions Transmitted Internationally Through Monetary Standards?" *Bulletin of the International Statistical Institute* 28 (2): 1–29.

Fleming, John M. 1962. "Domestic Financial Policies Under Fixed and Under Floating Exchange Rates." *IMF Staff Papers* 9 (November): 369–79.

Flood, Robert P., and Nancy P. Marion. 1982. "The Transmission of Disturbances Under Alternative Exchange-Rate Regimes with Optimal Indexing." *Quarterly Journal of Economics* 97 (February): 43–66.

Frenkel, Jacob A., and Assaf Razin. 1987a. *Fiscal Policies and the World Economy.* Cambridge, Mass.: MIT Press.

———. 1987b. "The Mundell-Fleming Model A Quarter Century Later: A Unified Exposition." *IMF Staff Papers* 34 (December): 567–620.

Friedman, Milton, and Anna J. Schwartz. 1963. *A Monetary History of the United States, 1867–1960*. Princeton: Princeton University Press.

Glasner, David. 1985. "A Reinterpretation of Classical Monetary Theory." *Southern Economic Journal* 52 (July): 46–67.

Graham, Frank D. 1922. "International Trade under Depreciated Paper: The United States, 1862–79." *Quarterly Journal of Economics* 36 (February): 220–73.

Hodgman, Donald, ed. 1983. *The Political Economy of Monetary Policy: National and International Aspects*. Federal Reserve Bank of Boston Conference Series No. 26.

Huffman, Wallace E., and James R. Lothian. 1984. "The Gold Standard and the Transmission of Business Cycles, 1833–1932." In *A Retrospective on the Classical Gold Standard, 1821–1931*, pp. 455–507. Edited by M. D. Bordo and A. J. Schwartz. Chicago: University of Chicago Press.

Ingram, James C. 1957. "Growth and Capacity and Canada's Balance of Payments." *American Economic Review* 47 (March):93–104.

Kenen, Peter B. 1985. "Macroeconomic Theory and Policy: How the Closed Economy Was Opened." In *Handbook of International Economics*, Vol. 2, pp. 625–77. Edited by R. W. Jones and P. B. Kenen. Amsterdam: North-Holland.

Keynes, J. M. 1971, 1980 [1913, 1940–4]. *The Collected Writings of John Maynard Keynes*. Vol. 1, *Indian Currency and Finance*. Vol. 25, *Activities 1940–4: Shaping the Post-War World: the Clearing Union*. Edited by E. Johnson and D. Moggridge. London: Macmillan.

Kindleberger, Charles P. 1984. "International Propagation of Financial Crisis in the Experience of 1888–93." In *International Capital Movements, Debt and the Monetary System*. Edited by W. E. Engel et al. Mainz: Hase and Koehler Verlag.

Klein, Philip A. 1976. *Business Cycles in the Postwar World: Some Reflections on Recent Research*. Domestic Affairs Study 42. Washington, D.C.: American Enterprise Institute (February).

Klein, Philip A., and Geoffrey H. Moore. 1985. *Monitoring Growth Cycles in Market-Oriented Countries*. NBER Studies in Business Cycles No. 26. Cambridge: Ballinger.

Laidler, David. 1982. "Jevons on Money." *The Manchester School* 50 (4): 326–53.

Levy-Leboyer, Maurice. 1982. "Central Banking and Foreign Trade: The Anglo-American Cycle in the 1830s." In *Financial Crises: Theory, History and Policy.* Edited by C. P. Kindleberger and J. P. Laffargue. Cambridge: Cambridge University Press.

Lucas, R. E., Jr. "Interest Rates and Currency Prices in a Two-Country World." *Journal of Monetary Economics* 10 (November): 335–60.

Mascaro, Angelo, and Allan H. Meltzer. 1983. "Long- and Short-Term Interest Rates in A Risky World." *Journal of Monetary Economics* 12 (November): 485–518.

McKinnon, Ronald. 1982. "Currency Substitution and Instability in the World Dollar Standard." *American Economic Review* 72 (June): 320–33.

Meade, James. [1951] 1965. *The Theory of International Policy* V.1 (Supplement), *The Balance of Payments*. London, New York: Oxford University Press.

Miles, M. A. 1978. "Currency Substitution, Flexible Exchange Rates, and Monetary Independence." *American Economic Review* 68 (June): 428–36.

Minford, Patrick. 1985. "The Effects of American Policies—A New Classical Interpretation." In *International Economic Policy Coordination*, pp. 84–130. Edited by W. H. Buiter and R. C. Marston. Cambridge: Cambridge University Press.

Mintz, Ilse. 1959. *Trade Balances during Business Cycles: U.S. and Britain since 1880*. Occasional Paper No. 67. New York: National Bureau of Economic Research.

———. 1961. *American Exports during Business Cycles, 1879–1958*. Occasional Paper No. 76. New York: National Bureau of Economic Research.

———. 1967. *Cyclical Fluctuations in the Exports of the United States since 1879*. New York: National Bureau of Economic Research.

Moore, G. H., and V. Zarnowitz. 1986. "The Development and Role of the National Bureau of Economic Research's Business Cycle Chronologies." In *The American Business Cycle: Continuity and Change*, pp. 735–79. Edited by R. J. Gordon. Chicago: University of Chicago Press.

Morgenstern, Oskar. 1959. *International Financial Transactions and Business Cycles*. Princeton: Princeton University Press.

Mundell, Robert A. 1968. *International Economics*. New York: Macmillan.

Nurkse, Ragnar. [1944] 1978. *International Currency Experience*. League of Nations. Reprint New York: Arno Press.

Oudiz, Gilles, and Jeffrey Sachs. 1985. "International Policy Coordination in Dynamic Macroeconomic Models." In *International Economic Policy Coordination*, pp. 274–319. Edited by W. H. Buiter and R. C. Marston. Cambridge: Cambridge University Press.

Rich, George. 1989. *Cross of Gold—Money and the Canadian Business Cycle, 1867–1913*. Ottawa: Carleton University Press. Distributed by Oxford University Press.

Stockman, Alan C., and Lars Svensson. 1985. "Capital Flows, Investment, and Exchange Rates." NBER Working Paper No. 1598. New York: National Bureau of Economic Research.

Svensson, Lars E. O. 1984. "Currency Prices, Terms of Trade and Interest Rates: A General-Equilibrium Asset-Pricing Cash-in-Advance Approach." *Journal of International Economics* 18 (February): 17–41.

Svensson, Lars E. O., and Sweder van Wijnbergen. 1986. "International Transmission of Monetary Policy." Institute for International Economic Studies, University of Stockholm, Seminar Paper No. 362.

Swoboda, Alexander K. 1979. "Comment." In *International Economic Policy*, pp. 204–208. Edited by R. Dornbusch and J. A. Frenkel. Baltimore: Johns Hopkins Press.

Taussig, Frank W. 1917. "International Trade under Depreciated Paper, A Contribution to Theory." *Quarterly Journal of Economics* 31 (May): 380–403.

Viner, Jacob. 1924. *Canada's Balance of International Indebtedness, 1900–1913*. Cambridge: Harvard University Press.

Wonnacott, Paul. 1965. *The Canadian Dollar, 1948–58*. Toronto: University of Toronto Press.

19

What's Natural About Unemployment?

Philip A. Klein

In 1945 William H. Beveridge published his book, *Full Employment in a Free Society*. He recognized full well that some unemployment is due to frictional, seasonal, and structural factors. He nonetheless found it relatively straightforward to state the employment goal of market-oriented economies: unemployment should be of short duration, there should, in general, be more jobs than people looking for them, and effective demand should be such that these objectives could be met (pp. 18–20). A healthy economy for Beveridge was one that, within the limits he delineated, would be naturally fully employed. Similarly Arthur F. Burns, writing in the early 1960s, recognized the same sort of definitional problems but had no difficulty stating the public policy goal as one of full employment in line with the Employment Act of 1946, then as now, our basic public policy statement on the subject of employment goals (Burns 1969, 186).

Defining Natural Unemployment

Today we are told that the economy suffers much "natural unemployment" and the implication is left that a goal of reasonably full employment is unrealistic. It is interesting to note the current definitions of "natural unemployment": it is the "rate that prevails in normal times"(Hall and Taylor 1986, 52); it is "that part of unemployment which would exist even at full employment" (Dornbush and Fischer 1984, 495); it is "the lowest level that can be sustained" and (again) "the lowest rate the nation can enjoy without risking an unacceptable acceleration of inflation" (Samuelson and Nordhaus 1985, 218). This last, as we shall try to show, is especially pernicious.

This paper is a revision of the paper "What's 'Natural' About the Unemployment Rate?" presented at a joint meeting of the American Economic Association and the Association for Social Economics, Chicago, December, 1987. I wish to thank Edward Coulson, the late Alfred Eichner, Robert Eisner, Robert J. Gordon, Will E. Mason, Monroe Newman, Warren Samuels, and the members of the Penn State Money-Macro Workshop for very helpful comments on an earlier draft.

All these definitions make whatever unemployment is included in the term "natural" appear to be inevitable and to be more acceptable than the consequences of trying to reduce it. Not infrequently, the term is used in such a way as to anoint a large amount of unemployment with the status of a genuinely natural event—unemployment is natural the way some people are "naturally lazy" or "naturally musical." (Alan Blinder [1987, 130] made a similar observation.) Lately (1988–89) the actual rate has fallen sufficiently low that the presumed "natural" rate must also be falling, but few if any seem especially anxious to suggest this.

Unemployment and Inflation:
The Conventional View

The current perspective began with Friedman's Presidential Address (1968, 8) in which he assumed "there is some level of unemployment consistent with equilibrium in real wage rates." If we abstract from the customary exceptions for seasonal and frictional unemployment, this can only mean that structural unemployment is a large (and secularly increasing) part of unemployment in the United States, and that it is more or less permanently to be regarded as beyond amelioration by conventional market forces. The only other possibility is that cyclical unemployment is perennially with us, but no one would argue that the economy is in perpetual recession.

This perspective toward the training and use of the labor force then colors all the subsequent discussion of "full employment" and low inflation as policy goals. Viewing these goals together, we find economists arguing that the "ideal" policy goal for prices is an inflation rate low enough to avoid any threat of acceleration in inflation (coupled with the implication that almost any inflation rate threatens such acceleration), while our unemployment goal becomes a secularly sliding scale to be, in effect, accepted at whatever the long-run average unemployment rate proves to be. That is, unemployment—of whatever level— can ex post be defined as "unnaturally low" if subsequently the economy suffers too much inflation.

One question that this approach leaves unanswered is why historically the United States should be plagued by so much more "natural" unemployment than many other market economies. If we accept the conventional explanations (job search is longer, the unemployed take their time about reapplying, etc.), why should this not be equally true about, say, the Swiss or the pre–1980 Germans with their very low unemployment rates? (Indeed, allowing for differences in definition, the U.S. unemployment rate was for much of the post-World War II period higher than that of most market economies. In recent years a number of European economies have had higher unemployment rates than the United States. Whether these recent higher European unemployment rates are regarded by economists as "natural" or merely actual is unclear.)

In sum, the term "natural" is pernicious itself because it leads to a perspective toward policy which suggests that we can and must live with however much unemployment is required to avoid "unacceptable" rates of inflation. It implies that rising natural unemployment is beyond reduction with macro policy and may well be the price that must be paid to avoid accelerating inflation.

If one thinks about it, inflation reflects merely a change in one of the measurement variables used to monitor an economy; and the economy in turn exists to serve its human agents. Unemployment, on the other hand, is a reflection of total loss of opportunity to participate in the productive activity of that economy by a significant number of its human agents. As such, unemployment ought to be rated at least on a par with inflation as an unfortunate economic consequence. The "natural rate" view regards any acceleration of inflation as worse than secularly rising unemployment rates. The argument is more insidious than it may appear at first blush. At what inflation rate does accelerating inflation become a significant threat? We are never told, except that this threat is almost always regarded by natural rate economists as presumptively a larger threat to the economy than existing unemployment which, however high, can always be defanged by pronouncing it "natural."

Unemployment and Inflation: Another View

The natural rate hypothesis does, to be sure, fit the "stylized facts" implicit in the notion of a shifting short-run Phillips Curve. It is not, however, the only interpretation which does so. There is, for example, nothing to suggest what inflation rate should be regarded as "natural." Accelerating inflation is painted, as suggested earlier, as seemingly imminent beyond even quite low inflation rates. In the first edition of his *Economics* text forty years ago, the youthful Paul Samuelson (1948, 282) noted that "An increase in prices is usually associated with an increase in employment. In mild inflation the wheels of industry are well lubricated and total output goes up. Private investment is brisk and jobs plentiful. Thus a little inflation is usually to be preferred to a little deflation." Times, to be sure, change, but this certainly sounds like there might be some low inflation rate which one could consider "natural."

In addition to Samuelson's appeal to logic, there is the empirical record. For example, the year-to-year change in the consumer price index in the forty-eight years after 1939 shows that deflation has occurred in precisely three years; an inflation rate under three percent has been recorded nineteen times, and a rate over three was experienced in twenty-six years. Whether or not zero inflation is "ideal," it is clearly not "natural" if by natural one means a condition typically found in the economy.

That being the case, there is no reason not to assume that the "natural rate of inflation" is something greater than zero. In his Presidential Address to the American Economic Association, James Tobin (1972, 8) commented that "the proposition that . . . the zero-inflation rate of unemployment reflects voluntary and efficient job-seeking activity strains credulity." That proposition is, of course, close to the Friedman position referred to above that the natural rate of inflation is that rate—obviously greater than zero—consistent with clearing markets. One could even suggest, not inaccurately, that the natural rate of inflation has been rising secularly.

If one postulates a non-zero natural rate of inflation, one can recast the entire argument of the shifting short-run Phillips curve to focus on a "natural" rate of inflation and an "inertial" rate of unemployment. Instead of a vertical long-run Phillips Curve at a "natural" rate of unemployment, imagine instead a long-run horizontal "natural rate of inflation." The precise rate of inflation is immaterial—but three percent is a not unreasonable estimate. (Empirically, for the entire period since 1960 it seems consistent with nonaccelerating inflation.) The short-run Phillips curves now apply to inertial unemployment rates and the shifts in the short-run curves occur because economic agents become accustomed to higher permanent rates of "natural unemployment." (One could even argue that the shifts in the short-run functions are policy induced as economists, among others, insist that the rise in the unemployment rate is inevitable because it is due to factors that cannot be easily eliminated.)

In such a world, efforts to reduce inflation below the "natural rate" lead to movement along a short-run Phillips curve which carries the economy below the natural inflation rate. (The economy suffers a recession, such as the 1981–83 episode, when we experienced a recession-induced decline in the inflation rate accompanied by large increases in the unemployment rate.) When economic agents have been persuaded higher unemployment is the price we must pay—when the "inertial unemployment rate" rises—inflation slowly drifts up again as, in fact, it has begun to do in the past year or so.

This explanation—shifting "inertial unemployment rates" accompanied by a "natural rate of inflation" substantially above zero—fits the "stylized facts" quite as well as the conventional "accelerationist" hypothesis postulating a secularly rising natural unemployment rate. But it has profoundly different policy implications. Instead of arguing that unemployment is the inevitable price we must pay for getting the inflation rate down, the "natural inflation rate" hypothesis argues that trying to reduce unemployment by depressing the economy is ultimately futile. Friedman (1983, 202) prefers to note that he knows of "no example of a country that has cured substantial inflation without going through a transitional period of slow growth and unemployment." Another reading of the same facts: no country has ever for very long (let alone permanently) rid itself of inflation via recession. The evidence is summarized in Chart 19.1, which shows growth cycles and inflation cycles for seven market countries in the period roughly since 1948. It shows fifty-six growth recessions and some fifty inflation rate cycles. (The latter are measured by changes in the consumer price index.)[1] A careful examination of Chart 19.1 shows that in no case has a decline in inflation occurred which could not be associated with a growth recession. In thirteen cases, these countries suffered recessions with no relief from inflation. The conventional conclusion, despite the thirteen failures, is Friedman's—namely that recession is the only way to bring down inflation rates. But another interpretation with more important policy implications seems equally (or more) compelling: in no case has a reduction in inflation brought about via recession ever lasted for long. In the overwhelming number of cases, inflation rates picked up again within a year of the end of the recession, and sometimes the inflation rate began rising even before the recession had ended.

With Table 19.1 it is possible to show quantitatively how short-lived has been the success in ridding market-oriented countries of inflation via recession. The United States has had nine inflation cycles since 1949; despite the low rates of the mid-1980s, in the absence of a shift to longer-run policies, a tenth inflation cycle may well be underway as of the late 1980s. In thirteen cases these countries suffered recessions which did not bring down inflation, but they have not had much success in the past fifty years in bringing down inflation without a recession. But Table 19.1 also shows that recession-driven deflations are ephemeral. In nearly 21 percent of the cases, inflation was rising before the recession had ended. Individual countries' records vary from Italy, France, and West Germany—which managed to restrain the outbreak of new inflation for close to a year and a half—to the other countries which have done less well. For all eight the average is eleven months. The question can be asked, is a year without renewed inflation worth suffering a recession? The evidence of Chart 19.1 and Table 19.1 suggests that periods of accelerating inflation are, in terms of frequency, quite as "natural" as periods of unemployment.

Conclusions

What can we conclude? The "natural inflation rate" hypothesis is as logical and explains the facts quite as well as the "natural unemployment rate" hypothesis. One points to the futility of trying to inflate an economy out of unemployment; the other to the futility of trying to depress an economy out of inflation. In the final analysis, both are incomplete, and as policy guides both are doomed to failure. Inflation and unemployment are not "natural," and both point to failures of the economy to perform in an acceptable way. There is, therefore, everything to be said for searching for ways to raise real growth rates, including investing in ways to improve the productivity of the labor force, especially by reducing structural obstacles to more efficient use of labor. In the meantime, the application of techniques designed to reduce the suffering associated with unemployment are appropriate temporary measures.

The tilt to public discussion of these problems is indicated by the current penchant for referring to the "full employment unemployment rate." Logically, one could also refer to the "low inflation 'zero' inflation rate" (i.e., that rate so

Chart 19.1. **Inflation Rate Cycles and Growth Cycles in Eight Market-oriented Economies, 1948–1988.**

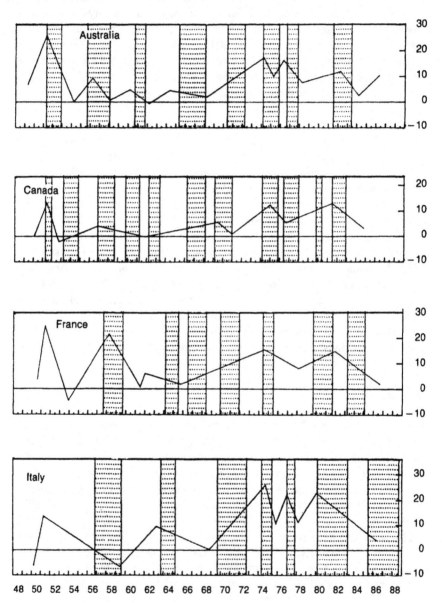

48 50 52 54 56 58 60 62 64 66 68 70 72 74 76 78 80 82 84 86 88

Note: Shaded areas represent growth-cycle recessions in each country.

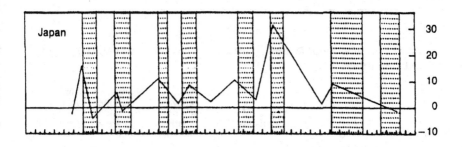

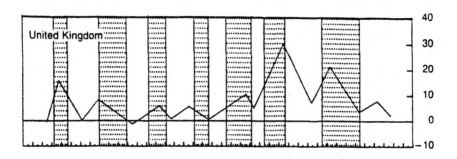

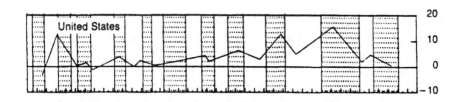

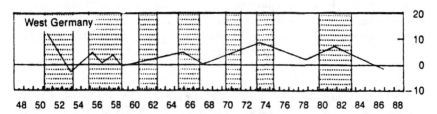

Note: Shaded areas represent growth-cycle recessions in each country.

Table 19.1

Length of Period without Renewed Inflation, Recession-driven Deflations in Eight Countries

Country	Period covered	Number of comparisons P	T	Average recovery w/o new inflation (months)	Number of inflations rekindled before end of recession	Number of recessions without decline in inflation
U.S.	1949–83	9	10	9	2	1
Canada	1950–84	5	6	8	1	5
Australia	1952–84	8	7	8	1	1
W. Germany	1953–86	5	5	16	1	2
U.K.	1952–83	7	7	9	1	0
Japan	1952–87	7	7	8	3	0
France	1959–78	4	3	19	0	3
Italy	1960	4	4	12	1	1
Total eight countries		49	49	11	10	13
					21%	26%
						(of all T comparisons)

Sources: Growth cycles and inflation rate cycles calculated at Center for International Business Cycle Research, Columbia University. Individual country turning point comparisons are based on information slightly updated from Chart 19.1.

low as to be achievable only with unacceptably high rates of unemployment).

It is time the economics profession declared its independence from the pernicious notion that our major macro problems are endemic, and that long-run amelioration of the cyclical impact which short-run trade-offs have on economic performance is permanently beyond our reach. If we stop being fixated on the idea that our only policy option is a short-run (and endlessly futile) choice between unacceptable inflation rates and unacceptable unemployment levels, we could focus on longer-run policies designed to foster feasible higher real rates of growth as well as lower unemployment rates. Indeed, lower unemployment rates are a fundamental component of higher real growth (via reduced structural unemployment as well as lower cyclical unemployment), and the latter in turn could be a major contributor to lower trend rates of inflation.

Notes

1. The change in the consumer price index is measured here by a technique often used by Moore's Center for International Business Cycle Research. Known as the "six-month smoothed technique," it consists of taking the ratio of the current month's index to the average of the twelve preceding months and annualizing the results. Calculated from seasonally adjusted data, it is designed to smooth out minor fluctuations and enable us to pick cyclical turning points which can be related to the growth cycle turning points

monitored at the Center for the countries under review. Table 19.1 ignores any measures of amplitude and focuses on depicting the resulting turning points in the growth cycles and in the changes in the CPI. In his original work with Kaish, Moore developed a leading inflation index which forecasts changes in U.S. inflation rate cycles with considerable success. My earlier study (Klein 1986) duplicated that effort for six of the other countries in Chart 19.1.

References

Beveridge, William. 1945. *Full Employment In A Free Society*. New York: W. W. Norton.

Blinder, Alan S. 1987. "Keynes, Lucas, And Scientific Progress." *American Economic Review* 77 (May): 130–136.

Burns, Arthur F. 1969. *The Business Cycle In A Changing World*. New York: Columbia University Press.

Dornbusch, Rudiger, and Stanley Fischer. 1984. *Macroeconomics*. 3rd ed. New York: McGraw-Hill.

Friedman, Milton. 1968. "The Role of Monetary Policy." *American Economic Review* 58 (March): 1–17.

————. 1983. *Bright Promises, Dismal Performance*. New York: Harcourt, Brace, Jovanovich.

Hall, Robert E., and John B. Taylor. 1986. *Macroeconomics*. New York: W. W. Norton.

Klein, Philip A. 1986. "Leading Indicators of Inflation in Market Economies." *International Journal of Forecasting* (2): 403–412.

Moore, Geoffrey, and Stanley Kaish. 1983. "A New Inflation Barometer." *The Morgan Guaranty Survey* (July): 7–10.

Samuelson, Paul A. 1948. *Economics*. New York: McGraw-Hill.

Samuelson, Paul A., and William D. Nordhaus. 1985. *Economics*. 12th ed. New York: McGraw-Hill.

Tobin, James. 1972. "Inflation and Unemployment." *American Economic Review* (May): 1–18.

Index

About the Contributors

ANIRVAN BANERJI is a Staff Economist at the Center for International Business Cycle Research at Columbia University. He has a B.Tech. in mechanical engineering from the Indian Institute of Technology in Kharagpur, an M.B.A. from the Indian Institute of Management in Ahmedabad, and an M.Phil. from Columbia University. He is currently involved in the continuing development of the CIBCR's Weekly Leading Index published by *Business Week*. His particular research focus is on reconciling standardization factors for weekly and monthly data for inclusion in composite indexes.

ERNST A. BOEHM received a diploma in commerce, a bachelor's degree in economics, and a masters degree in economics, all from the University of Adelaide. He obtained his doctorate at Trinity College, University of Oxford. He also has a master's in Commerce from the University of Melbourne. He has taught at the University of New England in New South Wales, at the University of Melbourne, and he was a Visiting Professor at the University of Pittsburgh. He is currently Senior Associate at the Institute of Applied Economic and Social Research at the University of Melbourne. He has been a Consultant to the Confederation of Australian Industry and also to the International Monetary Fund. He has been a Visiting Scholar at the National Bureau of Economic Research, the Brookings Institution, and the Center for International Business Cycle Research. He has published several books and many articles and is a leading expert on problems of Australian growth and stability.

MICHAEL D. BORDO is Professor of Economics at the University of South Carolina and a Research Associate at the National Bureau of Economic Research. He received his B.A. from McGill University, an M.S. from the London School of Economics, and a Ph.D. from the University of Chicago. He has taught at Carleton University and from 1981–1982 served on the staff of the U.S. Gold Commission. He coedited (with Anna J. Schwartz) the conference volume, *A Retrospective on the Classical Gold Standard*, and edited the conference volume *Money, History and International Finance* (forthcoming). With Lars Johung he coauthored *The Long-Run Behavior of the Velocity of Circulation*.

CHARLOTTE BOSCHAN is a Consultant to the Center for International Business Cycle Research at Columbia University. She has a Ph.D. in economics from Columbia, and has worked with Geoffrey Moore since 1951 when she became affiliated with the National Bureau of Economic Research. In the course of her work at the Bureau, she was associated with Victor Zarnowitz in the 1975 revision of the Commerce Department's cyclical indicators and in developing the procedure for combining them into composite indexes. She was largely responsible for constructing the Growth Cycle Program, including the method for determining turning points (the Bry-Boschan method) and the "flexible trend" underlying growth cycle analysis known as the Phase Average Trend. She has worked in labor economics as well. At the National Bureau, she started and managed the data bank, later known as Citibase. Her first professional job was at the Econometric Institute.

PHILLIP BRAUN received a B.A. with honors in economics from Oberlin College in 1981 and a M.A. in economics from Washington University in St. Louis in 1985. He is currently a Ph.D. candidate in finance and economics in the Graduate School of Business at the University of Chicago. He coauthored (with Stephen Mittnick) St. Louis Working Paper No. 84, "Structural Analysis with Autoregressive Models: Some Experimental Evidence." He was a Junior Economist at the Council of Economic Advisers in the Executive Office of the President in 1985 and 1986.

PHILLIP CAGAN received his undergraduate degree at UCLA and his master's and doctor's degrees in economics at the University of Chicago. From 1953 to 1955, he was a Research Associate at the National Bureau of Economic Research. After teaching briefly at the University of Chicago, he taught at Brown University from 1958 to 1962 before obtaining his current position as Professor of Economics at Columbia University. He was Visiting Scholar at the American Enterprise Institute in Washington D.C. from 1972 to 1987. He has written extensively in the area of monetary economics.

JOHN P. CULLITY has a B.S. in economics from St. Peter's College in New Jersey and his master's and doctor's degrees from Columbia University. His teaching career encompasses two years on the faculty at Fordham University before joining the Economics Department at Rutgers University in Newark, where he currently is Professor of Economics. He is also a Research Associate at the Center for International Business Cycle Research. He has worked widely in the areas of business cycles and forecasting. His recent efforts include working with Moore on the construction of a long-leading index.

CHANTAL DUBRIN is a Research Associate at the Center for International Business Cycle Research at Columbia University. She has been associated with

Geoffrey Moore since 1966, first at the National Bureau of Economic Research and then at the Center. She has a degree from the Ecole Polytechnique Feminine in Paris and a master's degree in economics from New York University.

EDGAR R. FIEDLER has a B.B.A. in business statistics from the University of Wisconsin, an M.B.A. from the University of Michigan, and a Ph.D. from the New York University Graduate School of Business Administration, the latter two both in economics. In 1956, he joined Eastman Kodak Company as a Statistical Analyst and from 1959 to 1960, he was a Sales Analyst for Doubleday and Company. From 1960 to 1969, he was Assistant Economist at Bankers Trust Company in New York City. From 1970 to 1971, he was Assistant Secretary for Economic Affairs in the Department of Commerce and also Deputy Director of the Cost of Living Council. From 1971 to 1975, he was Assistant Secretary of the Treasury for Economic Policy serving under Secretaries John B. Connally, George P. Shultz, and William E. Simon. He joined the Conference Board in 1975 and is currently Vice President and Economic Counsellor at The Conference Board. He is also Adjunct Professor of Economics at Columbia University. He is on a number of Boards of Directors and has published in various professional journals, for the National Bureau of Economic Research, and in the Conference Board's own magazine, *Across the Board.*

LAWRENCE R. KLEIN is the Benjamin Franklin Professor of Economics at the University of Pennsylvania, was the founder of Wharton Econometric Forecasting Associates, and is a former chairman of their Scientific Advisory Board. He is also Principal Investigator of Project LINK, an international research group for the statistical study of world trade and payments. Professor Klein is the author of many articles and books in economics, specializing in econometrics. He is past president of the American Economic Association, the Eastern Economic Association, and the Econometric Society. He is a member of the American Academy of Arts and Sciences, the American Philosophical Society, and the National Academy of Sciences. He has often been an adviser to the U.S. government and many international organizations. He is the holder of several honorary degrees from universities around the world and in 1980 was awarded the Alfred Nobel Memorial Prize in economic sciences.

PHILIP A. KLEIN is Professor of Economics at Pennsylvania State University. He obtained his B.A. and M.A. from the University of Texas and his doctorate from the University of California at Berkeley. He has taught in a number of colleges and universities both in the United States and abroad. He was for many years on the staff of the National Bureau of Economic Research and, at the present time, is Research Associate at the Center for International Business Cycle Research at Columbia University. He is an Adjunct Scholar at the American Enterprise Institute and several times has been an Academic Visitor at the

London School of Economics. He has consulted for a number of international organizations and has received three Fulbright Faculty Fellowships over the years. He has worked with Geoffrey H. Moore for more than thirty years, and they have published widely together. Klein has also written extensively on institutional economics and is a past president of the Association for Evolutionary Economics. He is currently an Associate Editor of the *International Journal of Forecasting*.

ALFRED L. MALABRE, Jr. is News Editor (Economics) for the *Wall Street Journal*. After beginning as a reporter for the Hartford *Courant*, he joined the Chicago bureau of the *Wall Street Journal* in 1958 and transferred to the London Bureau in 1960. Subsequently, he served as Bureau Chief in Bonn. He joined the New York bureau in 1961 where he has specialized in economics coverage. He was named News Editor in 1969 and has written a weekly outlook column since 1964, as well as a monthly column, "Tracking a Trend," which commenced in 1978. He is the author of four books and in 1988 received the George S. Eccles Prize for "excellence in economic writing" for his 1987 book, *Beyond Our Means*. His most recent book is *Understanding the New Economy*, published in 1988.

JEAN MALTZ is a Research Associate at the Center for International Business Cycle Research at Columbia University. She has worked with Geoffrey Moore since 1976, first at the National Bureau of Economic Research and later at the Center. Earlier, she worked with Melita Moore at the United Nations Statistical Office, Economic Affairs Department. She has a B.A. in mathematics from Wellesley College.

STEPHEN K. McNEES is a Vice President and Economist at the Federal Reserve Bank of Boston. He has a bachelor's degree from Swarthmore College and a doctorate from the Massachusetts Institute of Technology. He has taught at Harvard, Northeastern University, MIT, and Williams College. In 1982–83, he served as Senior Staff Economist for macroeconomic policy for the President's Council of Economic Advisers. His current position involves briefing the President of the Bank and the Board of Directors on the economy and economic policy. His major research interest has been on the evaluation of economic forecasts and assessing the role of macroeconomic models. He is currently an Associate Editor of the *International Journal of Forecasting*.

MICHAEL P. NIEMIRA is currently an Economist with Mitsubishi Bank in New York. Prior to this position, he worked as an Economist at Paine Webber, at Chemical Bank, and at Merrill Lynch. He has done graduate work in economics at Rutgers, studying with John Cullity, and has worked with Geoffrey H. Moore as well. He has contributed a number of articles to books and journals on business cycles and forecasting and is currently completing a book on economic cycles.

JOEL POPKIN is the President of an economic consulting company bearing his name and located in Washington, D.C. Prior to establishing the company in 1978, Dr. Popkin served as Director of the Washington office of the National Bureau of Economic Research, a member of the staff of the President's Council of Economic Advisers, and Assistant Commissioner for Prices of the U.S. Bureau of Labor Statistics. After obtaining his doctorate in economics from the University of Pennsylvania, Popkin's research interest has focused on the dynamics of business cycles, particularly wage and price movements. His work has renewed interest in the stage-of-process approach to studying business cycle developments. One result has been that the U.S. Producer Price Indexes are now reported by processing stage—finished, intermediate, and crude goods. He has published widely in his field.

ANNA J. SCHWARTZ received a B.A. in economics from Barnard College, and an M.A. and a Ph.D. from Columbia University. She began her career with the Social Science Research Council and has taught at Brooklyn College, City University of New York, New York University, and most recently (1984-1987) as Honorary Visiting Professor at the City University Business School in London. She has been on the research staff of the National Bureau of Economic Research in New York since 1941. She has published widely both independently and with Milton Friedman, having coauthored with him in 1963 one of the most widely cited books of the postwar period, *A Monetary History of the United States.* Subsequently, Friedman and Schwartz published *Monetary Trends in the United States and the United Kingdom: Their Relation to Income, Prices, and Interest Rates, 1867-1975.* With Michael Darby and James R. Lothian and others, she coauthored *The International Transmission of Inflation.* She has continued to publish extensively in the area of monetary economics. In 1981-1982, she was Staff Director of the U.S. Gold Commission and in 1987-88, she was President of the Western Economics Association.

WERNER H. STRIGEL received his doctorate in economics from the University of Munich. He began his career at the Bavarian State Statistics Office prior to joining the Ifo Institute for Economic Research in Munich in 1961. He was a Senior Economist and member of its executive board for many years prior to his retirement in 1982. While at Ifo, Dr. Strigel was codirector of CIRET (Centre for International Research on Economic Tendency Surveys), an organization devoted to the analysis of surveys of business cycles. CIRET has grown to include more than five hundred members from forty-three different countries and holds conferences biennially. Strigel has consulted for the European Economic Commission, and has lectured extensively internationally, having received an honorary doctorate from the China Academy in Taipei. Since his retirement, he has continued working and writing in the field of cyclical indicators and continues to act as advisor to Ifo.

VICTOR ZARNOWITZ began his studies at the University of Cracow and obtained an M.A. and a Ph.D. in economics from the University of Heidelberg. He was at the Graduate School of Business in Mannheim from 1949 to 1951 prior to coming to the United States, where he joined the National Bureau of Economic Research as a Research Economist in 1952. He was made a member of the research staff in 1963 and continues in that position currently. He taught at Columbia University from 1956 to 1959 prior to joining the University of Chicago. He was named Professor of Economics and Finance at Chicago in 1965. He has acted as an advisor to the Bureau of Labor Statistics. In this capacity, he was instrumental, along with Charlotte Boschan, in the 1975 revision of the business cycle indicators monitored monthly by the Bureau of Economic Analysis in *Business Conditions Digest*. He has written extensively in the fields of business cycle theory, measurement, and forecasting.

Printed in the United States
by Baker & Taylor Publisher Services